REVELATION AND THE MODERN WORLD

BEING THE FIRST PART OF A TREATISE ON

THE FORM OF THE SERVANT

BY THE SAME AUTHOR

THE COMMON LIFE
IN THE BODY OF CHRIST

A Study of some of the Biblical Materials
for a Doctrine of the Church

Fourth Edition

DACRE PRESS

REVELATION AND THE MODERN WORLD

being the first part
of a treatise on

THE FORM OF THE SERVANT

by

L. S. THORNTON, C.R.
D.D. CAMBRIDGE, HON. D.D. DURHAM

dacre press
westminster

FIRST PUBLISHED 1950

DACRE PRESS: A. AND C. BLACK LTD.
4, 5 AND 6 SOHO SQUARE, LONDON, W.1

PRINTED IN GREAT BRITAIN BY ROBERT MACLEHOSE AND CO. LTD.
THE UNIVERSITY PRESS, GLASGOW

In piam memoriam

PATRIS REVERENDI EDVARDI KEBLE TALBOT
HENRICI SCOTT HOLLAND FILII SPIRITVALIS
COMMVNITATIS RESVRRECTIONIS XVIII ANNOS
SVPERIORIS IN VITA RELIGIOSA DVCIS
PRVDENTISSIMI NECNON FRATRIBVS SEMPER
DILECTISSIMI HVNC LIBRVM DEDICAT AUCTOR

PREFACE

This book is concerned with the form of the Christian Revelation as it appears in its original setting. The inquiry is occupied throughout with two things, namely (1) the actual substance of the revelation and (2) its human context. The question is asked: what is the nature of the relationship set up between these two in scripture and in sacred history? When God speaks through human lips, when he acts upon the human plane, when he allows himself to be portrayed in the literature of one particular people, how in all this is the content of the message connected with its outward form? Upon our answer to that question will depend inevitably the kind of answers which we also give to the particular religious problems of our own time. Such at least is one of the dominant ideas which have determined the shape of the argument in the present volume. Around this general theme of form and content other subjects have grouped themselves. Here, too, some of the main topics which engage the attention of theologians are considered as problems of relationship.

Thus, for example, the author has, in the following pages, discussed the relation of the Old Testament to the New, of the special revelation in scripture to the wider revelation in the order of creation, and, again, of scripture to church tradition. Once more, he has found it necessary to examine the character of the nexus between revelation and the Christian order of society as well as the relationship which exists between both of these and the scientific culture of the modern world. Another matter which has received serious consideration is the question of biblical interpretation. The methods of critical analysis with which modern students of the bible are familiar stand in marked contrast with the traditional modes of exposition current in apostolic times and in the first ages of church history. Yet, since the traditional exegesis and its techniques are to be found in scripture as well as in the church, they form part of the material of which a scientific biblical theology must take account. A line of investigation such as this needs to be pursued sympathetically and objectively in a rigorously impartial spirit. No untested assumptions are permissible.

On the other hand, the investigator has, somehow, to bridge the gulf which lies between the world of modern knowledge and the fashions of thought prevailing in ancient times. He has also to take account of the transformations which that older world of thought underwent during the centuries of history covered by the biblical revelation. Here there are many pitfalls to be avoided; and no one who essays such a task can be sure that he has escaped them all. With such difficulties in mind the present writer has followed a method which can, perhaps, be illustrated by means of a metaphor drawn from the sea. In the story of St Paul's hazardous voyage through the Mediterranean to the island of Malta there came a moment when the 'sailors surmised that they were drawing near to some country'. So they performed the operation of taking soundings (Acts 27[27,28]). One sounding told them very little; but two soundings told them just what they wanted to know, with the result that, after precautionary measures, 'they all escaped safe to land'. So too, in the argument which follows, 'soundings' have been taken at a number of different points in our voyage of exploration. What this means can, I hope, be made clear in a very few words.

The bible is obscure to the modern reader because it was written a long time ago. Like the sea it has depths of which the surface-appearance gives little or no indication, even to the expert. If, then, we are to understand it rightly, we need the help of those forms of science which specialize in certain relevant studies. I refer especially to those sciences which have grown up round the comparative study of religion and of religious history, and which examine the workings of the human mind in the various stages of its social and spiritual development. These special studies provide the equipment of knowledge by means of which 'soundings' can be taken, so that we are not left at the mercy of surface-impressions. Here two points already mentioned may be recalled to mind. There is first a 'mental distance' between the past and the present. This suggests that special attention should be given to those phases of religious thought which are furthest removed from our own. But secondly, the bible and primitive Christianity together represent a whole series of such phases. If, therefore, we attend only to this or that part of the process we may reach very misleading conclusions. That would be like taking only one sounding to find out whether we were approaching land.

Even two soundings might have proved insufficient to direct St Paul's shipmates, if the floor of the sea had happened to be peculiar in its formation. Luckily, however, it gave them reliable indications of depth. So in the present volume soundings have been taken at three main points in the history of revelation. Citing them in their historical order these 'points' are (1) the mental habits and religious practices of the ancient Hebrews, (2) some peculiarities in the religious thought of Judaism round about the period of the Gospel story, and (3) typical workings of the early Christian mind a little after the period in which the New Testament was completed. Actually, however, for reasons set forth in the text (Chapter IV), the last of these three soundings has been taken first. Thus we have retraced our steps to the bible through the mind of the early church. In the course of this survey, moreover, the developments of later history have been kept in view; and in a final chapter a fresh attempt has been made to bring the conclusions reached into a setting of thought more nearly akin to the 'make up' of the modern world.

The thesis here unfolded may be regarded from three points of view. It is (1) an essay concerning the principles of biblical interpretation, (2) an enquiry into the Christian doctrine of revelation, and (3) an examination of one particular feature in that revelation as set forth in scripture, namely the prominence there given to the order of creation. Upon the last of these three points something further must be said, as it occupies a key-position in the argument. The creation-theme is closely related to the discussion of 'culture', as the human setting of religion, with which Chapter I is concerned. In that chapter the theme of creation is first opened up in section iv, where it is connected both with revelation and with 'creative grace'. In this way a background is suggested for the doctrine of man. Upon this latter doctrine there has been a fresh concentration of theology in recent years under the pressure of current events. Christian thought about man, however, needs to be carried further back, if it is to be soundly based. Moreover, it is precisely man's place in the plan of creation which is in question to-day. To the unity of that plan as it comes to fulfilment in the Christ there corresponds also a unity of the scriptures; and it is in terms of these two unities and of their interrelationship that we can most surely gain light upon the problems which beset the Christian society in the modern world.

One of the most urgent of these problems has to do with the very nature of the Christian society itself; and within that context there arises an important issue concerning the relationship in which 'Christendom' stands to that body of truth of which it is in some sense the trustee. The issue thus stated is dominant throughout Chapter III; and section v of that chapter is, in the author's mind, of crucial importance. For there we consider the character of the nexus uniting *any* form of human society to the knowledge by which it lives, the uniting bond being of such a kind that the two factors united (the society and its form of 'truth') are seen to be mutually dependent. So, as we pass from Book I to Book II that complex and enigmatic structure which we call Christendom is seen to occupy a mediating position between the revelation contained in scripture on the one hand and, on the other hand, that larger whole within which human life is set, and which throughout the present volume has been designated 'the order of creation'. If these considerations are kept in mind it is hoped that the interpretation of scripture undertaken in Book II under the guidance of St Irenaeus should present no special difficulties.

The reader has before him the first part only of a treatise to which has been given a single title taken from Philippians 2⁷. It is hoped that this will be completed in a second volume, containing the substance of the Scott Holland Memorial lectures delivered in the University of Leeds in 1943-44. The general subject of the second part will be: *The dominion of Christ*. To that further instalment the present volume is a necessary prelude. Biblical theology is entering to-day upon new and relatively untried paths. It seemed desirable, therefore, to attempt some elucidation of principles before plunging more deeply into the details of exegesis where probabilities are apt to depend so largely upon presuppositions. As the work proceeded, however, it became clear that Parts I and II would form a single whole. St Paul's great phrase: *the form of the servant* is as relevant to the general character of revelation as it is to the content of what stands revealed. I hope, therefore, that the Holland trustees will accept Part I as some small excuse for a delayed publication, in Part II, of the material for which they made themselves specially responsible.

As in a previous volume, so here I am heavily indebted to the work of many specialists in biblical scholarship and in kindred studies. Among these four names stand out pre-eminently in my own mind. They are H. Wheeler Robinson, J. Pedersen, S. H. Hooke and George Foot Moore. Under their authoritative guidance, greatly stimulated also by the no less illuminating studies of other workers in the biblical field, such as A. R. Johnson and Philip Carrington, I hope that I may have drawn attention to some theological aspects of this vast subject which deserve to receive fuller consideration. There is yet another department in which obligations must be mentioned. I am grateful to a friend and colleague, Canon F. W. Green of Norwich, for insisting that I must read the researches of F. Loofs into the sources used by St Irenaeus, for the numerous discussions which we have had together upon that subject, and for the trouble which he has taken in placing his own knowledge of patristics at my disposal. He is, however, in no sense to be held responsible for any use which I have made of this material.

One further piece of generous help by a specialist has been recorded in the appropriate place (p. 188, below). I am also greatly obliged to Father Geoffrey Curtis, C.R., and to the Reverend D. L. Popplewell for having read the whole of this work in manuscript and for many useful suggestions. I am once more indebted to the Dacre Press for undertaking the risks of publication. To Messrs. Robert MacLehose & Co. Ltd., and to their readers, compositors and printers, I am most grateful for the carefulness and accuracy with which their work is done.

L. S. T.

November, 1948.

CONTENTS

BOOK I
REVELATION AND CULTURE

BOOK II
CREATION AND ORTHODOXY

Chapter IV. THE STRUCTURE OF ORTHODOXY

BOOK III

THE FORM OF THE WHOLE

ABBREVIATIONS

AV   The Authorized Version of the Bible.

adv. haer   *Adversus haereses* = *Sancti Irenaei episcopi Lugdunensis contra omnes haereticos libri numero quinque.*

CQR   The Church Quarterly Review.

ET   English Translation.

EVV   English Versions.

ICC   International Critical Commentary (published by T. & T. Clark).

JTS   The Journal of Theological Studies.

LXX   The Septuagint Version of the Old Testament in Greek.

Moffatt, in conjunction with a scriptural quotation, indicates that the rendering is taken from *A New Translation of the Bible* by James Moffatt.

NT   New Testament.

OT   Old Testament.

PB   The Book of Common Prayer.

RV   The Revised Version of the Bible.

refs   references.

WH   The New Testament in Greek according to the text of Westcott and Hort.

Cross-references have usually been made by reference to chapters (Ch.), sections (§) and paragraphs (par.), so that:

> 'cp. Ch. I, § ii, par. 3' would invite a comparison with the third paragraph in the second section of Chapter I. Plural forms such as: '§§ ii and iii', 'pars. 6 and 7' have been employed, and also expressions such as: 'last 2 pars.' or 'last par. but two' to indicate the position of the paragraph(s) designated.

If no chapter is mentioned, it should be assumed that a reference to section and paragraph refers to the chapter in which the cross-reference is made.

Abbreviations used for titles of the biblical books are given in the Index under (1) References.

BOOK I

REVELATION AND CULTURE

CHAPTER I

REVELATION IN ITS HUMAN SETTING

i

What is the relation between revealed religion and its cultural environment? Two possible answers: (1) it transcends the environment; (2) it is the product of the environment. Neither of these answers is satisfactory. Revelation *masters* its environment because God identifies himself with human history in order to transform it. The form of the Servant prefigured in Jacob's wrestling (Gen. 32, Phil. 2[7]).

In the present work two quite distinct issues are deliberately brought together. The question: What is Revelation? may, at first sight, seem far removed from the problems of our present civilization and of its apparent break-down. The former, it may be said, is a matter which may be left to theological specialists, whereas the present condition and prospects of mankind are the concern of everybody irrespective of special knowledge or of religious belief. Yet this particular association of ideas should not seem altogether surprising, at least to students of religion. For in history religion and civilization have always been closely interwoven. Moreover, wherever we scrutinize more closely the precise character of this interweaving we find good ground for supposing that an all-important factor has been the claim of religion to possess an authority drawn from divine revelation.

But further, religion and culture[1] have in all ages shown

[1] In English, as spoken, we have no precise equivalent to *Kultur* as that word is used in German. Throughout the present work 'culture' refers to the total 'set-up' of life which has characterized some particular society in a given period of history. This total 'set-up' is much more comprehensive than 'culture' in the restricted sense of that word which prevails in English-speaking countries. This more comprehensive sense of the term has reference to the framework of life as it affects *every* member of society, no matter where

themselves to be mutually dependent. This reciprocal relationship might, perhaps, be defined by saying that religion has supplied to its more earthly partner motive and inspiration, whereas the latter seems to have provided for religion the organic forms in which it has come to outward expression. This point, if correctly stated, would clearly be of vital importance to any theorizing concerning Revelation. Accordingly, we shall find ourselves returning to the subject repeatedly as the argument of this book developes. Meanwhile, it has to be recognized that for Christians, at least, this mutual interconnexion between religion and culture has given rise to a number of problems which have proved to be very baffling. Here we must confine our attention to what directly concerns the theological issue of revelation; and in that context one affirmation may be made with some measure of confidence. This we now proceed to state.

In the modern period all the discussions concerning Christian origins have had behind them a difficult question, not always recognized and seldom, if ever, handled in a satisfying manner. This question may be formulated as follows: What is the precise relation of revealed religion to the contemporary forms of culture characteristic of the ancient world into which that religion came? Here the term 'revealed religion' need imply nothing more than the common Christian belief that there is a special revelation of the one true God enshrined in the scriptures of the Old and New Testaments. The question as a whole implies that, while this special revelation is the central theme of scripture, the bible also reflects and illustrates successive stages and types of culture, and that in these the revelation was, so to speak, embedded, so that through contact with them it came

he stands, for example, on the ladder of education. Moreover this framework (the outward order of things) is to be conceived as manifesting, in characteristic habits and institutions, the total bent of mental dispositions and social tendencies which are dominant in that particular cross-section of history. Obviously so wide a conception is capable of the most striking divergencies in its concrete embodiment. Our appreciation of such differences, again, will depend, for each of us, upon a broad knowledge of history such as cannot be conveyed in a note to a theological treatise. It is hoped, however, that the further indications given in the present chapter will set the reader on the right track towards the clarification of this difficult topic. Other clues will emerge as our theme unfolds. The illustration to be furnished in our next Section should be compared with one given below in Ch. VII, § ii, pars. 6, 7.

to expression. With these assumptions we have now to ask how far we, as Christians, are obliged to acknowledge a dependence of our religion, in its early history, upon the ancient phases and forms of culture with which it was successively associated? Or again, to what extent has such dependence, if it was a fact, been modified, transformed, or even perhaps obliterated, by some quality or power integral to that religion itself?

It will be convenient to indicate here briefly the attitude towards such questions which must be taken to underlie the argument of the present work.

Among influences affecting biblical and historical theology in recent times it is possible to discern two habits of mind which tend to arrive at very different results. One of these dispositions is accustomed to affirm the spiritual transcendence of the biblical religion over its environment, whereas the other tends to see that religion in all its manifestations as a product of its environment. The former disposition has generally characterized the Liberal school of theology, in some at least of its moods. In particular this attitude has accorded well with the antipathy towards 'natural religion'[1] which has been prominent in leading members of that school. Of the opposite tendency, on the other hand, we may say that it has been associated not so much with a particular theological tradition as with the application of scientific methods to the study of religious history. Finally, it must be said that traditional orthodoxy has hovered uneasily between these two types of thought, finding neither of them congenial to itself.

The summary statement of the last paragraph is inevitably too simple to cover all the facts.[2] Yet it is sufficiently true to illustrate broadly the nature of the problem which surrounds the theology of revealed religion to-day. In the present work the two tendencies to which reference has just been made are regarded as equally necessary and even as mutually complementary. Accordingly, in these pages no encouragement will be given to any view which assumes that either tendency is *necess-*

---

[1] The meaning assigned to this expression in the present work is more fully indicated below (Ch. VII, § i).

[2] For one thing 'the Liberal school of theology' needs to be more exactly defined. For 'Liberalism' in theology may mean a number of different things, and may even receive applications which appear to be contradictory. This issue will be further considered in the following chapters.

3

arily contrary to the true interests of religion. Nevertheless, if we are right in supposing that the two tendencies are complementary, that will imply that neither, taken by itself, is adequate to explain all the facts. It would seem, then, that there was in the Revelation itself some quality which enabled it, not simply to transcend its historical environment, but also, and more positively, to master it.

In this provisional conclusion there are several points which call for further scrutiny and elucidation. In the first place 'revelation', rather than 'religion', is the word selected to describe the determining factor in the situation envisaged. For 'religion' might suggest the various activities or experiences through which man draws near to God, whereas from the standpoint of faith the unique manifestations set out in the biblical record are to be attributed, not to any special qualities in the chosen people, but solely to the action of God himself. In other words, in a revelation of God the character of the revelation will correspond to the character of God. When, therefore, we speak of the activity of the revelation towards its environment we are, in reality, speaking of the way in which God acts upon the world in making himself known to man.

How, then, should we expect God to act upon the world? The answer to such a question could come only from the interpretation which faith gives to the bible as a whole. Our interpretation of the facts, therefore, will be partly dependent upon the theological presuppositions with which we approach them. This is a familiar dilemma of which more will be said later. At present it will be sufficient to remark that the dilemma warns us off from all forms of piecemeal construction which are not controlled by some degree of insight into the unity of the whole. It may also turn out to be true that 'the interpretation which faith gives to the bible as a whole' is something which carries us beyond the individual investigator in so far as it refers him (and all of us) back to the Christian community in which and for which the bible has specific authority.

In the provisional conclusion which we are examining there is one more expression which calls for fuller explanation. We spoke of the Revelation mastering its environment. This phrase might suggest a somewhat arbitrary procedure which did violence to the world of God's creation or to human nature itself.

4

To *some* theological presuppositions such a notion would apparently be congruous, but not to the standpoint here adopted. It is not in such a sense that the divine 'mastery' of environment is to be understood. For the present work, as its title implies, is concerned to emphasize the lowliness and condescension of God in his conduct towards man and towards the whole world of his creatures. If there is 'mastery' in God's modes of action towards the order within which he manifests himself, it is all of one piece with the action of Jesus Christ when he took a towel and girded himself to wash the disciples' feet. In that typical exhibition of the Servant's form we can see a wider revelation of God's total activity towards his creation, and therefore also a parable which sums up the whole method of divine revelation.

We are thus brought face to face with the mystery of the divine being which lies behind all that can properly be said about revelation. It is 'the high and lofty One that inhabiteth eternity' who dwells 'in the high and holy place, with him also that is of a contrite and humble spirit' (Isaiah 57^{15}). The truth here revealed cannot be confined to God's personal relations with sinners, even though it be there supremely manifested. The transcendence of 'the high and lofty One' and the separateness which is indicated by the word 'holy' point to a perfection which is most fully exhibited in condescension. God's greatness is shown in his intimacy with the lowliest of his creatures and in the care with which he has ordered their mutual relations in the world of his creation. But if this be so, then there is nothing in that world which is irrelevant to the revelation of the Creator, and no sphere or level of human life which could not be instrumental to such a revelation.

The way is now open to a clearer understanding of the sense in which the divine revelation may be said to have mastered the historical environment into which it came. Briefly, this may be summed up in a word by saying that the divine action adapted itself to, and even identified itself with, the given forms of history in order that by so doing it might transform their spiritual significance. The possibility of an explanation which sees the biblical religion as a product of its environment is due precisely to the fact that the divine action is perfectly adjusted to that environment, and that in all its manifold aspects. The fact that at almost any stage of the history the religion of Israel,

5

and not less the religion of the apostolic church, can seem explicable in terms of contemporary culture-forms, so far from militating against the truth of Christianity, bears witness to the completeness of the divine condescension. God's self-identification with the minutiae of contemporary life and thought is all of one piece with the doctrine of the incarnation.

Yet still, this is only a part of the truth. If the statement which has just been made were an adequate account of the matter we should have come perilously near to what one might call a pagan doctrine of divine immanence. This total adjustment to environment was a supreme work of condescension which left nothing as it was before. It was an agonizing conflict in which the Creator wrestled with his fallen world in order to redeem it; a conflict like that of Peniel[1] in which the divine wrestler emptied[2] his own strength into the human wrestler, in which, as on Calvary, God suffered defeat in order that Man might be victorious. God came down to the level of our trivialities in order that those same trivialities might be taken up into a context of surpassing significance. Such is the general character of revelation; and it carries this corollary, that nothing in scripture is too trivial to be relevant. For all the crudeness and the strangeness of its varied detail are in some sense organic to the new world which Christ has made in himself. To the implications of this language we shall return presently.

ii

A law of relation between religion and culture the necessary clue to our understanding of the bible, in itself and in its bearing upon our own world. For example, the relation between Paulinism and the mystery religions cannot be understood until the roots of both have been traced back to the cultural world of the Old Testament. Revealed religion has cultural unity with 'natural religion'; this it does not destroy, but masters, transforms and fulfils. St. Paul's eucharistic teaching illustrates the general working of the law.

[1] Gen. 32²⁴ᶠᶠ
[2] cp. the 'kenotic' phrase in Phil. 2⁷

6

Meanwhile, we have so far said nothing which would bring closer together the apparently unrelated topics of revealed religion and present-day civilization. For the 'contemporary' cultures to whose 'forms' reference has been made were contemporary with the period of history covered by the biblical writings. It is obvious, however, that if history shows a certain unchanging law of relationship between religion and culture, then a more exact understanding of that relationship as exhibited in the bible will provide an important clue to the problems of to-day in so far as they centre round the place of revealed religion in our own civilization. Moreover the clue may be expected to be like a lamp which throws light backwards as well as forwards. For if it is difficult to see contemporary history in its true proportions, anything like a main clue to the working of history may be expected to ease that difficulty by tracing out connexions with the past. Conversely, the difficulty of placing ourselves inside the biblical world and of seeing its happenings as the ancients saw them would be considerably lessened just so far as we were enabled to bridge the gap between their world and ours, so as to see precisely how the differences came to be. These observations will, to the trained historian, seem the merest commonplaces. What I am suggesting, however, is a particular and much needed application of a principle which in other spheres is already familiar.

Meanwhile the reader must be beginning to feel that he has had enough of these generalities, and that a specific illustration might help to clarify some things which have already been said. To such an illustration, therefore, we will now give our attention. Some years ago students of 'comparative religion' began to talk a good deal about the so-called 'mystery-religions' which came into prominence in the Roman Empire during the period of Christian origins. It was said, amongst other things, that St Paul had borrowed from this kind of religion, and that in doing so he had obscured the simplicity of the original gospel as taught by Jesus. This particular theory has now been very generally discredited. On the other hand, it is by no means certain that justice has been done to the facts which originally gave a handle to the theory. In other words, there has been a typical dispute between the two points of view referred to earlier in this chapter (Is revelation a product of environment or transcendent over it?); and it cannot be said that a satisfactory solution of the point at issue has been reached.[1]

It is not difficult to show that the religion of St Paul was no mere product of his gentile environment. It is a more difficult matter to decide to what extent his theology reflects that environment. But the problem must remain insoluble so long as we treat it in a piecemeal way. For different elements in the environment point to quite opposite conclusions. Thus we tend to discover an eschatological Paul, a rabbinical Paul, and a Stoical or Hellenistic Paul according to our particular predilections. Some of these varieties overlap at particular points; and there is always the possibility of individual reactions peculiar to the apostle himself. One of these reactions is definitely known. It is the intense indignation aroused in St Paul by any signs in his converts (as in Galatia and at Colossae) of that kind of syncretism (or hotch-potch) which makes an artificial amalgam between the religion of Jesus and some other religious system. This, it will be noticed, is the very thing of which he himself has been accused by some modern writers. Such negative evidence, however, cannot of itself furnish positive conclusions.

Our illustration has so far drawn attention to a particular instance of diverse conclusions following from differences of presupposition. This brings us back to a dilemma, from which, it was suggested, we could hope to escape only through some measure of insight into the unity of the bible as a whole, an insight which, in turn, would be dependent upon faith. Faith, as the gateway to a knowledge of God, would thus be the subjective condition of our capacity to find a unity in scripture. Such faith, however, would not be sufficient to deliver us from the dilemma of which we have been speaking. There must also be some objective ground in the facts themselves; otherwise we should become a prey to every sort of fancy. It is here, then, that the question of culture-forms becomes all-important. For if religion comes to expression in such forms, then it follows

---

[1] More will be said on this topic later. See below, Ch. III, § iv. In Ch. IX, § iv the writer has outlined his own solution of this particular problem. In the general pattern of mystery religions the believer attains union with a dying and rising god in a sacramental mystery. The superficial affinity with St Paul (e.g. Rom. 6, 1 Cor. 10, 11) is obvious.

inevitably that the unity of scripture will depend for its material factors upon some degree of cultural unity in the biblical world.

In the present work it will be assumed that a recent tendency to emphasize the unity of the bible is due, not simply to a theological reaction dictated by demands of faith, but at least as much to an increasing knowledge of the facts. A steady stream of literature is illustrating the theme of culture-patterns which throw light upon the biblical world of life and thought. Moreover, wherever these researches enter the biblical arena they tend to reveal previously unsuspected unities in the religion of Israel and by consequence in the background of the New Testament itself. The general effect of these researches upon our study of the New Testament is likely to be quite revolutionary. One of the most obvious gains can be succinctly stated in a few sentences. What I have called the piecemeal method of dealing with such a subject as Paulinism is doomed, and with it the controversies to which it gave rise. The question of St Paul's relation to the mystery religions, for example, could be adequately assessed only by carrying back both members of the parallel into the sphere of the Old Testament and of its multiple cross-connexions with the culture-patterns of the ancient world.[1]

At this point it is desirable that a somewhat fuller explanation should be given concerning the notion of 'cultural unity' as a factor upon which the unity of scripture may be thought, in part at least, to depend. Also, it will simplify the issue if, in our explanation, we start from a passage in St Paul's writings which is directly relevant to our main illustration concerning the mystery religions. In 1 Corinthians (chapters 8 and 10) the apostle discusses a question which had been raised concerning the social habits of the Corinthian Christians. Should they or should they not take part in dinner-parties held in the idol-temples of Corinth? Amongst ourselves such a practice would

---

[1] Some of these cross-connexions have been conveniently surveyed by a group of anthropologists in a collection of essays entitled *Myth and Ritual*, ed. S. H. Hooke (Oxford, 1933). This volume and its sequel (*The Labyrinth*, 1935) have raised issues which are still in debate. See (e.g.) *The Jewish New Year Festival, its origin and development*, by N. H. Snaith (London, 1947).

seem strangely incongruous, and, at least for the devout, incompatible with a Christian profession. Just so far as this is true, however, it provides evidence of a difference of outlook which has very wide implications. *We* have become accustomed to thinking of religion as something set apart from 'secular' activities, having, moreover, no necessary connexion with the conventional round of social customs. In the ancient world, however, religion was traditionally the framework within which all life was set. In this respect, at least, the unity of ancient culture was a religious unity in a sense which has to-day no precise counterpart in our western civilization. Here, then, is a mark of radical cleavage between ancient and modern types of culture.

By contrast with this cleavage between ourselves and that older world there are implicit in this section of 1 Corinthians certain presuppositions concerning the unity of ancient culture. Christians agreed with Jews in thinking that heathen idols were, in themselves, 'no-gods' and that their sacrifices were therefore empty of significance. But this did not mean that Christians no longer shared the ancient conception of sacrifice. Such an idea is precluded at the climax of St Paul's discourse,[1] and that by two distinct points in his argument. In the first place he declares— once more in agreement with Jewish opinion—that those who take part in idol-sacrifices are worshipping demons, and that to partake of food offered to idols is to hold communion with demons. Underlying this argument are presupposed, not only a demonology more or less common to the ancient world, but also general presuppositions of that world concerning the meaning of a sacrificial feast and concerning the way in which such feasts entered into the texture of social life. Secondly, the apostle here draws a three-fold parallel and contrast in which the Lord's Supper is aligned both with Jewish and with pagan sacrificial feasts.[2] The analogy would be immediately intelligible to St

---

[1] 1 Cor. 10[14-22]

[2] Thus, after referring to the cup and bread of the eucharist as a 'participation in the blood' and 'in the body of the Christ', he continues, in reference to the Old Testament sacrifices: 'Do not those who eat the sacrifices participate in the altar?' Finally the concluding statement that 'Ye cannot partake of the table of the Lord and the table of demons' covers all three sides of the comparison, since 'table of the Lord' as applied to the eucharist is taken from the prophet Malachi (1[12]), where it refers to the Jewish altar.

Paul's readers whether their spiritual ancestry was Jewish or gentile. The vast difference between the Lord's Supper and the pagan banquet (which began with a libation of wine offered to the local god) was a difference which pre-supposed a community of thought about the meaning of sacrifice as a religious institution and about the relation of this institution to the social life of the community through the medium of such commonplace events as the daily partaking of food. The apostle assumes that there is a truth about sacrifice exhibited in ancient religion, a truth which comes to its fulfilment in the Christian eucharist.[1]

iii

Religion is continuously assimilating material from its cultural environment; and therefore a supposedly 'essential core' of religion cannot be isolated from the cultural forms with which it is interwoven. The development of Israel's religion must be thought of as the growth of an organism in response to a divinely-ordained plan of revelation. The traditional character of this development and of its fulfilment to be re-examined.

The preceding paragraphs have drawn attention to the fact that a single religious institution like sacrifice could occupy such a central position in ancient communities as to provide an important focus for social life as a whole. Secondly, it has become clear that the rationale of this institution was in some sense shared with the heathen cults, not only by Judaism, but also by Pauline Christianity. But further, it is known that the institution in question goes back, relatively unchanged in character, through history to a remote past;[2] and finally, it will scarcely be disputed that its Pauline re-adaptation represents a very early stage of something equally central and continuous in the history of Christian worship. On the other hand, it is clear that the period of history spanned by the persistence of this institution in its ancient form was a period covered by many changes, including the rise and decline of a whole series of cultural types,

---

[1] To this subject we recur in Ch. IV, briefly at the end of § i, with further detail in § v. But a fuller explanation lies in the transformations of ancient religion explained in Ch. VII, § ii, and more completely in Ch. IX, § iv.

[2] cp. e.g. E. O. James, *Origins of Sacrifice* (London, 1933)

geographical and racial, national and international. Religious continuity, it would seem, provided a thread upon which such changes were woven. Yet the religious institutions, relatively unchanging as they might seem, were themselves subjected to continuous modification by the new social and intellectual factors which came into play in the course of the centuries.

These features of the interaction between religion and culture can be illustrated from the Old Testament.[1] Yet in suggesting that religion was itself the thread of continuity we must beware of understanding this imagery in a manner which over-simplifies the facts. For religion always appears in a human dress. Its unity is always expressed in terms of other unities which are its natural concomitants. Thus the similarity of pattern between the religion of Israel and the religious habits of Israel's immediate neighbours corresponded to natural laws of racial unity, to a community of traditions and of mental habits, as well as to a common level of cultural development. In this sense it is impossible to tear religion out of the external forms in which its inward unity is clothed, or to regard it as a thing-in-itself wholly independent of those forms. Later we shall seek to show that the attempt to isolate an essential core of religion from the external forms in which it was originally clothed merely results in an unconscious re-clothing of the supposed core in forms more familiar to the mind of the person who undertakes the hazardous operation.

It will be clear from what has been said above that the whole question of the relation between changing and unchanging factors in religion constitutes a difficult problem for theology. There are, moreover, other complications which have not yet been mentioned. In Christian tradition, for example, amidst all diversities of opinion there is general agreement concerning the finality and authority of the revelation enshrined in the scriptures. Yet that revelation was spread out over centuries of human development during which great changes of religious outlook occurred. The unity and finality of the revelation must therefore be of such a nature as to comprehend within its scope such changes. This inclusion of change within the unchanging is implied in the traditional doctrine that the Old Testament is

[1] This will be attempted later, especially in Book III of the present volume.

'fulfilled' in the New Testament. The modern epoch of critical analysis, however, has seemed to raise difficulties concerning the sense in which that doctrine of fulfilment can still be maintained. With a returning emphasis upon the unity of the bible, the whole of this subject is ripe for re-examination.

In the present work the doctrine of 'fulfilment' will be examined in what may be considered to be a representatively traditional form;[1] and an attempt will be made to throw fresh light upon such traditional teaching with the help of modern knowledge. In this way it may be hoped that some approach may be made towards a revaluation of tradition and also towards a fuller understanding of the issues involved. Meanwhile something further must be said in this opening chapter concerning the unity of revelation in scripture and concerning the manner in which that unity is here envisaged. This preliminary survey will also involve us in some further consideration of the meanings which are to be assigned respectively to 'revelation' and to 'religion', two words which have so far been employed without any precise discrimination.[2]

At certain points in the preceding pages, it will be remembered, the connexion between religion and culture was described provisionally in two quite different ways. First of all it was remarked that alongside its central theme the bible 'reflects and illustrates' successive stages and types of culture. Later it was suggested that the continuity of religion was like a thread upon which cultural changes were woven. The former way of speaking might suggest that the successive culture-forms had no closer connexion with religion than variations of scenery have with the train which passes through them.[3] The latter image, however, implies that in its passage through history religion enters into the texture of its human environment in such a way that a single pattern of life is woven out of the various elements through a unifying power which characterizes the religion in question.

A mirror in the train may have reflected each variation in the scenery; yet at the end of the journey the train may remain

[1] see below, from Ch. IV, § v onwards
[2] but see above, §i, par. 7
[3] Although this impression would not do justice to the statement on p. 2 when taken as a whole.

unaffected by the objects through which it has passed. By contrast, the pattern woven on the thread is a new unity in which none of the materials contributed have remained unchanged. If, then, we think of religious development in terms of this latter image, the various types of culture through which a religion has passed will be presumed to have entered into the structure of that religion in such a way that they will have contributed something to its total pattern. These successive types of culture may themselves pass away into decay and dissolution. On the other hand their respective contributions to the texture of that particular religion will continue to be operative factors in history just so long as the religion in question continues to be significant for human life. It is along some such lines as these that we shall best understand the relation in which the religion of the bible stands to the various cultural influences through which it passed.

Having reached this position, however, we must go a step further. Such a development of religion as we have been considering takes place in a living community of people. It is, in fact, the shaping and moulding of a common tradition which expresses that community's social life in its Godward aspect. The continuity of Israel's religion, therefore, was the continuity of a social organism in its response to divine revelation. In this respect the growth of an organism provides a more adequate analogy than we could find in the earlier illustration of a woven pattern. For every organism lives by virtue of its 'response' to the environment in which it has been placed by its Creator. By the correct response the organism assimilates to itself from its environment whatever is necessary to its development at each stage of its career. Moreover, at different stages its needs may be radically different, as the needs of the dragon-fly differ from those of the grub which it once was.

So it is with man, who alone among the creatures of earth can consciously direct his response towards his Creator. He also, at successive stages of his career, must needs assimilate from his surroundings very varied nourishment, material and spiritual. So too it was with the people of Israel who, in their spiritual life, were the recipients of God's special revelation. Their response to that revelation was conditioned at every stage both by the level of their own previous development and by the

14

character of the surrounding influences. So far, then, we have been speaking of religion as something subject to the laws of organic development. This conception, however, has now to be adjusted to our main theme. The continuity of religion must be brought into relation with the unity of revelation. The development of Israel's religion, however it be conceived, involved a continuous response to revelation. Here, once more, the analogy from organic life may still serve to guide our thoughts. The correct response of an animal to its environment is, biologically speaking, successful because that response corresponds not only to the needs of the animal in question, but also to the balance of forces at that particular point in nature's domain. Now for the theist 'the balance of forces' is simply one aspect of a providential order in which the plan of the Creator comes to fulfilment.

In the application of the analogy the balance of power in nature is replaced by a corresponding balance in history. In the story of the Hebrew people the believer can see a providential overruling of political forces. This divine overruling not only suffered Israel to survive as a religious group, but also provided, it would seem, at each period of Israel's history the conditions appropriate to its education and discipline at that particular stage. The detailed justification of such an interpretation cannot, of course, be undertaken here. But something further may be said concerning the connexion of events so understood with the divine plan of revelation in subordination to which the whole development of Israelite religion was being ordered and guided. To this subject our next section will be devoted.

iv

Revelation and religion correspond mutually as divine action and human response. For the Word of God is creative; and revelation is the sphere of creative grace within which the response of religion is made. The special revelation to Israel presupposes a universal revelation which is the correlative of man's creation in the divine image and the ground of his response.

The Christian doctrine of inspiration has been summarily defined in the saying that 'the Bible is the Word of God'. This is a forcible way of giving expression to the conviction that the revelation contained in the scriptures is in some sense to be identified with those scriptures. The precise sense in which such an identification is to be understood may perhaps be clarified by reference to something closely parallel which, in the preceding pages, has already been affirmed concerning the nature of religion. It will be recalled that we found it impossible to approve the idea of a sharp separation between the inward essence of Israel's religion and the external forms in which that religion was originally clothed. These external forms, it will be remembered, were part and parcel of that world of contemporary culture which Israel shared with its neighbours, the world in which all alike lived and moved. The attempted separation, however, would not only be highly artificial. It would also be a process which, negatively speaking, might be compared to the peeling of an onion, inasmuch as nothing would remain over from the operation. It was further suggested that positively, although unconsciously, the operation would be completed by the substitution of something more 'modern' in place of the onion peeled.

A similar objection may be urged against any attempt to distinguish the essence of revelation from the sacred literature in which it is enshrined. For all such attempts involve us in a process of discrimination by which we sit in judgement upon scripture and attempt to decide to what extent and in what degrees its various utterances are inspired. Here there is unlimited scope for every sort of subjectivity, before which the integrity of revelation must inevitably melt away. Moreover, if it be urged that individual judgement should be exercised in the acceptance of revelation, this claim can only escape presumption if it is understood in a sense which acknowledges the superiority of revelation over reason. It is for the Creator to decide in what manner he will reveal himself; and, God being what he is, the *manner* of revelation is not a matter upon which man can safely form decisions by his own unassisted judgement. The initial attitude of the religious man towards revelation is one of humility. For the mind needs to be attuned to the tones of the divine voice. Moreover the Word of God is not just so much information which we can assimilate and assess by purely intellectual processes. It is rather to be identified as an active

16

principle with that searcher of hearts so vividly described in the Epistle to the Hebrews ($4^{12, 13}$). It is now, as in the beginning, that power of God which gives life and light. It has the initiative; for it opens to reason doors of illumination and understanding which would otherwise remain fast closed.

The danger of prejudging the manner of revelation, thus briefly indicated, is a danger to which our own age has shown itself to be highly susceptible. This situation has arisen from the general character of our present civilization in ways which will be examined more closely as this enquiry proceeds. One, at least, of the reasons for bringing together the theology of revelation and the special problems of modern society will then, it is hoped, become apparent. Meanwhile, the parallel which we have just now drawn between revelation and religion suggests a congruity between these two which calls for fuller investigation. We have set side by side two modes of discrimination, each of which was held to be unjustifiable. Both modes of discrimination, it was maintained, tended to separate a supposed essence of spiritual activity from the outward form or vehicle in which it was manifested or conveyed. It must now be pointed out that the parallel can be extended a stage further. For the piecemeal method of procedure is implicit in both types of discrimination. As regards revelation it is this method which inevitably involves those who employ it in some measure of presumption. For how can we tell what parts of scripture are indispensable vehicles of revelation by contrast with other parts until we have grasped the revelation as a whole?[1] Is there, then, anyone who, outstripping prophet and apostle, dare claim to have reached that point of vantage?[2]

The congruity between revelation and religion, to which reference has been made, is of such a kind that it is not easy at first sight to say what sort of distinction can properly be drawn

---

[1] Naturally this objection can be urged just as strongly against the modern tendency to treat certain parts of scripture in both Testaments as having *a higher degree of inspiration* than other parts. By this method a silent presupposition is introduced which reduces considerable parts of both Testaments, in very varying degrees, to a secondary position, or again to an even lower level not greatly different from that once assigned to the 'epistle of straw'.

[2] St Paul repudiates any such claim twice over, in his repeated quotation of Isa. 40^{13} as rendered in the LXX (1 Cor. 2^{16}, Rom. 11^{34}).

between them. The difficulty has already appeared in these pages, as for example in our use of such a phrase as 'revealed religion', and that notwithstanding the contrast which was provisionally drawn between revelation and religion on pages 4 *ff*. There we referred to revelation as 'the way in which God acts in making himself known to man', whereas in ordinary speech 'religion' is taken at least to include the various activities by which man approaches the deity, whether directly in response to revelation or not. In modern practice, of course, both terms are sometimes used more vaguely without any necessary reference to deity. Speaking theologically, however, can we advance at all upon our earlier statement? For if revelation is essentially that which God himself does, must not religion then be understood to include the whole of what man does or experiences in receiving such revelation and in responding to it?

If there be indeed any such thing as 'religion without revelation' it can be left out of account in the present argument. For religion as understood in scripture always implies revelation, even though that revelation has been obscured, overlaid, or distorted through human perversity.[1] We must, however, go deeper. In the bible revelation is a correlative of creation. The Word, in giving life, also bestows light; and this light illuminates every man (John 1$^{4\ 9}$). With this teaching concerning the Word must be connected a corresponding doctrine concerning the Spirit. The inbreathing of the divine Spirit at creation (Gen. 2^7) is understood in biblical thought to mean that man is incomplete apart from the Holy Spirit. As in virtue of creation all men are enlightened by the Word, so only through the Spirit can they respond rightly to that illumination. Thus, as all religion presupposes revelation, so all genuine response to revelation is made under the influence of God's Spirit. But, once more, Word and Spirit are inseparable. When God utters his Word, his Breath goes forth. So when God calls us into existence he places us within the sphere of his uncreated light where our life unfolds to the warming influence of the rays. These, however, are not three successive acts, but three inseparable effects

---

[1] This, for example, is clearly the implication of St Paul's speech at Athens (Acts 17$^{26-29}$); cp. also the interpretation of Ps. 82 given in John 10$^{34-36}$

of that one creative grace which is the correlative of our nature, and *without which that nature cannot be itself.*[1]

The universal revelation here emphasized (which is at once the correlative of creation and an outflow of creative grace) is everywhere in scripture the presupposition of the special revelation given to Israel. The latter, however, forms the dominant theme, since it is the means through which the former comes to fulfilment under the conditions of a fallen world. This can be said without prejudging the question as to what would have happened if there had been no Fall. Taking the special revelation, therefore, as guaranteeing, and in a sense including, that wider economy which belongs to the plan of creation, we may now return to the questions posed in the last paragraph but one. The provisional answers there given must be judged to be, not indeed untrue, but for all that by no means satisfactory. For there a distinction between divine and human functions did not sufficiently preclude a division between the respective spheres of revelation and of religion; and this in turn might be understood to mean that religion, being the sphere of human activity, lay outside the scope of divine action.

Such a division into separate spheres would seem to imply that fatal misconception which has befogged the minds of controversialists in the debates concerning the respective claims of grace and freewill. So far from overriding freedom, grace has a contrary effect. For it is the sphere within which the will becomes genuinely free. Similarly, when we say that religion implies revelation, we must understand the correlation of these two factors as further exemplifying what is essentially the same mysterious truth. Revelation is the sphere within which religion comes to actuality. This conclusion was already implicit in what was said just now concerning the effects of creative grace. The life of man unfolds itself towards God under the warming influence of those rays of divine light with which it is surrounded, and towards which it turns as does a flower towards the sun.

V

The disparity between the biblical standpoint and modern estimates of religion. The Old Testament cannot be side-tracked

---

[1] In more technical language there is a coinherence of divine operations corresponding to the coinherence of Persons in the Trinity.

19

as unimportant; for (a) it manifests the lowliness of God, and (b) it shows the religious life of Israel as the sphere or organ of revelation's embodiment. The implications of revealed religion symbolized in the picture of the New Jerusalem.

In the researches of the modern anthropologist the human aspect of religion has inevitably filled the picture.[1] For in such scientific studies religion in all its manifestations may well appear as a product of the human mind, not radically different from other cultural activities which are interwoven with it. Indeed, the fact that ancient culture was commonly grounded in religious beliefs and held together in a religious frame would make it easy to suppose that at bottom religion and culture are the same thing, or perhaps two sides of a single many-sided mode of activity. This 'humanistic' way of regarding ancient religion can easily lead on to a further conclusion. Since the religious presuppositions of primitive peoples are no longer ours to-day, it is not difficult to conclude that religion, at least in any traditional sense, is obsolete. Moreover, the function of providing a basis for culture which was formerly characteristic of religion is apparently now supplied in other ways. Even if these substitutes for religion are not obviously successful in fulfilling the task assigned to them, yet the absence of any acceptable alternative makes people willing to believe that in the long run one or other of them (science, for example) will prove adequate to human needs.

It is noticeable that in this modern way of thinking religion is judged solely from the standpoint of its capacity to sustain society in its pursuit of earthly ends. From the traditional standpoint of religion itself, however, as judged both by its practices and by its official exponents, the primary purpose which it serves is the placing of man in right relations with God. Any benefits which accrue to man himself are in strict subordination to this primary aim. The difference of attitude here disclosed has serious consequences for belief. In the first place, the modern habit of regarding religion as a means to immediate human ends makes it extremely difficult to regard sympathetically primitive forms of religion in which beliefs, and the practices

[1] In this paragraph criticism is not directed against anthropology as such. On the contrary, its contribution will, in the ensuing argument, be found to be indispensable.

based upon them, are separated by such a great gulf from our own. Secondly, for that reason the Old Testament has in large measure become a stumbling-block; and this fact, in turn, directly affects men's attitude towards revelation, hindering the acceptance of the Christian faith in anything like its traditional form.

This difficulty cannot be overcome by a policy of concessions, which seeks to minimize the debt of Christianity to the Old Testament and to interpret the New Testament without regard to its primitive background. Such a policy would inevitably be self-defeating for reasons which cannot as yet be fully set forth. They will engage our attention more fully as we proceed. For the present it will be sufficient to recall the conception of revelation outlined in the first section of this chapter. There the Form of the Servant which Jesus took upon himself was understood to be of one piece with the whole of God's dealings with man; and the conclusion was drawn that there is 'no sphere or level of human life which could not be instrumental to such a revelation'. If we accept this conclusion, then what I have called a policy of concessions is seen to spring from an attitude which has already abandoned the central fortress of revealed religion, that is to say the lowliness of God as exhibited in the Form of the Servant.

If then we reject the policy of concessions, how shall we meet the difficulty which that policy has sought to overcome? If the concessionists had but known it, they were yielding ground, not at the weakest, but at the strongest point in orthodoxy. The ground abandoned in retreat might well have provided the *point d'appui* for attack. For the scandal of the Old Testament may be seen to be of one pattern with the scandal of the Cross, that greater scandal which we are now able to take for granted precisely because the Church has ever believed it to be glorious, even at times when she has not proved faithful to that belief. The stumbling-block which men find in the Old Testament is occasioned by those same tendencies of our fallen nature which brought the Son of God to Calvary. In brief, the pride of the human heart cannot stomach the humility of God. It is more congenial to find the revelation of God reflected in our own ideals and achievements than to follow the lowly track which that revelation has actually traced for itself in its slow movement through history within the limits set for it by man's capacity to receive.

Seen from this point of view the Old Testament is not primarily a record of disappointingly low achievements which we have long since left behind. It is rather, in the first instance, the story of God's self-appointed humiliation, whereby he fashioned for himself the chosen vessel in and through which he could redress the disorder of his creation. Here we may recall to mind two truths, already emphasized, which must now receive their application. First, revelation is creative of that response which we call religion; and secondly such creative grace of revelation can and does use human life at all levels as the instrument through which it acts. Revelation is not given *in vacuo*, that is, without a medium. It presupposes not only recipients but also organs of its manifestation. Such an organ is the order of creation itself; such also is man, the deputed head of that order. The latter, however, has the capacity to co-operate with deity by free response; and this response, just so far as it is rightly ordered, is, as we have seen, the product of creative grace.

This rightly ordered response to revelation is the essence of true religion. But further, we can now see that revelation is given, not only *to* those who make such religious response, but also *in and through them*. True religion, then, is the appointed organ of revelation; and it is in this sense that we may properly refer to the religion of the bible as *revealed religion*. This phrase epitomizes an important truth concerning revelation. The knowledge of God is given, we are accustomed to say, through the divine acts in history. We know what God is like by the *manner* in which he has dealt with us. In particular, this means that God did not leave men without guidance as to the nature of religious response. The biblical writers are unanimous in affirming that from time to time Israel received direction or re-direction concerning the ordering of its religious life. Under such authoritative sanction the orientation of the worshipping community towards God was embodied in concrete forms and institutions suitable to the actual development to which men had so far attained. The religion of Israel was thus both a deposit of revelation and the sphere of the divine manifestation. The Word of God in its coming to man generated an answering word as the means to its own fuller elucidation.

This conception of Israel's religious life as the given sphere in which God made himself known has still to be brought into relation with its 'fulfilment' in Christ. By way of transition to that subject let us notice how vividly our present theme is expressed in the picture of the New Jerusalem with which the canon of scripture closes.[1] Here the worshipping community, the People of God, is represented as the place in which the divine glory is manifested to the nations of the world. At the heart of this city-sanctuary is the source of its illumination, the Lamb of God, in whom is focussed the uncreated light of deity, and from whom that light is refracted forth with power to draw all mankind into its orbit. Moreover, the title of the central figure and the whole of the symbolism employed clearly serve to emphasize continuity between the two Testaments. The continuity indicated is such as to suggest a taking up of the old order into a new and final transformation. The discussion of this vital topic will round off the argument of the present chapter.

vi

Israel and scripture, as organs of revelation, can be understood only in terms of their cultural relations. Just so far as we are strangers to that cultural world we are deprived of a key which can unlock the New Testament. This complex culture-medium, transformed in Christ, must be viewed in wide perspectives of religious history.

In these introductory remarks we are confining ourselves to an indication of positions which are to be further elaborated in this work as a whole. Our general theme has been the unity of revelation as manifested in its human setting; and in that context two organs of such manifestation have been mentioned. These are (1) the religion of Israel as embodied and practised in the worshipping community, and (2) the records of that religion as embodied in scripture. But again, it was implied that the mutual relation between these two organs of revelation was dependent upon a third factor, namely the ancient environ-

[1] Rev. 21[10ff, 23-26]. The background is Ezek. 40ff, Isa. 60ff; and the scene is not heaven but a renewed earth, in accordance with prophecy.

ment of culture to which both Israel and the written word belonged. Thus it was indicated (in § ii) that the unity of scripture was dependent upon cultural unity, and again that in the ancient world the latter was, inevitably, a religious unity.

Next, we gave reasons for thinking that continuity of religion was comparable to an organic growth into which successive cultural elements were assimilated. The elements so assimilated, it was urged, were thus given permanent status as continuously operative factors in history. Finally, an identity of revelation, *in some sense*, was affirmed, both with revealed religion as practised in the worshipping community, and with scripture as the record of such revealed religion. The conclusion to which the argument is now manifestly moving was foreshadowed in the remark that, since the general character of revelation is one and undivided, scripture as a whole is organic to the new world which Christ has made in himself (p. 6). What that new world is was indicated in our reference to the symbolic picture of the New Jerusalem. Here 'revealed religion' has come to its consummation in him whose sacrificial offering is at once the heart of the true Israel and the nodal point of all revelation. Moreover, the entry of the nations into the holy city, bringing into it their glory and honour, suggests that very process of cultural assimilation of which we have been speaking.

From the foregoing statements it will be clear that the Israel of God, old and new, occupies a key position in what may be called *the order of revelation*. If, as we hold, the unity of scripture has its material basis in a unity of culture, the connecting link between these two lies in the historical continuity of Israel's religion. For the chosen people, in the development of its religious life, was on the one hand a focus of cultural unity in the slow process of the centuries; and yet again on the other hand it was, above all, the recipient of God's self-revelation and alike the object and the organ of his redemptive activity. As such it provided the constant and unbroken theme of scripture.

Under the new covenant the three factors just mentioned (religion, culture, scripture) have, in general, the same interconnexions as under the old covenant. Israel's religion is re-created in Christ. Yet the whole of its past is represented and even included in that transformation. This conclusion is required by all that has been said about organic continuity. If successive

24

layers of cultural patterns acquired permanent lodgement in the religion of Israel, then the Judaism of which Jesus Christ was the heir included the whole of this complex stratification[1]. Moreover, the reflexion of this manifold structure in the New Testament writings includes those final layers of cultural influence to which the first Christian interpreters of the Christ were themselves subjected during the century which followed the crucifixion. It is difficult to find any simple illustration which will give a convincing impression of the complex structure thus assumed to be present implicitly in the New Testament. There is, however, a certain kind of toy which is built up by placing one box or frame inside a slightly larger one and this again inside a third, the process being carried on in such a way that the last addition always includes all the other frames so far used. Thus, at the end of the process the largest frame is all-inclusive, and the whole structure is one.

The illustration, trivial as it is, may serve to indicate a single truth about the New Testament. It is the frame which is large enough to include in itself the whole legacy of Israel with all its diverse layers. As the written word, the New Testament includes within itself the Old Testament, not literally, of course, but by implication. This statement, however, refers only to the *written* word, that is to say, the record concerning the Christ and all that he signifies. For the unity of the New Testament is simply the unity of Christ the Word as that unity is reflected and reproduced in one of his primary organs, namely scripture. In the New Israel he has another primary organ for the manifestation of his unity; and each of these two organs of the Christ includes within itself the complex many-levelled structure of which we have been speaking. The bride of Christ sees her spouse, the Lamb of God, within the rich frame of scripture. But the nations of the world can see the Lamb only as he appears in the setting of the New Jerusalem, where his light is spread out over the bride's adornments and reflected in them.

The human setting of the revelation in Christ is, therefore, twofold; and this raises a fresh problem concerning the manner in which these two organs of revelation, the bible and the church, are interrelated. Discussions concerning this subject

[1] The 'heir' of the vineyard, however, found in it a richer inheritance than was known to the usurping husbandmen.

sometimes seem to be carried on without adequate attention being paid to the material factor which is the main connecting link between the two sides of the question. I refer, of course, to that complex structure of cultural deposits which is present alike in scripture and in the church. There is this, also, to be said. The point at which this structure was reaching its full development lies in the half-century or so during which most of the New Testament was written. This was also the period when the life and thought of the Christian Church was being moulded into classic form by the apostles and their immediate successors. In short, during that brief space the leaders of the church and the human authors of the New Testament are largely identical, so that one mind is reflected in both institutions.

In the opening sections of Chapters II and III attempts will be made to set forth some of the theological conclusions concerning revelation which appear to be implicit in these facts. At present it will be sufficient to emphasize one point only, namely this, that the normative interpretation of the Gospel took place under circumstances in which the interlocking of the worshipping community with scripture in a common cultural medium was at its maximum in every respect. But if this be so, then that common medium is clearly a key to the interpretation of Christianity the importance of which can scarcely be exaggerated. If such a key be either misused or neglected theology and the cause of truth must suffer a measure of damage and frustration whose consequences are too awful to contemplate. A slowness to recognize this key and its importance has already been responsible in some measure for some very serious mistakes in the sphere of biblical theology. Of these mistakes some notice must inevitably be taken in the present work; and that not for any satisfaction in the joyless task of negative criticism, but because the issues have been seriously clouded over and the true line of advance thereby obscured.

At this point a serious difficulty confronts us, a difficulty at which we have already glanced in these pages. The common medium of scripture and the primitive church is no longer shared directly by ourselves. A gulf yawns between our own civilization and the world of the New Testament. How then can we expect to build securely upon a foundation which we can scarcely hope to recognize? To return to our original metaphor, granted the importance of the key to which reference has been made, will it really turn in the lock when we insert it? Is it not more likely to become twisted by our unskilful handling, or even to slip out of our hands altogether? Two or three suggestions are here offered with a view to reducing this difficulty to less alarming proportions, even though it may not be thereby entirely removed. First, then, we recall that the common medium of which we are thinking is a structure slowly formed by processes akin to organic growth. Now in questions of exegesis interpretation will often go astray through our not knowing what we are to look for. If, however, we are looking for something which *ex hypothesi* has spread its traces over a background reaching into distant perspectives of the past, surely it should not be difficult to come upon those traces, if they exist. If, then, we have come to recognize even the bare possibility that such a complex structure is present in the New Testament, have we not already surmounted a large part of the obstacle confronting us?

The difficulty with which we are trying to cope is not, however, wholly due to the strangeness of the material medium in which primitive Christianity took shape. Another difficult feature of the situation lies in the fact that in the New Testament this medium has a cumulative character. Cultural elements which have been slowly assimilated into the religion of Israel during the centuries covered by Israel's history are now gathered cumulatively into one complex whole, so that any one of these factors *may* prove to be an important clue to any particular point in the New Testament. Our handling of this situation will, if it is to be successful, depend largely upon the extent to which we have mastered the literary habits of the New Testament authors. Literary habits, indeed, depend, in part, upon cultural factors; and this would seem to involve us in a vicious circle. There is, however, another consideration which enters in at this point, and which is of greater importance than anything yet said. When this new factor has been explained we shall see that it leads us on to a final suggestion.

The New Testament, as we have already observed, reflects the new unity in Christ, the unity of the new world which Jesus created in himself. To that new unity belong the writers of the

New Testament. Notwithstanding their human differences, they share one outlook through their common entry into that new world. Consequently their participation in what I have called the common medium has also undergone the same transformation. Their literary habits depend upon that medium *as it is reshaped in Christ*. These human factors are now controlled by the common orientation of Christians towards their Lord. We shall see later that the most primitive elements in the cultural medium operate in this fresh setting upon a new level. All this poses further problems, none of which, however, appears to be in principle insoluble. The new factor of which we are speaking may, indeed, prove to be the master-hand, which, superimposed upon ours, delivers us from much childish fumbling. If so, by guiding our inexperienced hands it may enable them to turn the crucial key in the lock.

Our final suggestion can now be briefly stated. The larger the canvas, the more easy will it be to see the picture as a whole, both in its proportions and in its detail. This principle has already been recognized in our reference to the backward-stretching vistas of the common medium which can be obtained in the pages of the Old Testament, and (it may now be added) in the stream of new light thrown upon that part of our subject by the sciences ancillary to history and pre-history. The canvas, however, may be extended forwards as well as backwards. Moreover, this forward extension is particularly desirable in view of what has been said about the new factor. The new world in Christ continues beyond the canon of the New Testament. The new Christian community did not suddenly change its habits when the last New Testament writer laid down his pen. Indeed, it would be reasonable to expect that the mental habits of the first Christian age would stand out more clearly, if we could watch them operating in a slightly more developed situation, if we passed, that is, from the first century to the second. For this reason special attention has been given in this book to the conception of revelation which emerges from a study of St Irenaeus.

CHAPTER II

REVELATION AND THE LIBERAL EXPERIMENT

i

Christ is the way, the truth and the life. But truth, though wholly given, remains mysterious. As the truth Christ fulfils all revelation. As the way he fulfils all religious response. Interdependence of these two factors, the truth and the way.

In the argument of the preceding chapter there was emerging a doctrine concerning the unity of revelation. Some of the implications of this doctrine can now be formulated more explicitly. For Christian faith all revelation finds its centre of gravity in the Christ. This truth, moreover, must be understood both exclusively and inclusively. Nothing can be put forward in competition with the exclusive claim of Jesus to be 'the way, the truth and the life'. But also, as the centre of gravity he is the norm towards which all fragmentary revelations are orientated, the *locus* within which they can be and are included. In him also revelation comes to its full concreteness. God is known in his works, but principally in that response to his fatherly love of which man is capable and through which the plan of creation is vindicated and brought to fruition. This creaturely response to divine fatherhood was fulfilled by the incarnate Son in man's proper form, that is the Form of the Servant. By his filial act our Lord gave to us an unparalleled disclosure of the divine life; and by that same act he opened to all mankind a way of entry into the life of response which is his, that life in which alone God can be truly known, loved and adored.

The very fulness of this divine disclosure, however, raises a difficulty with which we shall be largely occupied in the present chapter and in what follows from it. This difficulty may be stated in the form of a question which may have already occurred to some readers of Chapter I. If Christ is the fulness of truth, it may be asked, why should we concern ourselves at all with a less perfect revelation in the Old Testament and, more-

29

over, with all these complications of the cultural background? If God has given us all in his Son, and if, as St Paul says, 'we have the mind of Christ', what need can there be of anything beyond 'the simple gospel'? Will not that gospel be self-evidencing? The question thus posed represents a frame of mind congenial to the recent epoch of theology with its characteristic approach to religious truth. It is, therefore, highly germane to an enquiry concerning 'the Liberal experiment' which was made during that epoch.

It must be said at once that this problem of religious knowledge has two sides to it. God has indeed given 'all'; but how far are we capable of apprehending that 'all'? We rightly claim to know God in Christ; but in what sense can we know him? The answer to this question must inevitably be paradoxical. God is inscrutable; yet his glory is revealed 'in the face of Jesus Christ'. The knowledge of God, given in Christ, is available to us. Yet, inasmuch as it is inexhaustible in its wealth, it is also beyond us. St Paul says that 'his judgements are inscrutable and his ways beyond our power to trace out' (Rom. 11[33]). Yet we are also told that 'the unsearchable wealth of the Christ' is good news to be proclaimed (Eph. 3[8]). Finally, in Colossians two facets of this mystery are set side by side. Here Christ is described as 'the *mysterion* of God'. The phrase is technical and may be adequately paraphrased as follows: 'the secret which God has kept in his hidden counsel through the ages until now at length he has laid it open'.[1] On the other hand the apostle completes his sentence by affirming that in Christ 'all the treasures of wisdom and knowledge are *hidden*' (Col. 2[2,3]).

It will be noticed that in the foregoing statement I have referred to 'this mystery', where St Paul's use of the corresponding Greek word has a technical meaning which I have indicated in the paraphrase. In ordinary English 'mystery' can stand for anything which gives rise to perplexity and which calls for fuller explanation. Christian tradition, however, is familiar with the 'mysteries' of the faith. Such are the sacraments, or again the several articles of the creed.[2] This more theological use of the

---

[1] so Moffatt (*ad loc*) renders *mysterion*: 'open secret'. Cp. also the explanation given in Col. 1[26]

[2] The 'mystery' play, mediaeval or modern, has the same religious background.

word has a long religious history which goes back partly to the ancient 'mystery' religions and partly to the Old Testament.[1] In the passage from Colossians just now quoted it is the Jewish meaning which is primary, although we cannot exclude the possibility that for the apostle's readers the word would be coloured by the associations of contemporary gentile religion. The predominant suggestion of the word, however, is that of a divine secret which God reveals to the elect. Now any secret is 'mysterious' until it is explained. But the divine secret laid open in Christ is mysterious in a deeper sense. For although we have access to treasures of wisdom and knowledge in Christ, yet those treasures still remain 'hidden' in him!

The simplest way of explaining this language would be to say that the secret laid open to 'the saints' (Col. 1[26]) is hidden from the world, that is from those outside the church. There is much truth in this view; but it cannot cover the whole truth, inasmuch as the church and the world have from the first been closely intermingled. The knowledge of God in Christ is restricted and hindered by worldliness in the church. But secondly, what is laid open to the faithful in Christ is not thereby fully comprehended. 'The treasures of wisdom and knowledge' in Christ are that wealth which, as we have seen, is declared to be 'unsearchable'. For 'the secret of God', here identified by St Paul with Christ, partakes in that inscrutability which we acknowledge to be a characteristic of the divine life; and this continues to be true even though the secret has been laid open. But further, as God's secret, it is in God's keeping. Although manifested in Christ this mystery remains 'hidden'; and it is apprehended by those who are in Christ solely at God's sovereign pleasure, according as he sees us to be rightly disposed to receive it.

The problem which we are considering is by no means peculiar to the special revelation in Christ. There are parallels in other paths of knowledge; and these may help us to further insight concerning the conditions under which God may be known. While any form of knowledge makes some demands upon our nature, all special forms of knowledge involve a high degree of educational discipline. Moreover, at all the higher levels of knowledge, both in the arts and in the sciences, there are two further characteristics to be noted. In the first place the

[1] e.g. Dan. 2[17-30]

31

pursuit of knowledge is unlimited, not only in general, but in all particulars. In that sense the concrete objects of knowledge are always 'mysterious' and in some degree elusive. Yet, although never fully *comprehended*, they are progressively *apprehended* by those who submit themselves to the necessary conditions. This brings us to the second of the two further characteristics mentioned. The objects studied always impose their own conditions. Their nature determines the way in which we can know them. This factor carries a further corollary. Those who submit themselves to the discipline involved in their particular way of knowledge become by that very fact members of a cultural tradition, learners with others in a school of knowledge. To these various factors in knowledge we shall later have occasion to return. For the present it only remains to add that just so far as knowledge lacks the characteristics just mentioned it ceases to be significant except by way of warning.[1]

The bearing of these remarks upon our main theme is not difficult to see. The revelation of God in Christ is beyond our powers of comprehension, and in that sense mysterious. Nevertheless, although its mysterious character baffles us, yet, like all genuine objects of knowledge, it challenges us to put forth all our powers of apprehension that we may penetrate its secret. Here too, at the highest level, the universal law holds good, namely, that the path of knowledge is determined for the seeker not by himself but by the object of his search. At this point, however, the analogy cannot do more than point us to the threshold of the mystery. For in Christ the path of knowledge is not simply determined by the object of our search as effect is determined by cause, since in fact these two are here one. Christ is both the truth which we seek and also the way by which the seeker must go. The revelation of God is wholly given in the incarnate Son's response to the Father; and for us there is no other way of approach to the mystery of deity so revealed than that which is made available to us by our identification with the Son in that response.

1 When the concrete objects of knowledge are personal the analogy becomes more obvious. For (a) human personality, made in God's image, partakes in his inscrutability; (b) personal knowledge involves sympathetic appreciation of character, and (c) this is developed in a sphere of social relationships. For (a) see further Ch. X, § ii, below.

In particular, the manifestation of God in Christ demands and elicits a response from the whole of our nature; and this demand is more exacting and more comprehensive in its requirements than is to be found in any other way of life, religious or otherwise. In this respect the religion of Christ carries to its logical goal a characteristic feature of Old Testament religion. But, whereas under the old covenant the emphasis lay upon demand, under the new covenant it is the satisfaction of the demand in Christ which fills the picture; thus the old order created a problem for which the new order provided the solution. Accordingly, in Christ there is opened up in unexampled measure the possibility of a radical consecration for human life in its wholeness. There is also a corresponding possibility that in this thorough-going consecration a new and altogether higher measure of wholeness, unity and integration should be attained. Such a transformation of human life would have effects equally upon society as a whole and upon each of the individuals of whom it is composed.

Thus the fulness of revelation is reverently received and acknowledged in wholeness of response, the eternal interchanges of divine life between the Father and the Son being reproduced in those divine-human interchanges between God and man which are established in Christ. The unveiling of the Father's love in the obedience of the incarnate Son shows a complete mutuality of revelation and response, and at the same time constrains us to refer that mutual relationship back to the eternal life of deity. Moreover, on the two sides of this relationship there is a further correspondence of which we must take note. As God's revelation of himself is spread out universally over his works in creation and his acts in history, so also it is gathered up cumulatively in Christ by processes of slow preparation and of final transformation which we have already surveyed in outline. Similarly on the other side, there are possibilities of response to deity which lie hidden in the order of creation, which await manifestation in and through man, and which are fitfully exhibited in history. These also passed to realization through the lowly stages of revealed religion, until they were finally taken up into the wholeness of the Son's response to the Father. Into the orbit of this response we also have been taken; and thereby we too have access to his Father and ours.

There remains one further point to be made in connexion with the analogy drawn between the knowledge of God and knowledge in general. It was pointed out that those who submit themselves to the discipline involved in a particular way of knowledge are by that very fact bound together in a common cultural tradition. Clearly this also implies, at every point, dependence of the individual seeker upon the common tradition which that particular discipline creates. Once again, the whole of this common tradition is, on its side, determined as to its character by the nature of the objects investigated. The common tradition which lies behind the new edition of Liddell and Scott's Greek Lexicon, for example, is wholly distinct in character from that which operates in the proceedings of The Royal Society. Thus we find a dependence of the individual upon the relevant tradition and a further dependence of the tradition upon the objects of investigation. So also is it with the knowledge of God in Christ. But here once more the analogy fails to carry us further than the threshold of the mystery. For the common tradition into which the individual Christian enters is created by Christ in a manner for which no parallel can be found. The vistas opened up at this stage of our investigation are so large as to demand a fresh section for their further exploration.

ii

Christ is not only the truth and the way, but also the life. His simplicity is the simplicity of maturity, of integrity, of wholeness; and this wholeness is present in his Body, the church. The Body of Christ, then, is the sphere within which we can attain to the 'mature man, the measure of the stature of the fulness of Christ'.

The last stage of the analogy which we have been considering falls short of the Christian mystery in a way which corresponds closely to what we found before. As Christ is both the way and the truth, so also he is the life. He is not only the object sought by faith, but also the sphere within which the believer lives, the Body of which the Christian seeker is already a member. This scriptural phraseology identifies the redeemed community, including alike its constituent members and their common tradition, with him in whom the fulness of truth is given. But this language of newly-bestowed organic identity also reminds us that revelation is creative, and that the Creator-Word has re-created us in himself, in order that by inclusion within his filial response we may have access to the Father. It is a recurring theme of the Epistle to the Ephesians that access to the Father takes place in the one Body through knowledge of him who, being Head of the Body, is also God's only Son. Thus we are admitted not only to the *locus* of revelation, but also to its whole-ness, and that through identification with the Son in his wholeness of response.

Here we must return once more to the parallel drawn previously with the conditions under which knowledge in general is won. It will be remembered that the individual seeker finds himself associated with others in a common tradition of culture relevant to his own sphere of research. Moreover, the field of biblical scholarship is just such a sphere of research to which we can apply all that has already been said about knowledge in general. Now clearly the very basis of such a common tradition of scholarship is the complete freedom of each inquirer to investigate fully the facts relevant to his own special sphere. The common tradition draws its significance from the great elemental principle of all scientific knowledge, namely that every constituent member of such an association has, or can have, free access to the facts upon which a scientific judgement must be based. This principle of free access requires that we should make an important modification in our earlier statement concerning the individual seeker's dependence upon his cultural tradition. That tradition is not a mere link in a chain of causation, interposed between the individual investigator and the facts, as our original statement might have implied. The tradition is rather the setting within which the individual himself makes first-hand contact with the facts.

The tradition, however, is no merely passive medium; it has its own contribution to make. Thus, the correct assessment of the respective contributions of the individual investigator and of the tradition will often be no easy matter. These considerations must be borne in mind when we try to estimate the relation in which the individual inquirer stands to the unity of revelation in Christ. Here once more, however, peculiar factors intervene to limit the parallel which we have been drawing. There are two such factors, in particular, which may seem to open up for the Christian believer peculiar advantages to which nothing in the more general sphere of knowledge can be deemed to correspond. The first of these is the personal relation in which the believer stands towards God in Christ. The Christian revelation is above all things the self-communication of a personal Being to persons. When we read the gospels, we are reading about a person who is for us no distant historical figure, but one with whom we have a direct spiritual communion. On the other side of the analogy, however, the immediate contact of the investigator with the facts may be no more than the intermittent witness of the senses; and this, veridical as it is, cannot compare in depth and range with the sustained and ever-renewed communion of the Christian with his God.

This factor of personal communion has certainly been held in modern times (particularly under influences issuing from the Reformation) to weigh the scales down heavily in favour of the individual believer as against tradition. But there is a second factor, of equal importance, which comes in to reinforce the claim of the individual at this point. This factor is to be found in the special characteristics of the Gospel itself. In contrast to the religion of the Old Testament there is in Christ a great simplification. His yoke is easy by comparison with that yoke which, his chief apostle declared, 'neither our fathers nor we were able to bear' (Acts 15[10]). In place of a multitude of regulations one thing only is needful. In the context just now cited this one thing is variously described as the cleansing of the heart by faith and again salvation 'through the grace of the Lord Jesus'.

So far the simplification of religion introduced by our Lord corresponds closely to what has already been said about the primacy of personal communion with God. But there is also a further aspect of the new simplicity which takes us into the heart of the gospel story. It lies in the character of Jesus himself. There is in that character, as portrayed, a unity and consistency which defies analysis, although it is possible reverently to trace out some of its manifold aspects. There is, for example, spiritual assurance amounting to certainty concerning the ways of God. There is also a dominant serenity, which has in it none of the

Stoic negation of the emotional conflict, a serenity which embraces the stress and strain of life within a deeper unity. Again, there is a penetrating insight which cuts through the subtleties of Rabbinical casuistry and goes straight to the heart of the matter. Finally there is a tenacity of purpose which nothing can bend aside; and this in turn is directed by a clear perception of the end towards which purpose must be directed. Thus the various stages of the gospel story form together a single plan which corresponds to the unity of character unfolded.

In contrast to this simplicity and unity are set the misunderstandings, vacillations and failures of the disciples in the same gospel story, and the glaring faults and blemishes which stain the record of the apostolic church, not to mention the graver scandals and quarrels of later church history. Is it surprising, then, that the new and lighter yoke of Christ should be understood in terms of a direct imitation of, or reaching after, our Lord's own simplicity? Moreover, is it surprising that this striving after religious simplification should, in reaction from the complications both of theology and of institutional religion, express itself in a demand for simple directness and certainty in the sphere of religious knowledge? And does not one whole strain of thought in St Paul directly encourage such a view? If we already 'have the mind of Christ', does it not follow that we already have our finger on the pulse of reality? Thus by another route we return to the question raised near the beginning of this chapter.

Such a plea for simplicity raises many issues, some of which will be considered as we proceed.[1] Here we will confine ourselves to two or three main comments which will be closely related to the conception of revelation already outlined. First, then, the simplicity which is in the Christ, and which we in turn seek to have towards him (2 Cor. 11[3]) is a fundamental characteristic of religious response, perfect in him and indispensable in us. As such it is an essential pre-condition for all theological activity which is to have fruitful results. Moreover, it is not only a pre-condition, but also an accompanying factor which may preserve the inquirer from pursuing by-paths of false sophistication. Thus, if he perseveres and grows in *this* simplicity the

[1] The secular form of 'simplification' and its influence upon theology will be examined presently. See below, § vi of the present chapter.

seeker will be rewarded with increasing insight into the ultimate simplicity of that mystery which is the Christ. In all this, however, there is no immediate guarantee of final certainties such as might be possessed by initiates into a superior kind of knowledge. Indeed, that would be incompatible with the other strain in Pauline teaching which affirms that we must grow up into the truth. For 'at present we only see the baffling reflections in a mirror, but then it will be face to face' (1 Cor. 13^{12}, Moffatt).

The baffling character of our present experience is closely connected with the fact that revelation is given in wholeness of response. In Christ there is fulness of revelation, because in him the response was and is whole and entire. For that very reason all fragmentary revelations of the old covenant are gathered up into him, so that his wholeness is inclusive of all partial wholes. Similarly all possibilities of wholeness in mankind are included in him as treasure hidden, yet ready to be revealed in those who enter into his response. His simplicity, moreover, is just another aspect of his wholeness, his unity of response corresponding to the singleness of his character. We, however, are still far removed from the simplicity that is in the Christ, seeing that our response has that kind of immaturity which corresponds to a nature not yet unified.[1]

Thus we approach his simplicity from a lower plane and must needs contemplate it as a mystery into which we cannot fully enter. For a like reason his inclusiveness towards the enigmatic manifold of the Old Testament is inevitably strange to us, whereas the condescension whereby he includes our immaturity within the sweep of his response tends to be overlooked. This immaturity of ours may also too easily mislead us as regards both the meaning of free inquiry and the nature of religious certitude. Both topics will presently engage our attention more fully. Meanwhile there is one further aspect of our subject about which a final word must be said. The response of Christ, in its wholeness (although not in its perfection), continues in the redeemed community and in the tradition which that com-

---

[1] In scripture this kind of immaturity is traced back to man's fallen state. Thus it is a sign, not simply of an unfinished development, but of the disorder produced by sin. It had therefore no place in our Lord's human life. I have discussed this necessary distinction more fully in *The Incarnate Lord*, pp. 240 *ff*.

munity embodies. The qualification in parenthesis is all-important, and we shall return to it. Nevertheless that qualification does not cancel out the dependence of the individual upon tradition.

The parallel with knowledge in general still holds good. When all differences have been allowed for, it remains true that there is no sphere of human existence within which personal insight or experience can in themselves dispense us from entering into the continuity of that social framework within which our life is set. Our individual immaturities and their accompanying limitations can be overcome only in so far as we are assimilated into the whole Christ in his age-long activity. As he fulfilled the vocation of Israel, so also the life-structure which corresponds to that vocation can be completed only in his Body as a whole. The individual member of that Body has the mind of Christ, not as his private possession, but as a treasure common to all, something too vast to be duly appreciated in its richness by any single believer. The movement from the simplicity of immaturity to the simplicity of integration, maturity or wholeness, cannot be *per saltem*; it must come through growth and experience, involving a time-process.[1] Each of us enters into the liberty of God's children through *gradual* conformation of his whole being to that mystery which in community with others he adores.

So then we have access to all 'truth as it is in Jesus'; and yet, on the other hand, we have to become lowly learners in the school of the church where that truth is set before us. If the apostle can say that we 'have the mind of Christ' (1 Cor. 2^{16}), it is also said that we need to be perfected and built up until 'we all attain unto the unity of the faith and of the knowledge of the Son of God, unto a perfect man, unto the measure of the maturity of the fulness of the Christ' (Eph. 4$^{12, 13}$). We have here returned to a contrast already indicated in the paradox of hiddenness characterizing a mystery laid open. This paradox, however, is equally implied in the Johannine statement that Jesus is the way as well as the truth, as though he were both the seeker and the object sought. The reader will, perhaps, recall an earlier statement concerning what is in effect another aspect

[1] A treatment of this problem by St Irenaeus is set out below in a footnote to p. 146.

of the same problem.[1] It was there pointed out that the traditional doctrine of revelation involved an inclusion of change within the unchanging, and that the fulfilment of the Old Testament in the New Testament was one aspect of this truth.

Thus we are confronted with three fundamental forms, under each one of which a process of growth and development is seen to be included within the revelation of God's unchangeable perfection. The three fundamental forms are these: (1) the development of revealed religion in the story of Israel; (2) the earthly life of our Lord; (3) the growth of the Christian life in the Body of Christ. The entire biblical revelation is comprised within the unfolding of these three successive stages. Moreover, all the three parts are strongly interlocked and richly overlapping, with a single pattern of divine wisdom running through the whole. This point has already been noticed, so far as concerns interrelation between the first and the second stages, in what was said about the Old Testament being of one pattern with the lowliness of Jesus and with the scandal of the Crucifixion (Ch. I, §§ i and v). When once this point is thoroughly grasped, it is capable of throwing a flood of fresh light upon the connexion between Christ and the church. On the other hand, if this latter connexion, which is superficially familiar to us, is traced out apart from its profound continuity with Israel, formal orthodoxy may possibly be saved, yet not without grave loss of depth and perspective.

True insights with respect to the biblical revelation depend largely upon a right understanding concerning the interrelation of the three fundamental forms which we have been considering. It would be difficult to deny that to-day this issue has become crucial. Moreover, circumstances have combined to give to the problem a particular shape. The long period of critical analysis has tended to emphasize the diversity of parts in scripture in contrast to traditional emphasis upon the unity of the whole. In close connexion with this clash of interests (if we may so speak) there has arisen in the modern period another form of tension, namely the conflict between traditional beliefs and the claim of reason to investigate freely. The two forms of tension have not infrequently been actually coincident in practice. This has happened, for example, when free inquiry into the facts has

[1] see above, Ch. I, § iii, par. 3

apparently disclosed discrepancy or even contradiction between parts of scripture which were previously believed to be in harmony with one another. The mutual connexion between critical analysis and free inquiry will come in for fuller examination presently, as we seek to form a considered judgement concerning the great Liberal experiment in theology.

iii

The origin and nature of the Liberal experiment. Its strength and weakness. Its attempt to isolate a core of revelation which could be interpreted in terms of the contemporary idealism.

The argument so far developed may be summed up under two headings: (1) Religious revelation cannot be understood in separation from the cultural forms in which it is embedded; and (2) Christ can be known only as *the fulfilment of the entire organism* of revealed religion in its embodiments. From a general survey of such principles we turn now to the facts of an existing situation. In the course of recent centuries biblical scholarship has applied to the scriptures the modern techniques of scientific analysis and historical investigation. The critical view of the bible which emerged from this process has, during the past hundred years, precipitated a theological crisis in which we are still involved. The crisis has passed through three phases. In the first of these there developed a sharp, and even violent, conflict between the new view and the older, more traditional way of regarding the scriptures. The second phase was one of uneasy compromise between the new view and the old. Varying attempts were made to assign different territories or spheres of operation respectively to criticism and to religious belief. The third phase, upon which we have now entered, is still in its infancy and has not yet reached a coherent form. Negatively it represents an attitude of profound dissatisfaction with the results of the second phase. Positively it represents a renewed appreciation of traditional exegesis in certain of its aspects to which the exponents of compromise gave inadequate consideration.

These three phases of crisis correspond broadly to three stages in the recent history of biblical theology, but also to three attitudes of mind which may be, and indeed are, actually contemporaneous. Those of us who have passed successively through

41

the first two stages and beyond must inevitably desire both to justify our present attitude, and, if possible, to bring it into a more coherent form. Such is one of the purposes with which the present volumes are being undertaken. Let us first try to get a clearer view of the situation to which I have referred in terms of crisis and conflict.

The Christian believer who, in the course of biblical study, gives even the most general assent to the critical reconstruction finds himself involved in a dilemma. As a believer he accepts the scriptures as in some sense divinely inspired. On the other hand, as his investigation proceeds he finds himself forming an estimate of those writings in many respects widely different from that which he sees to be implied within the bible itself. Much which the biblical writers receive as history appears to him either to belong to the realms of myth and folklore or to consist of idealized pictures in which the history has been radically reconstructed in accordance with a later standpoint. Or again, books of the Old Testament whose authorship seems to be highly problematical and certainly composite are habitually referred to their traditional authors by the writers of the New Testament. Moreover our Lord and his apostles are represented as sharing such traditional opinions. Or again, the modern believer is often repelled by ethical standards and social customs for which the biblical writers who record them show no sign of disapproval. Finally the inspired authors have their own idioms of speech and their own literary habits. Behind these, in turn, lie psychological factors and processes of thought differing widely from those which operate in our own minds.

This catalogue of divergences could easily be enlarged. Enough has been said, however, to indicate the nature of the dilemma. The believer's mind becomes a sphere of conflict in which a clash takes place between two apparently incompatible worlds of thought to both of which he feels that he owes allegiance. Neither the one nor the other can be wholly renounced. Is it possible, then, to reach a *modus vivendi*? If so, how can the conflict be resolved? I have referred deliberately to two worlds of thought. For 'the biblical world of thought' is a reality of which we have to take account. This is a truth no longer open to question, the far-reaching implications of which are only now beginning to be understood. The phrase itself requires a good deal of explanation; and the subject is one to which we shall have to recur. Moreover the reality in question must be distinguished clearly from something else with which in the modern mind it may have come to be associated. 'The biblical world of thought', if it exists, is an objective fact quite distinct from those traditional modes of interpreting the scriptures which were operative before the critical reconstruction arose.

Traditional interpretations have the advantages which belong to tradition. They lie nearer to the ancient world, and therefore also to the biblical world, than systems which attempt to displace them. By virtue of their traditional character, moreover, they may and do retain elements which have genuine continuity with the biblical point of view. To say the least, such elements may constitute valuable clues which have sometimes been all too heedlessly flung aside in the supposed interests of modernity. On the other hand traditional interpretations have themselves been subject to the vicissitudes of history. The passage from primitive Jewish-Christian habits of thought to those which characterized the Church in the Roman empire, and from these again to the successive deposits, first of the mediaeval mind and then of its successors, this long-drawn-out process has given ample opportunity for far-reaching transformations. Some, at least, of these might be regarded as processes of dilution or of distortion, which prepared the way for their own dissolution. Finally, the disturbing effects of the critical reconstruction have forced the Christian consciousness to a recognition of something which traditional interpretations tended to conceal, namely the fact that 'the universe of discourse' in which we now live is radically different from that to which the bible belongs.

It has been pointed out that traditional interpretations of scripture are not to be identified with the bible's own account of itself. Nevertheless all pre-critical interpretations accepted (at least in intention) what *prima facie* seemed to be the biblical writers' meanings. By thus identifying themselves with what was supposed to be the standpoint of scripture they preserved continuity with the past, notwithstanding their natural tendency to introduce new features or to elaborate earlier stages of interpretation. The critical reconstruction, on the other hand, developing in conscious harmony with its own world of thought, has set forth a view of the bible which no longer professes to be that of the biblical writers. It is this new factor which creates a conflict in the believer's mind and which seems to place him in a dilemma. Accordingly, when this situation became manifest in the latter half of the nineteenth century, an attempt was made to resolve the conflict by means of a compromise. In that post-Hegelian age it seemed reasonable to suppose that a synthesis could be reached in which the tension between traditional beliefs and modern knowledge might be transcended without infringing the legitimate claims of either.

The problem of faith would reach its most acute form when what was believed to be the bible's own account of itself and, by contrast, the critical reconstruction were set over against each other in unrelieved antithesis. This might occur when each was regarded as all-sufficient in the sense that each seemed inevitably to claim the whole of the territory occupied by the other. In the new plan, therefore, a readjustment of boundaries was proposed. It was intended by this means to eliminate all overlapping claims. Henceforth faith and criticism were to occupy wholly different spheres. The spiritual message of the bible was to be recognized as true on the understanding that the critical interpretation of its earthly shape was accepted. The proposed compromise carried with it as an implication the vast, uncriticized assumption that what matters for faith is not the outward form of revelation but only its 'interior' content.

This was the essence of the 'Liberal' solution which reached its most logical expression in Germany towards the end of the nineteenth century. It marked what was doubtless believed to be a final concordat in the uneasy partnership between those who were in some sense the heirs respectively of the Renaissance and of the Reformation. This 'solution' has already, in the course of the present century, sustained so many serious shocks and setbacks that its supporters are everywhere on the defensive. It is all the more necessary, therefore, to make clear the contribution which Liberalism has actually made to the issue with which we are here concerned. The strength of the Liberal position lay in the conviction that reason is an ally of faith and that freedom to criticize is itself a matter of religious principle.

It followed from this that scientific criticism may properly be applied to the whole of the biblical material; and further that, in the interests of theology as well as of history, the critical in-

44

vestigator has an indispensable part to play. Here the function of criticism is quite distinct and definite. It has its own proper sphere which should not be invaded or usurped in the supposed interests of religious beliefs. This principle of free criticism is irrefragable. It remains quite untouched by the onslaughts to which Liberalism in all its forms has been subjected. Moreover, Liberalism was also clearly right in seeking for a delimitation of spheres. Nothing fruitful can result from giving dogmatic replies to critical questions. But if this is so, then the reverse proposition also holds good. No benefit can come from offering critical replies to dogmatic questions. In both cases the reply will have a spurious quality. Granted that faith and criticism have distinct functions which ought not to be confused, it does not follow that the delimitation of their respective spheres was rightly conceived in the proposed Liberal solution.

This was, in fact, the point at which Liberalism made its most serious mistake. It set out to preserve the unchanging essence of the biblical revelation; but it too easily, and even naïvely, identified that essence with the contemporary philosophic idealism of western man. In so doing it evaded the whole problem of historical religion, the problem as to how eternal truth can be manifested at all in the infinitely complex, slow-moving yet ever-changing processes of time and space. Moreover, by this too facile solution Liberalism also sinned against its own principle of free criticism. For if criticism is to be truly free it must be genuinely scientific. That is to say, it must defer always to the verdict of the facts. This principle was betrayed when Liberalism imposed upon the bible a conception of revelation drawn from quite a different source. The fact that the betrayal was unintentional merely serves to illustrate the melancholy truth that reason is all too easily prostituted in the name of reason. On this, its weakest side, Liberalism simply promoted a new kind of dogmatism. To that extent the Liberal theologian became a propagandist whose 'gospel' had no necessary connexion with the gospel history.

iv

The failure of Liberalism. This evasion of the whole problem of historical religion has fallen before the advance of criticism.

The impartiality of developing science opens the way to a new situation.

In the year 1910 Professor F. C. Burkitt published a short paper[1] in which he declared that Liberal Christianity was 'a compromise between traditional Christianity and present-day philosophy . . . formed by taking some things out of Christianity and some things out of our modern world'. He also expressed the opinion 'that the two elements are beginning to refuse to cohere' and that 'there is not enough of either element to stand by itself'. A generation has passed since this judgement was pronounced; and the time which has elapsed has served only to confirm the accuracy of the diagnosis. The Liberal compromise has collapsed irretrievably.[2] The system, as such, is dead; and, in the main, two causes have contributed to its demise. In the first place the particular philosophy upon which Liberals leaned so heavily has gone out of fashion. If not actually extinct, it no longer carries serious weight. In the second place, as Burkitt saw, science, with its strict impartiality, proved itself 'to be quite as ready to criticise and to destroy the presuppositions of Liberal Christianity' as it had been 'to criticise the presuppositions of traditional Christianity'.

The essence of the Liberal compromise lay in the idea that what matters for faith is not the outward form of the biblical revelation but simply its ethical and religious content, not the husk but the kernel, not the 'Hebrew old clothes' but the reality which they concealed, freed, as Harnack said, 'from all external and particularist elements'. It is this conception which has been destroyed by more recent scholarship. At one point after another form and content have been shown to be inseparable. The old clothes have proved themselves to be a body of flesh and blood without which the soul cannot exist on this earthly plane. In other words the revelation is manifested to us precisely in those 'external and particularist elements' which Liberalism sought to discard.

If this were all that could be said, however, we should have

[1] *The Failure of Liberalism*, Cambridge (Bowes & Bowes)
[2] For a recent estimate see the essay by Prof. T. W. Manson on *The Failure of Liberalism to interpret the Bible as the Word of God* in the volume of Edward Alleyn lectures entitled *The Interpretation of the Bible* (London, 1944).

no cause for satisfaction in so negative a conclusion. Theology is, after all, deeply concerned with the facts in which the revelation was given. But have we any reliable clue to the interpretation of those facts? In the hey-day of Liberalism such a question would have seemed unnecessary. For men were still living in that prolonged afterglow of the Renaissance when it was confidently expected that reason would unlock all doors and resolve all mysteries. The collapse of Liberalism, however, has left a void which has not yet been filled. Moreover, we cannot preclude the possibility that important conclusions of biblical scholarship which are still in possession of the field may prove to be untenable, at least in their present form. For, to quote Burkitt again, if 'scientific historical investigation seemed to be going hand in hand with Liberalism', this 'was partly due to the fact that so many of the investigators were themselves Liberal Christians'. Their presuppositions, therefore, belonged to the European world of the nineteenth century, not to the Jewish world of the first century.

It has to be acknowledged that the scholar can be naïvely complacent towards the presuppositions of his own age. He may even share the dangerous prejudice which counts contemporary wisdom to be in all respects superior to that of past ages. Such complacency will not fail to breed a provincial dogmatism which will discount ancient forms of thought as first 'obsolete' and then 'irrelevant'. Where this outlook prevails it becomes the biblical commentator's business to substitute a modern figure of speech for the ancient idiom, the latter being regarded as a 'metaphor' which is no longer suited to our needs. In such instances it is assumed that the substance of the revelation can be first identified in its simplicity, and then divested of its old garment and re-clothed in a new garment without loss of meaning. This was the working theory of Liberalism. As we shall see later, it actually does violence to the whole Hebrew way of thinking. Thus the ancient witnesses to the Word of God were gagged and silenced before ever they had a chance to deliver their testimony. The verdict went by default.

We have now to recognize that if theology is to be genuinely scientific it must resist the temptation to interpret its material upon the basis of premises drawn from any other world of thought than that to which the facts themselves properly belong.

It is just here that we are in some respects more fortunately placed than any previous age since the earliest period of Christian history. For through the accumulated labours of scholars the facts are more fully accessible now than at any time since that earliest period. A mere accumulation of knowledge, however, does not necessarily bring with it any clue to its profitable use. Indeed, the scientific habits of mind which characterize our modern world may prove to be a positive barrier separating us from the mental habits characteristic of that world in which Christianity took its rise, and to which its primary records belong.

It would be a complete mistake to suppose that these observations are directed against science. From another point of view, indeed, the impartiality of scientific thought is a primary safeguard against the dangers which are here under consideration. For science has her own way of correcting the mistakes of her devotees, of avenging herself upon those who misuse her resources. Perhaps we might say that the scientific machine has a way of consuming its own waste products. So far as modern biblical theology is concerned the crude over-simplifications of its earlier phases may be regarded as affording a parallel to similar mistakes in the corresponding epoch of the natural sciences. In both spheres faults have been overcome, partly by the impartiality with which science tends to correct her own errors, but partly also by the development of new sciences which effect a readjustment in the perspectives of human knowledge. On this last point something further must now be said.

Modern science began its career by mapping out that outer world which comprises the objects of sense. But as it passed on to survey the life of man, it found itself compelled to explore the inward workings of the human mind. In the result psychology has acquired such an important position that scarcely any aspect of human life and activity remains unaffected by its influence and by its special technique. Moreover the science of mind has taken yet wider flights. It has reached down into obscure underworlds, of animal behaviour on the one hand and of 'infantile' origins in man on the other. Again, it has also reached out to make novel contributions to the interpretation of history and of literature. Finally its entry into the intermediate realm of anthropology has done something towards bridging

48

the gulf between 'primitive' man and his more sophisticated heirs and successors. When we set this patient and sympathetic study of the human mind in all its aspects over against the partial collapse of civilization in the twentieth century, it is not surprising that there should have occurred a readjustment of outlook which has important consequences for biblical theology.

One of the less satisfactory features of the modern era has been, at least on some levels of thought, an unscientific attitude of depreciation towards the 'pre-scientific' epochs of history, coupled with an almost superstitious trust in modernity. While this point of view still lingers on in those whose critical faculties have been dulled by deep draughts of utopianism, the course of events is administering rude but salutary shocks to minds so sadly bemused. In the last century, however, the brilliant advances of science and the apparent stability of civilization gave some ground for such an attitude. It was, perhaps, not difficult during that period to regard ancient cultures as museums full of specimens of the past, objects whose value was to be judged solely by modern standards. Just so far as such influences prevailed contemporary fashions of thought became the final court of appeal against all that had gone before.

With such a background and with its own peculiar premises Liberal Christianity could attempt to justify its programme by claiming to rescue 'the Jesus of history' from a rubbish heap of irrelevant details. No such excuses, however, are open to ourselves. For *we* know that the revelation is given in the facts, and that no single fact, however strange and bizarre, is irrelevant. Again, *we* know that even the most primitive manifestations of human development are not to be regarded as dead relics of an obsolete past. For are not the barbarous habits of some obscure Semitic tribes among those precious facts in which the saving revelation was given? Finally, we may reflect that if any age of history is specially favoured by God, it is for the Christian believer that brief space of time when the Son of God appeared on earth in mortal form. In that sense at least Christian modernity must bow its head in lowly submission to the past.

V

The new path opening for biblical theology will lead to a more scientific attitude towards the medium of revelation. The

modern mind can no longer be the centre round which a theological unity is built.

Thus faith and knowledge alike point the way to a radical
re-orientation of mind with consequences possibly more far-
reaching than can as yet be envisaged. It is worth while, therefore, to indicate briefly at this point the change of perspective
which may be expected to characterize the biblical theology
of our time as it seeks to redress the mistakes of the past. In the
new outlook the centre of gravity will be found to have shifted
from modern fashions of thought to the mental world of the
bible. Instead of making his own mind, with its modern standpoint, the centre round which a theological unity is to be built,
the biblical theologian of the coming time will bend his thought
down to the mental habits of the inspired writers. He will then
seek to re-discover in their pages the modes in which *they* recognized and accepted the unity of revelation. As we have seen,
this readjustment has been, in part, forced upon us by the
development of those new sciences which are concerned with
the interior workings of the human mind and soul. But there
are also weighty theological reasons for giving a wholehearted
welcome to the change of attitude.

From this new point of view we shall study the unity of revelation as something inseparable from the mental world of the
scriptures. In such an inquiry, moreover, it will be recognized
that the two Testaments stand together. For among the primitive growths of Semitic culture, and in the soil of Hebrew religion, lie the roots of that Jewish tree upon whose fruits our
Lord and his apostles were nourished. There is only one world
of biblical thought, and that one world is mirrored in the New
Testament. We do not, of course, overlook here a complementary truth which is of primary importance for Christian faith.
If the one world of biblical thought is mirrored in the New
Testament, it has by some mysterious influence undergone
transformation in the mirror. This point has already engaged
our attention; and it raises issues to be considered in detail at
a later stage. For the present we are concerned with the unity
of revelation in scripture solely in its relation to scientific knowledge.

From these remarks it will be clear that the concept of a single world of biblical thought may be entertained upon two quite different levels. Of these the one presupposes the truth of Christianity, while the other requires no such presupposition. It is with the latter that we are now occupied. To the former level belongs the traditional doctrine that all the scriptures find their fulfilment and their unity in Jesus Christ, and that in him they are seen to be the Word of God to man. It is this doctrine which has seemed to be obscured and endangered, if not actually undermined, by the analytical processes of the critical movement with their manifest one-sidedness. There are not lacking signs, however, that biblical scholars are alive to this danger. It seems likely that the dispersive tendency of criticism will be balanced by an increasing regard for those factors which point to underlying unity. If this hope is realized we may be confident that nothing will be lost on the side of criticism. On the contrary, it may be expected to function more usefully as the proportions of truth are preserved.

In the new biblical theology, therefore, there will be no return to pre-critical devices for upholding the inspiration of scripture. For the new tendency has its roots in an objective survey of the facts. Traditional material will certainly be included in the facts surveyed. But if the new tendency owes something to tradition, it also owes something to reason and to the scientific spirit of free inquiry which is the mainspring of a genuine liberalism. The scientific basis for a new conception of unity in the bible will be found in the sphere of those newer sciences of mind such as anthropology and psychology. Indeed, important work in this field has already been done with most promising results. Not so very long ago religion was being represented as a 'pre-rational' product of human development. That is to say, it was regarded as a relic of the immaturity which characterized the childhood of the human race, something which was rendered obsolete when the age of reason arrived.[1] In due course, however, this superior attitude gave way to a genuine psychological interest. Primitive man was no longer regarded primarily as an irrational creature in bondage to obsolete beliefs. His mental life was still strange and enigmatic. Yet for all that it proved to be a fascinating object of study. His mental world was found

[1] For an examination of this thesis cp. C. C. J. Webb, *Group theories of religion.*

to have a unity of its own. Scientific analysis disclosed, not a collection of dead specimens, but a new field of spiritual activity. Here was, indeed, a world of most complicated patterns. Yet, at bottom, it was found to be psychologically one.

If we are to understand a man's behaviour we must find out what he is thinking. This is a hard won common-place which we take for granted to-day. To our grandparents it might perhaps have been intelligible as a practical maxim. If so, their application of it was certainly more restricted than ours. To the psychologist, at least, nothing human is alien. Moreover, his scientific objectivity is apt to have a strangely levelling effect. His researches have tended to emphasize continuity, rather than disparity, between civilized man and his primitive ancestry. Certainly in the present century *homo sapiens* has done little to disabuse the psychologist of this impression. The savage has been discovered lurking, with a savagery not appreciably diminished, in the mind of the sophisticated modern, and that not only in the confidential secrecy of the psychiatrist's consulting-room. The superior eminence of our contemporaries over earlier generations of mankind has thus been noticeably reduced. Meanwhile, as our own complexes prove to be surprisingly infantile in their origin, so the habits of our distant forefathers turn out to be surprisingly rational when seen in the context to which they properly belong.

With the application of these methods to the biblical material a new technique is called for. The nature of this technique may be indicated if we say that biblical research must inevitably become psychological as a necessary preliminary to the disclosure of its theological relevance. It is along these lines that we may look for a solution of the dilemma in which the believer in biblical inspiration seemed to have become involved. For example, in our reading of the dilemma the disparity of mental and spiritual development, as between the ancient Hebrew and the educated Anglo-Saxon or European of to-day, was seen to lie at the root of the difficulty. In the new situation, however, this disparity is already ceasing to be an awkward theological bugbear and is becoming instead an interesting scientific fact. We shall see later that in so far as the difficulty is genuinely theological it can be adequately resolved on its own level. But already some indication can be given of the line of approach.

In our change of attitude towards the Hebrew way of thinking we are passing from the negative fact of its 'obsoleteness' to the positive fact of its significance as a medium of revelation. What has now become important is the function of the Hebrew mind as the channel of communication through which God spoke, the instrument through which the divine voice still sounds. To change the metaphor, the outward form of revelation received its shape, colour and pattern from the biblical writers. They wove the garment in which the theophany is clothed, apart from which it cannot be manifested. For without that external medium of presentation the revelation would simply disappear from our ken, as surely as in a modern scientific romance 'the invisible man' was no longer seen when he took off his clothes.

vi

The defective technique of the Liberal experiment illustrated by reference to physical atomism. A possible bearing of this analogy upon the course of biblical studies.

Looking back we can, perhaps, see something of the process through which biblical studies have actually moved prior to the transition which we have just now been considering. The process has developed within limitations which were characteristic for the period in question, limitations which can be seen to have an extended background in the scientific rationalism of the modern centuries. We are thus brought back to further consideration of an analogy between the development of biblical studies and a corresponding development of the natural sciences.[1] An illustration will help to make this point clear. Until recently matter was commonly believed to be composed of separate, or 'discrete', elements, known as 'atoms' or 'particles'. Thus, in an article on 'atomic theory' published in the year 1909 we read: 'The belief that matter is granular in structure, that it consists of exceedingly minute discrete particles, is irresistible.'[2] Until the present century, therefore, with what-

[1] see above, § iv, par. 6
[2] *Encyclopaedia of Religion and Ethics*, ed. J. Hastings, Vol. 2, p. 210. The author was J. H. Poynting.

ever variations in detail, such particles could be regarded by the physicist as the ultimate objects of scientific analysis.

Moreover, the atoms, although not necessarily indivisible, could (so it might seem) be adequately known without being subjected to further division. In that respect they could be regarded as simple elements, and, as such, completely knowable for all practical purposes. From this point of view it would be easy to take one step further and to assume that matter, as the sum total of the atoms, could be completely comprehended. But further, whether or not that particular step was actually taken, the successes attending this typical phase of scientific investigation might readily lead to the assumption that an analysis of phenomena into their smallest elements was the most important part of knowledge. The fact that along these lines complete knowledge had not been attained would in no way diminish the prospect of ultimate attainment, since no insuperable difficulties had yet appeared upon the horizon.

With such a fascinating vista opening out it might well be thought desirable to extend the same technique of analysis to a wider world of facts, including literary records and the other human material with which the historian deals. Since, however, the method had won its most striking successes in the physical sciences, these would inevitably tend to furnish a pattern which would be reproduced when the new technique was employed in other spheres. As the physicist sought to identify the simplest elements, so the historian might be encouraged to search for elemental facts beyond which his analysis could not be carried. How far such an analogy between history and physical science is rightly drawn need not here concern us. The point is that just so far as physics furnished a pattern for other disciplines an incentive to a parallel simplification was introduced. Thus, the biblical investigator, amongst others, would be encouraged to suppose that the material upon which he was working might eventually be reduced to a collection of elemental facts in which there was no further mystery to be explored.

That biblical studies have been subjected to some such influences can scarcely be doubted. Just so far, then, as those studies were carried on, consciously or unconsciously, under a method of analysis so conceived they would be impeded by the same limiting factors which characterized the whole procedure. A collection of 'original facts' could not be an adequate representation of the biblical world of life and thought. As a *collection* it would be the sum of a number of separate (discrete) items. Regarded as *original*, in the sense of going to the root of things, the separate items of such a collection would be disappointingly inadequate. They would be mere external counters, surface phenomena lacking depth, and therefore incapable of revealing the real world of life and thought which underlay them.

Under such circumstances *discreteness* and *externality* were bound to be limiting factors, as it is clear also that they would be inevitable concomitants; for deeper analysis would destroy the appearance of separateness. The reality would be more like an archipelago in which surface impressions showed only a collection of islands divided from one another by the sea, where, however, diving operations would disclose the fact that the islands were actually mountain tops belonging to a connected range. When scientific exploration had been carried further it would eventually be realized that the bareness of the mountain tops gave no hint of the luxurious sea-plants and other living organisms which flourished in the world below.

This parable is applicable to both parts of our previous analogy, that is to say, both to physical science and to biblical research. In the former (physical science) the separate 'elements' now present the appearance of nodal points within a field of energy, each nodal point again, from another point of view, being found to comprise within itself a complex world within a world. So too, fuller knowledge of the biblical materials and of the mental activity which underlies them reveals a *cosmos*, an ordered human world, mysterious, yet ready to give a coherent account of itself so soon as it begins to be apprehended as a whole. The whole which reveals itself, however, is not that which the modern mind expected from first impressions of the facts. It shows a connected pattern wrought in richer colours than surface appearance could show.

The analogy between biblical methods of research and the technique of scientific analysis can now be carried a step further. The phase of physical science which furnished the analogy also provided a foundation for that fashion of thought in which matter was supposed to be like a machine. Let us consider what this implies. If we take a building to pieces, brick by brick, we

55

can see precisely how it was built up and of what units it was composed. Similarly the reduction of matter to its simple elements was a procedure which carried with it two implications. In the first place it was implied that the key to the structure lay in the parts alone. Consequently, if these were exposed in their simplicity the whole would be explained. Secondly, it was implied that the unity of the structure was like the unity of a machine. Now a machine has three characteristics which are, at this point, significant for our argument: (1) A machine can be taken to pieces, and so 'reduced' to its parts. (2) The parts, so reduced, can be seen in their individual significance. They are, in a sense, self-explanatory. (3) The parts can then be fitted together again into the frame to which they belong, a feat such as any small boy can perform with his 'meccano' set.

If we transfer these associations to a literary or historical inquiry two notions will be likely to predominate. On the one hand it will be assumed that in the very process of 'reduction' by the method of isolation the individual significance of each fact will be laid bare. In short, the facts will become *elementary* just so far as they are made out to be *elemental*. On the other hand a further assumption will follow inevitably. It will be taken for granted that the facts thus isolated and exposed can be fitted together again by a reverse process. It is at this point that we can put our finger on a flaw in the procedure. When a machine is reassembled some of the parts provide a frame into which the others are fitted. Where then does the frame come from in the process of reconstruction which we are considering? The answer to this question applies, once more, to both sides of the analogy. The frame into which the facts are fitted must be furnished by the mind of the investigator.

So far as the physical side of the analogy is in question the answer is not open to doubt. The procedure which has just been described corresponds broadly to that phase of scientific technique in which the elements were represented as having been arranged in a model. Moreover, scientists have, in recent years, shown themselves to be fully alive to the fact that the model or diagram in which they conceived the elements to be arranged was something contributed by their own minds. The model, however, has to-day fallen into some discredit for the very simple reason that the theory of discrete elements upon which it depended has undergone a complete collapse. Nature, it seems, has provided her own frame, and that too one having a degree of complication such that the scientific imagination cannot hope to comprehend it adequately. Moreover, exact science cannot afford to depend on an exercise of the imagination which is liable to prove misleading on some vital point. Accordingly the model has gone back into store and has been replaced by mathematical equations.[1]

Thus, on the biblical side of the analogy we can see that the arrangement of the facts in a framework contributed by the mind of the investigator was a procedure which could be justified only if the facts were, in their isolation, ultimate and complete. The framework into which the facts were fitted might, indeed, correspond in greater or lesser degree to the reality which was under examination. All that would be irrelevant, however, as a justification of the procedure adopted. For that procedure ruled out in advance the possibility that the facts selected already belonged to a single frame of reference proper to themselves. We can here begin to perceive the disastrous character of the mistake in which Liberalism became involved when it superimposed its own theory of revelation as a frame into which the facts had to be fitted.

But there was also another unfortunate feature of the situation which we are analyzing. The method adopted gave to the investigator an artificial control over the material with which he was dealing. The facts, extracted from their proper context and set in an alien frame, were like the museum specimens of which we have already spoken. The process of reduction had obscured their significance; for they were no longer functioning in their native habitat, the ecological whole to which as denizens they had belonged. As museum specimens they could contribute little or nothing to the disclosure of their real being. An object of knowledge thus isolated could not illuminate the knower. It was something which he had to illuminate as it lay passive under his inspection. So the facts took their colour from the torch turned on them by the investigator. In its bright light they looked familiar. He could, therefore, with confidence assign to them their places in a world of his own which he knew and understood. Nevertheless, the glare of that light cut off the

[1] see, however, the concluding par. of the final footnote to this chapter.

facts from the dark penumbra which was their genuine environment, the unknown and obscure world of their origin. Moreover, the context judged to be relevant to the facts was determined solely by the investigator's torch delimiting an area of illumination which was strictly circumscribed.[1]

---

[1] The statements about physical science in the concluding section of this chapter could be illustrated from *The Logic of Modern Physics* by P. W. Bridgman of Harvard University (New York, 1927). See especially his chapter II. In contrast to an earlier tradition of scientific rationalism the author propounds a radical empiricism for which nature is essentially mysterious and unpredictable. He holds that even 'the concepts of mathematics are inventions made by us in the attempt to describe nature', and again that in trying 'to invent concepts which exactly correspond to what we know about nature . . . we apparently never achieve success' (*ib.* p. 62). With this acknowledgement we may compare what the author has to say about the use of mental models and constructs. His cautious statements about the former which show signs of oscillation (contrast the pronouncements on pp. 53 and 97) are poles apart from the well-known dictum of Lord Kelvin (quoted on p. 45).

In the series of volumes written by J. W. N. Sullivan (in a style adapted to the needs of the unscientific reader) an even more radical attitude is apparent, e.g.: 'The present tendency of physics is towards describing the universe in terms of mathematical relations between unimaginable entities' (*The Bases of Modern Science*, 1928, p. 226; cp. *The Limitations of Science*, 1933, pp. 53 *ff.*, and *Science: A new outline*, 1935, p. 117). Here pictorial models have finally disappeared from the scientific way of knowledge. Moreover 'we cannot observe the course of nature without disturbing it'. Does this involve the conclusion that 'our data become useless in the very act of obtaining them'? Or does it rather divert us from 'entities' to 'operations' (from things-in-themselves to their mutual relations)? See *The Limitations of Science*, pp. 105-107, and cp. Bridgman (*op. cit.*, p. 222) on 'the operational character of our physical concepts'. See also below, Ch. X, § ii (penultimate paragraph and notes).

Yet another attitude is discernible in a paper *On Semantics and Physics* read before The Aristotelian Society in April 1949 by E. H. Hutten. Here models are retained, but reduced to a much more lowly status and subjected to constant revision. The following extracts are relevant. We are warned against the mistaken notion 'that we have "explained the nature of matter" by reducing it to its ultimate constituents' (p. 124); and we are shown a way by which 'we can free ourselves from the limitations of the model' (p. 128). For 'models carry surplus meaning which seriously impedes the improvement of knowledge'; they are 'semantic systems, though poor ones' (p. 130).

CHAPTER III

REVELATION, TRADITION, AND THE
SCIENTIFIC SOCIETY

A. Revelation and Tradition

i

Revelation and its integral form. There can be no manifestation of Christ without Christendom.

In the last chapter it was suggested that an essential feature of theological Liberalism lay in its unbiblical theory of revelation. This theory, it will be remembered, was characterized by an assumption that the outward form of revelation does not seriously matter. In the course of the argument, however, another fact came to light which must be closely connected with our estimate of the theory in question. What does not greatly matter is nobody's business, and is, in consequence, left to take its own course. If we do not concern ourselves about the form of revelation, that form will settle itself as best it can. Does not this mean, however, that in fact the question of form will be settled by existing circumstances? And is not this precisely what Burkitt meant when he said that Liberal Christianity was 'formed by taking some things out of Christianity and some things out of our modern world'? Thus it came about that the Liberal version of the Christian revelation was inevitably provided with a form by contemporary thought. Theological Liberalism, then, was closely (indeed, all too closely) connected with a contemporary situation which requires fuller investigation.

Here we touch upon an issue which has determined the whole plan of the present work. Theological problems cannot be adequately handled if theology is placed in blinkers. Yet the whole shape of our present civilization tends towards a departmentalism and a system of specialization which has that very effect. The scope of theology, as of other disciplines, tends to be

59

too narrowly restricted to its own immediate horizons. To this subject we shall have to return. Meanwhile enough has been said to explain why a phase of our argument which began with the Christian believer's reactions to biblical criticism must inevitably pass at this point to a wider survey, before it can profitably return to the special problems of biblical theology. Our survey, however, must once more start from revelation, with which, in this volume, we are especially concerned.

The Christian doctrine of revelation affirms a special divine activity to which there is a specific human response. The revelation, being not only special but also historical, was given in events that belong to the past. The response, however, by which the revelation is apprehended continues throughout Christian history and is itself historically conditioned. As the revelation was originally given through the medium of the Hebrew mind, so also it has been subjected to a continuous interpretation through the mediating thoughts of Christians. For in a revelation given to rational creatures interpretation is an inevitable part of response. But further, there is also a sense in which interpretation is integral to the revelation itself. For in the New Testament, at least, it appears that revelation and interpretation are complementary and even inseparable, as parts of a single whole.

If the New Testament is the final and crowning record of revelation it is also, and equally, the first chapter of Christian tradition. From one point of view these sacred writings may be identified with the revelation. From another point of view, and again with equal truth, they may be regarded as the traditional interpretation of the revelation, and that too in its normative form. With *this* traditional interpretation, then, which he finds in scripture itself every believer must inevitably desire to be at one. For thus he is made one with the revelation with which the interpretation manifestly identifies itself. The only alternative open to him is that which was adopted by Liberalism, namely, to affirm the separability of the revelation from the scriptural interpretation within which it was given.

In thus affirming the separability of revelation, however, Liberalism was in fact driving a wedge between a presumed core of revelation, on the one hand, and the entire organism of historical Christianity within which, on the other hand, that revelation was included from the beginning. It must be acknowledged that in taking this course Liberal theology was, from one point of view, simply reacting to an existing situation— and that, as it might seem, inevitably. To this point we shall recur presently. Meanwhile, let us be clear what it is that we are claiming. Our judgement upon Liberalism rests wholly upon the affirmation of a certain mysterious identity between the revelation and the form given to it by the writers of the New Testament. What this means we shall have to consider in detail at a later stage, when an attempt will be made to provide fuller justification for the position here taken.[1] We must now bring together two statements made in the present paragraph. We have spoken of identity between the revelation and two other entities, namely (1) the form given to it in the New Testament, and (2) the entire organism of historical Christianity. Is there a further identification involved here also?

In considering this question we have to remember that the interpretation which we find in the New Testament was the interpretation offered by the Christian community in the first century of our era, and that too as part of its response to the revelation. If then there is identity between the revelation and its scriptural form, this involves the consequence that there is also some kind of identity between the revelation and the response which is made to it by the community of believers as such, and that too in respect of the interpretative function of that community. The logical connexion here is no closer than the actual connexion which we find implicit in the New Testament. Moreover, there follows inevitably a further conclusion. If the revelation was originally lodged within a traditional interpretation which, in turn, is found to rest upon the early Christian community, is there any good reason for supposing that the revelation would continue to exist anywhere else than within such an interpretation? This question could, without change of meaning, be reworded thus: Is there any good reason for supposing that a revelation which from the beginning was identified with the beliefs of the Christian community could continue to exist outside that community? There seems to be no way of evading the conclusion that there is, in some sense,

---

[1] The detailed exegesis will be undertaken in the second volume of this work.

identity between the revelation and the beliefs of the Christian
community as such. In that sense, at least, there can be no
separation between the revelation and 'the entire organism of
historical Christianity', or alternatively between 'the gospel'
and 'Christendom'.[1]

The Liberal version of Christianity, however, was born into
a disrupted Christendom. The revelation which it offered, in
separation from any divinely given form, corresponded quite
simply to the fact that Christendom in its disintegration had
ceased to possess a single integral form. This was what I had
in mind in making the suggestion that the course taken by
Liberal theology was an inevitable reaction to an existing situation. In this sense the Liberal gospel bore unconscious witness
to the fact that Christendom and the Christ are complementary,
the one to the other, so that should the former suffer disintegration, the latter can appear, if at all, only in a ghost-like state,
in that condition of disembodiment which St Paul compared
to nakedness.[2] Such indeed was the Christ who appeared to the
Liberal theologians. Quite naturally, and with the best motives,
they hastened to dress him up in any clothing that could be
found to hand. Bereft of his proper body-garment, the indivisible seamless robe of the great high-priest, the Saviour was
hastily arrayed in the mantle of a nineteenth century philosopher. It is not surprising that a garment made for quite
another purpose proved to be both ill-fitting and unseemly.

ii

A law of deterioration operates in the disintegration of
Christendom and in the consequent fragmentation of truth.
Disintegrated religion breeds false simplicities which do not
correspond to the complex facts. The fragmentation thus begun
spreads to every department of life.

The line of thought which we have been pursuing has led us
to the notion that 'Christendom' is the high-priestly robe in
which Christ is manifested to the world. Obviously, therefore,

[1] 'Identification' in the above paragraphs corresponds to a Hebrew idiom
of thought. The fuller justification of such language will appear when the
idiom is more fully explained (below, Ch. VI onwards)
[2] following a Hebrew idiom of thought (2 Cor. 5$^{2-4}$).

the disruption of Christendom has set up a fatal obstacle to that manifestation. It is, again, the recognition of this fact which provides to all believers a supreme incentive for seeking the recovery of visible unity. For if there is an identity between the revelation in Christ and 'the beliefs of the Christian community as such', it would seem to follow that the truth of the gospel is literally divided up into parts by the divisions of Christendom. Moreover, this unnatural fragmentation of truth is unfortunately not the only, nor perhaps even the most serious, consequence of disruption which has to be acknowledged. For when such a living whole is divided into parts the original unity of life is not adequately represented by the sum total of all the parts living their respective lives in separation. Rather is it true that through the disruption of the original unity each of the parts becomes, by separation, less representative of those complexities which life involves than it was by its former share in the larger unity.

It appears, then, that the rending of Christendom by schism has had for one of its major consequences the working out of a law of deterioration. By successive stages the rich complexity of the original whole was reduced in the separate parts to simpler formations. Moreover, this kind of simplification was an impoverishment which involved yet another serious disadvantage. Like is drawn to like; so each of us makes response towards something to which his nature in some sense already corresponds. In a divided Christendom the parts, now oversimplified, find it more difficult to respond to the many-sided wholeness of truth, since in their divided state they no longer form a true counterpart of that mysterious wholeness. For Christian believers the matter may be stated more succinctly. Human nature is a complex thing containing in itself contrasted, and even contradictory, tendencies. Yet our Lord took this nature of ours in its completeness and made it his own, thus including all the contrasts and the complexities within himself. The church, therefore, which is his body is called to exhibit a similar inclusiveness of character. Only so can she reflect as in a mirror 'the truth as it is in Jesus', and so become like that which she reflects.[1]

[1] 2 Cor. 3[18], Eph. 4[21-24]. The precise relation of the church to Christendom will be considered later. See below, Ch. III, § v (last 2 pars.) and § vi, Ch. IV, § ii.

It is worth while, at this point, to take note of the fact that in the language of the New Testament 'salvation' means 'a making whole'. The state of salvation, therefore, is a state of wholeness in which we share by virtue of our membership in that 'whole' which is humanity redeemed in Christ. On the other hand the disruption of Christendom corresponds to the disintegration effected in human nature by its fallen state;[1] and, again, the divisions of Christendom are a means whereby that disintegration becomes still further entrenched, as it obscures the revelation in Christ and thwarts our due apprehension of it. Here there enters also a further consideration. Just so far as we are insensitive to the wholeness of truth, we take some fragment of it apart for our own purposes. We make it serve our own partial ends, thereby subjecting it to ourselves. Truth then seems to us to be simpler than it actually is; and we ourselves enjoy a spurious kind of simplicity in possessing it under a fragmentary form.

At each stage in this process the 'given' character of truth, as something beyond and above us, is steadily reduced, until at last it becomes a mere instrument of our subjectivity and of our lust for self-expression. The spurious simplicity here described is so far from being that simplicity of the gospel which is a genuine effect of the Spirit, that it may be more aptly compared to the Dead Sea fruit of a tree devitalized by the poison of its environment and the poverty of its heritage. The Liberal experiment in theology had in it something of that false simplicity; and this defect, in turn, may be traced to what might be called an impoverished spiritual ancestry.

The processes of disintegration which lay behind this particular movement in theology have been connected in the preceding argument with the breakdown of unity in Christendom. But obviously the formal breaches of communion which have occurred simply registered the breaking points of long-continued strain and stress when protracted issues reached at length their climacteric. We have to think rather of separative tendencies which gradually hardened into divergent presentations of truth.

---

[1] Thus the 'law of deterioration' began with the Fall of Man; and the process of salvation as 'a making whole' corresponds to the unity of creation. The principle of wholeness or 'totality' will be further discussed below in § viii of the present chapter.

The river of Christendom first bifurcated slowly into eastern and western streams; and when this bifurcation had become a settled fact, that fact, in turn, became the starting point of a fresh dispersive tendency in the west for which no compensating factor could be found. The quality which might have effected the necessary compensation seems to have mysteriously evaporated in the course of that original bifurcation, or possibly earlier still.

However that may be, as the intellectual life of Christendom developed and its institutions were elaborated, first racial and then individual factors received new emphasis. Moreover, as time went on the emotional, intuitive and imaginative elements in our nature tended to be forced apart from the more strictly logical processes of discursive reason. Whereas these various elements had previously been held together in some sort of balanced tension, they now began to be penned up in separate channels. In the result each of the elements in question acquired a new intensity both of activity and of emphasis. This, again, brought them into friction and disharmony through their mutually exclusive claims to pre-eminence. During this period of our western history faith became divorced from reason, while piety became a sort of thing-in-itself which might or might not be functionally related to the social organism.

Thus in the religious sphere the inward and the outward factors also ceased to hold one another in healthy tension. That 'complex of opposites' which is human nature is in itself the appointed meeting-place of this created order and of a yet more mysterious realm of spirit. Man is, therefore, so situated that this present world is for him symbolic of things spiritual. His mind is in itself a fertile source of symbolism and his entire being provides a natural basis for sacramentalism. As, however, the wholeness into which he was originally called was undergoing disintegration, so he himself was ceasing to be a single whole capable of receiving religious consecration in a sacramental order. The next stage in the process of dissolution followed inevitably. By a filleting process the spiritual and the material were separated off into parallel strata, as between which a condition of strict neutrality must henceforth be maintained.

This dualism had its repercussions in other spheres. Reason, now emancipated from the task of contemplating the *ens verum* of Christian revelation, had learnt to subdivide the knowable into distinct domains. It could thus, in practice, restrict its activities to the collection, analysis and arrangement of facts. In this way the contemporary contraction of faith to the inner world of religious experience had its counterpart in the restriction of knowledge to the outer world of sense experience. At the period when the modern era of biblical scholarship had its beginnings this 'empirical' limitation of reason and of rational activity was becoming a foundation principle of science. As to that, we have already seen, in the preceding chapter, something of the limitations under which that principle has operated.

After this fashion, and not at this point only, the religious withdrawal from the outer sphere merely enlarged the territory occupied by the non-religious or secular forms of humanism. Moreover, when the outer wrappings of religious belief are broken through, then faith becomes exposed to the full pressure of contemporary thought without other defence than its own interior vigour, just as soil deprived of its protective vegetation is thereby exposed to the disintegrating force of wind and weather. In the conflict of influences which were moulding the modern world the divided forces of religion fought a losing battle. Not only was the outer world handed over to the typical men of the later Renaissance and its aftermath (principally scientists and economists), but also the new religion of individual experience became diluted by the rising tide of idealist philosophy. Under such circumstances it was all too easy for the believer to identify the substance of the Christian revelation with some contemporary presentation of ethical and spiritual 'values'.

iii

A spurious simplicity subordinates revealed truth to ideas, and subjects theology to the spirit of the age.

Upon such a background it was almost inevitable that the biblical investigator's relation to the facts which he was examining should become one of artificial control. Moreover it is not difficult to see how perfectly *this* 'religious' simplification dovetailed into that more analytical kind of simplification which we considered in Chapter II.[1] There we saw that the facts, reduced to a spurious simplicity, were fitted into a frame of reference provided by the mind of the investigator. This frame of reference, again, was found to be a theory of revelation drawn, not from the world to which the biblical facts belonged, but from a philosophy contemporary with and congenial to the Liberal theology. We can now see more clearly how this theory of revelation was constructed. The inner world of religious experience, loosened from its traditional outer wrappings, readily coalesced with a 'spiritual' philosophy of ideas and values. This made it possible for ideas and values to be projected back upon the objects of religious experience. Thus, for example, Christ as object of religious experience became identified with ideas and values whose original *provenance* had no connexion with the Christian origins except such as might have survived the long drawn-out process of dilution and disintegration; and just how much could we suppose that to be?

The false simplification of facts was influenced by, if not actually drawn from, a contemporary technique of scientific analysis. Similarly the 'religious' simplification, arising from and reinforcing the whole process of disintegration which we have been considering, became, in its exiguous state, a mere appanage of the philosophy which happened to be in fashion at the time. The two forms of simplification, however, reinforced one another, when harnessed together to draw the Liberal chariot. If the biblical material be regarded primarily as a collection of facts which may be selected and arranged in such a way as to reduce them to elemental simplicity, then they may very possibly illustrate truth; but *they cannot present truth to us in a given form*. For in reducing the facts to simplicity we ourselves give them a form which suits our own ways of thought. Thus they become illustrations of an idea because we have imposed that idea upon them. The facts wait upon the idea, because the idea seems to us to be valuable. In this way the facts no longer confront us with truth as something to which we must submit; they have now become obedient servants of our own minds, or rather of those ideas and values which have taken possession of our minds. To this last point we must now give our attention.

[1] above, Ch. II, § vi

If what matters for Christianity is the interior content of revelation as experienced, by contrast with the outward form in which it was given, then logically all external facts become irrelevant, in the sense that no particular fact can be counted as relevant except so far as it is attested by experience. In practice, however, it is likely that significance will still be found in those particular facts which seem to support the religious simplification actually accepted. It must also be remembered that tradition disintegrates slowly even when the very idea of tradition as something fulfilling an important function is depreciated or actually disowned. But whether the disintegration be gradual or sudden, it will inevitably occur.

The Liberal compromise could readily adapt itself to varieties of religious belief, and could take a more conservative or a more radical form according to circumstances. These variations are, however, irrelevant to the main issue. Just so far as the investigator is in artificial control of the facts he has lost touch with the world to which those facts belong. Removed from their own proper frame of reference they no longer have sufficient stability to resist the alien interpretation which he puts upon them. Moreover we have now reached the point where it has become clear that the control thus exercised over the facts is not even freely exercised by the investigator. For his mind is dominated by the modern 'universe of discourse' to which he belongs, of which he is, consciously or unconsciously, the servant. This state of dependence upon the epoch to which historically he happens to belong makes it difficult for him to appreciate the possibility that the very different world to which the object of his study should be referred has rights of its own. Thus he overlooks the ineluctable claim of historical revelation to belong to its own period of history, and the corresponding claim of scripture to provide that all-important form of revelation without which and apart from which the revelation cannot be known.

The psychological difficulty just mentioned deserves rather more attention than it usually receives. It is, perhaps, peculiarly *our* difficulty in the sense that it is due, in part at least, to certain special features of the age in which we live. Modern civilization has for some time been supported by the sweeping successes of natural science. These successes, in turn, have impressed their own peculiarities upon the structure of society and, by conse-

68

quence, upon the outlook of the men and women who compose society. Mankind is to-day largely occupied with scientific knowledge and with the enhancement of power to which that knowledge opens the way. It is only quite recently that the double-edged character of this enhancement of power has forced itself upon our attention as something which might prove to be exceedingly dangerous.

These special features of our age have, however, all along carried with them a serious disadvantage, and that not simply to material security but quite as much to the whole spiritual outlook of mankind. Scientific knowledge is not the only form of spiritual activity open to man. In view of its destructive potentialities there would, perhaps, be considerable agreement to-day that it can scarcely be the most important of those activities which are open to us. There is, indeed, good reason for thinking that human society has, by its engrossment in scientific pursuits, become dangerously lop-sided in character. For one thing, the enhancement of power which science brings has made for the belief that within a measurable distance of time all human problems will be solved—solved, moreover, exclusively by scientific knowledge. This belief, again, is congruous with, if it has not actually generated, the modern notion of progress as an inevitable concomitant of human history. This progress-myth, in turn, has for its logical counterpart that attitude of depreciation towards the 'pre-scientific' epochs of history to which I have already drawn attention.

These characteristics of our time have tended to promote a certain kind of outlook, whose effects may be compared to those of a climate in a particular locality. The spirit of the age is like a mental atmosphere which all must breathe, no matter what their conscious, voluntary orientation may be. Yet, just so far as we are shut up within the spirit of our own age, we ourselves become vulnerable to all the influences which are hostile to that spirit. To be the creature of one age is to be the sport of all the ages, a victim of time and circumstance. The psychological difficulty which, we have suggested, is particularly *our* difficulty is simply an indication of the glamorous spell surrounding our scientific humanism. That spell conceals from us the inherent instability of a position which involves us in such subservience to the time-spirit.

69

For there is a psychological law whereby the complex of opposites which is human nature cannot express all its possibilities simultaneously. In comparatively equable times it tends to advance in spiral movements. But in times of crisis like the present it pursues a more zigzag course which may be likened to the swing of a pendulum. Just so far as these zigzag movements become violently contradictory one to another, the resultant discontinuity will undermine stability and produce a sense of frustration with its attendant dangers of world-weariness and pessimism. Something of this kind appears to be happening to-day on an extended scale; and the crisis of social security has also its theological counterpart. The sense of frustration has for some little time been apparent in biblical studies.

iv

An illustration of how this spurious simplicity in biblical theology fails to achieve its purpose. The gulf between radical scepticism and faith not bridged by the Liberal compromise. Biblical unity vindicated by the course of events in which tradition and science each played their part.

With such considerations in mind, therefore, we recur once more to the sphere of biblical theology where, as elsewhere, the wider situation has had its particular application. For example, it proved congenial to the outlook of the nineteenth century to emphasize the moral and rational factors in the teaching of Israel's great 'writing' prophets. The isolated grandeur of these lonely figures was then explained in terms of a 'progressive revelation' which reached its culminating point in Jesus of Nazareth and its fading after-glow in the apostolic age. This was the supreme example of that spurious simplicity which made the facts illustrate an idea imposed upon them. Jesus and his prophetic precursors attained a standard of ethical rationalism which received the gracious approval of their modern patrons. Other schools of thought, however, took charge of those parts of the bible which did not easily fit into this scheme. These steadily and persistently reduced the island bases in which the scheme still found a lodgement long after its main lines of defence had been broken through. Such destructive work has had its compensations. Jesus as the unsolved enigma of history continues also to be the ultimate mystery, and as such an object of faith.

This, however, is to anticipate. In some respects St Paul proved to be the Achilles heel of the Liberal interpretation. The treatment meted out to him has, indeed, a special significance for our present argument. Since the Reformation St Paul has been for many pre-eminently *the* apostle, that is to say, the father and true forerunner of Protestant theology. This estimate has become so deeply embedded that it is still the sheet-anchor to which much of our contemporary biblical scholarship is attached. The Liberal compromise found no difficulty, at first, in adjusting itself to this situation. St Paul was recognized to be pre-eminently the apostle of religious experience. This could be exemplified in his teaching, and not least in the circumstances of his conversion. Moreover, the latter also conformed to the type of the prophetic call;[1] and in the Acts of the Apostles Saul of Tarsus appears among the Christian prophets.[2] It was quite natural, therefore, to place the apostle in the line of that high prophetic series of which Jesus was the chief example. Thus the last of the series became the prophetic interpreter of his master in the gospel of ethical rationalism.

But eventually this solution proved to be too facile. On the surface of things the chief obstacle to the scheme lay in this apostle's teaching about the sacraments and in the way in which these are connected in the Pauline system with a high mystical Christology. It is not surprising, therefore, that a rival school of interpretation arose, which found in St Paul the inventor and originator of Catholicism regarded as a system of semi-pagan accretions obscuring the original gospel of Jesus. Some short-sighted persons supposed that this thesis would support the Liberal interpretation. For the theory that St Paul had paganized the gospel left the prophetic figure of Jesus in solitary grandeur, sharply separated from the whole aftermath of ecclesiastical history with its *chronique scandaleuse*.

In traditional Christianity, however, St Paul had been regarded as the first orthodox theologian, who had given to the Church an inspired interpretation of Jesus in his person and in his work. To this estimate the Protestant Reformers had also given their whole-hearted assent. Accordingly, for Catholics

---

[1] cp. Gal. 1 with Jer. 1   [2] Acts 13[1]

and for Protestants alike the attempt to drive a wedge between
Jesus and Paul was at once recognized for what it was, namely,
an attack upon a primary bulwark of faith. The new version
of Liberalism, therefore, tended to undermine any permanent
alliance between the respective heirs of the Reformation on the
one hand and of the Renaissance on the other. This was a real
parting of the ways. For the policy of compromise between the
old and the new, between tradition and rationalism, had provided Liberalism with its food and clothing; and now that
policy was ceasing to pay dividends!

To those who took seriously the new picture of St Paul as a
propagator of pagan ideas that picture was seen from the first
to form part of a larger canvas which included a repainting of
the central figure in the gospel story. In other words this particular way of applying the comparative method to the history
of religion involved a much more radical scepticism, not only
about the gospel of St Paul, but also (and in equal measure)
about the gospel of Jesus himself. This conclusion was, for good
or ill, an acknowledgement that the New Testament is a unity.
As such, in turn, it sounded the death knell of Liberalism. For,
as we have seen, the gospel of ethical rationalism could be read
into the bible with some show of plausibility only so long as it
was attributed to that select chain of prophetic figures who stood
out like a mountain range in contrast to the crude superstitions
of their contemporaries. The illustration which thus rises naturally to the mind is significantly akin to that of our previous
analogy with a passing phase in the story of physical science.
Here, as there, it is a new development of science which brings
about the transformation scene.

In the earlier illustration[1] it will be remembered that a group
of islands proved to be a submerged mountain range. In the
picture just now drawn it was implied that a mountain range
somehow becomes merged in the surrounding country. On
Liberal presuppositions this would be an intolerable application
of the principle that 'the lofty shall be brought low', and that
valleys shall be exalted to the level of the hills, a quite paradoxical quotation of prophecy against the prophets.[2] Yet the
prophecy is consistent with itself. For if 'all flesh is grass',[3] there
are, after all, no exceptions. God is the great leveller, whether

[1] above, Ch. II, § vi, par. 5   [2] Isa. 10^{33}, 40^4 [3] Isa. 40^6

he acts through by-gone Kings of Assyria and Persia or whether his chosen agent be a German professor of comparative religion in this twentieth century of our era. Moreover, if 'all flesh is grass', then he who 'became flesh' for our salvation fulfilled in his own person the prophetic doctrine that the lofty shall be brought low. In short, if the Lord of glory *did* take upon him the form of the servant, he did *not* do so in order to give a lesson in ethical rationalism. He came, rather, to make himself one with the lowly; but if so, then that rule of lowliness would, for him as for his apostles, hold good not least in the sphere of religious *praxis*.

We have here touched upon a vast subject, the implications of which can be unfolded only by stages. For the moment we must be content with a single observation concerning the contents of the last two paragraphs. They were not written in order to support the sceptical application of *Religionsgeschichte* to the New Testament. For once more the prophetic doctrine is applicable. The instruments of divine judgement are effectual only against the objects upon which that judgement is divinely directed. 'Shall the axe boast itself against him that heweth therewith?'[1] Science, as always so here, will show itself harmless towards the truth of the gospel, and therefore, also, towards those to whom that truth has been made known. The writing upon the wall passes sentence only upon those who are already found wanting. 'Daniel continues' into the new era. For the heavenly Judge has committed all judgement to one whose lofty lowliness (under the form of a Son of Man) is specifically 'Daniel's' secret.[2]

So far as concerns St Paul the two ways of thinking, the one traditional and the other radical, have, in the modern period, agreed only in making the apostle of the gentiles the originator of a new theological construction. In that respect, however, both systems of interpretation have been seriously undercut by a growing recognition of St Paul's debt to his former Jewish inheritance, partly in the sphere of eschatology, partly through the normal channels of rabbinical thought. Moreover, we are now witnessing a yet further stage of the retreat from earlier notions of his originality, as the dependence of the apostle upon pre-Pauline Christian tradition comes in for acknowledgement.

[1] Isa. 10^15   [2] Daniel's name means 'God is my Judge'

There remains, perhaps, only one more section of this withdrawal to be undertaken. For we have still to discover St Paul's obligations to the Hebrew way of thinking within the biblical *cosmos* of thought, when the latter is treated as a single whole.[1]

Thus the failure of the attempt to drive a wedge between St Paul and him whom he acknowledged as Lord and Saviour constitutes one more example of that neutrality of science by which all theories are ultimately tested. With that failure there was also laid bare the essential absurdity of trying to read a humanistic Jesus into the gospels by the simple device of ascribing all supernatural elements to the superstitious naïvety of the apostolic church. This *tour de force* belongs to a dead past. The bluff was called through the formation of more accurate estimates concerning the Jewish background and the whole of that complex world of contemporary beliefs and hopes, customs and traditions, in which Jesus and his first followers lived and moved and had their earthly being.

B. Christendom and a scientific order

V

A parallel between biblical theology and natural science. Each mediates between its given truth and a corresponding

---

[1] Those who embark upon this final stage of the journey might take as a starting-point the following statement of a modern Jewish scholar:

'Intensive research over many years has brought the writer . . . to a deep conviction that there is nothing in the teaching of Paul—not even the most mystical element in it—that did not come to him from authentic Judaism. To this opinion which I presented . . . some years ago, the great expert in Talmudic and early Christian literature, Prof. George Foot Moore, agreed' (*From Jesus to Paul* by Joseph Klausner, ET from the Hebrew, 1943, p. 466).

For both of these authorities, however, the above conclusion is (as we should expect) subject to important qualifications. Thus Dr Klausner held that 'most of the elements' in the apostle's teaching 'which came from Judaism received unconsciously at his hands *a non-Jewish colouring*' (italics as printed, *loc. cit.*); cp. also pp. 482, 483 of the same work. Again, the Note on 'Paul' in Dr Moore's *Judaism in the first centuries of the Christian Era, The Age of the Tannaim* (Vol. III, pp. 150 *f.*, Harvard, 1940) is the inevitable counterpart of his *dictum*, on p. vi of the same volume, that rabbinical Judaism is 'normative Judaism'. The Note bears unconscious witness (so it appears), not to any misapprehensions on the apostle's part as to the meaning of Judaism, but to *the transformation of Judaism* which St Paul experienced when he became a new creature in Christ.

social structure, since there is mutual dependence of the community and the knowledge by which it lives. The peculiarity of the modern community consists in the fact that it embodies a new scientific 'graft' upon the older organism of Christendom.

The placing of Jesus and the apostolic church together upon a common background where unsuspected unities are disclosed represents an important part of what I had in mind in the last chapter, when it was suggested that the dispersive movement of criticism had passed the zenith of its achievements.[1] It was also pointed out that a conception of biblical unity might be entertained which did not require the truth of Christianity as its presupposition. This, however, did not mean that such a conception could maintain itself apart from Christian faith. Such support as scientific researches may give to the notion of unity in the scriptures is naturally welcome to the Christian believer. But he will not expect evidence so gathered to carry him all the way. It may serve to clear the ground of encumbrances and to remove obstacles. But it cannot of itself unfold the full significance of that unity; nor can it show wherein its essential character is to be found.

This conclusion follows inevitably from what was said at the beginning of the present chapter as to the unity of revelation being rooted in the interpretation which it originally received from Christian faith. The interpretation was there related to the revelation as form to content in an indivisible whole, that whole, again, being inseparable from the community of believers in which it comes to concrete expression. It must now be pointed out that, in addition to all this, the first community of believers was either wholly Jewish or controlled by Jewish leaders. Its thought was Jewish, and as such was continuous with the thought of Israel through which the revelation of the Old Testament scriptures was given. The New Testament, therefore, presents us with an interpretation of the Christ which is organically related to the older revelation through the Judaism of the first Christian believers. As, then, the revelation was, from first to last, mediated in both its parts through the Hebrew mind, so the unity of its form (that form which is integral to the revelation) is essentially a Hebrew or Jewish

[1] see above, Ch. II, § v, par. 3

unity.[1] If then the unity of the scriptures has a natural foundation in the human characteristics of the chosen people, all the
phenomena dependent upon this comprehensive fact will inevitably disclose themselves to a genuinely scientific investigation. The facts, however, include the interpretations in which
they are, so to speak, embedded; and again religious beliefs are
among the facts which are integral to these interpretations.
Accordingly the scientific inquiry will inevitably be carried up
to the level of faith where the beliefs in question are accepted
as true. Moreover, all the implications of their truth, as seen
from the inside of those same beliefs, are proper matters for
scientific investigation. The truth or falsehood of the beliefs in
question, however, are not only outside the province of science;
they are also wholly irrelevant to the purport of the investigation which, within its own narrowly limited sphere, science, as
such, undertakes. In the same way the personal beliefs of the
scientific investigator are equally irrelevant, and in the same
sense. It follows that the biblical theologian can, without the
slightest diminution of scientific impartiality and objectivity,
carry out his researches with the underlying conviction that the
scriptures find their unity and significance in Jesus Christ.

For the Christian theologian this belief is not a provisional
hypothesis, but an article of faith. As such it may well place
him inside the beliefs lying at the root of the interpretation
which he is studying. When this occurs, however, it gives him
an advantage, because to that extent he is able to enter into
the mentality which he is seeking to know and understand. Any
other judgement upon such a situation would be formed in
defiance of elementary facts which belong to the workings of
science itself. This requires some further explanation in which
once more the principle of analogy will serve us.

The scientist's belief in an ordered unity of natural law provides the necessary foundation for his sustained attempts to
bring harmony out of apparent conflict. This situation recurs
whenever two groups of facts appear to be mutually incompatible. Similarly the theologian's belief that in Christ there is to

[1] This does not, of course, exclude other influences, which were in fact
continuously operating upon the religion of Israel, upon the Jewish background of Christianity, and, again, upon primitive Christianity itself, as it
reshaped its Jewish inheritance.

be found an ordered unity of the biblical *cosmos* provides the necessary basis for his special activity, a secure footing upon firm ground, when for lack of this he might prematurely abandon his task. On both sides a deep conviction of security sets the inquirer free from anxiety about the worth-whileness of his task and about the particular results which may be achieved. Moreover, on both sides of the analogy the belief in question is an article of faith, and has, therefore, to that extent a religious character. Again, on both sides this means something quite other than a generalization from observed facts, since no scientific generalization could possibly be adequate to carry the weight of implications involved in the belief.

Let us carry this parallel one stage further. Scientific presuppositions concerning the ordered unity of nature have been shaped and sustained within a continuous tradition of scientific culture. This tradition cannot validate the primary assumptions nor can it render them proof, either against mistaken application, or against an unduly restricted interpretation of their implications. Every detail in this statement has its obvious counterpart on the biblical side of the analogy and could doubtless be illustrated from the history of this department in theology. The statement is mainly negative, being designed to show that the limitations within which biblical theology must work are such as we might expect from the general character of scientific knowledge. In the opening sentence of the statement, however, there is something more positive to which attention must now be drawn.

The 'response' of the scientists to nature has matured along with the tradition which their achievements have brought into being. This tradition, in turn, as it has gathered strength, has moulded the whole outward form of the social structure to its own pattern. Eventually it has largely succeeded in impregnating society with its spirit. This series of interconnexions can be seen to correspond broadly (although in a very different sphere) with what was said at the beginning of the present chapter about the interlocking of revelation and interpretation in the tradition of the Christian community. In both cases a social life is built up round a certain response to reality and the outlook which is created in that response.[1] This requires fuller

[1] see also the analogy in Ch. II, § i above

consideration; and first let us glance at the scientific side. Modern society is built up round what may be called a scientific culture; and this culture, in turn, has two main characteristics. On the one hand, the social life of man to-day rests upon a basis of scientific achievements which determine the outward conditions of that life. But secondly, this fact, with all that it represents of human interest and preoccupation, inevitably tends to shape the typical mentality of modern man. Moreover, inasmuch as science does not correspond to all aspects of the human spirit, this situation has, as we have already seen, a narrowing effect upon man's outlook.

When we turn to the other side of this analysis we are confronted with a much more complex situation. For the scientific culture of the modern era, with its embodiment in our contemporary social order, represents a new departure; it is like a strange cutting which has been grafted on to an older tree, and which has thereby changed the character of the tree. This more ancient organism is Christendom, which again includes within itself a number of different elements. For it represents the transformation effected by the gospel of Christ upon several layers of the ancient and mediaeval worlds, and again the reaction of these successive human factors, in turn, upon the response of mankind to the gospel. Yet Christendom is something more than the total result of these mutual reactions, since it is the human family redeemed by Christ and re-formed by him into the new Christian community. As such, Christendom, now as throughout the centuries, has identity *in some sense* with that primitive Christian family of believers within whose embodied response the revelation of Christ was originally interpreted and thus manifested to the world.

This continuity of Christendom with the whole of its past, notwithstanding the transformations which it has undergone, conditions every aspect of the problem with which we have now to grapple. That problem, which is unfolding itself by stages, was already implied in the last paragraph. For it was there indicated that the 'Christendom' which has a mysterious identity with the original Christian community has also organic connexion, if not identity, with the modern social structure built up on the basis of scientific achievements. The connexion was implied in the illustration of the strange cutting grafted on to the old tree. Such an apparently paradoxical conclusion will require some further sections of this chapter for its unravelling. It will be noticed that we have now included in a single whole the two sides of a contrast which we had previously been developing.

vi

In so far as this new scientific society has lost the Christian *form* it has lost a vital relationship with the biblical revelation, the truth which corresponds to that form. Yet a function of science relevant to that revelation is to be sought and found in the continuing complex of Christendom.

The continuity of contemporary society with the Christendom of past history is as important as the obvious differences between them. There are large aspects of this subject into which we cannot here enter. Our immediate concern is with *revelation*; and the problem which arises under that heading must now be envisaged. Enough has been said already to make it clear that the bible belongs quite literally to a by-gone world, to which this modern age of humanism offers a whole series of contrasts. Notwithstanding these contrasts, there still survives in this outwardly secular order, and in spite of its secularity, a great deal of the genuinely Christian spirit and outlook. That spirit and outlook, however, are in themselves essentially formless, and that because the body corporate is no longer recognizably Christian.

Hitherto the recognized method of meeting this situation has consisted largely in attempting to instil into the modern order of life an increase of that spirit and a deepening of that outlook which can be called Christian. The weakness of this method has already been to some extent indicated in our analysis of the Liberal compromise and its effects. The best that could be hoped for along such lines would be a reinforcement of human plans by a breath of inspiration from above rather than the fulfilment of the divine purpose for man. At the worst, however, the inspiration might prove to be of a sort which did not truly come from above, but rather from an all-too-human source closely associated with those same human plans. For this method is simply a resort to the old device of putting a new patch upon an old garment.[1] The patchwork mode of applying Christianity to life involves an adaptation of the gospel to the apparent demands of an existing situation, whereas what is urgently needed is a conformation of human life in all its relationships to the demands of the gospel as those demands are manifested when revelation is apprehended in its integrity.

At this point let us recall what was said in the last section about the interaction between science and society in the modern world. This was compared to the mutual interdependence of two corresponding factors, namely the biblical revelation and the original community of Christian believers. What is common to the two situations here compared is the *mutual* dependence of the community and that by which it lives. If modern society depends upon science for the smooth functioning of its daily life, science in turn depends upon this scientifically equipped society for the possibility of its own continued activity. Science has thus framed for itself a social order which embodies its traditions and perpetuates them. On the other hand science itself is an interpretation by the human mind of an order with which that mind was confronted before science came into being. If we recall what was said earlier about revelation and the community of believers, the analogy will be seen to hold good. Strictly speaking, of course, the relationship in each case is threefold. As science mediates between society and the ordered unity of nature, so does theological interpretation mediate between the community of believers and the original revelation.[2]

In Christendom, however, the community of believers and the scientific society are intermingled. Moreover the latter has real continuity with the former in history, since the modern social order framed by science is to be regarded as an outgrowth of Christendom. In this way of speaking Christendom means, not the community of believers as such, but the whole complex of Church and Society as historically interlocked and mutually conditioning through the centuries. Yet this complex which has, at our end of history, its outgrowth of scientific culture, took its rise in Jesus of Nazareth and those whom he gathered about him in the first century of our era. Now, as then, the

---

[1] If modern secular society is of recent formation, its secularity belongs to the old order of fallen humanity.

[2] In this sense, of course, the whole of the New Testament is 'theological'.

revelation to which the first believers responded is the heart of Christendom; and Christendom itself is, as it were, anchored to that revelation through the continuing witness of the believing community. Yet through the disunion of that community, the consequent disruption of Christendom's outward form, and finally the new dispersive tendencies manifesting themselves in human nature itself, a wholly new problem has presented itself for solution.[1]

The problem was brought to light by the very failure of the Liberal attempt to solve it. Its nature, therefore, has already been adumbrated in previous pages of this work. In essentials it is sufficiently familiar. The revelation contained in the bible belongs to a world of thought which seems to be in almost every respect remote from the scientific humanism of to-day. How then can the one be made intelligible to the other? The patchwork method having manifestly failed, what other method is open to us? If Christ requires Christendom for his manifestation, and the outward form of society is no longer recognizably Christian, has not the revelation become once more a 'sealed book'?[2] And does not the problem involve us in a vicious circle from which there is no outlet?

The problem would certainly be insoluble if the two worlds were completely closed to one another. But to suppose that this is really true would be a strange conclusion for Christian faith. For it would imply that the Word of God, identified in the Christian revelation with the victorious human victim who was 'found worthy to open the book', had himself become imprisoned in a book, that he had, in short, suffered the fate reserved for his great adversary, namely, to be 'bound' and 'shut up' and 'sealed'.[3] The vision of the Lamb, holding in his hands the book of destiny and opening its seals one by one, has for the believer already received ample fulfilment in history. For him, therefore, the question at issue concerns not the power of the gospel but the salvability of our modern world.

[1] The reader is referred back to those parts of §§ i and ii in this chapter which are here summarized.

[2] Isa. 29[11]

[3] Rev. 20[1-3]; cp. 19[13]. The opening of the sealed book by the Lamb (Rev. 5) may be viewed as the act of God towards which the prophet was reaching out in the tragic situation of his own day (Isa. 29[9-24])

Must we then conclude that the prophetic oracle has now at length come true?

The Lord hath poured out upon you the spirit of deep sleep,
and hath closed your eyes, the prophets;
and your heads, the seers, hath he covered.

Is the book sealed only in the sense that a generation afflicted with blindness cannot read it? And if so, will a 'remnant' survive the catastrophe, as in the past?[1] These are questions to which we can return no clear answer. Our Lord himself is reported to have asked a similar question: When the Son of Man cometh shall he find faith on the earth? (Luke 18[8]). But if there are questions which cannot be answered, there are also considerations to be weighed which may well throw light upon our problem. At this point, therefore, we recur to the connexion between our present civilization and that complex of human history which we have called Christendom. For somewhere in that connexion we might expect to find interaction between the function of science on the one hand and, on the other hand, the revelation of Christ, which is the heart of Christendom.

vii

The positive function of scientific humanism. It is a large-scale attempt to face up to the complex realities of a *mysterious* universe. Moreover, its very failure to master nature through restricted forms of specialization witnesses indirectly to the order of creation as set forth in scripture.

In the preceding pages a good deal has been said about various mutual relationships, both of influence and of analogy, which may serve to connect the natural sciences with Christian theology. Moreover, since to-day all believing Christians are also members of the 'scientific' society, the significance of science for Christendom is obviously relevant to the problem which we are considering. Now, in emphasizing the idea that 'the modern social order framed by science is to be regarded as an outgrowth of Christendom' we did not of course forget the debt of the

[1] In Rom. 11[8] St Paul applies this oracle (Isa. 29[10]) to 'Israel after the flesh' by contrast with the new Israel of 'the election'.

western Renaissance to the scientific contribution of ancient Greece. In that respect the imagery of grafting a new shoot on to an old tree was by no means inappropriate. In principle, however, there was nothing new about all this. For Christianity inherited from the religion of Israel that assimilative function which takes hold of cultural elements from all available sources and turns them to its own purposes.

There is, however, another consideration which makes the illustration in question peculiarly appropriate here. Mediaeval Christendom sorely needed that new principle of scientific research, which, whatever anticipations may have occurred, was introduced for the first time on an extended scale during the period of the Renaissance. With a change of metaphor we might truly say that the streams of thought were running sluggishly, owing to a lack of water, when new fountains were mysteriously opened which provided an apparently inexhaustible supply. In this illustration 'water' stands for the materials of thought. At the dawn of the modern world men discovered by degrees that the materials of thought are infinite. Moreover, in the later stages of the present era it has become increasingly manifest that the complexity of order in nature is *also* infinite. In these two stages of discovery, taken together, there lie possibilities of a new understanding with regard to the mysterious character of revelation. Such a renewal of insight upon such a matter would prove profoundly salutary if only it could be brought to fruition.

It is, of course, an implication of Christian faith that the revelation of an infinite God has infinite significance, and again that this infinity of significance is being, and will continue to be, perennially unfolded before God's creatures.[1] It is also true, however, that finite creatures can never know the full extent of their own ignorance by contrast with the very limited knowledge which they possess. It is, for this reason, fatally easy for us all to be 'superior' in our attitude towards both the objects and the sources of knowledge, and by this false superiority to close

---

[1] This might seem to contradict the previous statement as to the infinity of the materials of thought being a relatively late discovery. The implication of faith, however, requires to be brought to actual manifestation; and this process was certainly impeded by mediaeval ignorance concerning the vast complexities of the universe as known amongst men of science to-day.

the very gates of knowledge to ourselves. The discoveries of
science, on the other hand, have revealed to us the bewildering
complications of knowledge and the immensities of our ignorance. Science therefore has, on the whole, provided a whole-
some discipline for that pride of reason with which modern
man started out upon his great adventures.

Moreover, this lesson in humility belongs to the very nature
of the task upon which science is engaged. For here the indispensable qualifications of the investigator are single-minded
devotion to truth and patient perseverance in pursuing it to the
end regardless of difficulties and disappointments. It is also a
matter of experience that a sustained tradition of scientific research can elicit these qualities on a large scale and can secure
the enthusiastic co-operation of a growing body of workers.
But further, such a tradition is inevitably controlled and shaped
by that ordered unity of nature which is its primary object of
faith. It belongs to the major certainties of the world disclosed
by science that every object of investigation has its own characteristics which cannot be changed by the standpoint of the
investigator.[1] Moreover, as we have already seen, it must be
acknowledged that in any inquiry the nature of the objects
towards which inquiry is directed will determine the whole
character of the undertaking. Nature has her own 'point of
view' which will not give way to ours.

A scientific tradition is then, by its very make up, a large-
scale attempt to face up to the realities of the universe. Nevertheless the fruits of this outlook could scarcely be garnered
solely under the inspiration of the discovery that the materials
of thought are infinite. For if these materials are in themselves
simple and uniform their infinity as objects of investigation
might prove to be no bar either to knowledge or to the power
which is based upon knowledge.[2] Just so far, however, as it is
now becoming evident that the complexity in the *order* of nature
is also infinite, considered as an object of investigation, we are
confronted with an altogether different situation. Moreover, as
science is now extended to include the whole of human life
within its scope, the total complexity involved is not only end-

[1] Although, of course, the mode of their manifestation may be, and is,
contingent upon that standpoint. See also above, Ch. II, § i, par. 6.
[2] cp. above, Ch. II, § vi

less in its range but also quite terrifying in the uncertainty of its potentialities.

Scientific man is confronted to-day with an ordered system which he once supposed that he could exploit for his own ends. Now, however, the course of events is showing him that the master-key lies, not in his own hands, but rather within that system of forces which he set out to control, a system which includes himself and his fellow men as well as the world of natural objects. We can now see that the universe is not anthropocentric; man cannot give form and shape to the complex realities which he uncovers. Rather he has a function to fulfil in a given order. For he himself is one of these complex realities. Thus it almost looks as if this epoch of scientific humanism had become an unconscious and unwilling witness to that order of creation which the Christian revelation affirms. The witness is indeed unintentional, and, in a sense, negative in character, yet for all that no less significant. Let us consider this briefly in a preliminary way. We shall return to the negative aspect again in the next chapter.

When modern man set out to control the resources of nature his increased mastery was won at a heavy cost to himself. For one thing, a scientific society is a society of experts, since the smaller the sphere of manipulation the more perfect that manipulation may become. The more restricted the class of objects investigated, the more intimate and microscopic might be the expert's knowledge of those objects. So specialization involves a reduction of the platform upon which human faculties are employed. This, again, must mean a narrowing of the horizons of knowledge and a corresponding restriction in the range of experience. The specialist does not necessarily need wide horizons or manifold experience at different levels of life to enable him to succeed in his appointed sphere. Even if he should have other interests, their inter-connexions with his special tasks might not be apparent. Nor would there be anything in his specialized function to suggest that such cross-connexions had importance. Thus, for example, the religious man might pursue his daily tasks in the laboratory, the office or the factory without considering what bearing his religious beliefs might have upon these several spheres or *vice versa*.

On the other hand specialization might promote a theory as

to the ultimate importance of its own form of knowledge which would be in inverse proportion to actuality. For if the smaller the sphere of knowledge the narrower the corresponding range of knowledge becomes, then the greater the mastery in such a compass the less significant that mastery might actually be, and yet the more delusive in its apparent perfection! In such a canalizing of human powers the consideration of life as a whole has been lost in the elaborate attention paid to the separate parts. Thus, in his apparent control over nature man's kingdom was seemingly complete; yet in fact it was a kingdom of shadows without substance. Moreover, in grasping at these shadowy controls the lord of the world became the slave of his own devices. Man assumed a Sisyphus-like task in taking the burden of creation upon his own shoulders. Its order became his to exploit. But in becoming its tyrant he lost control of that more interior kingdom which is himself. His 'dispersion' of his own being from its true unity was such that it could provide no adequate direction or control for external orderings. He thus became a slave to the disorder which he had generated, first within himself, and then in the larger *cosmos* to which he properly belonged.[1]

viii

A partnership between religion and science would unite two contrasted principles, the one concrete and personal, the other analytical and abstract. A scientific analysis of detail could lay bare in greater fulness the content of revelation towards which faith reaches out. On the other hand it is only the identification of faith with its object in Christ which can make possible a totality of response to the creative Word (Ch. III, § i and Ch. I, § iv).

[1] An illustration may, perhaps, serve to clarify the meaning of 'dispersiveness' (cp. above, Ch. III, § ii, par. 6). In the modern centuries the logical faculty (*ratio*) has become divorced from contemplative reason (*intellectus*) to the detriment of both. In a truly integral humanism the equipoise of these two rational activities would enhance their development so that each was carried to richer achievement. Such a humanism would be neither sophisticated nor frustrated, and that because intelligence was wholly worshipful and adoration wholly rational. Without the dispersiveness which we know, men might have enjoyed all life's treasures in their fulness.

We cannot rightly estimate the problem which we have been considering unless due weight is given to both the two contrasted aspects of our present epoch, of which the one may be called positive and the other negative. On the one hand man's capacity for uncovering the secrets of nature has acted as a great liberating and educative influence upon the human mind and spirit. On the other hand the loosening of this same capacity from its due relation to other factors in the total make-up of human life has threatened to frustrate its promise of achievement. Under such circumstances Christian faith has its own contribution to make; and it will be one which necessarily corresponds to the twofold character of the situation. This suggestion must now be developed more fully.

Let us begin by reminding ourselves of certain differences between what we may call respectively the religious outlook upon the world and the scientific outlook. Of these two the former is in its essentials closely akin to poetry, which often expresses it perfectly:

> The heavens declare the glory of God;
> and the firmament sheweth his handywork.

The psalmist's words are an admirable example of this poetic quality in the religious outlook. Religion sees the world in its wholeness, whereas science sees it in microscopic details. Again, religious faith sees the world as a whole in its relation to a personal God,[1] whereas science sees the details of things as instances of impersonal law. Science must inevitably take its own way; and in that way religion can appear only as a pattern of law exemplified by particulars. Religious faith, on the other hand, can recognize that the path of science is complementary to its own. The believer, therefore, can allow for the necessary function of science in his total appraisement of truth, and this recognition of science as an indispensable partner of faith is an essential feature of genuine theology to-day.

It is, however, no easy thing for this complementary relationship to be maintained in such a way that science enters into

---

[1] Compare the graphic picture of creation in such a passage as Isa. 48^{13}; and, again, for both the aspects mentioned in the text, Dame Julian's vision of 'all that is made' as a small nut in her hand (in the first of the *Revelations of Divine Love*).

theology in equal partnership with faith. Moreover, in a general summary, such as can be attempted at this stage of the argument, it would be difficult for any exposition to do justice to the immense diversity of the facts. Nevertheless, perhaps we shall not be far from the mark if we say that faith apprehends revelation in a 'totality', that is, in some given whole exhibited concretely. On this ground it is clear that the act by which a revelation of religious truth is apprehended cannot itself be analytical; nor can the attitude of faith which is sustained by and built upon such acts be an analytical attitude. Accordingly, in its acceptance of revealed truth faith needs that support which the critical exercise of reason alone can supply. Otherwise it is possible for something which is less than the whole to pass for the given whole without this fact ever coming to recognition.[1]

Generally speaking, it is a function of theology to ensure that the given whole presented for the assent of faith is subjected to a rigorous scrutiny. Such scrutiny must have an analytical character, and here also there are dangers to be avoided. But in the ideal partnership of faith and analytical reason science would subserve faith by disclosing the significance of details within a given whole of revelation without subjecting that whole to disintegration. Indeed it is clear that, if there is a genuine whole of revelation presenting itself to faith, only a rigorous analysis of details can bring out the full wealth of relations which the unity of that whole contains. Examples of such analysis will be attempted at later stages in the present undertaking.

At this point, however, we must take note of the fact that 'analysis' might, in such a connexion, have two quite different meanings. It could, for example, mean the logical articulation of truth in respect of its content as presented in some accepted or traditional form. In a historical religion, however, any theological issue raised may involve an enquiry into the relevant facts, conducted in accordance with the *modus operandi* peculiar to scientific research. Of these two methods we may say that

---

[1] In all this there is real correspondence with the psychology of everyday life. Each of us builds up a single world-picture out of experience; and this totality is continuously developed, enriched or corrected by fuller knowledge of facts adequately diagnosed.

the former would be appropriate for analyzing the implications of a particular interpretation placed upon revelation. By the latter method, on the other hand, the collection of facts and their scrutiny in detail will provide an array of stepping stones leading to the discovery of new and unsuspected facts. These, in turn, may, in a theological inquiry, be found to belong to that substance of revelation which is always inseparable from fact.

Now history, as an inquiry into facts, is founded upon scientific method and dependent upon scientific discovery. Like other historical disciplines, therefore, studies ancillary to biblical theology have, in the modern period, been subjected to that liberating and educative influence which has been the positive contribution of scientific humanism referred to at the beginning of this section. It is in this context, therefore, that we may hope through scientific discovery to attain 'a new understanding with regard to the mysterious character of revelation'.[1] Accordingly, whereas both the forms of 'scientific' analysis referred to in the last paragraph are necessary handmaids to faith, it is the second, or 'empirical' form, which has attained an altogether new significance during the modern epoch.[2] How then may we expect these new paths of discovery to lead us to fresh light upon revelation?

The question presupposes that partnership of science with Christian faith which is the proper concern of theology. To the problems of this partnership, therefore, we must now address ourselves. The idea of partnership itself suggests that the distinctive function of each partner is complementary to that of the other, and our preliminary definitions have already indicated that this is so. Let us, then, consider what this implies, and first on the side of faith. The believer responds to revelation in a concrete whole, and sees things as a whole in their relation to God. This *totality principle*,[3] as we may call it, is a dominant factor in the biblical religion of which more will have to be said later. It found its supreme application in the Christian

[1] see above, p. 83.

[2] The reader is referred to the final footnote of Ch. II above

[3] I see no reason why this useful terminology should be monopolized by its 'totalitarian' perversion. For its biblical application see below, Ch. V, § v (latter part).

belief that the whole of the biblical revelation is gathered up into a unity of fulfilment in Christ.

Here, at the apex of revelation, we see the cumulative instance of what is meant by 'revelation in a concrete whole'. The disciples did not receive revelation primarily in the form of abstract truths. They saw 'the glory of God in the face of Jesus Christ'. With that explanation, therefore, there will be no difficulty about a corresponding truth which may now be stated. The response of the believing community is a reaching out to totality in Christ; and this is quite literally a drawing of the parts to their places in the whole, since in the inspired interpretation the believing community, with its members, has identity with Christ. The principle of totality, as thus understood, gives form to the community of believers and characterizes its continuing response, round which, again, its whole tradition is shaped. From this point of view the totality principle illuminates that 'identity' which we found between revelation and its interpretation in the New Testament, and again between both of these and the community of believers.[1] For if Christ *is* the revelation, and we are his members, then we belong to the organism of revelation.

Indeed we might say that *totality* and *identity* are two aspects of one life-principle by which the creative Word calls into himself that response which he creates. In this connexion there is one particular manifestation of the totality principle of which we must here take note. It appears in that assimilative function which we have already explained in some detail,[2] by which, in Christendom as in Israel, elements of culture are taken up and shaped into conformity with the religious purpose which animates the whole. It is clear that in the ideal fulfilment of the totality principle along this line of advance all the possibilities of this created world-order would be gathered up into a unity in Christ. Thus would the principle of totality come to its final fulfilment, and this in virtue of the fact that the creative Word calls *back* into himself that capacity for response to which he originally gave a measure of independence. He recalls the responsive capacity of his creatures to fulfilment in the source

[1] see above, Ch. III, § 1
[2] in Ch. I, and see, in the present chapter, § vii, par. 1

from which it sprang, where alone its relative independence could find both justification and satisfaction.[1]

ix

The Christian doctrine of man shows the necessary foundation for a partnership between science and religion. Faith's yearning for a simple whole of truth clashes with the infinity of scientific knowledge. Yet in a Day of the Lord science might lead faith back to the *mystery* of revelation (Ch. II, § i). Total response to that mystery corresponds to the divine image in man, made perfect in Christ, the second Adam.

In the partnership which we are considering it is not difficult to see what are the mutual relations of function. The totality principle involves in the believer an attitude of dependence upon that whole towards which he reaches out in response. Moreover, this is a concrete and personal attitude. The whole man reaches out to the whole Christ for his completion. The believer seeks that salvation which consists in being 'made whole' by inclusion in the whole which is Christ. This is essentially the attitude of a creature towards the creator. The believer, however, also shares the creative function of the Word with whom he has identity. This privilege corresponds to another side of his being, whereby, as man, he is raised above the order of creation that, under God, he may master and control it. Here is a second aspect of human life, emphasized in scripture as having equal validity with the other; and it is in this connexion that we can discern a necessary relationship between the respective functions of faith and science.

For science is a way of knowledge by which the secrets of nature are mastered and controlled. Yet the whole of man's advance along this path of mastery is conditioned by his humble acceptance of nature as a given order of which the laws must be learned in order that they may be obeyed. Here faith is the servant of knowledge, with a limiting condition, however. For such knowledge is not given merely to be prostituted to a demonic rule, owning no will above itself. This may serve to explain the language adopted in a previous section, where our

[1] see above, Ch. I, § iv, last three paragraphs (creative grace)

present-day scientific society was referred to as an 'outgrowth' of Christendom.[1] Such it is, in one sense, by sheer continuity of history. But the phraseology inevitably provokes other considerations. If we do not accept the pathetic theory that modern man has 'outgrown' Christianity we are at least compelled to acknowledge that the order of life to which he now belongs has 'grown out' of its Christian form and has acquired a less lovely shape. If this particular outgrowth is ever to recover shapeliness of form it must needs 'grow in' to the matrix from which it took its origin.

Such a return to Christendom, however, would involve a new orientation which would not be confined to one side of the partnership. If the dispersive tendency of our nature is to make way for the harmony of that wholeness which is in Christ, then *the totality principle of faith must make room for the infinity principle of science*. The partnership will depend upon a firm alliance of these two principles. This brief statement must now undergo some expansion in order that we may go to the root of the matter. When the modern world 'outgrew' its mediaeval clothes it also lost the shape which could be recognized as the form of Christendom. Of these two facts the latter only was tragic, the former being merely inevitable; and the tragedy of which we are speaking was occasioned by a defective response of human nature as a whole in its reaching out towards the wholeness prepared for it in Christ. The defect, therefore, was essentially a defect of faith, which failed in its appointed task of bringing all the resources of our nature into the fulness of Christ.

History has long since passed judgement upon the mediaeval world, because in that world something of vital importance was left out. In our present terminology, something which was less than the whole was allowed to pass for the given whole.[2] This statement, however, is not directed towards those obvious abuses which in every age are deplored by all good men. Indeed, we are not concerned at bottom with the defects of one age more than of another, but rather with something much more radical to which our human frailty is in all ages exposed. It is that grave fault which is set forth in scripture under eschato-

[1] see above, Ch. III, § vi, par. 4. This image is complementary to that of the grafted cutting introduced in § v of this chapter (last par. but one).

[2] see above, Ch. III, § viii, par. 3

logical forms. The Day of the Lord comes, and finds men un-prepared for that which they had not expected. There was certainly something unexpected about the avalanche of scientific discovery when it came.

The Day of the Lord will doubtless always come in unexpected forms; and of this we were fairly warned in the gospel. Moreover, faith is always confronted with the mystery of the Christ; and it is the *mysteriousness* of revelation to which the infinity principle of science corresponds. Let us remind ourselves about that principle. The facts which may be discovered are not only unlimited in number, but also unpredictable in character. Consequently scientific research involves an element of surprise which cannot be forestalled. We are only now beginning to realize, for example, what is implied by 'the invention of invention' as a characteristic of scientific activity, that is to say, one invention leading on to others in something like geometrical progression without prospect of any limit to the process.

Nevertheless the process seemed, for a time, to give promise of complete mastery, practical if not theoretical, over the intractable in nature and therefore also over the major problems of life. Then surprise came again in double measure. For first the infinite complexity of the system began to disclose itself, particularly in physics; and then appeared also the monstrous capacity for destruction with which that system was arming man against himself. Thus at every new stage the unexpected happened. Human calculations were outmatched by the mystery of the universe. Yet the mysterious, in presenting its infinitely varied facets for our inspection, always confronts us in the guise of order. Thus the creative capacities of discovery and of manipulation with which man is endowed have led him back unexpectedly to a recognition of his creaturely dependence upon that system which believers call the order of creation.[1]

What then is the conclusion to which the theologian is led by such considerations? He cannot fail to be impressed by the

[1] It is perhaps unnecessary to add that this line of thought has been embarrassed, rather than helped, by recent incursions of well-known astronomers into philosophical theology.

'Creaturely dependence' will be considered more fully in the next chapter.

fact that, whereas faith ever yearns for simplicity and clarity, it is science which now presses us back to a recognition of the mysterious. Clearly this contrast could be more fully developed. On the one hand, faith starts from the simple unity of truth as found in Christ, and then seeks to gather into this higher unity all the complications of life and of the world as we know it. The *modus operandi* is from above downwards, the 'supernatural' seeking to include the 'natural' in its embrace. On the other hand, science builds up its world picture, tier by tier, from the base of the cosmic pyramid. Yet it was here, at the base, that intractable complexity first clearly disclosed itself, when the delusive simplicity of the atoms at last faded out of the picture.

Thus the infinity principle thrusts its way up from below, until at last it succeeds in disturbing the unnatural calm which all too largely pervades the blue dome of faith's airy stratosphere. In other words, the voice of science[1] is raised in stubborn protest against the believer's craving for a 'simple gospel' by which something less than the whole is allowed to pass for the whole. So also, the finger of a theology which is genuinely scientific points us away from all false simplifications, whether their labels be marked 'scholastic' or 'liberal', away from every form of 'Christianity not mysterious'; and so back at last to the infinite mystery in the *cosmos* of the written Word.

Of that biblical mystery something was said at the beginning of Chapter II. It was there pointed out that Christ is 'the mystery' in which total revelation is both met by total response and also exhibited therein. We are now in a position to carry this thesis a stage further. There is in each of us a capacity for response by virtue of our creation in the image of the divine Word. Such a capacity corresponds, not to this or that aspect of our nature, but to the whole of it. In each of us there are varying possibilities such as go to the making of artists, scientists or other human types. Yet none of these in itself, nor all of them added together, can make the whole man. For each in itself is only a partial representation of the divine image; and a mere addition sum will not produce the whole. Our Lord, however, came to earth to *be* the new Man, that is the Image

---

[1] Of science; but not, as yet, of the scientists. They for the most part tend to assume with naïve simplicity that the 'good news' of science will produce its own paradise, a 'kingdom of man on earth'.

in its created totality. Moreover, every believer, made *for* that image, has in him (by virtue of this fact) the possibility of correspondence to the pattern of totality in Christ. In his creaturely finitude, however, he needs to be confronted with infinity *in its complexity,* lest he complacently assume that he has comprehended it in the nutshell of his simple faith. It is this very complexity of infinity which the biblical sciences unfold before our eyes.[1]

[1] The biblical doctrine of 'the image' will be developed later in this volume under the guidance of St Irenaeus.

BOOK II
CREATION AND ORTHODOXY

CHAPTER IV
THE STRUCTURE OF ORTHODOXY

i

In the modern world *freedom from control* has largely displaced the positive Christian conception of freedom to serve in a given order. Man's dominion over creation depends upon his inclusion along with it in a creaturely relation to God. This complex fact was symbolized in the ancient institution of sacrifice (Ch. I, § ii).

In the last chapter the development of a parallel between theology and natural science made it clear that theology must inevitably seek to be in a positive relation to contemporary scientific culture. This is the indispensable first step towards interpreting the gospel to our time. We therefore attempted to define the nature of the partnership which should exist between faith and science by showing how their respective functions could be mutually enhancing. The partnership which would thus bear fruit in a scientific theology is, however, hindered and obstructed by the ambiguity which characterizes the scientific culture of to-day. This ambiguity has already been indicated in what was said about the 'negative' aspect of our epoch.

On the one hand scientific man, by his capacity for uncovering the secrets of nature, bears inevitable witness to the infinity and complexity, the inexhaustible wealth and the enigmatic character of nature's order. That is the positive aspect of scientific activity as regarded from the standpoint of religious faith. On this side the outlook of science generates characteristic virtues of its own such as patience, impartiality and open-minded respect for truth, readiness to co-operate and also to submit to criticism by those who are competent to judge. On the other hand the humanism of the modern world is 'secular' in the sense that man has replaced God at the centre of things. Such a statement represents a commonplace of contemporary Christian thought. Nevertheless there are aspects of this tragic situation which seldom, if ever, come in for the attention which the facts seem to demand.

A humanism which is secular in the sense defined quite naturally regards with repugnance the conception of a personal Being whose will originates and controls nature in such wise that its order is the expression of his purpose. For such a notion seems to set a limit to man's unfettered mastery over the natural realm. This, again, runs counter to the modern tendency to interpret freedom in negative rather than in positive terms. In our present epoch the ideal of freedom from control[1] has largely replaced the traditional Christian conception of freedom to fulfil one's function in a given order.[2] The modern era, however, originating as it did in a double revolt of faith and reason against the mediaeval system, was in the nature of things anti-traditional. For faith and reason alike freedom came to mean emancipation. But, further, in its 'dispersive' origins modern humanism was nourished, from its cradle upwards, upon atomistic presuppositions at all levels of thought. It is not surprising therefore that the doctrine of an order of creation receded into the background of a theology which largely shared the humanist outlook.

There is solid ground for believing that the 'given order' within which Christian freedom functions (and herein lies the true significance of Christendom) is itself bi-polar or double-faced. That is to say, from one point of view it is quite simply the order of creation as envisaged in scripture;[3] but also, it is that created order as manifested in and through the community of believers in which it comes to fulfilment. Meanwhile, let us take note that alike in scripture and in Christian tradition

[1] For some aspects of 'negative' freedom see *The Religious Prospect* by Dr V. A. Demant.

[2] The change was due to a prolonged obscuration of the primitive and scriptural conception of that 'given order' as it was elaborated in Christendom. For its liturgical aspect see the passage in 1 *Clement*, Chs. 40, 41, quoted by Dom Gregory Dix in *The Shape of the Liturgy*, p. 1, and in *The Apostolic Ministry* (ed. K. E. Kirk), p. 246.

[3] For the inclusive character of this concept see further below, Ch. VII, § ii, par. 3 with its footnote. See also the next note to the present paragraph.

man is brought into contact both with God and with his neighbour through the order of creation. That is the indispensable setting of religion and morals, of faith and conduct, of the interior life and of its external adjustments. Moreover, where this truth receives due recognition a triadic pattern of relationships is formed in which each of three factors (the interior religious life of man, his social relations, and the order of creation) supports the other two, and is supported by them.[1]

The truth of this contention appears in familiar facts of daily experience. In the world which we have known the arbitrary use of nature for our enjoyment of its wealth has been the counterpart of a correspondingly arbitrary treatment of man by his fellows. Going further back in the search for causes we note that an era of 'freedom from control' synchronized with a serious dislocation of that nexus between religion and morals which belonged, at least in theory, to the recognized tradition of Christendom. There were, indeed, strongly moralistic tendencies at work on both sides of the religious issue in the period of the Reformation and the Counter-reformation. Yet for all that the ethical influences of Christianity became increasingly restricted to the sphere of personal relationships.[2] This corresponded precisely to the humanistic glorification of human personality, and to the atomistic conception of the relation between persons. In that age of uprooting persons were already ceasing to be differentiated by membership in the complex hierarchical whole which is *both* Christendom *and* the order of creation. Instead they were beginning to become a collection of individuals. This, in turn, was the first step towards their eventual loss of individuality in mere collectivity, where in

---

[1] The biblical form of the 'triadic pattern' is indicated in the conclusion of the present section. Meanwhile it must be pointed out that in scripture 'the order of creation' is *not* 'nature', but the whole creaturely realm, including men and angels. It may, therefore, be thought of as the total area within which the other two 'factors' mentioned in the text are delimited by smaller concentric circles. The substance of the above paragraph will be more fully elaborated as the present chapter proceeds, especially in §§ ii and vi. See also p. 125, note 1, and for the complex of Christendom, Ch. III, § v (end) and what there follows.

[2] The facts have become familiar to English readers in the pages of R. H. Tawney's *Religion and the rise of Capitalism*. Much the same conclusions were presented by E. Troeltsch in *Die Soziallehren der Christlichen Kirchen*, which carried the story further back.

place of organic structure and function we see social colloca-
tions of definitely lower types. Such are the forms of aggregation
familiar to us to-day, the 'totalitarian', in which persons seem
to have become like parts of a machine, and the 'democratic',
in which persons sometimes tend to appear more like a collection of nails rattling loose in a box.

If we are to see these contortions of society in their due perspective we must place them upon the far-stretching background of history. The modern exaltation of man to a position
of superior detachment above 'nature', his refusal to acknowledge that he is bound up in one pattern with the world of
'natural' things, leaves him weakly exposed to exploitation by
the demonic forces which he has unleashed in his own being.
This state of things is in the strongest possible contrast to the
interpretation of human life which we find in the bible. For
in the biblical anthropology there is a profound sense in which
the contrast between man and 'nature' does not exist.[1] The
biblical epigram: 'all flesh is grass' gives perfect expression to
the idea that man is a creature among the creatures.[2] Yet this
identification of man with what lies below him is but one side
of a paradox, since upon him alone among the creatures has
been bestowed a conditional dominion over the rest of creation.

The condition under which this privilege is granted may be
defined by the statement that man is the high-priest of creation.
In this context the highest significance attaches to the ancient
forms of religious cultus. The sacrificial rites which were performed in the temple at Jerusalem conformed to a general
pattern common to the ancient world.   The evidence suggests
that from its first beginnings the religion of Israel had both an
identity with the surrounding forms of 'natural religion' and a
difference from them.[3] The difference is to be found not so
much in the spiritualizing of the 'natural' features as in their
inclusion within the unity of a revelation which came to its
total fulfilment in Christ. Within that unity the ancient system

---

[1] The reader is invited to compare what follows with the context in which
'all flesh is grass' was previously quoted (above, Ch. III, § iv, par. 6).

[2] 'flesh', of course, includes both man and the animals.

[3] see, for example, the recent Schweich Lectures by C. F. A. Schaeffer
on *The Cuneiform Texts of Ras Shamra-Ugarit* (London, 1939). For the sense
in which the expression 'natural religion' is used see below, Ch. VII, § i.

of sacrifice signified a balance of complementary truths. On the one hand it stood for a consecration of the natural world to God through its association with human life. On the other hand it also stood for a consecration of man; and this, again, implied and involved a mediatorial relation of man to the whole order of creation. The double truth may be otherwise expressed by saying that the ancient system of worship presupposed *man's unity with the rest of creation in a creaturely relation to God*. This presupposition, in turn, supplies the condition under which man's true dominion over creation is to come to its fulfilment. His creative headship is realized in creaturely service.

The phrase italicized in the last paragraph was framed to carry an implication which must now be unfolded. In the biblical conception of religion we have the supreme example of the triadic pattern of relationships referred to in an earlier paragraph of this chapter. Belief in God involves the corollary that worship is the highest act of which man is capable; and in this act man acknowledges himself to be a creature in the presence of his Creator. If, however, our interpretation is correct, the biblical doctrine of our human creatureliness exacts more from man than the acknowledgement of which we have just spoken. For the relation of man to God as Creator can be conceived in a highly individualistic fashion which would leave untouched such a cleavage between man and nature, as, for example, we find in modern humanism. On the other hand the biblical way of worship is here understood to imply that the act which unites man to God is also the act by which man is identified with the order of creation in the very purpose for which that order exists.

ii

The ambiguity of Christendom and its consequent disparities are sinful manifestations. Such are: (*a*) the age-long scandal of a church in which the divine plan is not fulfilled, and (*b*) the modern divorce between man and 'nature'. The latter disparity contrasted with the earlier witness of Natural Law to the unity of creation.

The act just now described, by which a threefold relation of identity is effected between God, man and creation, is in the

New Testament shown to be that all-embracing act of our Lord which brought back all things into a new harmony with the Creator.[1] Within the scope of this reconciling act, therefore, falls the given order of Christendom within which Christian freedom functions, and which we have described as 'double-faced'. If there is an ambiguity about the present outgrowth of Christendom, this ambiguity stretches back into the whole phenomenon of Christendom in history. Moreover, we cannot draw a circle round any part of Christendom, and say: 'the ambiguity is not here'. It penetrates therefore to the centre, to the heart of the sanctuary. The given order has two aspects. On the one hand it is clear that the place of new creation, where the act of Christ is abidingly effective, is pre-eminently the believing community. In *that* sense the Church is quite simply the given order of Christendom, the *locus* of man's self-identification with the divinely ordained plan of creation in its true, creaturely relation to God. Yet it is also clear that the given order is the fulfilled plan of creation, that Christendom is, in its proper meaning, the dominion of Christ over all things brought to its full manifestation. Such a fulfilment we do not see in history.[2]

The church, therefore, is an enigma to faith and an occasion of scandal to the world, a paradox of simple identity involving complex distinctions, the place in which the act of Christ is eternally fulfilled and yet also permanently unfulfilled. The conundrums occasioned by this paradox, alike for faith and for reason, have led to the various 'perfectionist' devices for getting over, through or round the difficulty. The paradox, however, is firmly rooted in scripture. Indeed, the unworthiness of Israel and of the elect saints is one of the most persistent themes of the bible. The truth of the matter begins to appear as soon as we recognize that the paradox becomes known in its terrible significance only in the light of revelation. The enigma is such only to faith, which can at least see plainly the difference between the two aspects of the church. Even the scandal to the

---

[1] Col. 1[20]

[2] As is pointed out in Heb. 2[6-8]. 'The fulfilled plan' is of course the true substance of 'the order of creation as envisaged in scripture' referred to in the fourth paragraph of the present chapter. This will be elucidated in Chs. V and VI. See especially Ch. VI, § ii, par. 2.

world is now possible only because the world is within Christendom. For so, all unconsciously, the world becomes subject to that light of the gospel which alone gives reality to the shadows.

It belongs to believers by virtue of their membership in the organism of revelation to discern the mystery of evil which invades the church, and to discern it in its character as 'sin'. But sin has ulterior consequences which extend beyond the interior life of the church. The mystery of evil also makes Christendom to be a complex, if not of opposites, at least of disparates. The disparity which thus arises from sin obtains between the potentialities of the given order as contained in what man is by creation and, on the other hand, the actualities of the given order as signified in the being of the church. For no ambiguity can make the church cease to be what she is by Christ's act, that is the place of reconciliation between God and all that he has made. Moreover, no ambiguity can deprive man of those marks of the divine plan which designate him to be the appointed agent through whom the possibilities of that plan are to be brought to fulfilment in all things.

These two inalienable facts together constitute, in their yawning separateness, a form of disparity which is in itself a testimony to the reality of Christendom. The lesion would not exist unless Christ had died for sinners. Modern man suffers like Malchus, the Jew who got wounded because Jesus was arrested.[1] The gospel has set in motion forces which leave nothing unchanged, for weal or for woe.[2] Moreover, the unbridged gulf at present fixed between the good news of which the church is bearer and, on the other hand, the contemporary orientation of our scientific society has its counterpart elsewhere. It corresponds to that other form of disparity which we have had chiefly in mind in this chapter, namely the modern separation between man and nature.[3] The frustration involved in this

[1] John 18¹⁰. Clearly the Jews in Christendom have also been in a unique sense the 'Malchus' of Christian history.

[2] The neo-pagan, for example, is inevitably frustrated by standards which he cannot make his own (e.g. if his Christian wife refuses to divorce him). But in a wider sense the whole torture of our modern world is due to the conflict of ideals set in motion by the Gospel, to be afterwards debased and hardened in ideological forms.

[3] see above, Ch. IV, § i, pars. 5, 6

separation has been the theme of much modern literature;[1] and for some, of course, the solution has been a return to pagan identity with *nature* without that transcendent principle which from first to last characterizes the biblical religion of identity with *creation*.[2] The separation, however, has come about through a change which we might call the fading out of Christian creatureliness.

This 'fading out' of creatureliness is significantly indicated by a corresponding change in our use of the word 'nature'. In modern usage this word commonly signifies the system of the world *apart from man*, unless the contrary is implied by the context or by an adjective prefixed. Thus we speak of 'the laws of nature' as a set of generalizations discovered by man, and frequently with the suggestion that such laws are significant primarily in relation to man's interest. Similarly we tend to regard 'the resources of nature' as so much material which man may legitimately exploit for his own purposes. Such exploitation moreover, is steadily intensified by scientific experimentation which is assumed to be capable of directing its activity to the most useful ends.[3] 'Freedom from control' has for one of its corollaries a freedom of scientific experiment which is ethically neutral. This is the counterpart of that contraction of morality to the sphere of personal relations which has already been mentioned.[4] A gulf has thus been created between science and morality, disparity breeding disparity.

The separation of man from nature thus inevitably issues in the exploitation of man through the medium of nature, the experimenter viewing his fellows simply as 'natural' objects to be treated on occasion like rabbits or guinea-pigs. Nature as a field of experiment sucks human beings into its maw by a new and diabolic process of 'identification'. This vicious circle in which the scientific society has already become entangled may be usefully contrasted with earlier ways of thinking and

[1] cp, for example, such writers as D. H. Lawrence, D'Ian Faussett and J. C. Powys. See also below, note 3 on this page.

[2] cp. above, Ch. IV, § i, last par. but one. See also Ch. I, § i, pars. 5, 6.

[3] On the relation of this to the order of creation see K. E. Barlow's *The Discipline of Peace* (London, 1942). The suggestive array of facts in this book can readily be disengaged from the essentially inconclusive philosophy of indeterminism with which the author has needlessly complicated the argument.　　　　[4] above, Ch. IV, § i, par. 5

speaking about the order of nature. Natural Law was a legacy of classical thought which Christian theology adapted to its own purposes. In its Christian form the conception implied that man and nature belong together in a single *cosmos*, that is, a system of order designed by the Creator for the mutual benefit of all its parts, the whole finding its fulfilment in the beneficent God who brought it into existence.

Here there is no artificial separation of man from nature, although the special position of man within the order of nature is fully recognized. In this way of thinking the moral and social life of man is subject to 'natural law' by the very plan of creation. Human nature, as such, carries within itself the witness of the part to the whole; for the laws which determine human welfare, at all levels of our complex being, are part of that wider plan to which all creation conforms. Man was created with the capacity to recognize his proper function within, and in relation to, the wider plan. Consequently the law of man's spiritual constitution, immanent in his nature as a whole, can be called *lex naturalis*. 'Nature' is here practically equivalent to the order of creation.[1]

The doctrine of Natural Law bears witness to the reality of human creatureliness, that is, to an aspect of truth which has so largely faded out of recognition in the modern world. Moreover, the importance of this doctrine far transcends the western and scholastic associations which have been its context in Christian thought. For example, that positive contribution of science to the treasury of truth which we called the 'infinity principle' is, for reasons already given, to be regarded as a natural ally of faith's recognition that man is a creature. We might expect, therefore, that the more this principle of science entered into the outlook of theology, the more the essential truth of Natural Law would receive reinforcement. On the other hand, we have to acknowledge that here as elsewhere

---

[1] In *The Laws of Ecclesiastical Polity*, Book I, Richard Hooker emphasizes the reasonableness of *natural law* by substituting for it the expression: 'law of reason'. This change of terminology may perhaps be regarded as significant of a changing situation. For the thirteenth century reason belonged to the nature of things. In the course of the succeeding centuries, however, increasing attention was given to the immense potentialities of reason as the instrument of discovery through which the nature of things is subjected to human control.

the language of theology cannot adequately represent the ineffable mysteries of revelation. It can, at best, point the way to them. So the terminology of Natural Law does not manifestly carry the associations which belong to the biblical doctrine of creation. The idea of 'nature' does not necessarily point to a creator; nor does the concept of 'law' suggest a revelation of the Creator's plan.

The doctrine of Natural Law bears witness to our creature-liness; but there are aspects of the biblical revelation concerning creation which that doctrine does not effectually cover. To these other aspects the Greek fathers bore testimony; and to this day the eastern churches do not, apparently, feel any need for the western doctrine. This fact, in turn, suggests that east and west have diverged in their respective insights concerning the mystery of creation. Such a divergence will inevitably have wider implications affecting the whole field of dogma. If so, then, this will be precisely one of the points upon which the divisions of Christendom have in part frustrated the proper functioning of Christian tradition and the adequacy of its witness to revelation.

iii

A parallel drawn between the second and the twentieth centuries. Marcion, orthodoxy and the post-Liberal inheritance.

The course of the argument which we have been following has suggested that defects in the modern approach to the biblical revelation have been closely connected, on the one hand, with the distorted character of our present civilization and, on the other hand, with a serious breakdown of Christian tradition. The ambiguity of Christendom has infected the pre-suppositions of faith, and nowhere more seriously than with regard to the doctrine of creation. In that respect the theological issue of to-day bears a close similarity to the fundamental issue confronting the church in the second century of our era. This may be most succinctly illustrated from the episode of Marcion and his heresy. For one thing, the cross-connexions between scripture, tradition and the doctrine of creation were deeply involved both in the heresy and in the orthodox reply. But secondly, the whole episode accelerated the formation of a permanent structure of orthodoxy, which from then onwards became definitely normative for Christendom, and that too at the period when church unity was as yet substantially unbroken. By this standard, therefore, our own aberrations may conveniently be brought to light and subjected to necessary correction.

There is, however, one further reason for submitting ourselves to such a historical test. In the second century the biblical world of life and thought which the church had inherited was for the first time brought under the full pressure of alien and hostile systems. Yet the Christians of that early period stood near enough to the first interpreters of the revelation to be still in some degree within the same mental world. They looked out upon horizons, enlarged indeed, but otherwise not greatly altered; and they reacted to dangers not very different from those which had already been adumbrated in the apostolic writings.[1] In these respects there is good ground for supposing that a parallel with the second century will provide a valuable check upon those unexamined assumptions of the twentieth century through which the revelation in Christ is approached to-day.

First, then, let us recall the salient facts. About a hundred years after St Paul began his missionary journeys a Christian presbyter named Marcion adopted a form of 'higher thought' which was in the fashion. He tried to combine the gospel with this other system; but in so doing he confused the Christian revelation of divine love with the 'spiritual' other-worldliness of contemporary theosophy. He rejected the Old Testament because its imperfections seemed to him unworthy of any connexion with the 'god of love' in whom he himself believed. He also made his own selection of Christian writings from St Luke and St Paul, being careful to include only such material as could give plausible support to his peculiar tenets. Marcion's treatment of the sacred writings had two immediate effects. It deepened in the catholic church a conviction that the Old Testament was an essential part of her own inheritance; and it hastened an official canonization of the New Testament in almost its final form. But behind the biblical issue lay deeper questions; and first, as to the nature of God. Marcion identified 'the God and Father of our Lord Jesus Christ' with the god of

---

[1] The church, however, was *no longer under Jewish leadership*. That was a new factor of primary importance.

contemporary 'higher thought', very much as some Christian intellectuals of the nineteenth century identified him with the Hegelian Absolute. This god of the second century intellectuals, moreover, was too spiritual to have contact with our gross, material world. Two factors may have contributed to the popularity of such an idea. In the first place, the old religion of nature had corresponded to man's creaturely dependence upon soil and weather, whereas the more sophisticated and complex civilization of city life under the Roman empire had obscured this dependence and detached urban culture from its primitive roots. A like phenomenon is a familiar feature of our own civilization. But secondly, the corruptions of the empire and its obvious injustice had turned men's minds away from earth to other-worldly forms of religion. 'Escapism' was in the air, then as now, and for like reasons. All this shows the parallel with our own time.

Since the god of love could have no contact with material things, Marcion, in accordance with another current opinion, assigned the work of creation to a secondary god, to whom he also ascribed the whole dispensation of the Old Testament. Two consequences followed: (1) The gospel could not be the fulfilment of the older covenant; for the two were in radical contradiction to each other. (2) The Christ of Marcion was divine, but not human. Like his 'Father' he could have no genuine contact with this world. He could not therefore redeem it; he could only save souls *from* it. Thus Marcion became an early protagonist of religious pietism. Confronted with this alien system of thought, and that too within her own borders,[1] the church developed a consciousness of that which was distinctive in her own tradition. The conflict with heresy brought to manifestation something which might be called the internal structure of orthodoxy. The church knew herself to be the chosen 'remnant', the true Israel of God towards which the prophets pointed. As such, she could not disown her past. In this attitude she was instinctively holding fast to a life-line upon which her continued existence depended. The connexion of the Christian church with the people and writings of the Old Testament was, however, only one section of a longer chain.

[1] Marcion was eventually excommunicated, and founded a church of his own.

The Old Testament, in turn, was firmly linked to this material world by virtue of its teaching concerning creation. This, of course, is not confined to the opening pages of Genesis. For the whole of the old dispensation is steeped in what might be described as the religion of creation. Thus we are able to discern a succession of links in that chain of orthodoxy which resisted the pressure of Marcion's fashionable arguments.

To this internal structure of orthodoxy we shall presently return; and we shall find reasons for thinking that the metaphor of a chain is in some respects quite inadequate to the character of that structure and to its consequent solidity. At present, however, we are considering a parallel between the second and the twentieth centuries. Certain obvious differences appear at once, which might suggest that the two situations should be contrasted rather than compared. For example, the main religious currents of our time, it may be argued, are concerned not so much with providing a way of escape from this world, as with giving support to a weakened civilization which is tottering to its fall. Once again, this is an age of humanism in which the humanity of Jesus is appreciated, even if misunderstood. In that respect, at least, the Liberal teaching has left an abiding mark which is not likely to be soon effaced. In the second century heresy denied the reality of Christ's human flesh. In the modern epoch men still find it easier to deny or to discount his deity. These considerations will serve to remind us that the parallel must not be over-pressed. None the less the differences are not quite so impressive as first appearances might suggest. Moreover, as we shall see, they do not directly affect the trend of our argument.

At this point we must make a short digression. For, if we are to understand the point of the second century parallel, a further discrimination has become urgently necessary with regard to the contemporary theological situation of our time. The system of theology which we call 'Liberalism' was, as a structure, completed about half a century ago; and the first cracks and fissures in the structure appeared in the first decade of the new century, that is, more than a generation ago. This structure now lies in ruins through the collapse of its foundations. The system, however, provided house-room for a number of false assumptions and bad mental habits; and some of these are still very much alive. For Liberalism was, as we have seen, simply the theological counterpart of that secular humanism which is still the tortured soul of our modern world. Moreover, the very different outlook which is now emerging is inevitably hampered by its unfortunate inheritance. The fact that we know ourselves to be living in a disordered world does not automatically remove the habits of mind which have made us appropriate denizens of that world. So the fact that theological Liberalism is now 'dated' does not in any way remove the processes of thought which that system has nurtured in us during its period of dominance. Nothing, indeed, would be more probable than that, in this way or in that, the old business would be carried on, even though it was conducted under a new name and sign.

One of the strongest points of resemblance between this post-Liberal inheritance and the heresy of Marcion is to be seen in the modern attitude towards the Old Testament. It is an undoubted fact that Liberalism could not find much use for the Old Testament as a whole, however much admiration it may have shown for certain elements in it. This followed inevitably from the Liberal presuppositions. For the 'Hebrew old clothes' were of no interest in themselves. The enlightened Christian idealist might certainly discard them; and then they could so easily be replaced by the garb of fashionable philosophy![1] What else was this but a repetition of Marcion's specious conjuring trick? Moreover, aversion from the Hebrew scriptures is a habit of mind which has assumed alarming proportions in the post-Liberal inheritance of to-day. Indeed, it is probably true to say that the popular version of Christianity is, in one way or another, deeply riddled with Marcion's antithesis between the two covenants. In this way the outworn gospel of Victorian *illuminati* still seems to peep out of the pages of the New Testament like a masquerading imp, to bedevil the minds of Christian people, so that they can no longer see the unity of scripture in Christ.

iv

The parallel developed and extended. Modern counterparts of Marcion's separatism and dualism. The gospel of creation replaced by a religious dilemma.

[1] see above, Ch. III, § i, last par.

The Liberal conception of Christ as the spearhead of human progress tended to mean that whatever preceded him was superseded; so that even where the earlier revelation commended itself to the Liberal mind as true, it was largely rendered superfluous by the gospel of Jesus. In this way 'progressive revelation' became a plausible cover for atomism in religion, an excuse for discarding everything in the religious traditions of the past which remained intractable to the fashionable ideology of the present. In such a system there could be no organic relation, for example, between the Old Testament and the New. For here the present does not carry the past along with it. Atomism travels light; *it has no luggage*.[1] Marcion's Christ was an isolated manifestation which had no relation to this world-order. The Liberal Jesus, on the other hand, was simply the most remarkable human atom of the series which the world-process has thus far thrown up. *Neither the one nor the other could take the process up into himself.* In this element of similarity between the two systems we see exemplified the saying that extremes meet.

It has often been noticed that, whereas other great historical figures are separated from their fellow men by their greatness, the Christ of the gospels, as known to us in traditional Christianity, has a greatness which brings him into kinship with all men. The Liberal experiment, however, reduced his greatness to that 'natural' kind which makes him to be one of 'the immortals',[2] those who have won for themselves a position to which lesser men cannot attain. From this point of view our Lord appeared as simply the most important of all the 'original facts' which Liberalism set out to investigate.[3] In the supreme instance, however, the difficulties of the technique adopted became too obvious to be overlooked. Some of these have been considered in the preceding chapters. There is, however, a more definitely theological dilemma implicit in the humanist piety of modern times, which is also directly relevant to the parallel with ancient heresy. To this, therefore, we now turn.

[1] For a twentieth-century exposition of this standpoint see *The Lord of Thought* by L. Dougall and C. W. Emmet (London, 1922). This book provided a perfect example of the Marcionite strain in Liberalism.

[2] *Die Unsterblichen* was the actual title of a series of German monographs published a few years ago. One volume of the series was devoted to *Jesus*.

[3] see above, Ch. II, § vi

If Jesus stood in solitary grandeur at the apex of human achievement, it would seem to follow that his spiritual isolation from his fellow-men disqualifies them from entering into his mind or understanding his purpose. Still more, then, should his acknowledged superiority have deterred his modern interpreters from identifying him with their own ethical ideals, thus making Christ in their own image. The great gulf which Liberalism set between Jesus and his brethren was the nemesis of a progressivist Christology. A Christ who climbs up the evolutionary ladder instead of coming down from heaven has not taken 'the form of a servant' in lowly self-humiliation. He has not made himself one with sinners; and he cannot, therefore, save them. The Jesus of the Liberal gospel could no more 'become sin for us' in the Pauline meaning of the words than the docetic Christ of Marcion and his fellow-heretics could become flesh. In both cases superiority spelt an aloofness which was an evasion of the world's burden. Thus the humanist heresy is in substantial agreement with its apparent opposite. For to evade the world's burden is the essence of escapism.

In designating the Liberal gospel as 'the humanist heresy' we have indicated that, in its theological aspect, the modern epoch ushered in by the Renaissance is a single whole. From this point of view, therefore, we are justified in extending our historical parallel somewhat further. Marcion's theology was not unlike that of certain thinkers in the eighteenth century who supposed that God had left the world alone to 'go by itself', like a piece of clockwork which, when wound up, continues to operate. On such a view God is believed to intervene in the world 'occasionally', in some such way as we ourselves act when we interfere with our watches once in a while in order to reset them to the correct time. In one respect the illustration of the watch fits the theory of Marcion more exactly than it fits the 'occasionalist' theology of the eighteenth century. For, as we interfere with a watch which someone else has made, so, in sending the Christ to earth, Marcion's god interfered with a world which he did not make.

The main purpose of this reference to 'occasionalism', however, is to draw attention to another point of similarity between the situation which confronted the church in the second century and that which has been characteristic of the modern epoch as a whole. The fashionable religious thought of his day was all in favour of the type of theory which Marcion propounded. The reason for this lay in the fundamental dualism of Hellenistic thought throughout the period in question.[1] 'Matter' and mind were set in radical opposition to one another; and religious salvation meant escape from the tomb-like prison of the body. A similar dualism was inaugurated by Descartes in the seventeenth century and succeeded in dominating the whole epoch which followed.[2] It is well known, for example, that Hegel did not know what to make of 'nature'. It represented a dark, irrational surd, an obstruction which refused to be resolved by the smooth flow of the Hegelian logic. Again, the religious philosophy of the period preceding the two world-wars commonly favoured the doctrine of immortality, but looked askance at the resurrection of the body. In this the moderns agreed with Marcion and his fellow-gnostics.

It will be noticed that the very different examples of dualism just now given agree in bearing witness to the modern separation between nature and man. For if a radical cleavage is made between the respective spheres of matter and mind, then nature will seem to belong to the former and man to the latter. The effect of the cleavage, therefore, is a debasement of nature by over-emphasis upon its materiality and an undue exaltation of man by over-emphasis upon his spirituality. Material things then come to be regarded as 'unspiritual', whereas human reason is exalted to a point where its dependence upon sense-experience is obscured. A further danger lurks in this situation. Man's dependence upon the mystery of nature, now implicitly reaffirmed by the 'infinity principle' of scientific discovery, is obscured by a humanist glorification of reason as the instrument through which discoveries are made. Thus the separation between man and nature, by undermining his proper dependence upon the order of creation, promotes in man a false independence towards the Creator. Occasionalism provided a good example of the third form of disparity which in-

---

[1] Stoicism was the exception; but then its origin was Semitic. In the modern epoch the system of Spinoza offers, in this respect at least, an instructive parallel.

[2] Even for Spinoza matter and mind *never meet*, since they are *parallel* modes of nature.

evitably accompanied the other two. To the double separation of man from God and from nature it added the notion of a corresponding gulf between nature and God. For the former was regarded as a closed system in which God could only be an intruder.[1]

In this respect occasionalism symbolized the whole epoch of secular humanism. The rival of the deity *here*, however, is neither nature nor the secondary god whom the ancients found convenient. In modern humanism it is man himself who has replaced God at the centre of things. The deity, expelled to the circumference, has become a stranger, not to nature only, but to the whole order of finite existence over which man has assumed the crown and sceptre.[2] In such a world the 'gospel of creation', of which the bible is full, is inevitably lost to view. Consequently religion seems to be driven on to the horns of a particularly futile dilemma. Either it must be restricted to a narrow form of pietism, that is, a piety which is out of relation to the contemporary world; or else it must become a veneer upon everything, a thin varnish to be spread over all and sundry without possibility of permanent manifestation in a form congruous with its own essential character.[3] In either case the secular framework remains unchanged. Under such circumstances pietism besets the path of orthodoxy, whereas the other alternative is no more than the practical application of the Liberal separation between revelation and its outward form. It is this second alternative which is proving itself to be,

[1] An alternative method of excluding God from 'intrusion' into the closed system of nature became characteristic of the nineteenth century. By this second method the deity was imprisoned within the natural order so that he could not act upon it in any way which would modify the fixity of the system. Thus nature acquired dignity through a divine immanence which had a religious appeal. On the other hand, God became scarcely more than a name for what nature either does or allows to be done. Existence could hardly fall into a lower category than this, if deity was to be allowed existence at all. Such, however, was the egregious compromise which provided the philosophical background for Liberalism; and it was this combination which constituted the main opposition to orthodoxy after occasionalism had been destroyed by German idealism.

[2] Or alternatively, as the last note has shown, the deity is 'firmly imprisoned within the system *which man allows nature to be*'. For, of course, 'the closed system' is a characteristic imposed upon nature by man.

[3] For a variation upon this imagery see above, pp. 79, 80.

in a variety of guises, the most characteristic and at the same time the most baleful part of the post-Liberal inheritance. Of orthodoxy and piety we must treat in our next section.

V

The function of orthodoxy in relation to Christian piety. The difference between ancient and modern piety illustrated from the eucharistic teaching of St Irenaeus. The doctrine of creation fundamental to the structure of orthodoxy.

Orthodoxy might be described as the mind of the church in its developing apprehension of the gospel. The substance of orthodoxy, similarly, could be defined as the gospel operating within the mind of the church as its formative content, and there manifesting its living and life-giving power of cohesion. For here cohesion is a self-communicating quality. The function of orthodoxy is exhibited in its capacity to hold together the parts of a whole which would otherwise inevitably fly apart in fragments under pressure from within and from without. The gospel offers to our broken humanity the salvation which consists in being made whole; and the integrating power of the gospel is exhibited alike in the continuity of tradition and through the function of orthodoxy in its relation to tradition. Since the tradition could be disintegrated through the infiltration of alien elements, orthodoxy is continuously on the watch to stem the flow of these infiltrations and to repair the breaches which they have made. For orthodoxy is an apprehension of truth in its wholeness and in its due proportions. Clearly then such a comprehensive and balanced apprehension is not the possession of any one individual. Thus to appreciate the wholeness of truth in its fulness can belong only to the whole. 'The truth as it is in Jesus' belongs to the whole Christ (Jesus and his church). We share in the fulness by membership in him, by partaking in the life of that whole.

Since orthodoxy holds together the parts in the whole, its coherence offers an inevitable challenge to successive fashions of thought, where these latter agree only in their acceptance of disintegration in one or other of the forms which it assumes. At an earlier point in the present chapter this cohesive power of orthodoxy was likened to a chain which holds other things together because in its own structure there is a coherence of its several links. Presently we shall attempt to give a more adequate form to this conception in terms of the actual reply made to Marcion's heresy in the course of the second century. For that period provides a classic example of the way in which orthodoxy shows its power of resistance to alternative forms of piety, when these are, in fact, its deadly rivals. Humanly speaking there were several alternative destinies open to the church during that time; and any one of these was reasonably probable. At the earliest stage the church might have become a Jewish sect with a few special tenets of its own. Later it might, as Marcion wished, have become one of the various 'gnostic' or theosophical sects which stood opposed to the Jewish inheritance of Christianity. Thirdly, at any time during this period, there was always the possibility of a compromise in which Jewish and Hellenistic or other elements were artificially combined.

The third alternative, sometimes called 'syncretism', was, in the early days of Christianity, a highly popular device by which rival sects pooled their assets and became united or blended for social and utilitarian reasons. This method of attaining religious unity is not unknown in our own day wherever theology is at a low ebb. There are, however, stern warnings against syncretism in the apostolic writings; and in obedience to such warnings the church steadfastly refused to barter her inheritance for a fashionable and highly attractive mess of pottage. Thus all the human probabilities proved to be mistaken; and the church pursued her own course. This turned out, in the long run, to be at once more inclusive and at the same time more exclusive than any of those alternative paths along one or other of which she had seemed destined to move. The Christians found the answer to their problem of faith in the significance assigned to Jesus by the tradition which they had received, and by which they lived. For them life within the tradition was a life of organic union with Jesus. Within this union, again, they found a whole series of unities differentiating their path sharply from the various tracks which crossed it.

In the modern world a phrase like 'union with Jesus', if it should convey any meaning at all, would probably suggest a purely personal experience. What further significance it might have would depend upon the religious background of those concerned. For some the experience in question would be connected primarily with sacramental acts which take place in church. For others, again, it would not necessarily be connected with common worship or with churchmanship at all. Whatever its precise associations, however, one thing could be said concerning such an experience with some degree of assurance. The Christian piety to which it belonged would be of a type, quite possibly more intense, but also quite certainly more restricted in range and character than the kind of piety which characterized Christians in the earliest centuries of church history. The difference here indicated is bound up with subtle changes stretching over long periods of time. Some of these changes have been noticed in the preceding pages of this book. Negatively the difference might be summed up in two ways. In the first place, as the church ceased to be predominantly Jewish the distinctively biblical way of thinking tended to be overlaid or altogether replaced by fresh developments drawn from new contacts in the gentile world. Secondly, the disintegration of Christendom into disunited parts and, again, the advent of modern humanism combined to effect a severance of piety from that deep-rooted identity with the order of creation in which the church had been nourished from the beginning. Both of these points have already claimed our attention. From the second century, however, we may hope to gain fresh light on the problem as a whole.

The two points of difference just mentioned are, in fact, deeply interconnected. For, of course, the biblical way of thinking belonged to a way of *living* in which piety was 'creaturely' in a sense already indicated.[1] Modern piety, in its estrangement from the characteristically biblical outlook, stands in definite contrast to the orthodoxy of the second century. This can be seen most clearly in the writings of St Irenaeus who, about a generation after Marcion's time, wrote his great reply to 'all the heretics'.[2] Among these he explicitly and repeatedly includes the followers of Marcion and 'those who are

---

[1] see above, Ch. IV, § i

[2] *Adversus haereses*, cited hereafter under Stieren's enumeration of chapters, etc. These correspond to the marginal references in Harvey's edition indicated by the abbreviation: 'Mass.', which, again, refers to the chapter-divisions of Massuet (the Benedictine edition).

like them'.[1] As an exponent of Catholic orthodoxy St Irenaeus stands out as the most representative teacher of his time. In him we find, comprehended in one massive whole, truths and principles which were conspicuously lacking in the Liberal experiment.[2] He is our most reliable guide to the structure of orthodoxy as it appears just after the last personal contacts with the apostolic age have been finally severed. In this way he is the authoritative exponent of a tradition which is continuous with the New Testament and which overlaps it. To him, therefore, we now turn.[3]

What piety meant for St Irenaeus is clearly manifested in his eucharistic teaching. This is incidental to the main argument in which he is contrasting orthodox beliefs with heretical 'spirituality'. The liturgical practice of the church is naturally common ground to St Irenaeus and to his Catholic readers. But his opponents also acknowledge its authority, at least by implication, inasmuch as they apparently share in that practice.

[1] adv. haer. iv.34.1 (Harvey iv.55.6). cp. also the following passages: i.27.2 ff; iii.11.7; iii.12.12; iii.14.4; iv.33.2

[2] During the period of Liberal dominance St Irenaeus could be dismissed as a 'traditionalist'. By contrast with Harnack's estimate the retreat from Liberalism appears in Brunner's more marked appreciation of this father (Der Mittler, 2nd edit., pp. 219 ff; ET pp. 249 ff). We have now, however, to face a new line of attack. For this see the next note.

[3] In Texte und Untersuchungen, Vol. 46 (edd. Harnack and Schmidt, 1930) there was published posthumously a treatise by F. Loofs dealing with the theological sources used by St Irenaeus in adversus haereses. From this it appeared that the author of that work was heavily indebted to a lost treatise against Marcion written by Theophilus of Antioch, that some of this material was 'taken over' verbally, and that other sources had been similarly, although less extensively, manipulated. In Loofs' treatise the source-criticism was carried through with impressive skill and ingenuity. It was also helped out with a thorough-going, if at times somewhat speculative, reconstruction of dogmatic history in its relevant aspects. Lastly, in a final summing up the contribution of St Irenaeus to theology was sharply depreciated. Loofs has most probably shown that in literary graces and in some other qualities Irenaeus was less gifted than Theophilus. He has, however, also revealed his own personal inability to understand the achievement of Irenaeus in its proper perspective. This may be regarded from two sides which are not unconnected.

(a) Methods of literary composition vary from age to age. The manipulation of sources in adversus haereses, if correctly analyzed by Loofs, shows a method not unlike that employed by the evangelists, St Matthew and St Luke. Again, the inclusion of earlier blocks of material within a single new

It can, therefore, be assumed as a point of departure from which to refute them. Accordingly, as against those who would tear the gospel out of the order of creation and make it purely other-worldly, he dwells upon the creaturely reality of the bread and wine which are offered to God in the eucharist. He then goes on to emphasize the processes of nature from which these offerings come, the sowing and harvesting of wheat, the planting and growth of the vine. For these bear witness to the God who created and nourished them. More than once he recurs to the thought that in the eucharist man offers to God the 'firstfruits' of the earth.[1] Here too he finds a fulfilment of the old covenant. For in his view the Christian eucharist is that 'pure offering' of the gentile peoples which is foreshadowed in prophecy (Mal. 1^{11}).[2]

Two points are to be noticed in this teaching. Irenaeus con-

work, without any attempt to harmonize contrasts or apparent contradictions, is a literary device with which criticism of the Old Testament has made us familiar. In such cases literary habits correspond to the entire cultural mould of the age to which they belong; and in that same cultural mould the outward form of thought is also shaped. Here we pass over to the second aspect of the 'perspective'.

(b) The theology of St Irenaeus is 'traditional' in a peculiar sense which corresponds to the whole character of the Christian culture in the primitive church. He did not create a 'system', because he evidently regarded himself as a defender and dispenser of traditions. Here the plural is all-important. He could give hospitality to diverse Christian contributions, provided they were serviceable for protecting the one rule of faith from the disintegrating forces of heresy. His emphasis upon the authoritative 'successions' of teachers in the church and his inclusive literary methods were thus two diverse indications of a single theological outlook. This will become clearer, I hope, when we have examined his doctrine of *recapitulation*, which lies at the heart of his system; for that doctrine corresponds very precisely to the functions of tradition in its relation to the *structure* of religious thought. In conclusion it must be pointed out that the theology of St Irenaeus has important aspects which have apparently escaped the notice of his modern critic. With these we shall be largely occupied in the present volume. For the rest, the sources are here regarded as ministering to a wider plan for which the Bishop of Lyons is alone responsible. Other aspects of the problems raised by Loofs will be dealt with in due course. See especially below, pp. 138, 167 (notes) and Chap. IX, § vi.

[1] quoting Deut. 16^{16}. But he is clearly influenced by the wide use of ἀπαρχή in the LXX version of the Pentateuch. This use of OT precepts is typical.

[2] *adv. haer.* iv.17.5,6; iv.18.1,4; v.2.3

nects the central act of Christian worship with the order of creation and its processes. But secondly he connects the eucharistic offering of created things with the religious cultus of the Old Testament. It is clear that, whereas the heretics must logically spurn all 'natural' religion as gross and materialistic, the tradition of the church, for which Irenaeus stood, was consciously in line with the religion of Israel at the point where that religion took into itself the whole world of creaturely things. All this, however, is part of a much wider argument about the relation of Christ to the order of creation. At the same time this specimen of the orthodox reply to Marcion *et hoc genus omne* shows how indispensable the Old Testament was to that wider argument. By his institution of the eucharist our Lord gave a fresh application to the Jewish practice of offering firstfruits. In the words: 'this is my body; this is my blood' he gave himself as the firstfruits by identifying his body and blood with those elements which are taken from creaturely things. By this identification he implicitly made two affirmations; namely, first, that his own flesh and blood are real and creaturely, and secondly, that every eucharist proclaims the oneness of Christ with creation, and therefore also the identity of his Father and ours with the Creator of all things.[1]

Thus the liturgical practice of the church with which every Christian was familiar was called into evidence to bear witness to all the great unities of theology. Herein was implied an analogy between the dispensation in which our Lord became man to redeem us and that earlier plan of creation to which we still belong. At this point the scope of the argument is enlarged to include the doctrine that we are members of Christ's body, 'of his flesh and of his bones'.[2] The reference to Genesis here belongs to the analogy; and the analogy itself presupposes the doctrine that Christ is creator as well as redeemer. For, says Irenaeus, he who feeds our bodies with his flesh and blood in the eucharist is also he who makes provision for the earthly needs of those same bodies in the order of creation. It is here clearly implied that creation and redemption are parts of a single plan. The two stages are not to be

[1] *ib.* iv.18.5 and v.2.2,3; in the latter passage he quotes 1 Cor. 10[16] effectively

[2] following a version of Eph. 5[30] which included these words from Gen. 2[23]

contrasted as though the former provided for the material side of our nature and the latter for the spiritual. So also the resurrection of the body has a close connexion with the eucharist within the context of our membership in Christ; and all these mysteries of redemption are grounded upon the order of creation as its completion and consummation.[1]

This teaching explains how it was that in her union with Jesus the church found a whole series of unities included; and it was unity of this high intensity which differentiated the church alike from syncretism and from heresy, although in different ways. Syncretism attempts to frame an artificial unity by amalgamating things which have no vital connexion with one another. Heresy, on the other hand, has an opposite tendency. It breaks up vital unities which are too vast and mysterious to suit its essentially narrow vision of truth. It is in the nature of things fissiparous because it makes a whole out of that which is only one element in the whole. Marcion and his friends solved the difficulties of faith by chopping up truth into little parts; and to this truth-chopping there are modern parallels. We do not divide the godhead into 'aeons'; but we have our own favourite ways of reducing unity to fragments. Such was the Liberal separation of revelation from its outward form, which in turn has been the source of other modes of fragmentation.[2] By contrast St Irenaeus was entirely occupied with the unity of the whole. He was concerned to show the forms under which that unity manifests itself.

[1] *op. cit.*, v.2.1-3

[2] Here it must be remembered that, as 'extremes meet', so heresy easily passes into its opposite, that is syncretism. For, when truth has been chopped up into pieces, these pieces have lost the original connexions which they once possessed in a living organism of truth. Thus they can readily be fitted into artificial combinations with pieces chopped off from other systems which have been similarly treated. The nearest modern parallels to the hotch-potch of heresies which confronted St Irenaeus are such systems as theosophy, anthroposophy and 'Christian Science'; for these also are artificial amalgams with claims to superior knowledge. In these systems, however, there is so little semblance of any Christian truth that their errors are easily detected.

Much more difficult is the problem presented by those 'modes of fragmentation' which may be described as a *Christian* legacy, partly from the disruption of Christendom and partly from the Liberal inheritance. The reader is here reminded of what was said earlier concerning the law of

vi

The threefold structure of orthodoxy further illustrated in the teaching of St Irenaeus. Three forms of unity interpenetrating in a single whole, namely scripture, Israel (old and new), and the created order.

Let us examine a further concrete example of his thought. In a certain passage he expounds that gospel parable in which 'the kingdom of heaven is like unto treasure hidden in the field'.[1] This St Irenaeus takes to mean that 'Christ is the treasure which is hidden in the scriptures', that is in the Old Testament. The exegesis certainly corresponds to his own use of the Hebrew scriptures, wherein, as he says, Christ 'was being signified through types and parables'. But is the exegesis correct? When we turn to the context in Matthew 13 we find four parables of farm life, in three of which 'the field' is prominent (the tares, the mustard seed and the hidden treasure). In the gospel explanation of 'the tares' the field is explicitly said to be 'the world'. Both arrangement and choice of words suggest that this is also implied in the parable of the mustard seed.[2] 'The field' in Matthew 13[44] would, therefore, naturally mean 'the world'; and this conclusion is actually accepted by Irenaeus![3] How then can the parable mean that Christ is the treasure hidden in the scriptures?

The answer to this question must be that Irenaeus sees two

deterioration operating in a divided Christendom (Ch. III, § ii). If each fragment of Christendom falls short in some degree from the wholeness of truth, then *any* combination of parts thus defective would have in it something, however slight, of that taint which characterizes all syncretism. Moreover, there is a further consequence. Every religious body has its own characteristic form of culture in which the corporate life of that body is expressed. Thus, any re-combination of parts, *unless it represented a radical re-integration into wholeness of truth*, would tend to undermine, and perhaps destroy, existing elements of religious culture without prospect of compensation for the loss incurred. This is the spectre which haunts all immediate programmes of Christian reunion to-day, a demonic power which could be exorcised only by a return of all into the truth in its wholeness, that is 'the truth as it is in Jesus'.

[1] *op. cit.*, iv.26.1, quoting Matt. 13[44]
[2] (*a*) The mustard-seed is inserted *between* 'the tares' and their explanation. (*b*) 'In his field' is repeated from the one parable to the other.
[3] His phrase may mean: 'the world is a field'. If so, it makes no difference to our argument; cp. also iv.40.3.

meanings in the parable; and when we turn to the preceding chapter of his book we can understand why this is so. For there he states that the relation of the Old Testament to the New is like that of sowing and reaping. The patriarchs and prophets sowed the seed of the word concerning the coming Christ; and the church reaped the harvest. But the one God provided for both, seed for the sower and bread for the harvester's food, 'so that sower and reaper rejoice together in the kingdom of Christ, who is present to all them that from the beginning were well pleasing to God'.[1] In the context the author is concerned to identify the Father of our Lord Jesus Christ with the creator of the world who is revealed in the Old Testament. Accordingly he depicts the unity between the two covenants in terms of the unity which obtains between two stages in the order of creation. Sowing and reaping are two processes in that one order. Such a duality of process offers an analogy to the duality of dispensations in which the one God has unfolded his purpose.

As there are stages in the farmer's handling of the resources of nature, so also there were stages in the sacred history recorded in scripture. Each of these two orders involved the co-operation of many persons, some at an earlier stage, some at a later. But in both spheres alike we can see a single divine plan unfolded under the providence of one and the same God. As surely as sowing and reaping belong to one operation, so surely do the two parts of the bible belong to a single divine economy. So far then there is analogy between creation and revelation. But the bold application which Irenaeus gives to our Lord's parable goes further. When he says that the scriptures are 'the field' in which Christ is hidden and in the same breath identifies 'the field' with 'the world', it is clear that *in some sense* he is identifying the 'order' of scripture with the order of creation.

Here we have to remember that St Irenaeus was familiar with the language in which the New Testament was written. For him, as for the apostolic writers, *cosmos* would have a double meaning.[2] The field which is 'the world' is also the

---

[1] *op. cit.* iv.25.3. The biblical texts cited are: Isa. 55[10], John 4[36 ff], I Cor. 3[6,7], 2 Cor. 9[10].

[2] For fuller explanation of this point see below, Ch. VI, § i, par. 2

'ordered beauty' which we see in creation. It was that same harmonious *order*, however, which this father also found in scripture. In both alike he found that unity in multiplicity which belongs to a single plan worthily unfolded. In both alike he read a gospel of creation which includes human life within itself. By this identification, therefore, the defender of orthodoxy is doing two things in one. He is demonstrating the unity of the biblical revelation. But he is also demonstrating the complete interlocking of the order of redemption in Christ with the order of creation which it presupposes. Moreover, he is bringing the two parts of his argument to bear upon one another for their mutual reinforcement. There is only one God; therefore only one revelation of boundless wisdom. It is to be found in the world which we see around us and also in the whole process of God's dealings with man in history. The clue to that one wisdom in all its manifestations is to be found in Christ and nowhere else. Moreover, both in the order of creation and in the record of scripture, Christ is *hidden* treasure, inasmuch as he is revealed only to lowly faith.[1]

But if St Irenaeus thinks of scripture in terms of the created order he does so because there is a third element in his thought interwoven with the other two. It will be remembered that at an earlier point in the present chapter the structure of orthodoxy was compared to a chain having three links. These were identified respectively with the Christian church, the dispensation of the Old Testament and the material world.[2] It was then suggested that the metaphor of the chain would prove to be inadequate, as not doing sufficient justice to the solidity of the orthodox structure. We have now reached a point in our analysis of second-century thought where we can see just how this is so. The weakness of a chain lies in the fact that if any single link gives way under pressure, then all the remaining links become useless. The whole chain is put out of action; for its strength lies in its weakest link. What St Irenaeus sees,

[1] cp. 'the mystery of God, even Christ, in whom are all the treasures of wisdom and knowledge hidden' (Col. 2³), and the comments on this text above, Ch. II, § i, pars. 3 *ff*

[2] above, pp. 108, 109. It will be noticed that the 'links' were stated in terms relative to the negations of Marcion, i.e. not scripture as such, but OT; not creation, but 'matter'. The reply of orthodoxy, however, took wider ground.

however, is a structure of a much more enduring kind. Here creation, scripture and the church are so fused into one whole that, although we can and must distinguish them, yet they cannot be separated. All metaphors break down, because we are confronted with something wholly unique.

The threefold structure of orthodoxy presented to us in the teaching of Irenaeus has this peculiarity: it consists in three forms of unity which interpenetrate one another. We may further define the mystery by saying that each of the three factors involved supports the other two and is supported by them.[1] Accordingly what was said about the church as 'the third element' at the beginning of the last paragraph would apply *mutatis mutandis* to the other two factors, that is, to scripture and to creation. We have already considered an example of this in the eucharistic teaching of Irenaeus. If he thinks of the eucharistic sacrifice in terms of 'firstfruits', he does so because in the New Testament Christ is the firstfruits of the new creation to which as his members we belong. Here in a single word scripture affirms the unity of the two covenants with one another in terms of the created order.[2] But also our connexion with this series of unities in the new creation is implicit in the same word.[3] The liturgical tradition of the church faithfully reflected the gospel of creation; and this, in turn, was like a thread upon which the unity of scripture was woven.

Another such thread was the identity of the Christian church with the true Israel, the people of God. How prominent this particular mode of unity is for our author may be seen in his teaching about the Hebrew prophets in their relation to the new covenant. Here again the threefold structure appears in a highly characteristic passage which is introduced with a quotation from St Paul.[4] Irenaeus cites the apostolic statements

[1] cp. above, p. 99, where the same law operates in another triadic relationship, that of human society. The order of creation is significantly integral to both these triadic patterns, a fact which indicates that the structure of orthodoxy, as here envisaged, is as broadly based as human life.

[2] cp. above, p. 119 with note 1

[3] For we have received the 'firstfruits of the Spirit', by which we are united with 'Christ the firstfruits'. The connexion between Romans 8 and 1 Cor. 15 is thus implicit in the eucharistic use of 'firstfruits' by Irenaeus.

[4] iv. 32 provides the prelude. Then follows the basic section: iv. 33.8-10, with which should be compared iv. 38.1-3 and v. 20.1, in order to get the whole context of thought.

about 'holding fast the head', that is Christ, 'from whom the whole body, compacted and joined, and through every joint of supply in the measure of each part, made increase of the body, unto the building up of itself in love'.[1] Irenaeus understands this law of growth in the body of Christ to include within its scope the dispensation of the Old Testament which 'bent to the service of God for their own profit those to whom it was given'. In other words, the gradual education of the human race in and through the people of Israel was part of that creaturely growth which is proper to the whole order of redemption. Two further statements are included in the paragraph with which we are now dealing. In the first of these Irenaeus points out, in effect, that if Israel's neck was bent under the yoke of the law,[2] this also involved a bending down of the deity to man's lowly level. In the second statement he significantly indicates that there is a single pattern in the developing organism of the Christ, and that this pattern already appears in the Old Testament, where 'the images of those things which are in the church are prefigured'. The full development is in some sense anticipated in the earlier stages. For the Christian doctrine of revelation both truths are vital.

A little further on in his argument, after referring to various factors in the life and constitution of the church, Irenaeus goes on to speak of the prophets of Israel, of whom he affirms that they were members of Christ's body. This passage is fundamental to our interpretation of orthodoxy in terms of three interpenetrating unities.[3] The preceding context is important. The author quotes from Matthew 5[12]: 'so persecuted they the prophets which were before you.' This indicates an identical pattern of sacrifice in the Hebrew prophets and in the Christian martyrs; for the same Spirit rested upon both. The sufferings of Christ were exhibited in the Israel of God before as well as after the incarnation, and that too in the *lives* of the prophets.[4]

---

[1] From the Latin version of iv.32.1, where Col. 2[19] and Eph. 4[16] are combined. Both the Pauline statements offer an antidote for heresy.

[2] cp. Harvey's note *ad. loc.* (Tom. ii., p. 255)

[3] iv. 33, 9.10. Possibly he is still thinking of the apostolic thesis in Eph. 4 where (4 [11–12]) 'prophets' appear in a list of ministries given for the building up of the church.

[4] The same doctrine is taught in the Epistle to the Hebrews, where Moses shares 'the reproach of the Christ' with Israel in Egypt (Heb. 11[26]).

'*In themselves* the prophets prefigured all these things.' By virtue of this fact they are seen to be members of Christ. Only when this point is established does Irenaeus go on to what he evidently regards as a corollary or consequence. Because the prophets were members of Christ therefore they fulfilled their particular functions. Prophecy is a *charisma* in the mystical body, as appears in the New Testament (Rom. 12⁶).

At this point, therefore, Irenaeus extends the doctrine of the mystical body retrospectively to the old covenant; and in so doing he applies the Pauline analogy in a fresh and most interesting way. The doctrine, as enunciated by St Paul, implies that the church is a creaturely organism in which the order of creation is reproduced and carried to its fulfilment in Christ. Irenaeus simply applies this principle to the elucidation of prophecy as a function of the mystical organism in its earlier stage of development. The *totus Christus* includes the Messiah *and* the *ecclesia*, Jesus *and* his church, being that one organism of redemption which embraces both the old dispensation and the new. This is the Israel of God, and yet also Jesus himself in his all-inclusive rôle. For the Head is also the Whole in whom are included all who belong to the true Israel. Some of these preceded his sojourn on earth in mortal flesh. Others followed after him in the order of time. But all alike are fulfilled in him. Accordingly Irenaeus sets the prophets of Israel in the company of the apostles, bishops and martyrs whom he has mentioned immediately before the passage now under consideration. All alike, fulfilling their several parts, contribute to the *character corporis Christi*.

There follows a fundamental application of the 'body' analogy. The prophets belong to 'the all' who make up the elect, 'the many' for whom Christ died. As members of 'the one man Jesus Christ' they have a specific function in his body.[1] It was their part to *preform* or *prefigure* him whom they announce in their prophecies. Here the author whom we are following employs the language of St Paul while he unfolds some of its implications in his own way. The two italicized words belong to the special terminology of Irenaeus. But there is much in

---

[1] For a fuller examination of this biblical language the reader is referred to what I have written elsewhere (*The Common Life in the Body of Christ*, Chs. X, XI; and also in an essay contributed to *The Apostolic Ministry*).

scripture to support them, as we shall see. The analogy is now developed as follows: The activity of the body as a whole is exhibited through the members. But no single member can exhibit the 'figure' of the whole man. So no single prophet could show forth the whole Christ. Each therefore prefigured in his prophecy that particular 'operation' of Christ which lay within the compass of his own special function as a member of the body.

The enumeration of prophecies which follows is dominated by this interpretation. Thus by a different route we return to the same threefold structure. The unity of scripture is thought of in terms of a single organism which is Christ and his church. Thus the entire Christian mystery is stated in biological terms; and scripture as a whole is seen to be an *organic revelation* conformed to the order of creation in its structure as well as in its scope, as that order in turn is conformable to Christ. Such was the reply to Marcion. If it can be justified, it will provide a welcome antidote to the neo-Marcionite tendencies of theology in our own day. Such a bold conception calls for a fuller investigation; and this will inevitably lead us back into that world of thought which is characteristic of scripture itself.

CHAPTER V

ORGANIC REVELATION

i

The organic conception of revelation and some western distortions which obscure it. The relation of this conception to the preceding argument and to the teaching of St Irenaeus.

In the preceding chapters we may seem to have wandered far afield. Our aim, however, has been severely practical. For the course of the argument has been determined by the present position of theology when seen in the context of a wider situation. At the heart of the theological issue to-day lies the problem of Revelation; and upon that subject we have now reached a point where some conclusions may be stated.

(1) In rejecting the Liberal doctrine of revelation we inevitably affirmed its opposite. If revelation is not separable from its outward form, then it must be manifested in and through that form. Moreover, so far from hampering theological freedom, the affirmation of this principle secures for theology its necessary safeguards. For example, only so far as the outward form of revelation is vital to faith, can faith itself be subjected to that discipline of knowledge which is indispensable for its healthy functioning. If the outward form does not matter, faith can take refuge in an inner sanctuary to which the critical faculty cannot penetrate. Thus faith and knowledge are driven apart. This intellectual discipline of faith was implied in the concluding stages of our third chapter, where we considered the relation of scientific inquiry to the function of faith on the one hand and to the mystery of revelation on the other. To sum up, it follows that there are two conditions under which the discipline of faith in the sphere of knowledge can have reality. In the first place, the outward form of revelation must be recognized as having vital significance for faith. But secondly, the scientific scrutiny of that outward form must be freely welcomed by the believer.

(2) There was, however, a further conclusion involved in our

repudiation of the Liberal theory. The entire Liberal 'quest of the historical Jesus' was, in effect, a search for an absolute core of revelation. If that search is held to have failed we are obliged to fall back upon the only remaining alternative. If the onion cannot be peeled we must accept it as it is. Revelation is given in the Whole. That is our second and equally inescapable conclusion. Where, then, is the Whole? In Scripture? Yes, certainly, and in Scripture as a whole. But here a further discrimination is necessary. It is not enough to say that the Word of God is contained *in* Scripture. We must insist once more that Scripture *is* the Word of God.[1] In fact it is now clear that Scripture as a whole is that Whole with which Revelation is to be identified. But if we say that Revelation has identity with the vessel in which it is conveyed to us, it is at once obvious that this is that kind of identity which involves distinction, like the identity of the divine and the human in the person of Christ, or again the identity between Christ and the Church. To the biblical background of this identity doctrine we shall return later.[2]

In evading the Scylla of Liberalism, therefore, we must not make the mistake of falling into the opposite error of bibliolatry, or 'fundamentalism'. Scripture is the Word of God only because, and as, it receives its fulfilment in Christ; and he has other organs for his self-manifestation, such as the church, the order of creation and that historical complex which is called Christendom. A question may properly be asked as to how these various modes of manifestation may be co-ordinated. This question, in turn, opens out into all the main problems of theology. We must, therefore, limit ourselves to a bare indication of its connexion with our present argument.

In the middle ages *the witness of creation* to the Creator was, in large measure, relegated to the sphere of Natural Theology. This left a problem of mutual adjustment as between the other organs or instruments of revelation. Moreover, such an adjustment would have to be made, if at all, in the territory which remained. It would have to be made in the sphere of 'revealed religion' thus restricted by sharp differentiation from the witness of creation. When the breaking-point came in the sixteenth century the respective claims of the bible and the church were

[1] cp. above, Ch. I, § iv   [2] see below, § v

set over against each other in direct opposition without any mediating factor. Such a mediating factor might have been found in the third constituent of the original whole, that is to say, in the witness which the order of creation gives to the purpose of God for his world. As it was, the Renaissance took charge of this third element in the whole, and in so doing inevitably secularized one specific aspect of the original revelation. The extent of the distortion thus effected could be rightly estimated only from the standpoint of the unbroken whole. It was on this ground that an appeal was made in the last chapter to the teaching of St Irenaeus. In the western world of to-day there are two forms of Christian orthodoxy, each of which has a certain inner consistency, although neither the one nor the other adequately represents the original whole. Thus Tridentine Catholicism and Protestant orthodoxy confront one another across an unbridged gulf, because that which might have held their opposite tendencies together first receded into the background, and then passed into a separate channel where it has largely lost its religious significance.[1]

In the earliest period of church history, however, we see the witness of creation, not as yet marshalled in a separate theological discipline, but entering as one factor amongst others into the unbroken witness of 'the whole'. That whole which we have here referred to in terms of 'revelation' has, it will be remembered, presented itself to us in other aspects. In our fourth chapter we thought of it in terms of a 'structure of orthodoxy' built out of three interpenetrating, unitary forms (creation, scripture and the church). As such it is the objective content of the faith which informs the mind of the church and preserves her from error.[2] That which stands 'revealed' in scripture is present in the mind of the church as the content of her thought and the formative power of her life. The relation of revelation to orthodoxy here corresponds to that of scripture to the church. Dependence is mutual. For, as the Israel of God, the church is present in scripture, being one of the great unitary forms which underlie the unity of revelation. This interdependence, however, of the revelation in scripture and of the

---

[1] Eastern Orthodoxy and Anglicanism register, each in its own way, a refusal to regard this purely western *entweder oder* as significant of 'the whole'.

[2] above, Ch. IV, § v, par. 1

orthodoxy which informs the church's mind presupposes also the third unitary form, that is creation.[1]

The statement just made implies that the interdependence of scripture and the church corresponds to and falls within a divinely ordered plan of universal scope. The plan is to be thought of as having been laid down when the world was created, although it comes to its fulfilment only in Christ. One aspect of this all-embracing conception confronted us in the belief of St Irenaeus that the Hebrew prophets were members of Christ. This inclusion of the Old Testament dispensation within the organism of Christ's body has the effect of making revelation 'progressive' in an organic sense. In this respect the theology of St Irenaeus had a depth of insight for which we look in vain in the more modern cult of 'progress' in any of its fashionable forms, whether secular or religious. In that theology the emphasis falls, not upon man's achievements, but upon God's condescension. Accordingly, revelation is not confined to the high points in man's response to the divine Spirit. It is found, rather, in the whole method by which God accommodates his greatness to our creaturely frailty. From this point of view human limitations are God's opportunity. Thus the imperfections of the earthen vessel in which the divine treasure is conveyed are themselves integral to the very nature of revelation itself. In other words human imperfections are constituent elements in a revelation given to sinful creatures. God condescends to the inadequate medium which we have prepared for him. He accepts men as they are, and manifests his greatness in the lowliness of the instruments which he employs.

This conception of revelation is 'organic' inasmuch as it conforms to the general notion of an organism, in which a single plan or pattern is fulfilled through the harmonious co-operation of its parts or members. The organism of revelation is not to be estimated by reference to the solitary greatness or perfection of its several members, but rather by reference to the manner in which these members combine to fulfil a single 'biological' pattern of unity. In such a conception the individual qualities of greatest significance are those which make it possible for the individual to fulfil his particular function in the whole.

[1] and the threefold web thus woven is historically exhibited in Christendom

Moreover the organic conception of revelation has a necessary relation to the time-process. This was well illustrated in the analogy from natural processes which St Irenaeus employed to indicate the interrelationship between the Old Testament and the New. As plant-life takes time to develop, so also does the spiritual life of man. Accordingly, if revelation was to be conformed to man's condition, it must needs pass through stages corresponding *pari passu* with the laws of his spiritual development. Once more, this implies that the slow movement of the chosen people from more primitive to more advanced levels of religious life and thought was itself a constituent element in the revelation, an element, therefore, having permanent significance.

If, however, we are to appreciate the full implications of revelation as thus understood we must bring together the two aspects of organic life referred to in the last paragraph, namely the functional and the evolutionary. In certain organisms organs are developed to serve a particular purpose; or so it seems to us. When they have fulfilled their functions these organs disappear in due course to be replaced by others. In such a case we should not say that the biological significance of the whole lay more definitely in the later phases than in the earlier. The interrelation here of function and process was clearly indicated in the illustrations selected from the pages of Irenaeus. As harvesting is neither more nor less important than sowing, so the biological significance of an organism does not lie especially in the earlier stages of its development nor in the later, but rather in the development as a whole. From the divine standpoint Moses and the prophets were as indispensable as the apostles and evangelists. The point may, indeed, be put more trenchantly. *If Marcion was wrong*, then the authors of 'The Priestly Code' were as indispensable as St Paul and St John. This conclusion accords well with a biblical principle to which we have already had occasion to refer, as illustrated in the prophetic oracle that 'the lofty shall be brought low'.[1]

ii

The relation of organic conceptions to the order of creation in the teachings of St Paul and of St Irenaeus. The parallel between the two creations—Adam and Christ.

[1] see above, Ch. III, § iv, par. 6

The interpenetration of three unitary forms in a single structure, as presented to us in the teaching of St Irenaeus, might be thought to rest rather heavily upon the Pauline conception of the church as a bodily organism. The possible relevance of such a criticism could be estimated only after a much fuller analysis of biblical material, such as we are to undertake in Part II of the present work. In the meantime we may take note of certain facts. In the first place, if St Irenaeus applies the 'body of Christ' language to the Old Testament dispensation, we have found that he also extends another biblical analogy, that of sowing and reaping, in a similar way. Moreover, his treatment of Christ's saying in John 4³⁷ ('there is one who sows and another who reaps')¹ appears to be substantially correct in view of the next verse. When our Lord says to his disciples: 'Others have laboured and ye have entered into their labours', it is reasonable to suppose that the 'others' referred to belong to the Old Testament dispensation. This would also give ground for the idea that our Lord's parables of sowing and reaping have a relevance which extends backwards in time as well as forwards. For this conclusion appeal could be made to other indications in the New Testament pointing to a presence and activity of the Christ in Israel prior to the incarnation.²

For our immediate purpose, however, it is of more importance to notice that the thought of Irenaeus is not tied down to the imagery of a single biological organism. His argument is directed against those who attributed the whole order of creation to a rival god. He is, therefore, concerned to show that the original creation and the new order in Christ belong to a single divine plan which has the one God for its author. At the roots of his thought lies the scriptural doctrine of the new creation. This means that for him there is in Christ a restoration of that 'order' which was imprinted upon creation from the beginning. The restoration, then, took place *in* Christ by virtue of his taking 'flesh'; and it follows from the scriptural idioms of

---

¹ In *adv. haer.* iv. 25.3 this becomes: 'one *people* which sows. . . .'

² e.g. 1 Cor. 10⁴, John 1 ⁹⁻¹¹, 8⁵⁶; cp. also Luke 24²⁷,⁴⁴. Such texts would naturally be taken to support the patristic identification of 'the Angel of the Covenant' with the pre-existent Logos, a theme characteristic of Justin, who greatly influenced Irenaeus.

thought that the renewal of the cosmic order is effected *in* that human organism of 'one flesh' which is both Christ and his church. Nevertheless the balance of New Testament teaching does not favour an exclusive employment of the 'body' image in our thought about the new creation. For behind this particular image lies a long series of analogies between Israel on the one hand and a variety of constituent elements in the order of creation on the other; and these have their counterparts in the New Testament. Moreover, whereas the doctrine of Christ's Body is, in scripture, *explicitly* unfolded only in the Pauline Epistles, St Paul himself uses the other analogies freely when it suits his purpose.[1]

We shall not be far from the mark if we say that in the outlook of St Irenaeus the wider implications of Paulinism are becoming explicit. We can see an earlier stage of the same process in St John's Gospel. For there the Pauline doctrine of Christ's Body has already become a fundamental presupposition which, at certain points, determines the form in which the story is presented.[2] But, of course, this is due, in part at least, to the fact that behind both these apostolic writers lies a Hebrew way of thinking which is common ground. One aspect of this Hebrew presupposition is the ancient feeling for man's creatureliness which sets human nature so firmly within the wider order of creation as almost to involve identification with it. It is precisely such a degree of identification which confronts us in St Paul's expositions of the 'body' analogy.[3] This may be seen partly in the ease with which he passes from the 'body' image to others drawn from a wider creaturely order and back again. Thus, in I Corinthians $12^{12\,\theta}$, having introduced the analogy of the body, he suddenly switches over to the conception of the Spirit as water moulding particles of dry dust into a moist compact soil;[4] and then he switches back again to resume the main theme. Probably he already has in mind here the picture

[1] e.g. I Cor. $15^{35\,\theta}$, Rom. $4^{17\,\theta}$, $8^{18\,\theta}$, $11^{16\,\theta}$, Phil. 2^{15}

[2] For details see my essay in *The Apostolic Ministry*.

[3] Here the question as to how far there is Stoic influence is not of primary importance. For the Semitic origins of Stoicism made it, in any case, an appropriate mediator between the Hebrew way of thinking and relevant factors in the Graeco-Roman world.

[4] For this use of ποτίζειν cp. Moulton and Milligan's *Vocabulary*, p. 531. The evidence was accepted by Moffatt in his recent commentary, *ad loc.*

in Genesis 2⁵⁻⁷ which he is going to use in chapter 15, the picture of the divine artist moulding Adam's body out of the wet soil. Similarly in that later chapter he passes from the imagery of sowing and harvesting to the heavenly bodies by way of the various forms of animal life, and so back again to Adam, covering the whole story of creation in Genesis.[1] All this too is comprised in an exposition of his doctrine concerning the resurrection of the body, as that in turn provides a fitting conclusion to his little treatise on the Body of Christ in its sacramental, mystical and ethical aspects.

One of the most characteristic features of apostolic thought might be described as a tendency to find the plan of creation manifested and fulfilled in Christ and the church. This, however, does not mean that creation itself is thought of primarily as an organism. For, as we have seen, the scriptural imagery is too rich, varied, and even heterogeneous to sustain without fluctuation a notion so uniform and so sharply articulated. On the other hand St Paul's teaching about the Body does introduce the organic idea into the theological thought of the New Testament. His contribution to that thought, therefore, did add a new element to the complex of biblical images concerning the order of creation. Moreover, whereas the organic terminology may owe much to contemporary influences of philosophic thought, the *nisus* of imaginative feeling behind it issues out of the Jewish nature of one who remained to the last a 'Hebrew of the Hebrews'. The confluence of these two streams, however, might have produced no more than a stagnant and insignificant trickle had it not been replenished with fresh and living waters flowing down from a higher source. In other words the Pauline introduction of the organic idea was fruitful because it gave intellectual expression to the new revolutionary fact which is the mystery of the Christ.

Paulinism, therefore, meant, from the first, a tendency to think of the new creation in organic terms. This opened for the gospel a door into the wider world of contemporary culture, and thereby made it possible for the Judaeo-Christian 'wholeness' of outlook to combat the disintegrating dualism of some

---

[1] 1 Cor. 15³⁵⁻⁴⁹; cp. 15²². Actually he changes the order, to suggest a gradation of seeds up to man, who then in his risen glory will shine as the stars. See further below in Ch. VI, § i, last 2 pars., and § v, pars. 2 *ff.*

contemporary thought on its own *terrain*.[1] The issue is already joined in the Epistle of St Paul to the Colossians; and the conflict reached its climax in the lifetime of St Irenaeus. It is in this connexion that the wider implications of Paulinism may be said to become explicit in Irenaeus. The Hebrew-Christian 'wholeness' is fully present still in the thought of this representative of the late second century. He has, indeed, completely escaped the current influences making for dualism in a largely hellenized world. St Irenaeus is thus the adequate exponent of a Christian theology which, while profoundly scriptural in essentials, interprets the substance of the gospel in a medium of thought characteristically and persistently organic in its mode of expression. The fundamental unity of the divine plan is never far from the author's mind; and the organic way of expressing that unity stands out more sharply than in the New Testament. Irenaeus represents a tradition which often takes a rhetorical form, as for example in the drawing out of parallels between the gospel and the story of creation. But these effects always start from something genuinely scriptural and remain remarkably true to the Hebrew way of thinking, thus preserving that remotely primitive background of thought which is included in the deep and distant perspectives of scripture.

A good illustration of what has just been said is to be found in the working out of a parallel between the creation of Adam and the virgin-birth of our Lord.[2] The starting-point is the key-idea of 'recapitulation' which comes from Ephesians 1^{10}, and which is understood in terms of the highly primitive 'repetition' *motif*. This *motif* is very prominent in scripture and will occupy our attention considerably from this point onwards. Here it involves the idea that the events of the first creation are repeated in the new creation. The repetition of a previous pattern of events is, so to speak, a hall-mark of genuineness. By it the divine activity can be recognized to be truly present and efficacious. Moreover the familiarity of the pattern ensures the possibility of a definite human response to something which can be known and appreciated for what it is. In the present instance 'repetition' is the means through which the effects of

[1] For another aspect of 'contemporary thought' see the concluding footnote of Ch. IX below.

[2] *adv. haer.* iii, 21.10 and *ff*

Adam's Fall are undone, and thus the order of creation is restored in Christ to its true harmony once more. 'Recapitulation' is a word which seems capable of several shades of meaning according to the precise context of thought in which it is used. Fundamentally it means that in the divine plan creation is to be 'summed up' representatively in Christ its true head, so that its whole wealth of significance is brought to fulfilment in him.[1] In this function of headship our Lord fulfils the part assigned to Adam in the story of Genesis. That is to say, as the redeemer Christ fulfils that universal high-priestly ministry, towards and on behalf of the world of creatures, which is the proper function of our human nature.[2]

Now in the language of scripture 'Adam' could signify the organic unity of the human race, partly because 'Adam' is, in Hebrew, the group-word for 'man' or 'mankind'. In the Hebrew way of thinking, moreover, Adam actually includes all his descendants within himself. For this reason St Irenaeus insists that 'recapitulation' is effected through the salvation of Adam. The whole race of men is to be restored in Christ to that headship over creation which is Adam's prerogative. The tragedy of creation lies in the fact that man by seeking to usurp divine prerogatives ceased to fulfil rightly his priestly service on behalf of the created world. The restoration of creation depends upon the restoration of man. For these reasons St Irenaeus frequently affirms that Adam is the lost sheep whom Christ came to seek and to save. Fallen man is thus regarded as a single entity; and the organic aspect of redemption is correspondingly stressed. It is in this context of thought, then, that we must understand our author's teaching concerning the parallel between the two creations, a parallel which is eventually carried far beyond the manner of our Lord's birth.

In Genesis 2[5] we read that before the creation of Adam, God had not yet rained upon the earth, and 'there was not a man

[1] Recapitulation passed through three stages represented by (a) the Epistle to the Ephesians, (b) Justin, (c) Irenaeus. In repudiating a connexion between (a) and the two later stages, Loofs (op. cit., pp. 357 ff) has misunderstood the significance of Eph. 1[10] in its relation to the epistle as a whole. Ephesians is actually a treatise upon recapitulation in some of its main aspects; e.g. the 'repetition' of Gen. 2 in Christ and the church is already adumbrated in 5[22] ff. To this we shall return.

[2] see above, Ch. IV, § i, penultimate paragraph

to till the ground'; so that the soil was *virgin* soil. In the next verse
we are told in the Greek bible that 'a fountain went up from
the earth and watered the face of the ground'. Irenaeus does
not mention this 'fountain'; but he may well have had it in
mind in view of the parallel which he now developes.[1] For as
Adam was formed by his Creator from virgin soil, so Jesus was
formed in his human nature from the flesh of a Virgin's womb.
Again, as Adam was shaped by the Word of God, so Adam's
shape was taken by the Word who 'recapitulates' Adam. Thus,
when the Word, from whom Adam received his form, himself
took that form, he did so by a creative act like the original act.
Why, then, did not the Creator again take the earth-mould
from the ground as before? Why was not the original act
exactly repeated? Why did he in the new creation shape the
human form 'from Mary'? The answer is that the original act
of creation had to be included in the new act. The pattern of
divine creativity must be repeated in identically the *same*
material. For only so could Adam be recapitulated in Christ
and the lost sheep restored to the fold.[2]

iii

The creation of Adam prefigures the total dispensation of
the Christ. Aspects of recapitulation: (*a*) Repetition of events;
(*b*) unity of process and end; (*c*) repetition of process.

St Irenaeus seems here to have in mind a number of different
aspects of the parallel, all of which he conceives to be important.
First of these is the act of the divine artist in forming Adam
from the dust of the earth. St Paul had contrasted the *earthly*
origin of Adam with the heavenly origin of Christ. But he had
also emphasized the *earthy* material of which 'the first man' was
formed.[3] The Greek bible, as interpreted by the apostle, would

[1] i.e. 'the fountain' watering virgin soil corresponds to the Holy Spirit
by whom the Virgin conceived. Cp. above, the reference to Gen. 2[5-7] in
Ch. V, § ii, par. 3. In EVV the fountain has become a 'mist'.
[2] The analogy is repeated by this author in *The Demonstration of the
Apostolic Preaching*, Chs. 32, 33, and by other writers.
[3] 1 Cor. 15[47]. In English the omission of the 'l' in 'earthly' suggests a
vital connexion between the two ideas thus distinguished. For the apostle
in this text draws out the exact significance of Gen. 2[7]. In the Hebrew

suggest to Irenaeus a double thought. Adam was of lowly origin, being 'earthy' of the earth. But also through his earthy body he was one with the 'earthly' order. Thus the story in Genesis identified the grandeur of creation with the materiality of creation's head. The high destiny of earth is linked inseparably with man; and the high destiny of man is bound up with his creatureliness. In this way the tendency of the New Testament to associate the order of creation with the new Man is, in the parallel which we are considering, extended backwards to its original association with the first man.[1]

So far we have been considering the material of which Adam's body was formed. We have now to consider the act by which it was formed. As the story is told, a Greek reader would think at once of an artist shaping a human figure with his hands out of some plastic material. So too St Irenaeus understands the verse. For he speaks here and elsewhere of the 'hand' or 'hands' of God by which the man was formed.[2] Moreover our own word 'plastic' is derived from the actual verb here used in the Greek bible to describe the divine act of 'forming' man.[3] Upon this expression our author fastens with remarkable tenacity. For throughout his treatise he refers to the 'formation' of Adam in language which recalls this particular feature of the narrative. It is as though he found in this phraseology a quite special theological significance; and perhaps we can guess at his thoughts. We have already seen one side of the picture. The handfuls of dust moulded into a clay figure emphasize the lowliness of man. But do they not also suggest a corresponding lowliness in God? If man is earth-born, that is so because his maker has willed it. This, again, suggests that

language 'Adam' may be presumed to come from the same root as 'earth' or 'ground' (*adamah*). Moreover, the Hebrew phrase: 'dust from the ground' (as rendered in LXX) is the source of the double thought in St Paul: (1) *not* from heaven; (2) of 'earthy' material.

[1] see above, § ii, par. 3. The double association of creation's order with both Adam and Christ is of course implicit in 1 Cor. 15. Cp. the last note to the paragraph of § ii just cited.

[2] see also *The Demonstration of the Apostolic Preaching*, Ch. 11. The theological significance of 'the hands' will be considered later. See below, p. 170 with note 4, and Ch. VI, § iv (latter part).

[3] ἔπλασεν, to which in *adv. haer.* correspond πλάσις, πλάσμα, and so also the translator's *plasmatio*

the very dust of the earth is precious in the eyes of the Creator as well as the sparrows and the numbered hairs of which our Lord spoke.[1] 'God saw everything that he had made, and behold it was very good.' From the divine standpoint nothing created is without significance; and in the new creation a like rule obtains. For we read: 'The base things of the world, and the things that are despised, did God choose'.[2]

The passage just quoted is one of several where those who are new creatures in Christ are, in the New Testament, described in language reminiscent of the original creation story.[3] We have already seen reason to suppose that Genesis 2[7] was in St Paul's mind in connexion with the 'body' image in the latter part of this same epistle. If, then, St Irenaeus was thinking along these lines the fashioning of Adam from many particles of dust would, for him, prefigure the act of new creation by which many members are united in the Body of Christ. This, in turn, would imply that the act whereby the image of God was imprinted upon Adam prefigured the vaster process which began when the Word became flesh, but which will reach its fulfilment only when 'we all attain unto . . . a full-grown man', that is, unto the fulness of Christ (Eph. 4[13]). There is also much elsewhere in this writer to suggest that the wider thought should be taken into account in the present parallel. In any case it will by now have become clear that in the working out of such an analogy between Adam and Christ, between the old order and the new, it is not simply detailed resemblances that matter, but rather the whole pattern of divine activity. The moulding of Adam's body is significant because by it the divine image is stamped upon man's nature. Nevertheless, the fact of the divine image in man is not to be understood rightly apart from the *process* by which it came to be.

On one side the strain of poetic myth running through the argument requires that, as in some ancient ritual, the acts by which Adam was created should be repeated in the events by which the Son of God became incarnate. Hence the archaic insistence that, in this solemn, factual symmetry, virgin-soil

---

[1] Matt. 10[29,30]   [2] 1 Cor. 1[28]

[3] 1 Cor. 1[26–28] begins with 'your calling' and ends with 'the things that are not' which God 'called' into the new existence. Cp. the similar language of Rom. 4[17], on which see my *The Common Life*, pp. 276 *f.*

prefigures a Virgin's womb.[1] On the other hand, at times the argument moves on quite a different level where the poetic pomp of repetition is replaced by the slow unfolding of an age-long drama.[2] Now in drama the significance of the culminating scenes depends upon their relation to all that precedes. The character of the *dénouement* follows from the gradual unfolding of the author's purpose; and this in turn depends for its execution upon the collaboration of all the actors, each making his contribution to the whole. Dramatic unity, therefore, is of the organic type. The end is implicit in the actual movement of the play as a whole; and that movement finds its final justification and explication in the significance of the end. From this point of view the Asiatic father sees strongly that aspect of scripture in which all that belongs to the first creation and to the old covenant is only the setting of the stage and the rehearsing of the scenes in outline before the real presentation of the play begins. Yet all those preliminaries belong to the reality and are of one piece with it. They are, indeed, included within it,[3] when the curtain at last goes up and 'the long story of man' is summed up in Christ before the intently understanding eyes of the spectators.[4]

The concluding sentence of our last paragraph echoes a phrase of St Irenaeus to which we must now pay attention. The picture of Adam as the lost sheep emphasizes the organic unity of fallen humanity. In that respect Adam sums up by anticipation the whole history of mankind. For 'we are all

[1] The 'repetition' is negative as well as positive. So there is a point-by-point correspondence between the events of the Fall and the analogous gospel events by which 'the knot' of sin was 'untied' (*adv. haer.* iii, 22.4; v. 19.1). The negative repetition *reverses* the tragic events of the former cycle, in order that the original work of creation may be restored.

[2] The emphasis in this sentence is upon 'the slow unfolding'. The reference to a 'different level' is not intended to deny dramatic character in 'the poetic pomp of repetition'. On the dramatic element in recapitulation see further the concluding footnote of this chapter.

[3] For another aspect of this oneness and inclusion, see below, Ch. VII, § v, from par. 5 onwards, where the dramatic analogy receives a different application; and again in Ch. X, § v, par. 6, where the analogy is applied to the compresence of creation with redemptive history and the inclusion of nature in grace.

[4] For the angelic spectators, of whom Irenaeus says interesting things in *The Demonstration*, 11, 12, cp. Eph. 3^{10}.

from him'.[1] Out of the brief story of Adam, therefore, as comprised in Genesis 1-3, there flowed the 'long story' of mankind.
This, in turn, was compendiously summed up in the brief story
of our salvation in Christ when the lost sheep was once more
found. Here we have a fresh elaboration in which the various
aspects of the recapitulation doctrine meet and overlap. In the
first form of that doctrine a 'compendium' of creation-events
is 'repeated' in a corresponding compendium of salvation-
events. In the second form, as we outlined it, Irenaeus is thinking of the whole dispensation of the Old Testament as a single
process prefiguring Christ, who, in summing up that process,
manifests its unity. It is this process which is represented by
his phrase: 'the long story of mankind'. The 'long story',
however, flows out of the short story of Adam and is already
symbolized by it. For the process by which Adam was moulded
to the image of God foreshadows the larger processes beyond.
This holds good in two respects. The moulding of Adam to the
image epitomized in advance the long story of mankind which
received its culmination when the perfect manifestation of the
image was given in the Word made flesh. But secondly, as we
saw, the creative act described in Genesis 2[7] foreshadowed the
whole of the wider Christian dispensation wherein regenerate
humanity is moulded to the perfection of the image which
already exists in the incarnate Word.[2]

The special characteristics of the saint's doctrine concerning
the image of God in man, as implied in the foregoing summary,
have yet to be investigated. For they are vital to this inquiry
concerning organic revelation. Meanwhile, it must be noticed
that we have now reached a third form of the recapitulation
doctrine; and here repetition of process overshadows repetition
of events. For the long story of mankind is a process of education
adapted to the frailty of man's condition; and in unfolding this
theme Irenaeus draws a striking threefold parallel in which
the divine method of dealing with man is seen to repeat itself.[3]
The kernel of the argument is the childlike condition of Adam.
This is the precondition of God's whole treatment of our race.

---

[1] *adv. haer.* iii, 23.2; for *longam hominum expositionem* see iii, 18.1

[2] above, Ch. V, § iii, par. 3 (quoting Eph. 4[13])

[3] *op. cit.* iv, 38.1-3; cp. *The Demonstration,* Chs. 12 *ff,* where the childlike
nature is also attributed to Eve

The story of revelation is the story of a divine accommodation; and as he developes this thought the mind of Irenaeus moves insensibly backwards and forwards between Adam and his descendants. In them the childlike Adam is clearly present. The process of shaping *him* is present in the education to which *they* are subjected. Finally, the Adam-process repeated in the race of men determines the form of the incarnation. Since we were children, God the Word became a child. Though he was 'the perfect bread' he, like a wise mother, gave himself to us for our nourishment in the form of milk. The passage closes with the coining of a delightful phrase: The Son of God,[1] perfect as he was, *shared in a co-infancy,* 'not for himself but on account of the man's infantile state, thus finding room for himself as man was able to make room'. He became childlike for the sake of the children to whom he came.[2]

iv

The 'co-infancy' of Christ with Adam. The relation of theology to the biblical forms of speech. Primitive wholeness preserved by the dominance of revelation over its environment.

The aspect of recapitulation which we have just described as a repetition of process might also be thought of in terms of interpenetration. That is a characteristic of this father's thought which we have previously examined at some length.[3] Here too the phenomenon is threefold, as before; but now the conception is stated differently. We have already pointed out that in the passage about 'co-infancy' the saint's mind ranges to and fro between the childlike Adam and his childlike descendants. We

[1] The variant: 'Word of God' may be the better reading (Loofs, *op. cit.,* p. 387, note 3).

[2] If Loofs' analysis is accepted (*op. cit.,* pp. 420-423) the thesis first took shape as a relatively simple, but profound, statement of Christ's conformity to the immaturity of Adam without the more complex notion of 'the many' included in 'the One'. The latter, however, was integral to the recapitulation theory of Irenaeus; and its introduction by him transformed the original thesis.

[3] In Ch. IV, § vi. As we proceed it will become clear that the interpenetration is here threefold in respect of its modes: (*a*) Adam and his members; (*b*) Christ and Adam; (*c*) Christ and his members. The second mode of interpenetration, (*b*), will be examined more fully in Ch. VI.

must next take note of the fact that there is a corresponding fluctuation of thought perceptible in respect of the third term, namely the childlike Christ.[1] The incarnation is a divine accommodation to the weakness and immaturity of man. That is clearly a prevailing idea in this passage. But just how much is included here within the scope of the incarnation? And how is the childlike Christ conceived to be related to Adam and to his descendants?

In the first part of this chapter[2] the author is undoubtedly referring to the fact of the incarnation – Christ's 'human visit' or 'sojourn in human guise', as it is called. A comparison between the infancy of our Lord and the childlikeness of Adam would, therefore, suitably resume and develope that earlier parallel between the creation of Adam and the birth of Christ which we have previously considered. As the argument proceeds, however, it becomes evident that St Irenaeus is thinking in terms of 'the whole Christ', that is, not simply the earthly life of Jesus, but rather Jesus *and* his church as united in the one mystical organism. The allegorical statement that 'the perfect bread of the Father' gave himself to us in the form of milk is a way of describing the incarnation. But it leads on quite naturally to the spiritual nourishment of the church, and, again, to the slow growth of the Christian life.[3] Thus the coming of Christ to man was conformed to our condition of immaturity throughout the whole story of God's people. Finally, in the actual reference to the co-infancy the range of thought is extended even more widely. This is indicated by the precise language used. In a simple reference to the incarnation we should expect the writer to say that the Son of God 'became our co-infant'. His words, however, are as follows: 'The Son of God was sharing infancy with the man on account of the man's infantile condition'. Here the pattern of human sonship is repeated because the divine Son has penetrated to the core of our creaturely being.

But further, there are two points to notice. In the first place, if we confine our attention to the opening words of the sentence

---

[1] For 'the One' and 'the many' see § v of this chapter

[2] iv. 38.1

[3] This is illustrated from 1 Cor. 3[2]: 'I fed you with milk, not with meat; for ye were not able to bear it.'

the imperfect tense of the verb[1] would naturally suggest a gradual growth and education of Jesus from birth to manhood. If St Irenaeus had this in mind his key phrase contains a reference to those glimpses of the holy childhood which are imparted to us in St Luke's Gospel. Following the evangelist our author is then teaching that Christ made himself one with the people of God by sharing their spiritual development. The childhood and growth of Jesus would thus be of one pattern with the slow education of the human race. It would be part of his whole self-accommodation to human immaturity. But secondly, when we look at the sentence as a whole we notice that the conditions of childhood are said to be shared by the Son of God with 'the man'; and here the reference can only be to Adam. For the very next sentence refers to 'the man' as having been 'lately made' (by contrast with his Creator). This is a clear reference back to the starting point of the whole passage, where the childlikeness of Adam is explained in closely similar language. Finally, the 'co-infancy' sentence opens with an explicit reference to Adam's condition in 'the beginning'.[2]

It would seem not unreasonable for the modern reader of St Irenaeus to reinterpret such a statement as this to himself and to his contemporaries by the simple expedient of substituting phrases like 'mankind' or 'human nature' for 'Adam' or

[1] συνενηπίαζεν. The translator rendered this by a perfect (coinfantiatum est), thereby narrowing the range of meaning to the historical event of our Lord's conception and birth.

[2] It will be convenient to set out some of the points in fuller detail. The passage as a whole opens (iv, 38.1) with an answer to what must have been a typical objection among the heretics of the day: 'Why should not man have been created in a state of maturity?' The reply turns upon the double meaning of τέλειος. Such 'maturity' is a form of 'perfection' impossible in things created; for they are 'recently generated'. God, indeed, had the power to bestow upon man such perfection. 'But the man [i.e. Adam] was unable to receive it; for he was a child'. At this point the author seems to be preparing to say that the recapitulation took place 'in the last times' on account of Adam's immaturity. This is required by the sequence of thought and suggested by the participial clause ('having summed up all things into himself'); for Irenaeus constantly associates recapitulation with Adam. The sentence in question actually begins along that line of thought; but it is completed with a sudden switch over from Adam, 'the child', to us, 'the children'. This abrupt substitution seems to indicate that in the mind of Irenaeus the two terms are interchangeable. So then, 'our Lord came to us' in a manner suitable to our immaturity. The delay, therefore, was due

'the man' throughout. The sense of the passage would then be twofold. First, the incarnation was in essence an accommodation of God's infinite perfection and majesty to our finite limitations; and secondly, the method of the incarnation was the method which characterizes the whole of God's dealings with man. So far as general statements go this interpretation is certainly not untrue. Nevertheless it cannot be regarded as an adequate equivalent of the ancient cycle of thought which it seeks to summarize. For no abstract generalization can possibly do justice to the scriptural concreteness of that original. The primitive 'wholeness' which belongs to the biblical world of thought is faithfully preserved by Irenaeus, whereas it is dissipated in the general statement.[1] The thought of this father is most likely to be correctly appraised if we remember that he is working upon traditional interpretations of biblical material. This means that his thought moves *within* the biblical forms of speech;[2] and however free he may feel to give his own interpretations, this condition holds the field. For these forms of speech are a frame of reference which belong to the substance of revelation. While in no way impeding the movement of his mind they provide an outward vesture for his imaginative thinking. Thus the *corpus* of revelation has passed over into his

to the need of a preparatory education stretching over 'the long story of men'. The statement about 'the perfect bread' giving himself to us as milk, which follows immediately, is explicitly interpreted to mean the incarnation. So far the argument is straight-forward except for the sudden identification of 'us' with Adam. The next sentence, however, extends the nursing metaphor to cover the habitual nourishment of our life in the church; and this, in turn, introduces (38.2) the Corinthian Christians as typically slow learners in the school of the incarnation. Then, quite suddenly, we are back again at 'the beginning' with the newly-created Adam receiving Christ as his partner in co-infancy!

[1] This raises a difficult problem concerning the general statements of theology and their relation to scripture. Into this we cannot enter as yet; for our present concern is with the *content* of revelation. Only by returning *to* that content can we hope to discern rightly the methods by which it may best be safeguarded.

[2] If Irenaeus owed the 'co-infancy' phrase verbally to his Antiochene source, then the compresence of Adam with Christ (in *some* sense) was already there implied in the imperfect tense (see above, p. 146, note 1). If we accept this assumption, it follows that the biblical idiom (on which see below, § v) was by that means transmitted through Semitic Antioch to the West, where, however, it was eventually obliterated by the Latin translator!

theological thought without breach of continuity and without loss of integrity. If we are to understand him, therefore, our interpretation must also keep within the same traditional orbit.[1]

Accordingly, when we enter into the argument about Adam and Christ, as presented by St Irenaeus, we are entering into a cycle of primitive Christian thought which goes back to St Paul. As such, it is a cycle within which is preserved more than one stratum of culture. For many influences had played upon the long biblical and Jewish-Christian tradition of which St Paul was both heir and interpreter. As to all that, moreover, there is a preliminary consideration which we shall do well to bear in mind. It is now widely recognized that in the Pauline treatment of the comparison between Adam and Christ the details of the comparison are determined not so much by theories about Adam as by the significance of the revelation in Christ. In other words, Christian beliefs were not subordinated to contemporary ideas. On the contrary, current notions about Adam were adapted to fit the primitive apostolic Christology. As a magnet, by its mere presence, draws to itself objects in the environment which are amenable to its influence, so did the gospel of Christ, through the medium of those who acknowledged its sway, draw into its orbit materials of its

---

[1] Even so, however, we encounter difficulties which were not wholly surmounted. Thus, in the passage under consideration, after the scriptural metaphor of a mother suckling her infants (cp. 1 Pet. 2^{2,3}) the author continues: 'that, having been accustomed to eat and drink the Word of God, we might be enabled to possess the bread of immortality which is the Spirit of the Father'. This corresponds to the thought of John 6$^{51-58}$, which, in the light of 6^{63} (cp. 4^{24}), *might* be understood to mean that sacramental feeding upon the incarnate Word prepares for a heavenly banquet of the Spirit. Such an interpretation would approximate to that 'Spirit-Christology' which did not distinguish the divine nature of Christ from the Holy Spirit. The second century was involved in a difficult transition of terminology, a passage from Hebrew to Greek idioms of *thought* and from Jewish to Christian presuppositions of *faith*. The complications may be illustrated from the following: In Lam. 4^{20} 'the anointed of the Lord' is called 'the breath of our nostrils'. In modern idiom this could be understood to mean 'the life and soul of our nation'. In LXX, however, we read that 'the breath of our face' is 'Christ the Lord'. The echo of Gen. 2^7 (cp. Eccles. 12^7) would easily suggest an identification of 'Christ' with 'Spirit of God'; and this actually occurs when the passage is quoted by Irenaeus (*adv. haer.* iii, 10.3: *The Demonstration*, 71). Spirit-Christology will be explained more fully in Ch. IX, § vi.

cultural and intellectual environment lying ready to hand. Again, as the magnet supports the objects which are attached to it, so too did the gospel of Christ hold together the materials thus drawn into its orbit, thereby giving to those materials a new unity of form through which its own significance could be expressed. If, as we may reasonably presume, this principle of development continued to operate during the second century under the still surviving influence of apostolic tradition, that would sufficiently explain the preservation of 'primitive wholeness' in the thought of St Irenaeus as indicated in the last paragraph.

V

The One and the Many in primitive Christian thought. Hebrew psychology throws light upon the obscurities in Irenaeus. The Hebrew 'striving after wholeness' interacting with the organic idea.

It has by now become clear that the phase of patristic theology which we have been examining can become intelligible only when it is interpreted from within the biblical world of thought to which it still properly belongs. As we anticipated at the end of the last chapter, the study of St Irenaeus presses us back to scripture, particularly to St Paul, and through him eventually to the most ancient layers of Hebrew tradition. This conclusion has been forced upon us step by step, until in the 'Adam' typology it became inescapable. Organic revelation means, amongst other things, an organic unity between scripture and church tradition on the one hand, as it also involves on the other side a massive interconnexion of scripture itself with the whole world of facts contained in the ancient cultures. This far-reaching continuity of revelation which sends us back from the patristic theology to primitive Hebrew psychology must now be subjected to closer scrutiny; and it will be convenient to begin at the point where the present digression led us away from the text of St Irenaeus.

It will be remembered that a peculiarity of the passage introducing the idea of 'co-infancy' lay in sudden oscillations of thought, from Adam to his descendants, and back again quite suddenly to Adam. The two themes remain distinct, and yet they seem to merge into one another. In short, Adam is both distinguished from his descendants and also identified with them. This double relationship, although presented somewhat abruptly, ought not to surprise us. For it is a leading feature of the parallel between Adam and Christ as originally drawn by St Paul. Here we are on ground familiar to the anthropologist.[1] Hebrew thought moved on a primitive level after a fashion common to other primitive peoples. According to this way of thinking a living man is not a soul dwelling in a body, but rather an animated body, a 'psychical whole', whose various mental activities are identified with corresponding parts of the body. The Hebrew idiom of thought refers to the man in terms of some particular part of his body to emphasize some particular function of his nature, just as we say 'I see' when we are referring to a purely mental illumination. But further, as the individual man expresses himself in parts of his body, so also he is 'extended' in things or persons outside himself. Thus Elisha sends his staff to raise a child to life; and a man's servant or deputy is 'as himself'. That is to say, a duly authorized representative is thought of as having actual identity with his principal. Of more immediate relevance to our present purpose, however, is that form of 'extension' by which a man is identified with his family, his household, his tribe or even larger social units. In this form of extension the man who is the natural head of a social group may be thought of as including the other members of the group within himself.

On the other hand neither the 'head' nor the 'members' in such a group lose their individuality. Each may be thought of separately, if occasion serves; and this double relation of identity and distinction gives rise to that very phenomenon of *oscillation* which we have noticed in St Irenaeus. There are plenty of examples of this in the Old Testament,[2] as when the messengers of Moses to the king of Edom begin their speech with the plural

---

[1] For what follows the reader is referred to the classic essay by H. Wheeler Robinson in *The People and the Book*, ed. Peake (Oxford, 1925). A convenient summary of the literature bearing on Hebrew psychology is given by A. R. Johnson in his small monograph: '*The One and the Many in the Israelite Conception of God*' (Cardiff, 1942), from which one or two phrases have been included in the text above.

[2] A number of these are quoted in detail by A. R. Johnson (*op. cit.*, pp. 8*ff*).

'we' and then change over to the singular 'I'.[1] In such passages
the social group is thought of alternately as a number of individuals and as a single person. This is precisely the situation
which has confronted us in the pages of Irenaeus. For example,
the conception of Adam as the lost sheep of the parable implies
that his salvation is a purely personal affair. Yet the insistence
on an identity of substance between the virgin-flesh of Mary and
the virgin-soil from which Adam was formed implies an identity
between Adam and his descendants. Moreover the necessity
that Adam, as the lost sheep, should be saved rests upon the fact
that his salvation carries with it universal consequences. This
is expressed by saying that Adam is recapitulated in Christ.
The fact that Adam is both 'the one' and 'the many', both an
individual and the whole race, renders this idea intelligible.
The literal inclusion of Adam in Christ by physical descent, so
that the original earth-mould of Adam's body is present in the
flesh of the sinless Saviour—this literal fact carries with it the
literal inclusion of all Adam's descendants in that flesh which
was nailed to the cross. For this reason St Paul was able to say
that 'One died for all, therefore the all died'.[2]

We can now begin to see how the various aspects of recapitulation cohere together. When Adam is thought of as an individual who is literally included in Christ, then the solemn
reversal of the events which comprised the Fall in and through
the events which comprised the Redemption becomes a perfectly straightforward conception. The knot which was tied is
literally untied. For the reverse process is carried out upon
identically the same material. When, however, the mind of St
Irenaeus oscillates back to the thought of Adam's many
descendants, he then has to envisage a process moving to its
culmination through the centuries. Similarly the idea of co-
infancy has two aspects. If Adam is 'the one' who is included
in 'the One Man Jesus Christ', then the childlike Adam is
literally taken into the Child who was born at Bethlehem, so

[1] Num. 20[14-21]; and see on this passage Johnson's note (*op. cit.*, p. 15).
[2] 2 Cor. 5[14]. The question as to whether the 'literal' fact of material
identity is scientifically admissible is wholly irrelevant, since the revelation
was given in the thought-processes of its own era. As we have already
noted, a historical revelation must be historically conditioned. This unalter-
able fact raises no difficulty *unless* the revelation is regarded as capable of
separation from its outward form. Cp. above, Ch. II, § iii, par. 4.

that the 'newly created' condition of Adam is 'repeated' in the newly created humanity of Jesus. The first 'beginning' is, indeed, both included and repeated in the new 'beginning'. On the other hand, whereas the long education of the human race was epitomized in the growth of Jesus from birth to manhood, it is also now repeated in a new form in the slow re-education of redeemed humanity, that is, the many members of Christ's body the church.

At this point we return to that aspect of recapitulation which may be described as *interpenetration*.[1] It has, once more, two sides to it.[2] The summing up of Adam in Christ includes all Adam's descendants; and in this notion time is altogether transcended. We must beware, however, of identifying this conception with the philosophical idea of a transcendence of time by eternity. For eternity in the philosophers' sense is an idea foreign to the Hebrew mind. What is envisaged in the Hebrew conception is rather the inclusion of the time-process in a single all-inclusive fact or event. This is a characteristic manifestation of the Hebrew 'striving after totality', as it has been called,[3] whereby every phenomenon is referred to the 'whole' to which it belongs. Adam is the 'whole' to which all men belong; and Christ is the whole to which all are transferred by inclusion of Adam in Christ.[4] On the other side of this doctrine of interpenetration is the idea of 'the many' who are included in the whole. These are spread out through time; but the Hebrew mind does not envisage the time-process as a causal

---

[1] see above, Ch. V, § iv, par. 1, with notes

[2] In § iv of the present chapter, par. 1 (with notes), interpenetration was found to have three 'modes'; and, again, running through these modes there appeared two aspects, namely, 'the One' (Adam or Christ) and 'the many' members of 'the One'. In the text above 'two sides' refers to these two aspects, consideration of which was resumed ('two themes') in par. 2 of the present section.

[3] J. Pedersen in *Israel, its life and culture I-II* (ET, Copenhagen and London, 1926), p. 123. This valuable chapter on the Hebrew conception of 'the soul, its powers and capacity' is of equal importance with the essay by Wheeler Robinson.

[4] In Rom. 5 and 6, seen in the light of Rom. 11, it might seem that the essential Pauline idea was simply one of transference *from* Adam to Christ. But the inclusion of Adam *in* the transference is involved, not only in 2 Cor. 5, but also wherever the 'old Adam' is conceived to be present in the members of Christ, as in Col. 3[5-9] and in Eph. 4[22].

sequence, since it does not think, as we do, in terms of a logical chain of causation. On the contrary, all the details are related to one another by their dependence upon the whole to which they belong.

This dependence of many items upon a single whole may be illustrated by considering a variety of instances. The context of the individual may be his social group, say the people of Israel. But if we are to grasp this particular totality, it must be seen in the light of history. For the unity of Israel's history is the divine purpose implicit in all its details. The wholeness which is sought is the concrete fulfilment of that purpose as envisaged in the prophetic pictures of the future. Again, consider the following pregnant analogy:

A Hebrew sentence is like the Hebrew idea of personality;[1] its parts are vividly and picturesquely set before us, but they are co-ordinated, rather than subordinated to one central idea, and the nature of the co-ordination is often implicit rather than explicit.[2]

Here the single sentence is implicit in its many parts; and similarly the total significance of a story in the Old Testament is often implicit in the details rather than explicit in any single statement.[3] In fact, biblical speeches frequently take the form of a historical survey in which the argument is implicit in the form of the narrative.[4] Yet the 'whole' which Israel sought was given in Christ; and this fulfilment inevitably introduced a new emphasis upon 'the One' in whom 'the many' now exist. Thus the shadowy figure of Adam takes colour in St Paul under the illumination which streams from Christ; and again a new word (*soma*) is found in the Greek language to express the 'central idea' of Christ's *body*, for which no Hebrew word would have been sufficiently comprehensive.

The transformation introduced by the coming of the One for whom Israel looked is a subject which we have yet to consider. We have, however, already noticed one of its effects in

[1] This 'idea of personality' was described near the beginning of the present section: 'an animated body, a psychical whole, whose various mental activities are identified with corresponding parts of the body'.

[2] Wheeler Robinson, *op. cit.*, p. 380

[3] Pedersen has given illustrations, e.g. the story of David (*op. cit.*, pp. 183-190).

[4] The perfect example of this is the speech of St Stephen in Acts 7.

that sharpening of the organic conception of the Whole which, starting from St Paul, reaches its zenith in St Irenaeus.[1] Thus the Hebrew idea of the Whole became fused with the Greek concept of an organism. We can see the fruits of this fusion, at both ends of the period we are considering, in the beginnings of a distinctly Christian philosophy of history—in Romans 9-11 on the one hand, and, again, in the characteristic emphasis upon the progressive education of mankind which we have found in the teaching of St Irenaeus. Nevertheless this fusion has not, even in Irenaeus, overcome the oscillation between the One and the Many. Its effects are seen, rather, in a more markedly organic way of regarding both factors. 'The long story of men' is now a progressive development, and the organic unity stressed in the recapitulation doctrine is a living whole which includes this development, or at least may be thought of as doing so. The qualification with which the last sentence concluded is important. For, inasmuch as the Hebrew oscillation is still present in Irenaeus, he sometimes writes as though 'the many' are included in 'the One', and sometimes he leaves them side by side. The passage which includes the prophets in the Body of Christ seems to belong to the former class, the 'co-infancy' passage to the latter.

In both types of thought, however, the other type seems to be present. When he places the prophets within the Body of Christ Irenaeus has much to say about the preparatory character of their dispensation, as though men were not yet ready to receive the fulness of truth in Christ. On the other hand the fluctuations in the co-infancy passage suggest that recapitulation of Adam in Christ is so conceived that the incarnation itself is here brought within the orbit of the Hebrew 'extension' idea. Theology is familiar with the doctrine that there is an 'extension' of the incarnation in the church. If the word 'extension' is here given a meaning which corresponds to Hebrew thought it faithfully reflects the Pauline doctrine that Christ is 'extended' in his members. If, however, the Hebrew conception of the whole-and-its-details is also introduced, then the extension of the Christ will be thought of in terms of *context* rather than of causal *succession*. Christ is then seen to be that Whole which includes all the people of God in its context. As

[1] see above, Ch. V, § ii, par. 5

(in Wheeler Robinson's analogy) the sentence is implicit in its parts, so Christ is implicitly present in the unfolding story of his people, as that complete Word in which all their several contributions find significance; with which, therefore, in a sense they are identified, whatever their temporal relation to his earthly life may be. When once the idea of a causal succession has retreated into the background, making room for Hebrew presuppositions, then the Whole is no longer thought of primarily in terms of temporal order. Thus the redeemer, by penetrating into the orbit of the Adamic social group, has made his own human range co-terminous with that orbit. Conversely, by the same fact he has also gathered up the vast multitudes of humanity into the brief *compendium* of our salvation which he enacted in his earthly life.[1]

[1] It has been suggested to me that in the preceding chapter (as also in subsequent chapters) the dramatic character of the recapitulation theme, as unfolded by St Irenaeus, might with advantage have been more strongly emphasized. Moreover the continuity of this theme with the biblical *cosmos* of thought might seem to indicate that, in this respect at least, what is true of the former would also hold good for the latter. Some of the special characteristics which in the present work have been identified with distinctively Hebrew idioms of thought must certainly have wider connexions, not only in the Semitic world, but also in the psychology of all peoples belonging to the same general level of culture. Poetry and drama, however, belong to all cultural levels. As I understand it the suggestion which we are here considering would imply that the outward form of the biblical revelation is essentially dramatic, and that by virtue of this fact a door stands open giving direct entry into the biblical world of thought. If this suggestion is soundly based, then a clue to the distinctively biblical modes of representation would be provided which might not ineptly be compared to a pair of magnifying glasses. By its means the eyesight of the twentieth century man could be adjusted without difficulty to what in the present volume I have called 'the deep and distant perspectives' of scripture.

The possibility that such an aid to the imagination might greatly ease the difficulties envisaged in the present work must not be overlooked. Nevertheless, it must be said that by this means the problem of a historical religion given in the forms characteristic of a particular time and place might all too easily be by-passed. An illustration may help to make this clear. If the 'repetition' *motif* is a feature common to all drama, repetition is also a fact of nature which recurs at every level of the universe. In ancient religion these two forms of repetition are believed to be inter-dependent, so that by performing certain acts man can cause corresponding events to occur in nature. This magico-religious significance of dramatic repetition is implied in the recapitulation doctrine; and it must be said that, not at one point but at many, it implies an interpretation of human life and its setting wholly different from that which commonly obtains in our modern world. If, then, every characteristic idiom of Hebrew thought and representation could be illuminated from the correspondingly concrete modes of presentation by which, in the arts, the barriers of time and space are overpassed, there would still remain *in every instance* a vital difference between the two sides of the analogy. To ignore the cultural chasm still remaining would be to repeat the errors of the Liberal experiment in a no less devastating form.

On repetition in nature see further, Ch. VII, §§ i and ii, and, from another point of view, Ch. X, § iii onwards.

CHAPTER VI

THE FORM OF REVELATION

i

The literary expression of the repetition *motif*. Redemption presented in terms of the creation story, and with identical idioms of speech. The manifold order of the new *cosmos* is included in the One New Man.

The prominence given to Adam in early Christian thought had its counterpart in the conception of a renewed or restored creation. This idea, in turn, became a focus of the repetition *motif*, so that the new creation was believed to be a repetition of the first creation as presented in the narratives of Genesis. The new creation, thus envisaged in terms which go back to Genesis, was evidently a major preoccupation of the apostolic church, as it is never far from the thoughts of the New Testament writers. The evidence for this fact accumulates as we learn to look for it, and as we come to know for what we should be looking. For in the New Testament a great theme of this kind is like the Hebrew sentence. That is to say, the theme as a whole is often not explicit; it is implicit in a large number of details, any one of which may be overlooked if we are not aware of the theme. Moreover, details of this sort are recognized by a close attention to language; and here the English reader labours under difficulties. For a Hebrew idiom of thought which has passed through Greek, and possibly Latin, before it gets rendered into English, may never survive the process at all! Again, the Hebrew mind often formed important connexions of thought through the varied associations of a single word.[1]

A familiar illustration of this appears in the story of Eve's

---

[1] It has to be remembered that in primitive thought words are active instruments ('spells') with potent effects. The more meanings a word could have, therefore, the more important and dominating it would seem to be.

creation. In the English versions of Genesis 2²² we read that
the rib which the Lord God had taken from the man 'made he
a woman'. But the margin of the Revised Version draws
attention to the fact that the Hebrew reads: 'builded he into a
woman'.¹ Other examples of this idiom in the Old Testament
represent a wife as being built up by having children.² Similarly,
a man and his family form a 'house' which has been so built.
From this double meaning of 'building' proceeds a whole train
of associations to which we shall return later. For the present
it will be sufficient to indicate briefly the bearing of this
sequence of thought upon the creation-theme. A body can be
built like a house; but by another idiom a body can be thought
of as a garment of flesh put on at birth and taken off at death.³
Once again, the Greek word *cosmos*, meaning 'order', usually
stands for the world-order or 'the world'; it can, however,
mean that outward ordering which we call 'adornment', such
as personal ornaments or beautiful clothes. Thus it is that the
same word may stand for 'world' and for 'garment'; and since
the body is a garment, the three ideas (world, body and garment) become interchangeable. So the Wisdom of Solomon
(18²⁴) speaks of 'the whole world' being upon the high-priest's
garment;⁴ and we can see at once how the *garment* of Jesus,
our high-priest, is the new *world* of the new creation, that is to
say his *body*. Here, again, the two aspects of 'building' recur.
The Body is both a 'spiritual house'⁵ and also the new Eve, the

¹ The Hebrew idiom is preserved in LXX, so that the idea would be
familiar to every reader of Genesis in the primitive church. J. Skinner
(ICC), *ad loc.*, draws attention to an Egyptian parallel where 'the operation was actually likened to the building of a wall'.

² e.g. Gen. 16², 30³; in Ruth 4¹¹, where EVV. preserve the idiom, the
wives build 'the house'.

³ see above, Ch. III, §i, last par. and note. The passage there referred to
(2 Cor. 5¹⁻⁴) combines 'body-house' with 'body-garment'. Again, the Book
of Job contains both idioms, body-house in 4¹⁹ and body-garment in 10¹¹;
and in both these instances the context in LXX contains significant echoes
(Job 4²¹, 10⁸,⁹=Gen. 2⁷,¹⁵).

⁴ Philo called this garment 'a copy of the whole heaven' because the
'breast-plate' upon it was believed to represent the twelve signs of the
Zodiac. See the striking passage in *De Somn.* I 214, 215.

⁵ 1 Pet. 2⁵ᶿ. Here, as in Heb. 3⁶, the 'house' is a family-group. But the
language of 1 Pet. 3³ᶠ comes very near to the *soma-cosmos* imagery (see next
note).

bride of the second Adam; for these two, as 'head' and 'body' make one 'flesh'.[1]

All such associations of thought contribute to that outward form from which the biblical revelation is inseparable. In the 'new creation' theme, moreover, we have found the subject taking shape along two distinct lines, namely the one organism and the manifold order. On the one side there is Adam recapitulated in Christ; on the other side is the order of creation which furnishes many biblical analogies to the church, the congregation of the true Israel.[2] The oscillation between these two sides does not mean that they are regarded as two parallel, but separate realities. That would be to import our modern 'dispersive' logic into the Hebrew way of thinking. It may possibly be true that the sharpening of the organic conception, in St Irenaeus if not in St Paul, made the unity of the two forms of imagery more difficult to maintain. If so, that would account for the abrupt character of the transitions from one to the other, which we have noticed in this father's teaching.[3] If, however, we read the creation story in Genesis from a standpoint which has in mind the characteristic Hebrew idioms and presuppositions we shall be obliged to recognize that it carries on the face of it many suggestive thoughts about the new creation in Christ. Some of these, at least, must have been familiar to the first Christians. Such suggestions, again, will depend upon the ease with which transitions were made through verbal associations from one side of the story to the other, from the order of creation to Adam or Eve and back again—from the *cosmos*, for example, with its multiplicity to the *body* of the man or the woman with its unity of outward form. If such considera-

[1] Eph. 5^{22}ff. In Eph. 2-5 the body of Christ is first a temple and then the bride of Christ. In 1 Peter 3^{3,4} the *cosmos* of the Christian woman is 'the hidden man of the heart'. Here the new man (Christ) 'adorns' the woman, whereas in Rev. 21^2 the city *built* in heaven is '*adorned* as a *bride* for her husband'. Such combinations of verbal associations could be varied endlessly.

[2] see above, Ch. V, § ii

[3] In the co-infancy section (iv, 38, 1-2; see above, pp. 143ff) the abrupt transition was apparently *introduced* by Irenaeus when he made a considerable insertion, thus breaking the smooth flow of his Antiochene source. Here source-criticism can give no satisfactory answer to the questions which present themselves. Why was such a violent change introduced at all? And why was the change carried through with such peculiarly sudden transitions of thought?

tions as these are well-founded we shall have gone a long way towards understanding the unity of scripture as envisaged by primitive Christianity.

The second chapter of Genesis, as being more graphic and pictorial than the first chapter, would in large measure provide the *imagery* of Christian thought about the new creation in Christ. At the same time Genesis 1 fills out the details and provides reflexions upon the meaning of the story which follows. For, of course, the first Christians would read the two chapters as the work of one author, and would therefore interpret the one by reference to the other. We have already found indications pointing along these lines, and we shall find them fully confirmed as we proceed. At this point, then, it may be useful to analyze the creation-story of Genesis 2, as we may suppose that it appeared to the first age of the church; and clearly it falls into three main divisions, namely (1) the creation of Adam, (2) the creation of the animals, (3) the creation of Eve. Thus we get a threefold scheme, with two sides, corresponding to the one organism and the manifold order. Genesis 3, being the sequel to the story, provides one or two extra details:

Genesis 2^{5b-8}, 3^{19b}	(1) The One has *identity* with creaturely substance.	The many are earthy units of like nature with the earthy One.
Genesis 2^{9-20}	(2) The One has *headship* over (and kinship with) creaturely order.	The many are living beings of diverse kinds under the One living being.[1]
Genesis 2^{21-25}, 3^{20}, (5^{1-4})	(3) The One has *extension* in a new creation.	The many are the human complement included in the One.

We have already noticed that in writing 1 Corinthians St Paul's thought seems to be coloured at more than one point by details of the creation narratives.[2] In chapter 15, moreover,

---

[1] 'Living *nephesh*', the designation of Adam in Gen. 2^7, is introduced (somewhat awkwardly) in 2^{19} to designate every animal named by Adam.

[2] Besides Ch. 15 the more obvious examples of this are 1^{26} *ff*, 6^{13-20}, 11^{3-12}. It is suggested that 12^{12-14} be added to the list.

he is clearly combining elements from both of these. In verses
45-49, for example, it appears to be explicitly assumed that
'the image of God' mentioned in Genesis $1^{26, 27}$ was imprinted
upon Adam by the method described in Genesis 2^7. The
underlying thought here is that, as the image of Adam was
transmitted to members of Adam's family (Gen. 5^{1-3}, 9^6), so
the restoration of that image in Christ to its true state of glory
is now being transmitted, in turn, to those who belong to *his*
new family. There is, however, implicit in this chapter as a
whole the further idea that a new *cosmos* has come into being,
and that it is situated in the risen body of Christ. The members
of that Body correspond, in the new creation, to the different
kinds of 'seed' and 'flesh' which were subordinated to Adam's
headship in the manifold order of the first creation. The language of 1 Corinthians 15^{35ff} is here full of interest. The
argument starts from an analogy between human 'seed' and
corn-seed, and then goes on to make human 'flesh' a sub-
specimen of 'all flesh'. This places man well within the creaturely order; and there he still remains when he is, a little later,
described as a 'living being' (verse 45)[1]. For in Genesis 2^{19}, as
we have already indicated,[2] the same phrase is applied to the
animals; and this emphasizes their kinship with Adam (as
shown in the second line of the diagram). That kinship is also
stressed in another way in the original story. Plants and
animals come 'from the ground' like Adam. They therefore
share the 'adamic' nature; or, conversely, Adam shares their
'earthy' nature, since Adam's name might mean 'earth-man'.[3]

Thus Adam was of one substance with the whole creaturely
order, sharing with the animals the breath-life of earthy flesh.
Notwithstanding his special prerogative, therefore, 'the first

---

[1] Here the Hebrew phrase quoted from Gen. 2^7 (viâ LXX) defied translation. For *nephesh* is a 'psychical whole' which may be identified with the
living body. Even where, in distinction from the body, *nephesh* = breath-soul
the centre of reference still remains in the body as the seat of personality.
'The Hebrew idea of personality is an animated body and not an incarnate
soul' (Wheeler Robinson, *op. cit.*, p. 362). 'The soul of man is a soul of flesh'
(Pedersen, *op. cit.*, p. 176).

[2] see the last note but two

[3] see above, p. 139, note 3. The slight variations of language in Gen.
$2^{7, 9, 19}$ seem to have no special significance, the 'dust' being mentioned only
at man's creation, as being the first of the series.

man' has identity with the manifoldness of the *cosmos*. His animated body is recognized to be what is sometimes called a 'microcosm',[1] a world in miniature, in which the larger world of created things is representatively included.[2] The text already cited from Wisdom (18[24]) had here another application. The badge of man's high-priestly relation to the order of creation is the erect figure in which the image of God is manifested.[3] The image is shown in the upright body, a 'garment' reaching down to the feet (like the high-priest's vesture); and in its representative character this body-garment might be said to have upon it the whole *cosmos* in substance and animation as well as in order and beauty. How much of this was in St Paul's mind we cannot tell.[4] It is not without interest, however, that the Epistle to the Hebrews (2[5-18]) connects our Lord's high-priesthood with the fulfilment of Adam's destiny as outlined in Psalm 8, and that, moreover, in developing his theme the writer uses language reminiscent of that same context in Wisdom.[5] We may now sum up this section by saying that, in the primitive Christian view which we have been exploring,

---

[1] Philo speaks of 'the man' as 'the little world' (*De Plant.* 28; the whole section is highly relevant).

[2] The idea of the microcosm is implicit in the *soma-cosmos* theme of the contemporary Stoic philosophy. Moreover there are parallels in that philosophy to the fact that Christ, like Adam, is both 'head' and 'body' of his world (cp. W. L. Knox, *St Paul and the Church of the Gentiles*, pp. 160 ff). From another authority come the following suggestive definitions of relevant Hebrew idioms of thought: 'the body is a perfectly valid manifestation of the soul', and ' "a man's head" is the same as a man' (Pedersen, *ib.* pp. 171, 174).

[3] cp. Augustine, *de gen. cont. Man.* 1.17, quoted by Skinner (*op. cit.*, p. 32, note) in reference to Gen. 1[26] *f*

[4] In Vol. II of this work we shall find reason for connecting the next chapter of Wisdom with the preceding chapter of 1 Cor.

[5] Wisd. 18[20-25] (interpreting Num. 16[46-50]) attributes the victory of the high-priest over 'the destroyer' to 'the weapon of his liturgy', that is, to 'prayer and propitiation'. Heb. 2[14-18] connects our Lord's rescue of the holy seed from the devil's clutches with a like ministry. Later the writer of the Epistle actually introduces the destroyer (11[28]) from his earlier LXX appearance (Exod. 12[23]). This might well have been suggested to him by 1 Cor. 10[1-14] which, starting from the Exodus, summarizes the story of Israel's 'temptations' and 'falls' before 'serpents'. Here St Paul warns the Corinthian *ecclesia* that the destroyer's sword is ready to exclude them also from the promised land of the new creation, if they 'repeat' Israel's repetition

Christ, as the new Adam and high-priest of the world, includes within himself the order of creation in respect of both its matter and its form. He has identified himself with its substance and with the manifold law of its life.[1]

ii

The interpenetration of creation and Christ involves the mutual dependence of the Old Testament and the New. The conception of a mutual dependence between two factors, higher and lower, enters significantly into the Irenaean conception of the image of God in man. The image co-extensive with man's rôle as the microcosm of creation.

Our present line of investigation will show how natural it was for St Irenaeus to believe that an inclusion of Adam in Christ carried with it a summing up of all things in Christ. It helps us to understand why the statement that Adam 'was a child' is immediately succeeded by the statement that 'on this account also our Lord came to *us* in the last times, having summed up *the all things* into himself'.[2] The incarnation was, for Irenaeus, a recapitulation of the whole creation because he understood that doctrine to imply some such interpretation of Genesis as we are now putting forward. The recapitulation statement of Ephesians 1[10], which is the key to this father's theological scheme, was for him a summary of the whole Pauline version of Genesis 1-3 as both reversed and fulfilled in Christ. On this interpretation, however, 'fulfilment' means that the story of Christ and the church is already wrapped up in the story of Adam and Eve; and this way of understanding the typology is certainly in accordance with the technique employed in the great nuptial passage of Ephesians 5[22-33]. For there the

---

of the primal rebellion (cp. Gen. 3[24]). The association of Gen. 3 with other 'serpent' passages in the Pentateuch by Philo (*Leg. All.* II. 71-108) provides a literary parallel.

[1] For the subject-matter of the preceding section the reader is also referred to an article by L. H. Brockington on: *The Hebrew Conception of Personality in relation to the Knowledge of God* (JTS Vol. XLVII, Jan.-Apr. 1946, No. 185-6).

[2] *adv. haer.* iv, 38.1

coming revelation concerning the divine bridegroom and his mystic bride is conceived to be already present in the unopened 'secret' of the ancient story.[1]

Such a conception throws fresh light upon the use made by Irenaeus of such words as 'prefigure' and 'preform'. When Adam's body was being moulded the very body of the coming Christ was already being shaped. For, as St Augustine later remarked, 'in the old the new lies hid'. The patristic standpoint here opens up profound questions concerning the relation of the incarnation to the divine plan of creation. For primitive Christian thought there is only one plan which includes both mysteries. Creation and incarnation appear to us as two distinct stages, of which the second (that is, the incarnation) is the divine answer to the disaster of the Fall. The distinction, however, must not be pressed to a point where the incarnation begins to seem like an after-thought which was not included in the original plan. Such a notion cannot be squared with the teaching of a passage like Ephesians 1^{3-14}, where the Christians are told that God the Father chose us in Christ before the foundation of the world, and 'foreordained us unto the adoption of sons through Jesus Christ', or again with the renewal of this way of speaking in Ephesians 3^{8-12}.

It was a commonplace of Christian belief in the first age of the church that the plan of creation can be clearly understood only in the place where it is completed, that is in Christ. This corresponds to the other half of St Augustine's saying, quoted in the last paragraph: 'In the new the old lies open'. The saying was, doubtless, intended to apply in the first instance to the relationship between the two parts of scripture, the Old Testament and the New. But clearly it is capable of wider application. To the interdependence of the two Testaments corresponds the interdependence of the two creations; and the connecting link between the two applications of the saying is to be found in Christ. For, as we have learnt from St Irenaeus, Christ is the Whole in which scripture and creation interpenetrate. In both scripture and creation, however, the interdependence of

---

[1] The *mysterion* referred to in Eph. 5^{32} is a divine secret which was originally lodged in the oracle of Gen. 2^{24} (= Eph. 5^{31}). It is now, however, unsealed by the act of God in Christ, so that in Jesus and his bride its full meaning is at last laid bare.

'the old' and 'the new' is mutual. If 'the old' becomes manifest
'in the new', it is equally true that 'the new lies hid in
the old'.

This complete mutuality of interdependence has important
consequences which we shall have to follow up in detail. For
the present we will confine ourselves to its bearing upon the
doctrine of the divine image in man. This, as we shall see, is
closely connected with our present thesis concerning Revelation. But first it seems desirable to say a few words in explanation of the phrase just now used: 'complete mutuality of inter-
dependence'. Two entities may be complementary to one another in the sense that each is indispensable to the other, and
yet they may occupy two different levels in a hierarchical scale
of being. Thus the Old Testament is indispensable for our
understanding of the New Testament; yet the gospel of Christ
cannot be reduced to elements drawn from the Old Testament
any more than life can be reduced to its chemical constituents.
A 'Judaizing' of Christianity is as mistaken in the one sphere as
a 'materialistic' explanation of life would be in the other.
There is, however, an opposite pair of errors which is not less
deadly, and often more plausible. This consists in mistaking the
transcendence of the 'higher' factor over the 'lower' for *inde*-
pendence of it in a sense which nullifies their *inter*dependence.
That was the characteristic error of Marcion, as it is (in a
measure) of pietism in all ages, and not least to-day.

These considerations bear directly upon the doctrine of the
divine image in man. By virtue of that image imprinted upon
his nature man stands at the head of creation. Yet in scripture
this headship is linked indissolubly with Adam's earthliness.
It is somehow inseparable from the fact of his kinship (yes, in
a sense, even of his identity) with the whole material order of
the world. His representative character as microcosm is as
fundamental as his unique pre-eminence; and, once more, the
two factors are interdependent. In view of these considerations
we should expect a balanced doctrine of the image of God in
man to be as much concerned with one of these factors as with
the other. This is precisely the point at which, once more, St
Irenaeus faithfully reflects the teachings of scripture. For that
very reason, however, his thought will seem strange to those
who are familiar with the doctrine in question mainly in its

later western form as shaped by the dominant influence of St Augustine.

For since the fifth century of our era western thought concerning the image of God in man has moved along lines marked out by the greatest of the Latin fathers. Through the method of psychological analysis Augustine sought and found traces of the Trinity in the soul of man. This concentration upon a psychological analogy has two inevitable effects which can be epitomized by saying that the human side of the analogy is confined to the *interior* life of the *individual*. When the soul is abstracted from the body it becomes, not simply an abstraction in our thought, but from other points of view an object relatively detached and to that extent inaccessible. Through the body the soul has contact with its environment. Apart from the body the soul is not so much a person as an 'individual', an entity set apart from the social organism. To say this much, however, is not necessarily to pass judgement upon the Augustinian experiment. It is easy to see dangers long after the event; and a return to the 'wholeness' of primitive Christianity must not be allowed to degenerate into a complacent habit of indulging in prudential 'post-mortems' upon the actual course of Christian history. Such retrospective tutiorism would overlook the fact that there is an element of risk in all courageous thought as in all noble living.

But further, the Augustinian analysis, notwithstanding its self-imposed limitations, illustrated an important truth which holds good for all applications of the analogy from the human to the divine. The *de Trinitate* exhibited fundamental distinctions within an organic unity of the human soul, the unity being as fundamental as the distinctions. We have only to extend this principle more widely so that it includes the whole of human nature in its integrity, and we then have in our hands a valuable clue which will serve us equally well within the orbit of the main Jewish-Christian tradition. That tradition received its classic expression in the first formative period of Christian theology, which may be said to reach from the conversion of St Paul to the death of St Irenaeus. Within that epoch we find, both in its earlier and in its later phases, *substantially* the same treatment of the doctrine concerning the divine image. This will become clearer as we proceed to unfold some aspects of the

doctrine as held by St Irenaeus and to compare his teaching
with that of the New Testament[1].

iii

Revelation and the doctrine of the image. Differences of preoccupation and of aim, as between the Augustinian teaching and
the earlier tradition. Presentation of the doctrine by St Irenaeus:
(a) the image of God in man; (b) the image of God in Christ;
(c) the manifestation of the image in Christ perfects and fulfils
the image in Adam.

In comparing the teachings concerning *the divine image in man*
which we find respectively in St Irenaeus and in St Augustine
we must limit ourselves strictly to what is relevant to the scope
of our argument concerning *revelation*. Confining ourselves,
therefore, to the connexion between these two themes, we may
begin with one general observation, namely, that the revelation
with which Christians are concerned may be considered either
in respect of its possibility or in respect of its actuality. By this
I mean that there are open to us two alternative preoccupations. We may be occupied primarily with the question: how
is it possible to know and to understand the revelation as given?
Or again, we may address ourselves chiefly to the consideration:
what was the mode in which the revelation was in fact given?
Here we may say, at the outset, that the former question corresponds broadly to the plan of St Augustine's *de Trinitate*, at
least so far as it falls within the scope of this discussion, whereas
the latter question fits more closely the treatment of the divine
image in man which characterizes the writings of St Irenaeus.

Now it sometimes happens that the substance of a theological
interpretation is closely connected with, and even partly determined by, the manner in which the theologian envisages his

[1] Among the sources used by Irenaeus there were differences, both of
terminology and of emphasis, upon this subject. Under both headings the
differences correspond to a broad divergence between the Semitic and the
Hellenistic ways of thinking and speaking about human nature. The source
which Loofs has designated IQA has a quite Hebraic standpoint. Man is
'flesh'; the 'image' is imprinted upon this 'flesh'; and the 'likeness' is to be
attained eventually under the transforming influence of the divine Spirit.
The distinction here made might seem to be supported by the fact that, in

task. So it appears to be in the two instances which we are at present considering. What we may learn about God, by way of analogy between the divine and the human, will inevitably be other than that which we may learn by considering the actual facts of revelation as set forth in scripture. An interpretation of revealed truth by the light of natural facts scientifically analyzed will yield results quite different from those which are reached by contemplating the very form of revelation as originally given.[1] These considerations should serve to put us on our guard against being content to register the more obvious differences between the two types of thought which we are here contrasting. It has, for example, already been pointed out that the Augustinian analogy is limited to traces of the Trinity in the human soul, whereas St Irenaeus finds the image imprinted upon the whole man. Again, it is sometimes said that the later doctrine sees in man the image of the Trinity, whereas the earlier patristic tradition teaches that man is made in the image of God the Word. In both the examples just given it could, indeed, be shown that the difference is by no means unqualified.[2] But it is more important to note that for our present purpose such details are quite subsidiary to the difference of plan already indicated. Accordingly at this point we pass on to review the treatment of the doctrine in question as presented in the writings of St Irenaeus.

It will be convenient to unfold the teaching of this father in three stages which may be summarized as follows: (1) The image of God in man; (2) the image re-created in Christ; (3)

LXX, Gen. 5[1-3] does not repeat 'likeness' from Gen. 1[26]. Where this source is not in use, however, man is 'spirit, soul and flesh (body)', as in 1 Thess. 5[23]. Moreover, the Antiochene document (which, in the opinion of Loofs, represents the lost treatise of Theophilus) makes no distinction between image and likeness. Both are connected primarily with freewill (*adv. haer.* iv, 37-39). It cannot, however, be safely assumed that an Antiochene author would have repudiated the Irenaean thesis: *non pars hominis* (v. 6.1); i.e. the image is in the whole man. It was *this* primitive doctrine which retreated into the background under the Augustinian influence.

[1] The former appeals to the wider revelation presupposed in scripture. Yet its selection of natural facts can at best bear witness only to some one aspect of the revealed Whole.

[2] e.g. see above, p. 162, note 3, and the sentence of the text to which the note is appended; see also below pp. 169, 170, particularly the quotation from *adv. haer.* v, 1.3, citing Gen. 1[26].

the interrelation of (1) and (2) and their connexion with the saint's total doctrine of revelation.

(1) In *The Demonstration of the Apostolic Preaching* St Irenaeus remarks that 'man is a living being compounded of soul and flesh' and that 'he must needs exist by both of these'.[1] A little later he explains the implications of this statement in terms of the 'image' doctrine, and the statement is so important that a fairly full quotation is necessary. Speaking of the Creator he says:

> Man He formed with His own hands, taking from the earth that which was purest and finest, and mingling in measure His own power with the earth. For He traced His own form on the formation,[2] that that which should be seen should be of divine form: for (as) the image of God was man formed and set on the earth. And that he might become living, He breathed on his face the breath of life; that both for the breath and for the formation man should be like unto God.[3]

Here we note that the equiponderance of 'soul' and 'flesh' in the earlier passage is elaborated in the later statement in a whole series of important phrases. For first, the earthy material of Adam's body is dignified with two noble superlatives. 'Purest and finest' may suggest that the author is thinking in terms of his favourite analogy with the Virgin-Birth of our Lord as developed both in his larger treatise and also in the smaller work from which our quotation is taken.[4] Secondly, there is here no room for a dualistic doctrine of man, since the divine power is actually mingled with the earthy substance. Moreover, the phrase 'in measure' seems to indicate that the divine power was tempered to the lowly material, so that the purity and fineness of the latter might not be absorbed by the deity, but rather might be brought to full manifestation. Thirdly, 'manifestation' is the appropriate word; for it was the Creator's purpose that the divine form should become manifest in the human *plasma*. Thus it is evident that in describing the

[1] *The Demonstration*, Ch. 2 (ET by J. Armitage Robinson from the Armenian version (London, S.P.C.K., 1920)).

[2] Robinson notes that the word here used in the Armenian is 'equivalent to *plasma* or *plasmatio*'.

[3] *op. cit.*, Ch. 11 (Robinson's rendering)

[4] *op. cit.*, Ch. 32; cp. above, p. 137, note 2, and last par of Ch. V, § ii, with notes.

creation of man the author already has in view the incarnation. Further proof of this will appear presently. But it has previously been pointed out in the present work that the whole treatment of the Adam theme by St Irenaeus implies a profound unity of creation and the incarnation.[1] Fourthly, the image, to be perfect, must be living as well as visible; so life was supplied by the divine breath. As visibility points forward to the incarnation, so breath suggests the activity of the Holy Spirit.

In other passages St Irenaeus teaches that 'perfect man' consists of 'spirit, soul and flesh' and that in such a man the soul which is mingled with flesh 'assumes the Spirit of the Father'.[2] It only remains to point out that for this author 'the hands of God' are the Word or Son of God and the divine Spirit, 'to whom the Father speaking said: Let us make man to our image and likeness'.[3] The sentence last quoted makes it clear that Genesis 1[26] was understood to be addressed by the Father to the second and the third persons of the Trinity. Irenaeus, therefore, is saying that man is made by the Holy Trinity in the image of the Trinity. Moreover, the identification of 'the hands of God' with the Son and the Spirit suggests that our author is thinking of the deity in the anthropomorphic language of the Old Testament. He is content to rest in the form which revelation has received in scripture, because it *is* the given form through which God speaks. In this respect the concreteness of scripture corresponds to the concreteness of the incarnation where the image of God is finally manifested.[4]

(2) Writers of the first formative period, that is, the first two Christian centuries, do not sharply distinguish between an order of 'nature' and an order of 'grace' as was done in the western middle ages. They prefer to contemplate the original

---

[1] see above, from Ch. V, § ii onwards, and especially Ch. VI, § ii, first 3 pars. This 'profound unity' is one of the basic truths to which the present volume is devoted. It will occupy us continuously from here onwards.

[2] see *adv. haer.* v, 6.1 and v. 9.1

[3] *ibid.*, v. 1.3; cp. iv. pref. 4 and v. 6.1

[4] 'The hands of God' are apparently taken over from Theophilus. But there is a similar terminology in the *Clementine Homilies*. Details are given by J. A. Robinson in his English edition of *The Demonstration* (p. 53 note). In the homilies Wisdom is identified with the Holy Spirit, as by Theophilus and Irenaeus. The Spirit as 'hand' could be inferred from Ezek. 8[1-3], and again as 'finger of God' from a comparison of Luke 11[20] (=Exod. 8[19]) with Matt.

plan of creation as made manifest in Christ. Thus St Paul finds the *perfect* manifestation of the divine image only in Christ and its *complete* manifestation only in the general resurrection of the just.[1] To this corresponds the whole treatment of the subject by Irenaeus, for whom, as we have seen, the process by which the image is moulded in history is vital to the significance of the image as actually manifested.[2] There is a movement of revelation which corresponds to the movement of the Hebrew mind in its grasping after totality. Christ is the Whole in whom the divine image is perfectly shown. This showing forth of the Whole, however, requires as its context the details proper to the whole.[3] All history thus comes to be regarded as a single act of the divine artist, as described in Genesis 2[7], and as fulfilled in Christ. In him, the last Adam, is to be found the one visible image which is *not* an idol; and its formation by 'the hands of God' comprehends the total activity of the Blessed Trinity towards finite being.

Accordingly, as the incarnation is implicit in the saint's doctrine of man, so his doctrine of creation enters deeply into what he has to say about the perfection of the image in Christ. We have already seen that for him the end is implicit in the beginning as truly as the beginning is summed up in the end. Consequently the incarnation is regarded as completing what was begun in Adam. This, as we shall now see, is brought out in the graphic phrase with which the quotation from Genesis

12[28]. Again, in Ps. 8[3(4)] the deity is addressed with reference to 'the heavens, the work of thy fingers'. So, whereas in the Clementines the Spirit (= Wisdom) is 'stretched out as hand' to create (*Hom.* xvi. 12), in *The Demonstration* (Ch. 26) we read: 'the finger of God is that which is stretched forth from the Father in the Holy Spirit'. This is said with reference to the Ten Words 'written with the finger of God' (Exod. 31[18]). Moreover, as early as the *Epistle of Barnabas* (xiv. 2) the author, in his quotation of this phrase from Exodus, significantly adds to it the two words: ἐν πνεύματι. In the light of these facts it is possible that in the NT parallel to Exodus 31[18] (2 Cor. 3[3] =Jer. 31[33]) St Paul is thinking of the Holy Spirit as the finger of Christ, who in turn would be the hand of God writing creatively upon human hearts. On this point Loofs has a good note (*op. cit.*, p. 439, note 1). On the whole subject cp. addit. note B (3) below, which in turn prepares the way for a discussion in Ch. IX concerning the wider phenomena of Spirit-Christology.

[1] 2 Cor. 4[4–6], Rom. 3[23]; 1 Cor. 15[49], Rom. 8[23,29]; Phil. 3[21]
[2] see above, Ch. V, § iii   [3] see above, Ch. V, § v (latter half)

1[26] is introduced.[1] Having contrasted the creation of an
'*animal rationale*' in Adam with the completion of a 'perfect man'
in Christ, he goes on: 'For Adam did not ever (*aliquando*) escape
the hands of God to which the Father speaking said, Let us
make man to our image and likeness'. Here it almost looks as
if the person of Adam is regarded as persisting until it comes to
fulfilment in the person of the incarnate Son. The image, as
shaped in the age-long process is, in its first formation, no more
than a creature distinguished from other creatures by its endowment with reason. As such it was indeed the work of the
Father's hand (the Logos),[2] reflecting pre-eminently the divine
reasonableness which characterizes the whole order of creation.

Yet, after all, this was only 'the beginning' of the work. 'In
the end' the hands of God, Word and Spirit, 'united to the
ancient substance of Adam's formation, produced a living and
perfect man'. This final result of the divine artist's age-long task
was effected by the Father's good pleasure in the virginal conception (as described in John 1[13]).[3] Thus at last, in the incarnation of God's only Son, Adam, who had never escaped the
divine hands, was finally moulded 'according to the image and
likeness of God'. In the passage which we have just summarized
the identification between Adam and Christ is pressed to a
point rendered necessary by the identification of the *plasma* of
Genesis 2 first with the former and then with the latter, at two
stages of a single process. Elsewhere, however, as we have
already seen, oscillation from the One to the Many carries St
Irenaeus back to sharper distinctions. In considering one such
passage we shall be led further afield into his doctrine of
revelation. At this point therefore we pass to the third and last
stage of this inquiry into his teaching concerning the image of
God in man.

[1] The quotation referred to occurs in *adv. haer.* v. 1.3, and is given above
on p. 170.

[2] In *The Demonstration*, Ch. 5, it is said that 'since God is λογικός, therefore
by λόγος he created the things that were made'. This reflection of God's
rationality in a settled order was to appear most clearly in man (the play
of words being preserved in the Armenian, as Robinson notes, *ibid.*, p. 74n.).
Similarly the adorning of the *cosmos* by the Spirit was to be crowned by the
human spirit fashioned into the divine likeness.

[3] *adv. haer.*, v. 1.3; Irenaeus apparently followed the singular reading in
this text: 'who *was* begotten'. Cp. in *adv. haer.*, iii, 16.2 and iii, 19.2.

(3) It is noticeable that in the development of his theme the saint seems to emphasize especially the manifestation of the divine image, 'that that which should be seen should be of divine form'. This visibility of the divine form is evidently crucial to his doctrine. Thus in a summary of 'our faith' in *The Demonstration* he contrasts the invisibility of the Father with the incarnate state in which the Son is both visible and tangible or palpable.[1] A further development of this idea appears in the following statement:[2]

In the former times it used to be said that the man had been made according to the image of God, but it was not (in fact) being shown. For the Word, according to whose image the man had been made, was still invisible. Moreover, because of this he (the man) easily lost the likeness. But when the Word of God became flesh, he confirmed both. For indeed he truly showed the image, having himself become that which was his image; and he firmly re-established the likeness, having conjoined the man with himself in likeness to the invisible Father through the visible Word.[3]

In the recently recovered Greek text the last phrase becomes 'the Word who is being contemplated'.[4] Accordingly we may profitably compare (and contrast) this statement with St Paul's picture of the Christian, both contemplating and reflecting as in a mirror the glory of the incarnate Word. The redeemed man is transformed into the likeness of the perfect image which he sees in Christ. For he himself is a mirror in which that image is reflected. Christ, who is the image of God, is refracted forth as content from the lives of his members. Thus the image in which they were made is reconstituted in them *ad similitudinem* because they are in Christ.[5] By contrast Adam appears defenceless through the invisibility of his archetype, the Word whose image he bears and to whom he must be conformed. Thus he falls a prey to counter-fascinations, and easily loses the 'likeness' for

---

[1] *The Demonstration*, Ch. 6

[2] Here, as elsewhere, the English rendering of *adv. haer.* is my own.

[3] *adv. haer.* v. 16.2   [4] Loofs, *op. cit.*, p. 250

[5] 2 Cor. 3^{18}-4^6. In this passage St Paul seems to have in mind the story of our Lord's Transfiguration and, of course, the theophany to Moses on the mount, when the 'glory' with which man was 'crowned' (Ps. 8) appeared for a brief space on the face of the lawgiver (Exod. 34). Upon this theme see further below in Ch. VII, § iv, par. 1, and § v, par. 8.

which he was destined. Another point of connexion between the apostle and the doctor of the second century must also be noticed in our comparisons of these two utterances. St Paul teaches that the Christ is the very image of God in which Adam was made. Man, therefore, is but the image of the original image; and the glory with which man was crowned in the beginning was a portion of that glory which in its fulness belongs to God's Son. Adam was, so to speak, the understudy of the divine Word, who eventually took upon himself the rôle assigned to his deputy. He 'showed the image' only by himself becoming 'that which was his own image'.

At this point we become inevitably aware of another factor in the scheme which St Irenaeus is setting forth. The re-creation of the image in Christ is represented as bringing to light the incompleteness of the original 'formation'. If man easily fell because his archetype was not yet made visible, then it appears that disaster overtook the Creator's plan before it had been brought to maturity. Nevertheless the Fall could not alter the divine purpose; it could only make manifest the need for the fulfilment of that purpose in Christ, a fulfilment which was pre-destined from the beginning. The incompleteness of 'the man' and his utter dependence upon the divine 'hands' which he could never escape, these are essential features of the Creator's plan which decisively condition its glorious consummation in Christ. In this aspect of the saint's doctrine the contrast between the immaturity of the first formation and the final perfection of the image in Christ is heavily stressed, precisely as in the section dealing with co-infancy.[1] Yet here, as there, the oscillation towards dualism does not undo the complementary thesis of a mystical identity between Adam and Christ, of an interpene-tration between the order of creation and that Christological mystery of redemption whereby creation is restored.

iv

Further aspects of the teaching of St Irenaeus: (1) The mystic place of man's abode, in creation and in Christ. (2) The hidden work of the Creator-Word laid open in its visible completion by the incarnate Word.

---

[1] iv. 38.1-3; see above, Ch. V, § iv

The primitive Christian conception of two orders, the old and the new, summed up respectively in Adam and in Christ, has now been shown to have two aspects. Sometimes the emphasis rests upon the fundamental unity of the two dispensations. Interpenetration is so far-reaching that each factor can be stated in terms of the other. Adam is identified with Christ in the sense that we know the significance of the 'Adam' figure only when we see it concretely realized in the Christ. So also the new order in Christ is the fulfilment of everything which preceded it in the divine plan, because the *character corporis Christi* is stamped upon the plan as a whole from the beginning. On the other hand, sometimes, as in the passage last cited in full (*adv. haer.* v. 16.2), the interrelationship is seen to involve a contrast between the inferiority of the old order and the superior excellence of the new. Then there occurs an 'oscillation towards dualism'.

Neither aspect can cover the whole truth; and when that situation arises the imagination is baffled in its search for an adequate picture. At this point, however, we may call to mind a parallel instance which we have already encountered. In Chapter V, § v (last two paragraphs) it was pointed out that in the thought of St Irenaeus 'the many' were sometimes included in 'the One', whereas in other passages 'the many' and 'the One' were left side by side. Upon this phenomenon of oscillation it was remarked that 'in both types of thought the other type seems to be present'. If the reader will turn back to the further explanation there given he should be in a position to interpret rightly the duality of picture-images with which we are now dealing. Two further illustrations of this *interpenetration* phenomenon (Adam-and-Christ) and of its duality, as they appear in the pages of St Irenaeus, must now be given.

(1) Let us begin by taking note of the peculiar language used by St Irenaeus in reference to the world of the first creation, in a section the context of which has already been examined. It is the section of *The Demonstration* which immediately follows the passage already cited concerning man's creation from 'the purest and the finest' earth . . . that 'for the breath and for the formation man should be like unto God'.[1] The saint continues

[1] see above, p. 169

his description with a double reference, to man's freewill and to the end for which he was made, namely, 'that he might rule all those things that were upon the earth'. He then goes on to speak of 'this great created world'. This, we are told, was prepared by God before the formation of man; and again, that it was 'given to man as *his place*, containing all things within itself'.[1] This last phrase introduces a familiar biblical theme which goes back to the story of Jacob.

In Genesis 28 we read that Jacob 'met the place' and dreamed of angels ascending and descending upon it. This and other passages in the Pentateuch gave rise to the rabbinical opinion that 'the Place' was a name for God.[2] Accordingly, in John 1[51] 'the Son of man' is identified with 'the place' upon which angels ascend and descend. In view of these facts the details which follow in the passage from *The Demonstration* now under consideration are, to say the least, significant. The description continues as follows: 'There were in *this place* also with (their) tasks the servants of that God who formed all things; and the steward who was set over all his fellow-servants received *this place*'. St Irenaeus explains that 'the servants' are angels, and 'the steward' an archangel. The threefold repetition of the 'place' phraseology in connexion with angels certainly looks like an echo of Genesis 28, possibly under the influence of St John's Gospel.

St Irenaeus, however, goes on to say that God prepared for man '*a place* better than this world . . . and its name is Paradise'. Moreover, there 'the Word of God' walked and talked with the man continually'.[3] We are once more reminded of mystical words in St John's Gospel. Jesus says: 'I go to prepare a place for you' (14[2]); and this place can be none other than Jesus himself in his risen glory. St Irenaeus, therefore, would see in Jesus the 'place better than this world' of which Paradise was

---

[1] This arrangement of order is Robinson's (*op. cit.*, p. 80). Unlike the German translations it follows the Armenian exactly. His own suggestion, however, (p. 80, note 3, concluding sentence) sadly misses the point. See further, additional note A.

[2] The following passages are also relevant: Exod. 3[5,8], 23[20], 33[21]. To these we must add the significant alterations of Exod. 24[10,11] in LXX. See also below, p. 177, note 1, and cp. S. A. Cook, *The Religion of Ancient Palestine in the light of archeology* (Oxford, 1930), p. 18.

[3] As God talked with Jacob in the incident just now mentioned.

only a type.[1] If his thoughts were running on these lines the author of *The Demonstration* may well have included in his typological scheme the remaining incidents of Genesis 2, which he next records (chapter 13), that is, the naming of the animals and the 'building' of Eve. In this picture, moreover, Adam dwelling in Paradise is represented as a new-born child, a type, surely, of the new-born Christian dwelling in Jesus in whom he 'should grow and so come to his perfection', being provided with all 'necessaries of life'. It scarcely needs to be said that the phrase 'better than this world' symbolizes man's unfallen state, and is not, therefore, to be understood as denying the good of this earthly creation. In actual fact Paradise is here described as containing all the good things of this present world, but in an ideal form. The paradise of the mystical body is indeed the world of this creation raised to its true perfection in Christ. This interpretation is further supported by the threefold application of the mystic 'place' language to *this* world before it is applied by the author to 'a place better than this world'.[2]

(2) There is, however, another sense in which the new creation in Christ is 'better than this world'. It was indicated in the passage which we quoted *in extenso* towards the end of our inquiry into the teaching of St Irenaeus concerning the image of God in man.[3] In our brief comments upon that section it was pointed out that the re-creation of the image in Christ brings to light the incompleteness of the original 'formation'. But we also observed that the contrast thus stressed between the first and the second creations was not allowed to override the complementary truth of a mystical identity between them. This positive doctrine of continuity is very emphatically and strikingly expounded in the context of the passage in question. St Irenaeus is, throughout that part of his treatise, following up the characteristic notion that the image imprinted upon Adam was made more fully manifest when brought to complete visibility in Christ. In the chapter which immediately precedes the extended quotation he illustrates this truth by a most interesting

[1] In John 14[2] there is a clear echo of Exod. 23[20], where 'the place prepared' is the land of promise. In an earlier 'place' passage (Exod. 3[8]) that land was described as 'flowing with milk and honey'.

[2] see below, additional note A

[3] *adv. haer.*, v. 16.2; see above, pp. 173*f*

treatment of the miracle recorded in St John's Gospel, where our Lord heals a man born blind.[1]

The method of healing employed by our Lord in this incident suggests quite naturally the method by which the Creator shaped Adam to the image. There is, however, a difference. For there the whole man was shaped out of the wet earth-mould, whereas here our Lord makes clay and anoints the eyes. The difference corresponds to the fact that the blind man needs only restoration of sight that he may be a whole man. This person, moreover, was born blind. There was a defect in his original creation which took place *secretly in the womb*.[2] St Irenaeus suggests that the man was deliberately left defective in his first creation, in order that the Creator-Word who then made him secretly might afterwards complete his creation openly before the world. In the course of the argument the author employs certain texts which struck him forcibly; and their interest for us lies in the clues which they give to the working of his mind. Now the dominant motive of this father, we must remember, is the urgent necessity of proving that there is only one God, and he too the Creator who through his 'hands' made all things. For this was the doctrine denied by the heretics of the day.

By the very nature of things, however, the work of creation is secret. Who is there whom we can call in as witness to this mysterious activity? Yet the divine operations continue ceaselessly from generation to generation. Faced with this dilemma, St Irenaeus fell back upon prophetic oracles which suggested to him that the Creator would at length be openly identified. First among these we may place the saying of Isaiah 66[14]: 'The hand of the Lord shall be known to those who fear him'. This promise follows another which might be understood as predicting a resurrection of the dead.[3] Accordingly St Irenaeus

---

[1] John 9. See *adv. haer.* v. 15.1-3

[2] The italicized phrase covers two distinct points in the Irenaean thesis which we are about to expound. For the second see below, pp. 179*ff* with note 1 on p. 181.

[3] In LXX, where, in the preceding sentence, Irenaeus would read: 'Your bones shall rise up (ἀνατελεῖ) like a plant'. This verb (ἀνατέλλειν) could be applied to (*a*) the rising of heavenly bodies, and (*b*) the springing up of plant life. In Zech. 6[12] it is used (with its noun) in the second sense, of Zerubbabel, as the messianic Branch (lit: 'Growth') of David's stock. In

passes on at once to the miraculous resurrection of Israel in Ezekiel 37, a passage which is prefaced by the statement: 'The hand of the Lord came upon me'. The 'hand' is here understood to be the divine Word, by whom the Father made the worlds, and by whom the dead are now raised to life when Christ, the Word incarnate, calls them forth from the tomb (John 5$^{24-29}$, 11$^{39-44}$).[1]

Further, on glancing down the column of his Greek bible, following Isaiah 66^{14}, St Irenaeus would come upon the text in which the prophet Jeremiah is told: 'Before I *formed* thee in the womb I knew thee' (Jer. 1^5). This the saint proceeds to quote, applying it to ourselves with the remark that 'the Word of God forms us in the belly'. Here there arises a linguistic point. The word used in this passage for 'formed' is the same, in both the Hebrew and the Greek, as that which is used in Genesis 2^7 for the forming of Adam. Moreover, the man born blind in John 9 was framed in the womb by the Creator-Word, as was Jeremiah.[2] With these facts in mind we turn to our Lord's answer to the disciples before he healed the blind man: 'Neither this man sinned nor his parents, but that the works of God might be manifested in him'. The Creator, then, permitted the birth of a blind man so that God's works might be manifested in the bestowal of sight through the incarnate Word. The plan of the two creations is, therefore, one.

The first creation was left incomplete in order that its completion by the incarnate Word might reveal unity of authorship. It follows that the man born blind is himself a type of Adam as well as of the new-born Christian. Fallen man was re-created

---

Luke 1^{78} the noun is used in the first sense, of the messianic 'Dayspring from on high'. St Paul has both forms of imagery closely interwoven in his description of the general resurrection, and that too as part of a thesis concerning the messianic rising of Jesus, the new Adam, a rising in which the Branch typology was fulfilled (1 Cor. 15$^{35-49}$). The two meanings of ἀνατολή are beautifully combined in the double messianic title of Rev. 22^{16}.

[1] The rising of bones in Ezek. 37 might appear as a sequel to Jer. 23^5: 'I will raise up (ἀναστήσω) a righteous Growth to David'.

[2] Gal. 1^{15,16} is also quoted. Throughout this section Irenaeus connects the completion of creation alternately with phenomena of birth and of resurrection. The New Birth is implicit in this collocation. See next note.

by the Word who originally made him; and every sinner initiated into the family of the new Adam is redeemed from the blindness of sin in which he was born. He is re-created and cleansed by baptismal rites, and brought back with rejoicings into the flock of the Good Shepherd (John 9[6,7], 10).[1] Here the familiar picture of Adam as the lost sheep restored is seen by the Bishop of Lyons on the background of those pastoral and sacramental acts which he himself was accustomed to perform amongst his own flock.

In the sacramental life of the church the incarnate Word continues to 'show the whole from the part'.[2] The 'enlightenment' of sinners in baptism witnesses perpetually to the ceaseless work of the Creator. We cannot doubt that in his use of the text from Jeremiah St Irenaeus was thinking in terms of the

---

[1] The anointing before washing in 9[6,7] corresponds to the very primitive 'sealing' of Syrian-Christian neophytes with the Spirit by means of unction *before* their baptism with water. For the baptismal relevance of John 9 see Hoskyns, *The Fourth Gospel*, pp. 407*ff.* See also below, p. 286, note 4.

[2] *adv. haer.* v. 15.3. In his use of this phrase Irenaeus appears to be affirming that the forming of Adam by the Creator-Word was 'shown' in the healing of the blind man. This could have a double significance in reference to John 9 and 10. As the healed eye is a part or member of the body, so the blind man, who *is* that body now restored, is himself a 'member' of Adam. Thus the creation of Adam is completed by Christ in a son of Adam (Ch. 9) and ultimately in the flock of Christ (Ch. 10)

At this point we recall the characteristically Irenaean identification of Adam with the lost sheep which the Good Shepherd restored to the fold. Can it be that this particular collocation of images represents an Asiatic tradition associated with the sequence of thought in John 9 and 10? The OT background of John 10 is primarily Ezek. 34; and the last verse of that chapter, according to the Hebrew text, could read thus:

'Ye are my sheep, the sheep of my pasture; ye are Adam, I am your God'. The English rendering: 'Ye are men', correct as it is, does not carry over the double nuance of 'Adam' from the original (see above, Ch. V, § ii, penultimate paragraph). With the rendering which has just been suggested, however, the final section of Ezek. 34 reads like a return of 'Adam' to Paradise. This takes place when 'David' (the messianic king) leads Israel, the Lord's flock, back into the Holy Land. Further, on this view the strongly attested reading: 'Son of Man' (John 9[35]) acquires new significance. In the Greek bible this title sometimes renders the Hebrew 'Son of Adam', as in Ps. 8 (quoted in Heb. 2[6*ff*]). Without entering into the subtleties of Johannine Christology we can say that in John 9[35] 'Son of Man' may represent a fusion of the 'second Adam' *motif* with our Lord's messianic claim, a

new birth. The prophet sanctified in the womb was a type of the regenerate Christian in whom the image of the eternal Son is reproduced by a birth from the new Eve, the true Israel of God.[1] The economy of the incarnation is itself an integral whole; and the new creation in its wholeness makes visible the secret plan of the Creator, that single plan which pervades all his works.

In his treatment of this incident in St John's Gospel St Irenaeus has fastened upon a characteristic feature of the gospel narratives, and one which is fully exhibited by the fourth evangelist. Upon this subject we must at present confine ourselves to two or three concluding sentences. The Johannine 'signs' have a mysteriously fascinating quality by virtue of the fact that here events recorded as sober history are found to carry symbolic effects which are mystical, sacramental, theo-

___

fusion which is characteristic of NT theology (for fuller details see my essay in *The Apostolic Ministry*). Moreover throughout Ezekiel the prophet is addressed as Son of Adam (= Son of man) by the deity, one instance (35^2) occurring in almost the next line to the 'sheep-Adam' combination of 34^{31}. Thus the title of our Lord revealed to the blind man in John $9^{35\vartheta}$ would, by virtue of its associations with Ezekiel, prepare the early Christian reader of St John for a connexion between 'Adam' in Ch. 9 and the messianic flock in Ch. 10. These considerations, if soundly based, would throw fresh light upon the sequence of thought in John 9 and 10 as understood by the Asiatic school. Jesus is the promised Son of Adam (Gen. 3^{15}, Luke 3^{38}), who, although destined, like Abel (Gen. 4^{1-12}), to be a smitten shepherd (Zech. 13^7 etc.), yet restores and completes the original Adam-image in every member of his flock. It only remains to add that this line of thought receives corroboration from the Hebrew text of Ezek. 36^{24-38}, where after baptismal cleansing the Adam-flock returns to the garden of Eden. This also involves a miracle of resurrection (37^{1-14}), so that John 9-11 is roughly parallel to Ezek. 34-37.

[1] Thus John 1^{13}, quoted in *adv. haer.* v. 1.3 as though it were read with the singular construction, requires the better-attested plural to bring out the full force of the teaching which Irenaeus found in the fourth gospel (see above, p. 172, with note 3). But also Jer. 1^5 is quoted in order to connect the man born blind with the creation of Adam. Gen. 2^7 has been cited in the preceding paragraph. Jer. 1^5 brought a verbal echo of that text into a description of a human birth. Whether consciously on the author's part or not, this conjunction of texts has the effect of reviving the analogy between the creation of Adam and the Virgin-Birth of our Lord, that birth which, in turn, is the ground of our sacramental regeneration (see above, Ch. V, § ii, last par.). Moreover, this conjunction of *ideas* is true to the collocation of *mysteries* in John 1^{12-14}.

logical, and ultimately cosmological in their significance.[1] By this means the whole life of the new creation in the mystical body is, *for us*, thrown back into the gospel history. By the same qualities the whole order of the first creation is taken up into that 'place' which is 'better than this world', that place where all the defects of the world as we know it are replaced by the perfections proper to the complete manifestation of the divine image, that place where God is made to be truly visible in the work of his hands.

V

A summary of conclusions. The extension of the image of God in Christ. The Christian meaning of the creation-story: the relation of individual Christians to the image in Christ's Body, Kingdom and Family. The social aspect of the image shows mutual submission to be the counterpart of privilege in the new creation.

Here let us pause for a moment to take note of some conclusions which have emerged in the present chapter concerning the form of revelation. We may summarize them as follows: Christ, as man, includes within his being the manifold order of creation. He has identified himself with it in respect of both its substance and the law of its life. Secondly, in so doing he has identified himself with man's vocation to be the agent in and through whom God is made manifest as visibly ruling over his creation. Thirdly, the form of revelation is, therefore, essentially the form of Christ, as minister of his Father's purpose. From this standpoint we may say that the flesh of Jesus is the sphere in which Adam's dominion becomes effective once more. For

[1] It does not follow that the evangelist consciously intended these effects. We must leave open the possibility that he was concerned only to produce a simple record of facts; always supposing that he would do so in accordance with the literary habits of his time and place, and of the Christian community to which he belonged, equipped, also, with the power of the Holy Spirit's guidance and inspiration. The qualifying clause, however, is sufficiently wide to leave room for great varieties of interpretation—for any in fact which do not simply prejudge the historical issue. The effects, if not consciously intended by the evangelist, would issue from the given revelation of the Word, bearing its own testimony in and through the facts thus faithfully recorded by the inspired author.

the orchestra of creation produces harmony only when the divine conductor himself wields the human baton. Fourthly, there is interdependence between creation and Christ. As regards the function of the new Adam this has two aspects. On the one hand he transcends and controls the manifold order which he has made his own. Yet, on the other hand, he moulds it to the divine purpose only through subjection of himself to fulfilment of its laws. As the image of the Father made flesh, he exhibits all the creaturely characteristics proper to the *soma-cosmos* of the New Man.[1] For the dominion of Adam is bound up with his creaturely condition as the earth-born man who is moulded from earth to the image.

We shall have to take account also (and more fully later) of the complementary fact that what is true of Christ as the New Adam is true also of the church in respect of her identity with Christ. As the new Eve she is, by virtue of that identity, the matrix of the redemptive process in its perpetuation through history. But she retains her character as 'help-meet', and fulfils her maternal function in the new creation, only so far as she exhibits those same creaturely characteristics to which her divine bridegroom has subjected himself. The theme of the new Eve, about which the New Testament has a good deal to say, corresponds to the third line of the threefold scheme into which we analyzed the second chapter of Genesis in the diagram on p. 160. The One New Man, who has identified himself with the creaturely substance and placed himself at the head of the creaturely order, has also 'extended' his own person in a new creation through the 'building' of his bride and the subsequent birth of a holy seed.

At this point in the narrative of Genesis the story of creation might seem to carry within itself a suggestion of further creation chapters yet to be unfolded.[2] Here was a definite hint of a plan not yet completed; moreover, the hint would seem to be underlined in the subsequent promise of the woman's victorious seed

---

[1] For *soma-cosmos* (world-body) see above, in Ch. VI, § i, the second and the last pars. with notes

[2] From another point of view the duplication of the creation-story (1^1, 2^4) might in itself suggest that Genesis $2^{4\theta}$, *as the second recording of creation*, was in reality the story of the new creation in Christ told beforehand *in mysterio*. Cp. above, Ch. VI, § ii, par. 1, with the note on Eph. 5^{32}.

(3^{15}) and in the statements about the reproduction of 'the image' in Adam's descendants ($5^3, 9^6$). Certainly the whole of this last section of the creation-story received close attention from Christian writers of the early centuries. At present, however, we are concerned only with its relation to the primitive doctrine of the image, regarded as a vehicle of early Christian thought concerning the form of revelation. We have already had occasion to refer to St Paul's treatment of this subject;[1] and we have found one important point in which St Irenaeus builds upon apostolic foundations. So far from retracting the divine image to the limits of the human soul, this father agrees with St Paul in *spreading it out*, and that too not simply over the whole of human nature, but also over the whole order of the new creation as *gathered up* into the new Adam and again *extended* in his new family of redeemed mankind.

The three phrases employed in our last sentence to indicate the range and scope of the divine image may be seen to correspond respectively with the three parts of the creation story in our diagram (on p. 160). For first, in the story of Adam's creation the many units of earth are 'gathered up' into the form upon which the image is printed. So too the many units of mankind redeemed are gathered up into the body of the new Adam. The many units are completely undifferentiated in their common lowliness of origin, of size, and consequently of the place assigned to each. Yet all are built in to that structure wherein the perfection of the divine image is manifested. The image becomes visible, not primarily in the units as individuals, but rather in the whole to which they all belong. Yet, for all that, each of these lowly fragments of the whole partakes in the glorious form which is traced upon the entire formation.[2]

The divine image cannot become fully visible in individual units as such, precisely because it is 'spread out' over an *order*, the order of the new creation. In the creation story creatures of diverse kinds become an ordered kingdom through subjection

---

[1] see above, Ch. VI, § i, par. 5, on the teaching of 1 Cor. 15, and the further references to the Pauline doctrine of the image on p. 171, with note 1.

[2] So too with the image of Antichrist depicted in the dream of King Nebuchadnezzar (Dan. 2); all the great empires which contribute to its formation partake in the blasphemous pretensions characterizing the whole sinful idol; all alike share its dreadful fate.

to the headship of one who shares their earthly origin and yet transcends it. So too in the new creation there is a manifold order which is much more than a collection of units. The company of the elect are ordered according to their respective vocations to fulfil a diversity of functions. The two scriptural images which delineate this kind of unity are, first, the theocracy of Israel, a visible kingdom with its officers under the king, and secondly, the body of Christ with diverse organs responding to the head. Once again, the image of God in the new Adam is rendered 'visible and palpable', not in the head alone, but in his response as shared by all the members, a response which is differentiated according to the laws of organic unity. It is worth while to reflect upon the ethical implications of this doctrine of 'wholeness' in its primitive form. The holiness of God is rendered visible in the whole Christ, Jesus and his church. For the revelation of deity is not shut up in sacred books, but embodied in a holy community which persists through history.

The early church did not regard holiness or sin apart from the reality of the one organism in which God's holy Son became incarnate to reveal his Father's glory. Consequently her ideal of perfection was exemplified especially in the martyrs, who exhibited the passion of Christ in his mystical body. They were made perfect (Heb. 11[40]), not in the individual progress still to be charted in as yet unwritten text-books of the future, but by their share in 'the testimony of Jesus', the *marturia* of the whole Christ. Similarly sin was a matter for public discipline; for the corporate witness of the church was all-important. Its centrality had not yet been disturbed or upset by later engrossments in the cult of individual sanctity. Accordingly the 'great church' was not deceived by the plausible arguments in favour of perfectionism which were advanced by the early puritan movements. It still held fast to that many-sided mystery which St Irenaeus, as rendered by his translator, calls the *character corporis Christi*.[1]

The individual units which, in the first creation-picture, were characterized by uniformity of lowliness have now, in the

[1] The phrase is actually used in reference to one of its possible applications, namely ministerial succession as guarantee of a tradition traced back to the teaching of the apostles (*adv. haer.* iv. 33.8).

second picture, become significantly differentiated according to
the manner in which they contribute to the whole. For the
perfection of the individual is seen to lie in the fulfilment of
his vocation within that one organism in which alone the perfection of the image can be manifested.[1] The third picture,
however, takes us to a yet more intimate level of unity. For
here the Many form within the One a family, a family being that
which combines identity of life with the richness of personal
relationships. Through the creation of the new Eve out of the
very side of her sleeping spouse[2] the divine image, as *character
corporis Christi*, is not simply and solely spread out over the whole
extent of the new creation. It is also actually reproduced in
each of the individuals who together comprise the holy seed—
that holy seed which is continuously begotten from the mystical
union of Christ and the church. It is this reproduction of the
image in the members of Christ which alone gives their full
significance to the two earlier pictures in the creation story.
The identity of status between all the members, suggested by
the first of the three pictures, is now seen to be an identity of
honour and privilege, which gives promise of a yet more
glorious identity of destiny when 'the image' has grown to
maturity in 'the likeness'.[3] Privilege is here cradled in lowliness,
as the new Adam was himself cradled in lowliness in the crib
of Bethlehem.

The privileges of the lowly provide the ethical theme of
many passages in the New Testament which are observed to
have a 'subordinationist' tone. The connexion of these with
the creation narratives will occupy us later. Meanwhile, passing
from the first creation-picture in our diagram to the second, we
may ask: In what sense does the extension of the divine image
in the family of the new Adam enhance the significance of that
given order in which the response of all the redeemed is
'differentiated according to the laws of organic unity'? In other
words, when we superimpose the idea of the family upon the

[1] This definition of individual perfection corresponds to what was said in
Ch. IV, § i, concerning 'freedom to fulfil one's function in a given order'.

[2] This interpretation of John 19[25-37], familiar to patristic scholars, will
come in for fuller consideration in Part II of the present undertaking.

[3] cp. the quotation from *adv. haer.* v. 16.2 above, p. 173. For the critical
view of 'image' and 'likeness' see Skinner, *op. cit.*, p. 32. See also the note
at the end of § ii of the present chapter

other two concepts of the organism and the kingdom, what difference does it make to the notion of the 'extended' image which we have been considering? Once again St Paul seems to provide the answer to a question which has been prompted by the teaching of St Irenaeus. For the supreme privilege of the lowly lies in their mutual submission to the pattern of the given order, so that it is reproduced in themselves. This pattern exists in its perfection in Christ, having been wrought out by him in his mission of filial obedience and lowly service unto death. The reproduction of this pattern in the family of the new Adam constitutes the renewal of the image which was imprinted in the beginning. To be incorporated into the family of the New Man is to 'put on the new man which is being renewed according to the image of him that created him'.[1] Thus to be clothed with the extended image of deity in Christ is to become an integral participator in that image as actualized in the redeemed society; and this in turn means to be taken into the response of 'the perfect man' to his Creator, the response of the incarnate Son rendered through the Spirit to the Father. So by his rebirth into Christ the redeemed man is renewed in that image of the Trinity according to which he was created.

Thus it has become clear that although the image cannot become fully visible *in individuals as such* it is reproduced in redeemed *persons* by virtue of their identity of life with the new Adam. Its pattern becomes visible in them, as a family likeness is visible; and its social aspect becomes visible in their personal relations with one another. This social aspect of the image corresponds to the spiritual significance of the mystical union between Christ and the church, as that in turn is the divine-human counterpart of the eternal relations in the life of the Blessed Trinity. The pattern of the image is in its essence social; for the image is constituted in God the Son, and its significance lies wholly in the filial relations of the Son with the Father. To be made 'according to the image' is to be made 'in the Son' according to the pattern of his sonship. To be regenerated into the life of the new Adam is to re-enter his filial life of obedience to the Father in that new order of family relationships which he has constituted in his Body. This is the

[1] Col. 3[10]

187

new world of the extended image to which fuller consideration has yet to be given.

Additional Note A.

St Irenaeus on 'the place better than this world'

It seems desirable that some of the finer points in *The Demonstration*, Chapters 11 and 12, should be examined more fully. Dependent as we are upon an Armenian version of the original, it is worth noticing that the 'place' terminology is, on the whole and in spite of some variations, supported by modern translators. See: *Texte und Untersuchungen* (Harnack-Schmidt. Leipzig, 1907) 31 Band, Heft 1, p. 7; *Patrologia Orientalis* (Paris, 1919. Tome xii. Fasc. 5), p. 668 (English) and p. 762 (French).

Having had the fortunate opportunity of consulting Mr S. Topalian (lecturer in Armenian, Turkish and Persian in the University of London) I have formed the conclusion that, of the five modern translations from the Armenian version, that of Armitage Robinson is, in this section, the most accurate. His fourfold rendering: 'place' corresponds in each instance to *vair* in the Armenian. As to the original Greek, the Armenian-Greek dictionary suggests that *vair* probably represents τόπος, although χώρα is a possibility. Of these the former has all the biblical associations of 'place' referred to in the text. The latter, however, is used by Philo in a sense exactly suiting the first occurrence of *vair* in Chapter 11 (for refs. see below, p. 240, note 1); and this sense, in turn, corresponds to the above-mentioned biblical associations. We may compare the definition of deity in Hermas, *mand.* 1, 1, where the χώρα concept is aptly expressed by means of the corresponding verb and verbal adjective. This definition is twice quoted by St Irenaeus in *adv. haer.* (ii,30.9; iv,20.2), the second time as 'scripture'; and there the translator renders: *omnium capax, et qui a nemine capiatur.* Cp. also F. Loofs in *Texte und Untersuchungen*, 46.2, p. 15. A third citation occurs in *The Demonstration*, Ch. 4; and here Robinson gives the Greek text of Hermas in a footnote (*op. cit.*, p. 73). Our interpretation of St Irenaeus along these lines, however, does not rest wholly upon a single point of verbal exactitude. For the entire passage (Chs. 11, 12) seems to be most carefully constructed.

We have already noticed this with regard to the earlier portions of Ch. 11. (1) If 'He prepared a place better than this world' (Ch. 12) echoes John 14² (= Exod. 23²⁰), then clearly a similar significance should be attached to the statement (Ch. 11) that the first place 'given to man' was also 'prepared by God'. (2) The impressive

phrase: 'this great created world', the 'place containing all things
within itself' seems to be moulded to correspond with what is to be
said later about the better place and its excellent supply of all things
necessary to the life of man. Moreover, the aspect of the *cosmos* as
the receptacle which contains all things is precisely one of the
points of which we have found reason for thinking that it is transferred by St Paul (e.g. in 1 Cor. 15) to his conception of Christ's
mystical body. (3) This *cosmos* 'was given to man as his place'; but
not (as Robinson supposes) 'to have all as his own'; that would be
a piece of modern humanism quite remote from primitive Christian
thought! On the contrary, the true reason had been carefully stated
by St Irenaeus in the preceding sentence of Ch. 11. There we are
told that man was 'made by God for this end, that he might rule
all those things that were upon the earth'. Thus the appointed ruler
of the first creation was in 'his place' as fitting into the divine plan
and as fulfilling his specific function in that plan. In this respect
Adam typified the indwelling of the Word in a better place which
was to come, that place where the Word incarnate now reigns over
Adam's restored dominion 'until all things are put under his feet'
(1 Cor. 15²⁵). The Word, like his stewards, angelic and human,
'received this place' (end of Ch. 11).

(4) According to our author the man was at first 'alone' in his
place, apart from the invisible company of angels. When, however,
he was transferred to Paradise (a detail suggested by the transition
from Gen. 2⁷ to Gen. 2⁸) he was no longer alone. The parallel with
Jacob continues. For now, in addition to the angels, the first man
enjoyed the companionship of God's Word. At this point the typological character of the whole description comes to the surface and
becomes overt. The communion of the man with the Word in the
better place is explicitly stated to be a 'figuring beforehand' of 'the
things that should be in the future'. (5) If the mystical body of
Christ was thus foreshadowed in the garden of Eden (for this cp.
adv. haer. v. 20.2: *plantata est ecclesia, paradisus in hoc mundo*), there
are also parallel statements made concerning man's 'place' in the
first creation. Of these we must now take note. In the first instance
the description of the archangel as 'the steward who was set over
his fellow-servants' looks like an echo of the parable in Luke 12⁴²⁻⁴⁶.
If so, we have a characteristic 'backward extension' of new creation
thoughts into the old order (on which see above, Ch. V, § ii, par. 1).
But secondly this 'steward-servants' *motif* leads on to a description
of man's relation to the angels in the first creation. This, again, is
reminiscent of St Paul's teaching about 'the heir' who 'as long as
he is a child is no better than a slave, though he is lord of all, being

under guardians and stewards' (Gal. 4^{1,2}). The parallelism thus
effected between Adam and Israel is, in the result, most instructive.
By means of the Pauline reminiscence there recurs an association
of ideas which we have encountered in the theme of 'co-infancy'.
The child-like Adam, 'secretly appointed lord' of the angels, must
(unlike them) 'grow and come to perfection'. The Pauline reminiscence serves to recall the essential fact upon which the apostle
and the Asiatic father are here at one, namely that this growing to
perfection took place through the schoolroom discipline of Israel's
long story. Yet Irenaeus places this growth within the 'place better
than this world' which typifies the new creation in Christ. Thus,
once more, as in his treatment of the prophets (above, Ch. IV,
§ vi, concluding pars.) Irenaeus brings the Old Testament within
the orbit of the incarnation. This, again, is but one element in a
picture which shows the two creations as distinct, yet interpenetrating.

BOOK III
THE FORM OF THE WHOLE

CHAPTER VII
THE ORGANISM OF REVELATION

i

Two modes of revelation, given in the spheres of nature and of history, overlapping in man. The structure of religion and the organs of revelation. Israel's religious development may be understood in terms of a dialectical conflict between diverse factors answering to the complexity of the material facts.

In the course of the last three chapters we have, as it were, taken a cross-section of the traditional doctrine concerning revelation, as that doctrine is presented in the writings of St Irenaeus. Our exposition, however, has been in some degree also a vindication, in as much as we have been able to show that the methods employed by St Irenaeus in his handling of scripture are methods which are, implicitly or explicitly, present in scripture itself. Further confirmation of this fact will appear as we proceed. Meanwhile, it remains to draw out more fully for ourselves and for our time the significance of this teaching in some at least of its far-reaching implications. In undertaking this task we shall need to remember that the scriptural revelation is relevant to our time by virtue of the fact that it has *continuous* relevance to all times and to the changes which time brings. For the Christian conception of revelation implies the inclusion of a changing order within a process of divine disclosure, a process, moreover, which in itself has an unchanging character.[1]

---

[1] above, Ch. I, § iii, par. 3. Change inevitably characterizes a creaturely world. Yet that world remains an *order* of creation, expressing as it does the unchanging purpose of deity. It will be argued presently that creation and revelation are two aspects of the same activity (cp. Ch. I, § iv.). So, whereas the *process* of disclosure (revelation) corresponds to a changing world, yet that process always reflects the unchanging character and purpose of deity.

Here the concepts of *order* and *process* are of equal importance; and the definition within which they are comprised applies alike to the unfolding story of Israel in scripture and also to that wider revelation which is given in the *cosmos* of creation. The revelation, alike in scripture and in creation, is wholly given, and in that sense is final and complete. Yet the process *in* which the revelation is given is in neither case complete. In the first place, the mysterious secrets of nature are being continuously unravelled before us. For on the one hand these mysteries belong to what is plainly an unfinished process of natural development; and on the other hand, in the sphere of know-ledge, the possibilities of this unfinished process provide material for a never-ending inquiry.[1] So also the unfolding story of Israel is extended in the unfinished drama of church history; and here the spouse of Christ continuously awaits the final manifestation of him in whom the 'secret' of God was once for all disclosed.[2]

The parallel just now drawn between revelation through creation and revelation in scripture was sketched in a bare outline which could not do justice to the deeper issues involved. There are, in fact, important differences between these two modes of revelation as given to our apprehension. Alike for the scientist and for the theologian 'nature' is an order which discloses its character in a process.[3] Of that process we are, one and all, contemporaries and, each in our measure, eye-wit-nesses.[4] Scripture, on the other hand, is the record of a process the key to which (speaking temporally) must be said to lie not in the present but in the past, that is to say in the historical events of the gospel story. Thus, whereas both modes of revela-tion exhibit a changing order in a process which has an un-

---

[1] see above, Ch. III, §§ vii and ix

[2] see above, Ch. II, § i

[3] The reader is reminded of an earlier discussion concerning the 'faith' of the scientist in an 'order of nature'; see above, Ch. III, § v. The 'human' sciences cannot be excluded from this sphere. See next note.

[4] The reader is asked to remember that the 'wider revelation given in the *cosmos* of creation' must be taken to include human nature, in some of its aspects, within its scope, notwithstanding the fact that the same human nature enters into the special sphere of historical revelation recorded in scripture. This is another facet of the interpenetration of forms which was described in the last section of Ch. IV and elsewhere in Book II.

changing character, there is a radical difference between the two modes, at least so far as concerns our temporal relation to them. There is, in short, a difference between man's place respectively in the *process* of history[1] and again in the *order* of nature. For our relation to the former is serial in a sense which has no counterpart in the latter. In the historical series we are contemporaries only of the historical present, whereas in certain respects we have membership in an order of nature which, notwithstanding its process, is in its totality simultaneously present.

The difference between the two modes of revelation, therefore, rests upon a corresponding contrast between nature and history. The changes which characterize nature (as such) trace patterns of recurring uniformity. Within these cycles of recurrence variations, extensive as they may be, are broadly subservient to uniformity of pattern. In history, however, it might seem that uniformity tends to disappear amid the never-ending novelty of variations. Whereas repetition belongs to the very fabric of nature as we know it, 'history never repeats itself'. This dictum, nevertheless, must not be understood in a sense which lifts man out of his place in the order of nature. For man is the meeting-point of nature and of history; and that means that he is included in both. The freedom which gives to him his pre-eminence, and to history its special character, is a gift which crowns nature for its reinforcement. As we saw at an earlier stage in the argument, freedom finds fulfilment in a given order which includes man along with nature in a single plan of creation.[2] Man's creaturely status, therefore, involves him in the recurring uniformities of nature, so that the rhythms of his complex being, at its various levels, correspond to those uniformities and are conditioned by them. This implication of our creaturehood enters inevitably as an important factor into the spiritual life of man in all its manifestations.

The lines of thought pursued in the preceding paragraphs

[1] In English idiom 'history' can mean (1) the actual course of events (*Geschichte*) or (2) the account given by historians concerning (1), i.e. what in Germany is called *Historie*. Broadly speaking (1) is to (2) as the order of nature is to the natural sciences. In the present argument 'history' means the actual course of events.

[2] Ch. IV, § i

open up large issues concerning the theology of revelation and, in particular, concerning the manner in which revelation enters into and determines the life of the church.[1] In this final stage of our argument concerning *Revelation and the Modern World* we shall hope to gather up the threads of the two preceding stages. In accordance with the scriptural conception of the Word as essentially creative, Revelation is here conceived to be a mode of divine activity by which the Creator communicates himself to man and, by so doing, evokes man's response and co-operation. By such action on the part of the Creator, everything belonging to man's creaturely status, and all the products of his human achievement within that status, are drawn into the orbit of the response divinely evoked. The result is a complex historical structure magnetized and held in being by that unique interchange of communication between God and man.

From one point of view this structure might be taken to be as wide as religion itself. It would then be understood to include all the diverse embodiments of the religious spirit which have appeared in history. In that sense it would correspond to the universal revelation which, it was suggested, is 'at once the correlative of creation and an outflow of creative grace'.[2] In our earlier discussion of this theme, however, it was pointed out that the special revelation to Israel was the means through which the wider revelation comes to fulfilment under the conditions of a fallen world. From the latter standpoint the complex historical structure created by the divine activity of the Word is the organism of revelation envisaged in scripture, that is to say, the Israel of God as fulfilled in the Christ and in his church. Within the structure so defined scripture itself, as the written repository of revelation, occupies a position, and fulfils a function, without parallel in its authority. The pre-eminence proper to scripture, however, is not imperilled but safeguarded when the written word is seen to be organically related to other organs of revelation. Of these there are two which call for special consideration in the present chapter. These are (1) the 'natural religion' which scripture itself presupposes, and (2) tradition in that holy community with which scripture is so largely preoccupied.

[1] see the Preface, p. x, and the Synopsis of Contents, Ch. III, § 5
[2] see above, Ch. I, § iv, pars. 5 and 6

It will not be possible, nor indeed desirable, to keep these two topics sharply separated from one another in our discussion. For, in the first place, tradition is an important factor in all human societies and therefore in all manifestations of religion. Moreover, the traditions of Israel and of the Christian church have been continuously conditioned by that process of assimilation from environment of which we have already taken note in previous chapters. But secondly, this age-long process of assimilation makes it impossible to discuss the special revelation and its traditions in isolation from the facts of 'natural religion' which belong to the wider revelation. At this point it is desirable that something further should be said by way of definition in regard to the terms which are being used, particularly the expression: 'natural religion'.

The religion of Israel is distinguished from that of its neighbours, in part at least, by a greater emphasis upon history. The prophets appeal to the wonderful works of God in Israel's past history as evidence both of his faithful love and of his power to protect Israel in the present. This factor of historicity received, of course, an altogether higher significance under the new covenant. But, without entering as yet upon that vast topic, it may be said that the historical character of the biblical religion differentiates it sharply from the natural religions to be found everywhere in the ancient world. The other religions are *natural* in the sense that they find the presence of divinity manifested in phenomena of nature rather than in events of history. Their deities do not intervene in human affairs by unique historical acts. Rather, they are always presumed to be present in nature's recurring cycles of uniformity. This identification of deity with all that is and all that happens is the basis of idolatry, there being no compensating factor of transcendence adequate to redress the balance. Nevertheless, despite their distortion of truth, the testimony of the natural religions to a universal revelation cannot be simply discounted.[1] Scripture itself constantly affirms a witness to the Creator in the works of his creation; and this is the truth towards which the natural religions were blindly groping.

But further, scripture also shows that throughout Israel's

[1] cp. Acts 17[23]: 'What therefore ye worship in ignorance, this set I forth unto you.'

history the religion of nature, as defined in the last paragraph, was in constant interaction with, and influence upon, the more distinctive religion of Israel.[1] It is difficult to do justice to the complexities of this subject in the space at our disposal. For on the one hand the critical estimate does not permit us to form any precise conclusions concerning the original character of the Mosaic religion. On the other hand recent researches are showing convincingly how great was the debt of Israelite religion to the forms of religious culture by which it was surrounded. We may, however, surely say that the conflict which developed between the prophets of Israel and Canaanite religious *praxis* had, in some degree, the character of a dialectical process. In that process the transcendent religion of the prophets could triumph only by including within itself much of that to which it stood, or appeared to stand,[2] in formal opposition.[3]

Such a verdict upon the religious history of Israel could be unwelcome only to those who are able to assume that the whole truth of Israel's religion was comprised within, and conveyed through, the institution of prophecy, regarded as a channel of revelation. Any assumption of this sort, however, would involve us in that selective attitude towards the written word which we have found reason to repudiate on the ground that it inevitably substitutes human ideas and opinions for the authority of divine revelation.[4] From every such over-simplification of the issues we must needs return to the greater complexity of the actual facts, where no single element in Hebrew religion can be presumed to have an exclusive right to represent the whole.[5]

[1] That is, the prophetic type of religion which, with its appeal to history, set Israel apart from her neighbours.

[2] The qualification has become important in view of a changed attitude towards OT prophecy. For this see *The cultic prophet in Ancient Israel* by A. R. Johnson, Cardiff, 1944.

[3] For a detailed illustration of this process see below, § ii, pars. 6 and 7; and, for a more complete picture, Ch. IX, § iv.

[4] see above, Ch. I, § iv, par. 2. The changed attitude mentioned in the last note but one suggests that the said 'ideas and opinions' were in fact ill-founded, one-sided and misleading.

[5] cp. the judicious estimate of this matter in Prof. D. C. Simpson's Foreword to *Myth and Ritual*, especially p. xiii, note 2, with the paragraph to which it is appended.

ii

The tensions and interactions of biblical religion correspond
to that 'complex of opposites' which is human nature. The nexus
of nature with history in one order of creation illustrated from
typical transformations of Israel's religion. Dependence of
religious response upon ' direction' (*torah*).

For the theory of a simple conflict between true and false
forms of religion we have now substituted an alternative conception according to which different religious factors were held
in tension by the balancing of their diverse claims to recognition. This alternative conception has the advantage that it
corresponds to the complexity of human nature itself, a complexity which is due, in part at least, to the fact that here there
enters into the situation man's mysterious power of choice.[1]
Freedom to choose between two possible courses of action super-
venes in us upon that balance of forces which elsewhere determines the uniformities of nature. Broadly speaking the two
aspects of our nature correspond respectively to the *traditional*
and to the *prophetic* aspects of religion. Of these the former ensures continuity with the inheritance of the past, whereas the
latter addresses itself to the necessity of facing a present crisis
of decision. Thus traditional religion conforms itself to the given
order, whereas genuine prophecy summons men to choose
between the will of God and the powers of evil in each new
situation which arises. Both these factors are necessary to the
health of religion. For right decisions men stand in need of
guidance from the old wisdom of former generations, in order
that tradition in turn may be reshaped to meet the perpetual
challenge of the new.[2]

The course of this exposition has by now made it clear that
tradition occupies a position in human life conformable to our

[1] cp. above, the 'complex of opposites' in Ch. III, § ii, par. 7

[2] It is to be noticed that prophecy is not necessarily opposed to tradition.
It may, indeed, recall men from the allurements of a fashionable progressi-
vism to the genuine traditions of their past, as Israel was recalled by her
prophets from the idolatrous fashions of the passing present to the original
Covenant of Sinai-Horeb. So also in modern times men like Kierkegaard
have summoned Christians to the traditional duty of moral decision as
against the specious Hegelian suggestion that whatever is coming-to-be is
its own justification.

place in the plan of creation. Since man is a microcosm of creation[1] it is inevitable that the element of routine in accordance with a recurrent pattern, that element which is so characteristic of nature, should have its place also in the life of mankind. In this sense traditional religion conforms itself to a given order which bears some analogy to the order of nature. The analogy was indicated at the beginning of the present chapter in our remarks about the two modes of revelation, and especially in the fact that both spheres of revelation, namely scripture and creation, could with equal veracity be described in terms of 'a changing order'.[2] By way of illustrating further the meaning of that term we may at this point recall to mind that passage in the treatise of St Irenaeus against the heresies (discussed at length in our fourth chapter) where this father draws a parallel between the agricultural operations of sowing and reaping and the unity of organic development manifested in the nexus between the Old Testament and the New.

It is to be noticed that the parallel just cited from St Irenaeus is a parallel between natural process and historical continuity. This is, of course, only a partial statement of what is involved, since the nexus between the two Testaments is something much more mysterious, indeed more metaphysical, than what is ordinarily implied by historical continuity. Nevertheless, allowing for these deeper considerations, the possibility of such analogies is a further reminder that, however much we may emphasize the contrasts between nature and history, there is no actual gap between them. For these two spheres of being overlap in man, in whom they are firmly locked together in one order of creation.[3] We propose now to indicate ways in which this interlocking of the two spheres is manifested in the religious traditions of Israel and of the Christian *ecclesia*. In so

[1] see above, in Ch. VI, § i, last par. with notes, and § ii, par. 5

[2] The reference to man's place in the '*process* of history', etc. (par. 3 of § i above) was not intended to suggest that history is all process and nature all order! *That* differentiation was concerned solely to indicate two aspects of man's place in the spatio-temporal series.

[3] The reader will note that in this way of speaking the order of creation is conceived to be capable of including within itself both the realm of nature and the process of history. Such appears to be the scriptural standpoint. Indeed, our Lord's parables of farm life are all evidence for this; cp. again, in the present volume, the first half of Ch. IV.

doing we shall be illustrating more fully what is implied in the Irenaean conception of a single organism of revelation in which there is mutual interpenetration as between creation, scripture, and the church.

'Archaeological evidence', we are told, 'shows that there is no break in the cultural history of Canaan separating the period of Hebrew occupation from that of Canaanite occupation. The sites, objects, and natural phenomena which had been sacred to the Canaanites became in time sacred for the Hebrews also'.[1] Here, it may be remarked, we have the proper starting point for those discussions about St Paul's relation to the mystery religions of his time, at which we glanced in the first chapter of the present work. The historical religion of Israel which culminated in the death and resurrection of the Christ had its roots deep down in ancient forms of natural religion to which Israel gave new historical associations. In the instance which has just been cited the new associations were mediated by means of stories ('cult legends') in which the sacred sites of Canaan were declared to have been the scenes of revelations 'from Jahveh himself to the ancestors of the Hebrew people'.[2] A notable example of such a 'cult legend' ('explaining' the origin of a Hebrew religious cult in a particular place) is to be found in the story of Jacob's dream at Bethel (Gen. 28).

In the instance just quoted the historical element is so slight as to be actually problematical. We cannot say how much of these patriarchal 'sagas' can strictly be called history. There are other stories in the Old Testament, however, where the historical ground under our feet is much more solid, where also the transformation of natural religion by means of new historical associations becomes, for our present purpose, much more significant.

There is no story in the Old Testament which has proved more significant both for Judaism and for Christendom than the story of the Exodus of Israel from Egypt. At the heart of this story as told in the book of Exodus stands the account of the Passover festival and its original inauguration. With this the

[1] Cited from p. 108 of *In the Beginning* (being Vol. VI in the OT section of the Clarendon Bible) by S. H. Hooke, Professor Emeritus of Old Testament Studies in the University of London (Oxford, 1947).

[2] *op. cit.*, p. 108; cp. also *ib.* p. 19

narrative also associates a divine command to keep the feast of unleavened bread. These two ritual observances, however, are now believed to have been in origin two distinct spring-festivals of natural religion, having, in their earliest forms, no connexion with Israel's departure from Egypt. Their re-association with the story of the Exodus had the effect of combining them into a single commemoration of that historic deliverance. Thus it came about that an annual commemoration of redemptive history first supervened upon the nature-cults and eventually superseded those earlier cults in the national memory and consciousness.[1]

In this way the God who intervenes in history to save his people displaced the gods of primitive nature-worship. In the transformation, moreover, the ancient ritual was not simply annulled, although undoubtedly its general character became changed in certain respects. Until the fall of Jerusalem in A.D. 70 the lamb was still sacrificed in the temple-court and the sheaf of the firstfruits was still waved before the Lord. Thus the gifts of the Creator to man were still gratefully acknowledged. Nevertheless, as the Creator he was known to be no mere personification of natural forces; he was acknowledged as the Lord of heaven and earth who controls the course of human history, and who, in his people, will bring about the fulfilment of his own ineffable purposes. The ancient rites of the Semitic 'cult-pattern' were thus, through their re-association with Israel's history, prepared for their last and final transformation. This took place when the Word of God, incarnate in human form, became the Lamb of God and offered himself as the firstfruits of a new creation.

The two examples which we have selected to illustrate the interlocking of nature and history in a changing order of religious development have one obvious feature in common. Both the local sanctuaries and the national festivals were important because ancient religion was essentially a matter of ritual acts. The right things had to be done in the appointed

[1] The reader must be warned, however, that the historical problem is extremely complex. For evidence of this he should read Additional Note I in *Israel, its Life and Culture III-IV*, the second volume of the series, by J. Pedersen (Copenhagen and London, 1934-1940). Vol. I was cited above, near the end of Ch. V.

places and in the correct way. The feature common to our two examples was, therefore, no fortuitous accident of choice. Religion was made up of concrete acts which were the proper and approved responses to the will of the deity. This external character of religion was of one piece with the concreteness and objectivity of all primitive life. The welfare of the community was conceived to depend upon a whole network of such external responses, all precisely conditioned in time and circumstance. Moreover, any unauthorized violation of the traditional régime would be regarded as an invitation to disaster, and would probably meet with condign punishment.

In a changing order change would, of course, inevitably take place. Its justification, however, in important matters would always be the revealed will of the deity. The community, therefore, was utterly dependent upon those who were the recognized interpreters of the divine will. Priests, prophets, and elders were the necessary channels of direction. 'Direction' (*torah*) was thus the indispensable means to the continued existence of Israel as the people of Jahveh. With the introduction of this word we enter upon a fresh stage of our investigation. In what follows, however, it should be remembered that the progressive transformation of Israel's religion, examples of which have been given in preceding paragraphs, is, from another point of view, to be identified with that process of assimilation of which we have previously spoken. The permanent 'direction' of Israel's religious life[1] has to be seen on the background of that 'complex stratification' of cultures which is somehow represented both in the pages of the New Testament and in the very being of the Christian church.[2]

iii

Torah, which declares the divine will to man, is identified (*a*) with revelation, (*b*) with its organs (scripture and tradition), (*c*) with the divine Wisdom whereby the world was created. So also the recognized teachers of *torah*-wisdom are identified with

[1] That is, the expert guidance showing the way in which they were to 'walk' (cp. St Paul's precept: 'Walk in the Spirit').
[2] see above, Ch. I, § vi

the deity in his fatherly relation to the holy community, securing to it the given Whole in and through a continuous historical succession.

In the English versions of the Old Testament the Hebrew word *torah* is rendered 'law'.[1] This is unfortunate, as 'law' inevitably suggests a written code of statutes having legal force, whereas the Hebrew word is not primarily legal in its associations, but rather religious and educational. Moreover, *torah* carries no necessary implication of a written document. The root meaning of the verb is 'to throw'; and this suggests that its second meaning ('to direct') may be derived from the 'casting' of lots, which was, among the Hebrews, a recognized method of ascertaining the divine will.[2] There are, of course, other possibilities. But in any case the earliest associations of the word would be with those primitive methods by which the recognized leader or accepted expert sought to discover the divine will in order to 'direct' aright his clients or followers. After the settlement in Canaan the recognized authority or 'instructor' (*moreh*) in all matters of the cultus would be a priest at one of the sanctuaries, and eventually a member of the Zadokite priesthood in the temple at Jerusalem. So the prophet Haggai was divinely instructed to ask for *torah* from the priests of the post-exilic temple concerning a matter of ceremonial uncleanness (Hag. 2[10𝑓]). So also the prophet Malachi, writing in the following century, says: 'The priest's lips should keep knowledge, and they should seek *torah* at his mouth: for he is the messenger of Jahveh of hosts' (Mal. 2[7]). In both of these instances the *torah* is given in oral form; and from time immemorial oral instruction was the normal form of direction, long before any written scripture came into being.[3]

The true 'instructor', however, was Jahveh himself, who through his chosen agents directed the responses of Israel to

---

[1] RV margin sometimes has 'teaching' as an alternative.

[2] In their first (recorded) official act after our Lord's ascension the apostles obtained *torah* by this method (Acts 1[15𝑓]), on which see my article: *The Choice of Matthias*, in JTS, Vol. XLVI, No. 181-2.

[3] 'Natural religion' also had its *torah* experts, good and bad. In OT, for example, Melchizedek represents the former and Balaam the latter.

his successive revelations. The prophets 'call their own utterances *torah*';[1] and in the relatively late book of Daniel God is
said to have given *torah* 'by the hand of his servants, the
prophets'.[2] Again, the author of Psalm 78 summons 'my people'
to give ear to 'my *torah*'; but a little later he remarks that
Jahveh 'appointed *torah* in Israel', thus acknowledging the
source from which his own instruction comes (Ps. 78[1,5]).
Eventually *torah* was in a special sense identified with the five
books of Moses, although a Jewish opinion is cited to the effect
that the Prophets and the Writings (that is the rest of the Old
Testament) are also *torah*.[3] But the fundamental meaning which
covers all these variations is 'religious instruction' whether
written or unwritten.[4] An important form of such instruction
was the family *torah* imparted by parents to their children; and
this is emphasized especially in Proverbs and Ecclesiasticus.
Torah therefore could have a wider or a narrower connotation. Thus it *could* mean simply the true wisdom of life
which comes from God. Even 'the *torah* of Moses' might cover
a great deal more than the Pentateuch, including the oral
'law' which Moses 'received' and the scribes of later ages
expounded.[5]

It follows that in its wider connotation *torah* could be identified quite simply with Revelation—'all that God has made
known of his nature, character, and purpose, and of what he
would have men be and do'. On the other hand, since revelation
has its organs, 'Torah in one aspect is the vehicle, in another

[1] G. F. Moore, *Judaism*, Vol. I, p. 263. With this statement agrees H.
Wheeler Robinson, *Inspiration and Revelation in the O.T.* (Oxford, 1946),
p. 204 with note 3.

[2] Dan. 9[10]. Actually the plural form ('directions') is here used.

[3] Moore, *op. cit.*, Vol. III, p. 81, note 28. This wider use seems to be
reflected in NT, e.g. John 12[34]: 'We have heard out of *the law* that the Christ
abideth for ever.' Here the Greek phrase represents *torah*; and the reference
is most probably to messianic promises such as 2 Sam. 7[13], Pss. 72[17], 89[28]
and especially Isa. 9[7], some of which are more explicit than anything in
the Pentateuch. See also John 10[34] and Rom. 3[19], the latter referring back
to a catena from Psalms and Isaiah.

[4] Commandment and statute are included in it, and distinguished within
(not from) it (*ibid.*).

[5] In rabbinical teaching it was held that Moses received on the
mount the whole 'unwritten law' of Jewish tradition as well as the
written law.

and deeper view it is the whole content of revelation'.[1] It will be observed that this estimate, by a foremost authority, corroborates the view outlined earlier in this volume that revelation cannot be separated from its outward form, and that scripture can be quite simply identified with the Word of God. There is, however, another issue raised by the formula just now cited. For 'the vehicle' of revelation is not scripture as such but *torah*, that is a traditional body of instruction in the holy community, of which scripture is a transcript. 'And we ought not to assume that the oral tradition ceased to function when the transcript was made, or even that the written transcript then became primary. The transcript may be regarded as a cross-section of the living tradition at a given time and place'.[2] In *torah* as vehicle of revelation the contrast and tension between scripture and tradition has not yet emerged. Scripture is one form of tradition, its literary form; whereas tradition in its wholeness is 'a living biological phenomenon'[3] to which that literary form belongs and without which it cannot be understood.

The identification of *torah* with Revelation was formally expressed in Jewish thought through its developed doctrine of 'wisdom'. The words of Deuteronomy 4[6]: 'this is your wisdom' refer, in the immediate context, to Israel's observance of the Mosaic statutes and judgements. But the words were also understood to involve an identification of *torah* with the divine wisdom. 'Since this law, the distinctive wisdom of Israel, was revealed by God, it, like all true human wisdom, was God's wisdom of which so much is said in the Proverbs and other works of the Jewish sages'.[4] This brings us back to the connexion between revelation and the order of creation, of which we have already treated in the present work. Moreover, Dr Moore's way of putting it also brings 'all true human wisdom' into the same context, a suggestion which opens up wide vistas for theology. We remember also that in the New Testament there is a 'Wisdom Christology', concerning which much has been

---

[1] Moore, *op. cit.*, Vol. I, p. 263

[2] Dr. Philip Carrington, Archbishop of Quebec, *The Primitive Christian Catechism* (Cambridge, 1940), p. 3. To this book I am deeply indebted in what follows.

[3] Carrington, *op. cit.*, p. 4

[4] Moore, *op. cit.*, Vol. I, pp. 263 *f*

written. Clearly the identification of *torah* with divine wisdom is pregnant with consequences, some of which have been for judgement as well as for salvation.

These issues must be unravelled by stages; and first as to the connexion with creation. From Proverbs 8 onwards the Wisdom of God is personified as God's companion and partner in his creative works. For Jewish interpreters Wisdom is both the co-architect and the 'instrument' with which the world was created.[1] Thus *torah* is identified, both with the divine wisdom which planned and executed the creation of the world, and also with the 'plan' upon which the creation was framed. It follows that the Law of Moses (that is, the contents both of the Pentateuch and of the oral law) existed before the foundation of the world. So finally comes the logical conclusion of this line of thought: 'God studied Genesis and created the world to correspond'.[2] These ideas are already explicit in the book of Jesus the son of Sirach (Ecclesiasticus) about 200 B.C. After describing Wisdom's divine origin, premundane existence, omnipresence in creation, and tabernacling in Israel, the writer continues: 'All these things are the book of the covenant of God most high, the law which Moses commanded' (24^{23}). Thus the book of the Law is personified, receives divine attributes, fulfils cosmic functions and carries out a historical mission. This is the Jewish form of the doctrine concerning the organism of revelation which we encountered in the pages of St Irenaeus. For the book to which such qualities are ascribed is still the transcript of Israel's traditions as well as the divinely given counterpart of the created world. Creation, scripture and tradition meet in one instrument of revelation.

'The world was created for the *torah*', that is for a religious end laid down and clarified in 'the distinctive wisdom of Israel'. If then the revelation is identified with its vehicle, Israel's traditional and codified wisdom, what status should be assigned to the teachers of this wisdom, the human agents of revelation? For the rabbinical answer to this question we are not left in doubt. 'The word of the Lord' is identified with scribal tradition. Deuteronomy (17^{8-13}) requires implicit obedi-

---

[1] Moore, *op. cit.*, Vol. I, pp. 266 *f.* The whole of this chapter on 'The perpetuity of the Law' is of outstanding interest.
[2] *ibid.*, p. 268

ence to the enactments of a rabbinical court. In the case of a
'contumacious elder' the Mishnah says: 'The matter is more
serious concerning words of the Scribes than words of the *torah*'.[1]
The supremacy of the written law is not challenged; for in the
passage from Deuteronomy just cited decisions are expressly
remitted to the appointed judges, who are therefore bound to
interpret scripture, and do so with the authority of Revelation.
We shall find a parallel situation in the New Testament with
regard to apostolic tradition. There is no way of escape from
this duality. Once the written transcript of tradition is canonized, authority in the holy community becomes bi-focal.
Moreover, there is another aspect of this question (concerning
the status of the recognized teacher in Israel) to which we must
now give our attention.

We have already noticed a psalmist's use of the expression
'my *torah*' side by side with a recognition that *torah* was divinely
appointed. This way of speaking inevitably raises in another
form the same problem: What is the relation of the human
teacher to the divine Wisdom? To take refuge in the inspired
authority of the writings in question does not carry the issue
far enough back.[2] For in the opening chapters of Proverbs the
same formula is put into the mouth of a human father address-
ing his son. Moreover 'hear the instruction of thy father' is
paralleled with 'forsake not the *torah* of thy mother' (Prov. 1[8]).
As we read these sections we cannot fail to conclude that in
some sense the instruction given by parents to their children
concerning the conduct of life is here identified with divine
Wisdom. For example, the language used in the great *Shema*
passage of Deuteronomy concerning the Mosaic precepts
(Deut. 6[6–8]) is echoed in Proverbs, where the same exalted way
of speaking is applied to the family instruction: 'Bind them
about thy neck; write them upon the table of thine heart'.[3]
Here is a probable explanation: 'This *torah* is thought of as
ultimately coming from God'. 'It follows that the father has a

[1] *Sanhedrin* xi. 3, quoted twice by Moore, *op. cit.*, Vol. I, p. 262 and
Vol. III, p. 81, note 27

[2] A Jewish solution of the problem is cited by Moore (Vol. III, p. 81,
note 28). This takes the expressions, of 'Asaph' in Ps. 78[1], and of 'Solomon'
in Prov. 4[2] *et al.*, as evidence that these 'Writings', along with the Prophets,
belong to canonized scripture, and are therefore *torah* in the later sense.

[3] Prov. 3[1–3]; cp. 1[9], 2[1,2], 4[4,21], 6[20–23]; cp. especially 6[22] with Deut. 6[7].

godlike status in reference to the son, and the honour paid to parents is a form of the honour paid to God'.[1] The fifth commandment belongs to the first table of the law.[2]

In Psalm 82 the rulers of the nations are addressed by the God of Israel in these words: 'I said, ye are gods, and all of you sons of the Most High'. Our Lord's comment on this text, as reported in John 10[34,35], is as follows: 'He called them gods *to whom the word of God came*'. With this way of speaking Dr Carrington's interpretation is in full accord. Moreover it is in accord also with a Hebrew idiom of thought to which we have previously referred, by which a person is identified with his representatives through an 'extension' of his personality in them.[3] So 'the word of God came to a son through his father, as it had previously reached the father in like manner through *his* father'. This 'didactic succession' in genealogical continuity from one father to another is already emphasized in Proverbs (4[1–4]). The combination of these two notions—(1) the divine status of the father in relation to the son, and (2) the idea of a succession by which teaching is handed down from father to son—was destined to become a factor of great importance, not only in Judaism but also in the Christian church. It explains, for example, the emphasis which St Irenaeus lays upon the succession of 'elders' in the church as a safeguard of orthodoxy. This use of the word 'elder' to signify one whose teaching carries authority in the community goes back into the Old Testament. The office of elder is traced back to Moses (Exod. 18); and the tradition of God's 'marvellous works' in Israel (another technical phrase)[4] is rehearsed by Joshua to the elders (Josh. 24) to whom the tradition is handed on.[5] These elders are reminded of 'your fathers' (the patriarchs), and become in

---

[1] Carrington, *op. cit.*, p. 4 and notes. It also follows that honour paid to parents is a form of that fear of the Lord which is the beginning of wisdom.

[2] This appears (e.g.) in the order of Lev. 19, where the precept about honouring parents precedes those concerning idolatry and worship.

[3] cp. above, Ch. V, § v, pars. 2*f*; and for the application to the deity see also A. R. Johnson's book, *The One and the Many*, etc., especially pp. 32 *ff*. For Carrington's thesis note the significant parallelism of Ecclus. 3[6].

[4] On 'marvellous works' see my note on p. 240 of *The Common Life*.

[5] The rehearsal in Josh. 24 is repeated in Neh. 9.

turn fathers of those who succeed them. Accordingly, when the office of 'teaching elder' became established the godlike status of 'fathers' was transferred to these professional teachers, who assumed the 'divine father-son relationship as the basis of their teaching'.[1]

Thus divine wisdom is *continuously* embodied in the holy community through its succession of recognized teachers, just as it is *once for all* embodied in the canon of scripture. We see here the two sides of what is involved in response to divine revelation. That revelation is always given, not only to, but also in and through response.[2] The marvellous works of the Exodus, in which Jahveh made himself known to Israel, required the co-operation of Israel through Moses as the medium in and through which the works took place. So also the continuous response of Israel through prophets and teachers was the medium in which the revelation was continuously unfolded. On the other hand the revelation, although given continuously in history, has also a finality which even in the Old Testament is cumulative. This characteristic of the revelation was ultimately reflected in the closure of the Hebrew canon of scripture so that nothing further might be added.[3]

The revelation was given in the story of redemptive history. This we ventured to call a 'changing order',[4] because the changes wrought by history were ordered to a master-plan. In the process, moreover, there was something which did not change, namely the character and the purpose of God and the divine activity in which these were manifested. So the revelation gradually unfolded in the history was from first to last a revelation of that all-satisfying Whole towards which Israel ever strove. At every point, therefore, in the redemptive history the Whole sought and desired was present to be pos-

[1] Carrington, *op. cit.*, pp. 4 *f*, and the whole of his Chapter VII

[2] see above, Ch. I, § v, penultimate par., and Ch. II, § i, par. 1

[3] Probably the New Testament writers did not realize that they were adding a new volume to scripture. It took a century at least for the idea of a New Testament to become explicit. The Christian church was at first wholly occupied in showing how Christ fulfilled 'the scriptures', i.e. the OT. When Irenaeus wrote *The Demonstration* the latter idea summed up his whole conception of doctrine.

[4] see in § i above the conclusion of par. 1 and the first sentence of par. 2, and also in § ii, the second note to par. 2

sessed.[1] Indeed, redemptive history did not end with the closure of the canon; for the treasure of the Whole was like a rich deposit, to be handed on successively through the ensuing ages. Thus a *corpus* of historical revelation, permanently enshrined in scripture, but also dwelling in the heart of the community, is extended through time. Thus, too, the serial succession of time is gathered up into the finality, into the once-for-allness which characterizes the historical revelation. Here we see looming up in outline the first sketch of an answer to the problem which emerged at the beginning of this chapter when we were comparing two modes of revelation, the problem of the relation between the present and the past in a historical religion which looks back to a past foundation.

iv

Revelation is always creative, as creation is always revealing. Revelation is inseparable from the instruments which it creates for its embodiment. By that embodiment, therefore, revelation takes on a creaturely character; and in a fallen world its organs are both humiliated and exalted. In the story of revealed religion a single pattern of humiliation is unfolded.

The Jewish identification of *torah* with the wisdom by which the world was created implies that divine revelation is essentially creative. That implication had always been present in the Hebrew conception of the Word; and it carries consequences which we shall have to consider later. 'Direction' given through a genuine channel of revelation had in it the character of a word from the Lord.[2] Accordingly, the present paragraph should be compared with what was said in Chapter I concerning the complementary character of the two forms of divine activity which we call respectively 'revelation' and 'creation'.[3] This was connected with the characteristically

[1] cp. the various utterances of Jewish teachers concerning the presence of the Shekinah with those who study *torah*, e.g. *Aboth*. iii, 7, quoted by Carrington, *op. cit.*, p. 10

[2] cp. the repeated formula of the written *torah*: 'The Lord *said* unto Moses'

[3] Especially the paragraph (5 in § iv) which concludes with a reference to 'creative grace' as a 'correlative of our nature'

Hebrew conception of the divine Word as both illuminating and quickening.[1] In Genesis 1 created life is called into existence by successive utterances of the divine Word. These, however, were preceded by that original going forth of the divine Word in which there was light. The *fiat lux* of Genesis 1[3] may well have been in the mind of the psalmist who wrote: 'The opening of thy words giveth light' (Ps. 119[130], RV). Moreover, a few lines further on the writer prays: 'Make thy face to shine upon thy servant; and teach me thy statutes' (verse 135). The object of this double petition seems to be the giving of a personal theophany such as was granted to Moses on the mount of revelation (Exod. 34). The mental illumination proceeding from the uttered words of God is to be accompanied by a physical irradiation proceeding from the divine face to the human suppliant. There is a difference, however, in this respect between the mediator and his disciple. What was conveyed to Moses directly when he received the written law is stored up for this psalmist *in* that written law. The *torah*, like the face of God, gives light; and the uncovering or manifestation of the *torah* 'lets light break forth from it'.[2] When the words of the *torah* enter the heart they will have this effect, as surely as the original going forth of the Word, at the beginning of creation, was an epiphany of light.[3]

At this point it will be advisable to tabulate some conclusions concerning revelation:

(1) In the biblical tradition revelation and creation are completely complementary notions. Revelation is always

---

[1] The double imagery of light and life may have been associated with the ancient belief that the heavenly bodies were living beings. This belief was common to the ancient world, although in the development of Israel's religion these luminaries were dethroned from the position of deities to that of created lights (Gen. 1[14–19]).

[2] This way of connecting two verses of Ps. 119 was first suggested to me by Briggs (*The Psalms*, Vol. II, p. 433, in ICC). The parallel with Moses is my own contribution, following St Paul's combination of Exod. 34 with Gen. 1 in 2 Cor. 3, 4.

[3] The versions of the psalter in AV and in the Book of Common Prayer each contribute something to the exegesis of Ps. 119[130] along with RV. The PB version has: 'When thy word goeth forth'. AV has: 'The entrance of thy word giveth light'. Compare these with RV cited in the text above. From the divine mouth words 'go forth' into the 'open', and then 'enter' the heart of the devout suppliant to illuminate him.

creative; and conversely the Creator is ever manifested in his creative activity. This unity in the modes of divine activity carries with it also certain other unities, as follows:

(2) Creative revelation is mysteriously inseparable from the vehicles which it creates for its own embodiment. This must be connected with the principle that revelation is always given to, in, and through response.[1] For God is known in his works, but principally in that human response to fatherly love by which the plan of creation is brought to fruition.

(3) There is complete harmony and unity between the plan of creation as a whole and the true order of human life as set forth in the vehicles of special revelation (Israel and *torah*).

(4) Through its embodiment divine revelation takes on a creaturely character. Creative revelation involves intimate union of the Creator with his creatures and ultimately of God with man.

Our fourth point implies the completion of creation in the Christ, in whom alone creaturely response to divine fatherhood was fulfilled.[2] Creaturely character, however, has been disturbed by the disorderly intrusion of sin; and this fact conditions the whole plan of creative revelation as actually unfolded. Creaturely response was fulfilled by the incarnate Son in man's proper form, that is the form of the Servant; and in a fallen world, 'subjected to vanity', the response in that form involved the costing death of the Redeemer as the price of fulfilment.

Some of the four points which we have just enunciated resume earlier stages of the argument or have been sufficiently illustrated. To others we shall find it necessary to return. For the present let us consider more fully the complications introduced by sin into the plan of creative revelation. In a disordered world the creative activity of God becomes recuperative and redemptive. That whole relation of intimacy with his creatures whereby deity is manifested takes on a more sombre and desolating form, and yet also one which, in the final issue, is seen to be both majestic and glorious. The pattern of humiliation and exalta-

[1] above, p. 208, with note 2
[2] As was stated above (Ch. II, § i, par. 1). Thus was disclosed that final paradox of the divine plan: the creativity of creatureliness.

tion which the church has always found in the story of the
Redeemer is seen to be of one piece with all that goes before
and with all that follows after in the history of the city of God,
from the first *fiat* of creation to the last trumpet of judgement.
Of this St Irenaeus has shown us something. We have now to
consider further in what sense such an extended pattern of
humiliation and exaltation has stamped itself upon the story
of revealed religion.

It will be convenient to take this in two stages, beginning
with the backwards extension[1] of 'humiliation', that is, the
anticipations which the form of the Servant receives in the dispensation of the old covenant. Our estimate of the Old Testament, however, (as always) is provided for us in the apostolic
writings; and here we come upon one of the great paradoxes of
New Testament teaching, namely, its contrasted attitudes
towards the Law of Moses. Let us first take another glance at
the high estimate formed within old Israel. We have seen how
greatly the author of Psalm 119 valued the spiritual treasures
of the written *torah*. Here is a further example of this attitude
to *torah* in the psalter:

> The law of the Lord is perfect, restoring the soul:
> The testimony of the Lord is sure, making wise the simple.
> The precepts of the Lord are right, rejoicing the heart:
> The commandment of the Lord is pure, enlightening the eyes.
>
> (Psalm 19[7,8]).

It is significant that the writer goes on (in verse 9) to identify
torah with 'the fear of the Lord' which elsewhere is called 'the
beginning (or chief part) of wisdom' (Prov. 1[7], 9[10]). With this
we may compare the following association of ideas which Dr
Carrington finds in 'the rabbinic school' of the later Judaism:
'The learner coming to school is 'approaching' the fear of the
Lord, the teacher is endued with godlike honour, and 'wisdom'
is itself a grace from God; there is, in short, an element of real
presence'.[2]

It is not surprising, then, that our Lord himself should have
sanctioned this exalted attitude, both towards the written law,

---

[1] For an explanatory illustration showing the meaning of this phrase, see
above, Ch. IV, § vi, last three paragraphs.
[2] *op. cit.*, pp. 9, 10, with the relevant footnotes

and also towards 'the didactic succession' which was its living complement. For the former we have evidence in this saying from the great sermon:

Think not that I came to destroy the law or the prophets:
I came not to destroy, but to fulfil.   (Matt. 5[17]).

For the latter we have in the same gospel the recorded saying: 'The scribes and the Pharisees sit on Moses' seat. All things therefore whatsoever they bid you, these do and observe' (Matt. 23[2,3]). On the other hand the sentence continues: 'but do not ye after their works; for they say and do not'.[1] This corresponds broadly with St Paul's teaching. On the one hand the law is declared to be holy and spiritual (Rom. 7[12,14]). On the other hand its teaching is said to be 'weak through the flesh' (Rom. 8[3]), that is, rendered ineffective through the moral weakness and perversity of human nature.[2] It cannot, therefore, be held to stand on the same footing as the promises of God which never fail (Gal. 3[16 ff]).

The contrast between promise and law, thus introduced, explains in part the lowly position assigned to the Law by St Paul, notwithstanding his high regard for its teaching and his resolute rejection of the idea that the Law is 'against the promises of God' (Gal. 3[21]). Here, again, we must notice the agreement of the apostle with his Lord. Jesus set the law of creation above the Mosaic permission of divorce, the latter being simply a concession to 'the hardness of your hearts' (Mark 10[2 ff]). So St Paul says that the Law 'was added because of transgressions' (Gal. 3[19]). It was a disciplinary expedient by which the divine plan was adapted to the needs of a sinful world. It was, as an institution, temporary and preparatory. It corresponded only to one stage in the education of the human race, a stage of immaturity like adolescence in the individual. The Law was not effective as an instrument of salvation. For although it could show men the path it could not recover to

---

[1] The other synoptic gospels agree in substance with St Matthew. Thus, both St Mark and St Luke tell us that, after healing lepers, Jesus directed them to fulfil the precepts of the Law laid down for such cases (Mark 1[44], Luke 5[14], 17[14]). Again Matt. 15[1–14] is, if anything, more severe than Mark 7[1–13] in denunciation of a corrupt *torah* tradition. Once more, Luke 10[25 ff] agrees with Matt. 5 in first appealing to the Law and then developing its spirit ('Love thy neighbour') in a way which transcends 'the letter'.

[2] A more exact parallel to Matt. 23, however, is to be found in Rom. 2.

them the power of walking along it. It could not undo the catastrophe of sin or quicken the spiritually dead. In Judaism, therefore, men were kept 'shut up' in a state of pupilage no better than slavery until Christ set them free.[1]

This statement does not refer primarily to the fettering effects of Pharisaic legalism. For that aberration was itself symptomatic of an attitude which treated the disciplinary instrument as a self-justifying end. This attitude, in turn, might seem to be the logical consequence of a doctrine identifying the human vehicle with the divine Wisdom which created the world. The problem therefore was not primarily moral but rather cosmological. As such, then, the apostle treats it in accordance with assumptions common to his age. In the thought of the ancients the heavenly bodies were living beings which controlled men's fate in this lower world.[2] In contemporary Judaism these intermediary powers were identified with the angelic hierarchies. From this point of view the angels would also be identified with the cosmic 'elements' as 'elemental spirits'. In the course of his argument St Paul simply calls them 'the elements' (Gal. 4[3,9]). Accepting a current Jewish opinion that the Law was given to Moses through angels (3[19]; cp. Acts 7[53]) he declares that submission to the Law involves subjection to the rule of these subordinate spirits. In calling the latter 'elements' he makes the punning suggestion that such 'elemental' beings (having identity with the simple elements of *the world*) cannot take their disciples beyond the bare elements, that is the ABC, of *religion*. For Christians to submit to the minutiae of the Jewish law would be a return to 'the weak and beggarly elements' of a schoolroom régime which they should have outgrown.[3]

How lowly then was the Law, and how humiliating the status to which Israel was reduced! And what a transformation in the outlook of one who had formerly 'boasted in the law'![4]

[1] Gal. 3[21–26]; 4[1–5]; cp. also 4[21]-5[1], where the apostle adapts to his own theme a current piece of allegorization. See Philo, *De Congressu*, 1-24, etc.

[2] cp. the third note to par. 1 of § iv above

[3] The whole argument is strange to us because, despite Platonism, the ancients knew nothing of the absolute contrast between 'matter' and 'spirit' introduced by Descartes in the seventeenth century.

[4] Rom. 2[23]. In the light of Ch. 7, Rom. 2[17–24] reads like a confession of the writer's own past folly.

But now, see how the argument concludes. If Israel was subjected to servitude there was One who came to share that
servitude: 'God sent forth his Son, made of a woman, made
subject to law, that he might redeem those who were subject
to law, that we might receive the adoption of sons' (Gal. 4^{4,5}).
The humiliation of Israel was, after all, only a prelude to the
greater humiliation of God's Son; yet it was also of one pattern
with that greater humiliation. How perfectly, then, does the
'co-infancy' teaching of St Irenaeus fit in with the arguments
of St Paul![1] Our Lord himself received on his shoulders that
yoke which Israel had first refused and then misused.[2] These
considerations, moreover, will be found to illustrate further our
four conclusions concerning revelation, put forward earlier in
this section, and particularly the unities to which attention
was called under points (3) and (4), with the appended reflexions concerning sin and its consequences.[3]

The true order of human life, to which we referred under
point (3), is inseparable from the larger plan of creation within
which it was originally set. The disruption of the former by sin
involved the disorder of the latter. But further, the method of
restoration must inevitably be accommodated to the gravity of
the total disorder. Thus the 'elementary' discipline of the Law
corresponded to the disorders of 'the elements'. In this respect
all the vehicles or organs of revelation were, as St Paul elsewhere expressed it, 'subjected to the vanity'.[4] This characteristic of a fallen world also illustrates our fourth conclusion concerning revelation and the crowning manifestations of unity to
which it called attention. If, as was there said, the divine
revelation takes on a creaturely character by becoming embodied, then it also follows that 'the vanity' to which 'the
whole creation' was subjected by the Fall must necessarily
enter into the dispensation of recovery throughout its entire
range. We have seen one application of this truth in the lowly
limitations of Israel's servitude to the Law. But at every stage
a single pattern of humiliation was being unfolded. The most
crucial 'moment' in the mystery of 'the vanity' was expressed
by the apostle in his statement to the effect that 'him who knew

---

[1] cp. also the Addit. Note A, par. 4, above
[2] For the former see Hos. 10^{11ff}; for the latter, Matt. 23
[3] above, pp. 210f　　　[4] Rom. 8^{19ff}

215

no sin' God 'made to be sin on our behalf' as the indispensable means whereby 'we might become the righteousness of God in him' (2 Cor. 5[21]). Even so, this is not the whole account of the matter. There still remains to be considered the forward extension of Christ's humiliation, the reproduction of its pattern in his mystical body and in his members.[1]

V

The principle of transformation in its scriptural forms. Israel dies to live in Christ; and Christ as Wisdom lives in Israel's story. As a whole present in its parts, Jesus has identity with the Old Testament types. They in turn are glorified in him and lead to him. This relationship illustrated from the Transfiguration and from the mission of St John Baptist.

In the scriptural theme of redemption we have now traced back the humiliation of the Christ into the story of Israel, at least in respect of its most treasured possession, that is, the Law of Moses. We have next to consider a corresponding 'extension' of our Saviour's exaltation in the same sphere. If Israel's abasement was an inevitable prelude to the mission of the lowly Servant, then there must be a sense in which Israel shares also in the Servant's glory. The fulfilment of the old covenant in the new suggests that somehow the old enters into the new and is thereby transfigured. But what exactly does this imply? The idea of transformation has recurred frequently in the present work. In our first Book (Chapters I-III) it appeared under the guise of *assimilation*, that is, the process by which,

---

[1] It is noteworthy that in Rom. 8[20] 'the subjection' is effected by God himself as a first step in the work of restoration. The reference is to Gen. 3[16-19]. A second step (as Galatians shows) was the corresponding subjection of Israel to the Law. The third step in this series was the subjection of the Son himself to 'the vanity', when by a human birth he became subject to the Law and (for our sakes) to its curse (Gal. 3[13]), making his great act of redress under that lowly condition (Gal. 4[4,5], Rom. 5[18-21], Phil. 2[6-8]). In this filial act of obedience Christ's members, as partakers in his Sonship, are permitted to share (2 Cor. 10[3-5]). Accordingly, it has to be remembered that, emancipated as we are from 'the vanity' of the Law into the liberty of sons (Gal. 3[25-27] *et al.*), we are still subject to the birth-pangs of the new creation, while we await the full fruition of our sonship (Rom. 8[22-30]).

both in Israel and in Christendom, revealed religion has gathered into itself the resources of its cultural environment. Where such a process justifies itself, the organism of revelation is enriched with new treasure without in any degree losing its own proper character or weakening its own distinctive functions. Moreover, the process has a cumulative force which enables the organism to resist the hostile influences threatening its vitality. Thus, by dominating its successive cultural phases this 'living biological phenomenon' acquires the balancing qualities of toughness and elasticity which give to it a time-transcending character.

In every such process of religious assimilation, as in all life, the elements assimilated lose something of their original character, and pass into a new form through the reassociation which has taken place. Examples of such reassociation were given earlier in the present chapter when we were considering the subsumption of ritual factors from the surrounding nature-religions into the historical structure of revealed religion. The original rites died to their earlier associations in order that they might live anew in the higher context of redemptive history. It will be remembered, however, that the process of 'dying to live' occurred more than once in the same ritual factor. The paschal festival of nature-religion received first a Jewish and then a Christian form. This adds something altogether new to the picture drawn in our last paragraph. We remember that there are some natural organisms, the continued existence of which depends, not only upon successful assimilation of external elements, but also, in due time, upon a radical transformation of the organism itself. The change of the caterpillar into the butterfly provides an obvious example of a characteristic feature in the order of nature, which in turn furnishes an analogy to the mysteries of death and resurrection.

The law of 'dying to live' is so persistent in the rhythmic cycle of nature that it has had a prominent place in all natural religion. In the light of recent research we are beginning to see how deeply it enters into the religion of Israel. But its supreme exemplification in the *praeparatio evangelica* lay not so much in developed Jewish beliefs concerning individual destiny as in the prophetic doctrine of Israel's own death and resurrection. Of this we can distinguish two forms, which in turn suggests two different, but complementary, views of the relation in which the Christ stands to the old covenant, and ultimately to the order of creation. The first form of the prophetic doctrine is exemplified in the vision concerning the valley of dry bones (Ezek. 37^{1-14}), where the state of death is followed by a miraculous resurrection to life. The second form of the doctrine is one in which, while humiliation issues in exaltation, the state of humiliation is itself seen to be glorious, so that glory is referred back from the end to all that precedes it. This is exemplified in the Servant song (Isa. 52^{13}–53). Between these two conceptions there is a difference of emphasis. The former interpretation puts the emphasis upon the End in which the divine plan is seen to be vindicated, whereas the latter interpretation fixes attention upon the character of the plan as a whole—a Whole containing within itself its own justification. This requires fuller elaboration.[1]

In the first form of the doctrine the national life has been destroyed by a national apostasy. Yet Israel is raised from the dead by a creative act of God. In the context, and elsewhere, it is made plain that judgement, repentance, and cleansing from sin are indispensable preliminaries to restoration. The predestined glories of the covenant thus depend upon a 'return' to God which is itself a work of God. In the second mode of presenting the truth Israel's destiny is fulfilled in expiatory sacrifice, in such wise that glory is found in reproach, life in death, riches in poverty, a marvellous work of God in an object of the world's contempt. Common to both these conceptions is also another factor. The exaltation of Israel has for its counterpart a corresponding transformation of Israel's environment in the world of nature. This is in accordance with the scriptural view that nature and history fall within one plan of creation, so that the sin of man has cosmic consequences and, conversely, the redemption of man carries with it a restoration of harmony to the universe.[2] There is, however, once more a distinction to

---

[1] The two interpretations are not sharply separated. They are like two paths which often cross or two shades of colour which easily blend into one another.

[2] cp. above, § ii, par. 3 with note, and p. 211, conclusion (3). See also H. Wheeler Robinson, *Inspiration and Revelation in the Old Testament*, pp. 28-33, for a valuable discussion of this topic.

be observed here between the two types of doctrine which we are considering. In the former type transformation belongs to the future; the restoration of the earthly paradise will take place in an Age to Come. In the latter type the transformation is concurrent with the present fulfilment of Israel's mission. The miracles of the original exodus from Egypt are repeated in a literal 'return' to Zion.

How then will these two moods of prophecy bear upon the truth that Israel came to fulfilment in the Christ? From the human standpoint Israel's story was a failure apart from the good news of Jesus who fulfilled the Servant's mission.[1] But then from the same standpoint that mission of good news was itself a failure apart from the resurrection on the third day. For the writers of the New Testament, however, Jesus *is* the true Israel, so that Israel died in him upon the Cross and rose again in a new form when Jesus rose from the tomb.[2] If then Israel died and rose again in Christ, it follows that everything characterizing Israel's covenant with God underwent a like transformation. In that 'everything' would be included 'the oracles of God', that is the scriptures of the Old Testament with which Israel was 'entrusted' (Rom. 3[2]). Thus the *torah* passed into the glory of the Christ as part of the treasure which he established for and in himself by the victory of his death and resurrection. But again, Jesus is the Servant of the Lord in whose mission the true *torah*-wisdom is enacted so that 'the many' are thereby justified (Isa. 53[11]). The fulfilment in him of the true way of life carries with it not only a transformation of Israel but also a restoration of creation's order and harmony. In short, Israel is fulfilled in the Christ because he is the divine

---

[1] In Luke 4[17–21] Jesus reads aloud in a synagogue the opening words of Isa. 61, a passage in which a prophet proclaims himself to be, not only a Spirit-anointed herald of good news, but also (61[3 ff]) *the actual inaugurator of a new age*. Jesus, newly anointed with the Spirit (Luke 3[22]), identifies himself and his mission with this oracle, which for the first Christians would coalesce with the 'Servant' oracles in the same book (Isa. 40*ff*) to form one picture. It would probably also be connected with the promise in Deut. 18[15 ff], as in Acts 3[13–23]; cp. Acts 7[37], John 1[21–23].

[2] For fuller details I must refer to what I have written elsewhere. The argument is parallel to that concerning the old Adam, for which see above, Ch. V, § v, par. 5, with the note on inclusion of Adam in Christ—The new Adam includes the new Israel.

Wisdom in and through which the world was originally created.[1]

This doctrine of fulfilment implies that Christ is the End, that is the goal of Israel's history, because he is the Beginning by virtue of his identity with Wisdom.[2] The connexion between end and beginning is clearly taught by St Paul (for example, in Col. 1[15θ]); and it carries with it an implication of deity. For it corresponds to a prophetic title of Jahveh (Isa. 41[4], 43[10], 44[6]). The implication is made fully explicit in the Revelation of St John, where the divine title, 'Alpha and Omega, the first and the last, the beginning and the end' is ascribed equally to God and to the Lamb (1[8,17], 21[6], 22[13]). The identification of our Lord with Wisdom has, moreover, another important aspect. Wisdom, by virtue of her creative functions, is present everywhere in the works of God. She fills the world; but Israel is her special care. For the works of God in redemptive history fall within the divine plan of creation.[3] So in the *Wisdom of Solomon* this personified figure is present as Israel's guard and guide throughout the desert wanderings. It follows that the doctrine of 'Israel fulfilled in Christ' is part of a wider thesis. Christ as Wisdom was personally present throughout Israel's history.

When, therefore, St Paul teaches that Christ was the rock which provided water for the people in the wilderness, he is simply giving a Christian application to current Jewish teaching. According to the Hebrew idiom of identification Wisdom is 'extended' in the rock, as Moses in his rod or Elisha in his staff. Similarly the water from the rock is water of wisdom ('spiritual drink').[4] In this way of speaking Christ is seen to

[1] This 'Wisdom Christology' is prominent in 1 Corinthians and in Colossians. It is implicit also in the 'fulfilment' thesis (e.g.) of Rom. 10[4θ]. For the use there made of Deut. 30[11-18] can be illustrated from Baruch 3[24θ], a typical exposition of the Wisdom-*torah* doctrine, of which more will be said later.

[2] In Prov. 8[22] Wisdom is declared to be 'the beginning' of God's ways in creation. (RV margin correctly renders both the Hebrew and LXX).

[3] Wisd. 8[1], 10. For the author of this book the nature-miracles which assisted Israel, at the Exodus and after, are simply an indication that there is in 'Wisdom' a single providence of God controlling both the order of nature and the course of history, so that all creation co-operates with the divine acts of historical redemption.

[4] 1 Cor. 10[4], and cp. above, Ch. V, § v, par. 2

be not only the goal of all revelation, but actually its substance. He takes up the chosen people and its scriptures into himself because he is the Whole of which they are parts. In this divinely composed historical drama Jesus is not simply the principal actor; he is the whole action in which each of the actors in turn plays his part. So St Paul asserts that the scripture 'preached the gospel beforehand to Abraham'; and he finds in Jesus the promised seed of whom Isaac was only a type.[1] Observe, however, that this degradation of Isaac into a mere type of the true Seed gives to Abraham's son a more glorious significance than he could ever have in Judaism. Once more we see that in the single pattern of scripture humiliation in the Lord's service *is* glorification.[2] The Old Testament and its contents are, in the light of their fulfilment, seen in new and more radiant colours. In the view of the apostolic writers the colours were always there; but they could appear in their true grandeur only when the Light of the world had manifested them within the aura of his own incarnate glory.

It is this conception which clearly dominates the synoptic account of our Lord's transfiguration. Moses and Elijah are seen in the light which surrounds the figure of Jesus. According to St Luke (9^{31}) they 'appeared in glory'.[3] That is to say, these

---

[1] Gal. $3^{8,16}$, Rom. $4^{17}\theta$

[2] This is one application of our Lord's saying: 'Whosoever humbleth himself shall be exalted' (Matt. 23^{12}, Luke 14^{11}). The identification of types with their counterparts under the new covenant is further elaborated in Gal. 4^{21-31}.

[3] There is here a verbal echo of Exod. 24^{11}, where in LXX the same verb is used. In the Hebrew text of Exod. $24^{10,11}$ it is twice stated that Moses and his companions 'saw God'. LXX, however, reads as follows: 'They saw the place where God stood', under whose feet was 'a work of bright sapphire' like the firmament of heaven in form and clarity. Again, for the second reference to 'seeing God' LXX substitutes: 'they appeared in the place of God'. For St Luke Jesus, transfigured in his mortal flesh, is the bright Place where God has taken up his stand on earth. For this mystical use of 'place' see above, Ch. VI, § iv, pars. 3 *ff* and notes. But the 'place' of deity, thus designated, is extended so that its radiance includes the representatives of the Law and the Prophets. The 'glory' in which Moses and Elijah 'appeared' in the gospel story is the glory of 'the place' in which Moses had once 'appeared' on Mt. Sinai. Exod. 24^{10} had already been thus expounded by Philo in his identification of the mystic Place with the Logos (*De Confus.* 95, 96; *De Somn.* I, 62). See also below, Ch. VIII, § iii, par. 5 (*site* of creation) and note. In the historical emphasis of his 'topology' (as we may

two typical representatives of the old covenant seemed to the three apostolic spectators to be included in the glory which streamed from the central figure. To this conception the same evangelist adds a corresponding image in his account of the Emmaus walk when the risen Lord appeared to two disciples and 'beginning from Moses and from all the prophets he interpreted to them in all the scriptures the things concerning himself'. Upon this experience their own comment is given in these words: 'he opened to us the scriptures'.[1] Returning to the transfiguration-scene, we notice that whereas two evangelists speak of 'Moses and Elijah' St Mark reverses the natural order and speaks of 'Elijah with Moses'. This should be connected with the question and answer during the descent from the mountain.[2] 'Elijah came first and restores all things' *could* mean simply that the prophecy of Malachi (4^5) has been fulfilled in the person of John the Baptist, in whose mission the restoration of all things begins.[3]

On the other hand, the emphasis of our Lord's words in Mark 9^{13} falls upon the parallel between the martyrdom of the Baptist and the approaching passion of the Son of man (cp. Mark 6^{14-16} and note 2 on this page). The last of the prophets fulfils the scriptural pattern of glory through humiliation. In so doing he sums up law and prophecy in his own person, showing

call it) St Luke mediates fittingly between Philo and St John in the total economy of revelation.

[1] Luke $24^{27,32}$; cp. the repetition of the same phrase in 24^{45} where, however, it is 'the mind' which is 'opened'. The colours were always there; but Jesus alone could reveal them.

[2] Mark 9^4 with 9^{11-13}, cp. Mal. 4^{4-6} (LXX), where the order has been reversed by the translators, so that 'Moses' gets the final word from this pre-eminently cultic prophet! For St Mark, however, the reversed order signifies not the finality of Moses but the primacy of the new Elijah. Moreover, than John 'there hath not arisen a greater' (Matt. 11^{11}: ἐγήγερται). Does not Matthew's use of this expression reflect the typology of Mark 6^{14-16}, where John is made to prefigure the death and resurrection of Jesus (ἐγήγερται ... ἠγέρθη)? Matthew has the second of these two words in 14^2 (=Mark 6^{16}).

[3] If, however, Lake and Cadbury are right in their contention that the verb here rendered 'restore' (with its corresponding noun in Acts 3^{21}) refers to 'establishment' of prophecy, our Lord's words in Mark 9^{12} would mean that all OT scripture comes to fulfilment or completion with the mission of the Baptist. See *The Beginnings of Christianity I*, Vol. IV, p. 38, and my comment in JTS, Vol. XLVI, No. 181-2, p. 55.

their substance to be a foreshadowing of the Christ. He 'completes' the divine plan by ushering in the 'restoration'; and this he does by enacting in his own life's blood the Servant's mission. On this view John, as *Elias redivivus*, embodies the Law in its true character, exhibiting its ancillary function in relation to the Christ. It was precisely this aspect, moreover, which St Paul emphasized in his picture of the Law as a nursery-slave leading young Israel along the road towards the school of the promised Redeemer (Gal. $3^{23\,\textit{ff}}$; cp. 4^3). St John seems to be hinting at the same truth in his account of the Baptist's witness. This appears first in the scenes at the place of baptism (John 1^{19-39}). Here John is (1) the voice heralding the good news of divine promises to be fulfilled (Isa. 40), (2) the witness who saw the fulfilment enacted in the descent of the Spirit upon the Son of God, (3) the 'cultic prophet' pointing to the sacrificial Lamb, (4) the nursery tutor handing over his tender charges to the true Servant that they may learn to take their part in the Servant's Mission.[1]

In a later scene the farewell lesson of the old covenant is repeated (3^{27-30}), when the last genuine representative of old Israel's *torah* assigns to himself the part of the bridegroom's friend who acquiesces joyfully in his own 'decrease'. As the stars wane before the sun, so the old order pales before the new.[2] This quenching of all created lights, however, is not the end. For the Law and its ministries belong to the Israel which died and rose again in Christ. Moses and the prophets live again in the new Israel where their testimony is joyfully received; for, as Jesus is reported to have said of the former, 'he wrote of me' (John 5^{46}). This reference to Moses follows a final Johannine reference to the new Elijah,[3] the whole section in Chapter 5 corresponding to an earlier treatment of the same theme in the Prologue (1^{1-18}). In the Johannine writings Jesus,

---

[1] For 'cultic prophet' see above, p. 196, note 2

[2] This imagery is highly relevant to the Elijah prophecy of Malachi 4. For here Elijah heralds the day of the Lord when 'unto you that fear my name shall the sun of righteousness arise'. The 'sunrise', moreover, is to bring healing (cp. Isa. 53^5). So the reference to John as 'the lamp which burneth and shineth' (John 5^{35}) follows upon a typical narrative of healing (5^{1-16}), the connexion of Ἰησοῦς with ἴασις being a continual undertone of healing miracles in NT.

[3] see the last note

as the Lamb of God, is the uncreated Light of the world who, in mortal form, has inaugurated the new creation with the life-giving flame of his own sacrificial fire. In the prologue, which presupposes the mystery of the Transfiguration, the fourth evangelist agrees with St Mark in giving to 'a man sent from God whose name was John' the priority over Moses ($1^{6,17}$). Here, as in 5^{35}, 'John' is a created lamp, shining in the firmament of the new creation (Gen. 1^{14f}), but with a glory wholly reflected from 'the true Light which lighteneth every man' (1^{6-9}). In this aspect of the prologue we are shown the vehicle of special revelation as a torch directed towards the incarnate source and focus of all revelation. But John is not only a lamp. He is also a 'voice'; and through his mouth we hear the genuine message of Israel, old and new. This is given in the concluding verses of the prologue (1^{15-18}): Jesus as Israel's End has become her new Beginning. For he always was her source, being in himself the whole fountain of 'grace and truth' from which her every part was filled with heavenly treasure. So the organism of revelation can be defined in its wholeness and in its unity; it is the embodied response of the Son, in whom alone the Father stands revealed.[1]

[1] The difficulty of regarding verses 16-18 as an utterance of the Baptist disappears if John is the 'Voice' heralding the Lamb (1^{23}). For his mystical identification with the true Israel qualifies him (in the mind of the evangelist) to speak for the Bride concerning the Bridegroom in the wholeness of the one organism (cp. 3^{31-36}).

CHAPTER VIII

THE EXTENDED IMAGE

i

The *movement* of revelation through Israel to Christ and the Church involves personal embodiments. The *proportions of* revelation are re-adjusted in the primacy of the prophetic forerunner over Moses, and of the Word over *torah*-wisdom. The Word seeks embodiment; yet although identified with its several instruments, it passes beyond them to its Christological goal.

In the preceding chapter the conception of a single organism of revelation with its interpenetrating forms was further developed, the outline sketch derived from the teaching of St Irenaeus being filled in from biblical sources. Our object, however, was not solely to fill in the outlines, but perhaps even more to suggest the process of development through which the living structure of revealed religion has passed in the course of redemptive history. The significance of process is, indeed, integral to the doctrine of revelation as here set forth. For, so soon as it is recognized that the content of revealed truth is inseparable from the form in which it has been given, it follows inevitably that the meaning of the divine disclosure can be apprehended only in the historical unfolding of that form. Here, once more, we move along lines laid down by St Irenaeus, for whom the characteristics of the divine image in man are made manifest through the manner in which man is moulded to the image. This emphasis upon process, moreover, is in line with the whole tendency of modern biblical studies, such as *Formgeschichte*, with their concentration upon 'setting in life' (*Sitz im Leben*). That tendency, again, was illustrated at two points in the last chapter. I refer first to the light thrown by anthropology upon the development of Israelite religion in the transformation of nature-cults, and secondly, at the other end of the story, to the bearing of Jewish 'background' upon the New Testament in its record of Judaism transformed in Christ.

The way is thus opened for a fuller consideration of all that is involved in that 'moving picture' of cosmic process which St Irenaeus drew out from the scriptural theme of the divine image. It is a story in picture-form, which shows the image imprinted upon man, only to be partially effaced by the Fall; then restored again in Christ to its full perfection, and eventually extended in him throughout the entire universe of redeemed creation. This topic will occupy the remainder of the present volume; and as we approach it we shall do well to recall what was said earlier about three fundamental stages of revelation and their close interconnexion.[1] The intervening chapters, from the introduction of St Irenaeus onwards, will have made clear how deep that interconnexion is. Israel, the Christ, and the Christian church are so intermingled[2] that our understanding concerning the relations between any two of these mysterious factors depends upon the degree of insight which we can attain in regard to the corresponding connexions of each or both with the remaining factor. We shall be able to see clearly the character and functions of the Christian church as bearer and steward of God's Word just so far as we are able to envisage accurately the multiple relationship of the church which arises from the interweaving of those three strands in the single garment of revelation.

Here it must be laid down as axiomatic that the mission and functions of the Christian church are as vital to an adequate doctrine of revelation as either the preparation of Israel for the Christ or even the gospel story itself. This must be so, not simply because the church through identity with Israel in Christ enters into the substance of revealed religion; but also because without the embodiment of our Saviour in Christendom he must ever remain hidden from the world. Revelation is not simply a deposit of truth laid up in scripture. It is in essence the activity of God's Word. Indeed, it *is* the creative Word of God himself in his characteristic activity, whereby, in one and the same movement of creativity, he brings into

[1] Ch. II, § ii, last two paragraphs
[2] This word makes one more attempt to diagnose 'interpenetration'. Characteristically Hebrew modes of thought mix themselves with the words of our Lord and shape the forms in which his life in the church is interpreted, so that all the 'three fundament stages' occupy the same ground.

existence an ordered *cosmos* and also illuminates that given order with his own rays of uncreated light that thus it may serve as a mirror of deity. Revelation is the manifestation of the Word of God in his living embodiment in human history. The embodiment never ceases to be living, and therefore revelation can never be simply a deposit of past events. Moreover, even though accessible to the present in the record of scripture, it would, in that form, still remain a deposit of past events unless the written record were interpreted in a human embodiment. Without that present embodiment there would be no present contact with the Word incarnate. The further elucidation of this theme can best be effected by a return to the Johannine prologue and to those reflexions upon it with which the last chapter ended.

In the gospels the new Elijah takes precedence over Moses, because the Baptist is understood to be the personal embodiment of Israel as precursor of the Christ.[1] This corresponds to a constantly recurring factor of Hebrew prophecy. Hosea, Isaiah, Jeremiah, Ezekiel—each in turn identifies himself and the incidents of his personal or domestic life with this or that feature of Israel's contemporary history. His personal life takes on a symbolic character representative of Israel, while still maintaining its original character as his personal life. In each case the prophetic record oscillates to and fro between the two aspects which are found in a single sequence of events, or alternatively between the two sets of events which are mysteriously blended in the prophetic consciousness.[2] It may well be

[1] For St Mark and St Matthew see above, p. 222, with note 2. St Luke gives more space to the Baptist and to his relationship with our Lord than any other gospel. He traces the parallelism of life back to the beginning (Ch. 1); and includes a pre-natal greeting of the new Israel by the old (1^{39-45}; cp. also the significant witness of priesthood to prophecy in 1^{76-79}). He affirms that there is 'none greater' (7^{28}), and repeats the 'resurrection' saying of Mark 6^{16} in a variant form ($9^{7,8}$). On the mount, however, he retains the historical order (9^{30}) and omits the subsequent reference to the Baptist (Mark 9^{9-13}); for there he is about to present the actual life-stories of Moses and Elias as complementary types, equally fulfilled in Christ ($9^{51}\theta$). For this see further my JTS article already mentioned, and Dr Farrer's essay in *The Apostolic Ministry*.

[2] see especially Hos. 1-3, Isa. 7^3, $8^{1-4,18}$, Jer. $16^1\theta$, 32, Ezek. $24^{15}\theta$; and for the connexion with the prologue of St John see the end of Ch. VII above with the concluding note.

that the picture of the suffering Servant (Isa. 50[5f], 53) is best understood from the same angle, the prophet in that instance being anonymous. With this group of phenomena should be connected other incidents in the prophetical writings, closely similar in their general character, but introducing a further notion of far-reaching significance. In this second group of incidents[1] the actions of the prophet embody, not simply contemporary history as such, but, in particular, a word of the Lord determining the course of that history. The Word of God is thus identified with the prophet's actions with creative effects for good or ill. Yet the Word also *goes beyond* the prophet, since no mortal man can adequately contain such an 'extension' of deity.[2] Here is the point at which we can begin to see the relevance of the Baptist to the prologue of St John's gospel.

For on this side a primary presupposition of the prologue is the same as that which we find expressed in the theological preface to the Epistle to the Hebrews, where the completeness and simultaneity of God's utterance in his Son is contrasted with its diversity and multiplicity in the prophets. Once more, the fulness of grace and truth in the incarnate Word (John I[14,16]) corresponds precisely to the Pauline conception of the Christ as the One in whom the *pleroma* of the godhead dwells (Col. I[19]). Moreover, each of these great statements associates the finality of the revelation in Christ with his cosmic functions in creation. Yet, whereas both divine sonship and cosmic activity are central for all three writers, the special characteristic of the prologue is its definite adoption of the Logos-Christology in preference to the earlier, Pauline dependence upon Jewish wisdom teachings. The relevance of this familiar theme to our present argument can now be briefly indicated. Whilst the creative functions of the Son could be stated in terms either of Word or of Wisdom, the former could more easily be associated with the prophetical form of revelation, whereas the latter had in later Judaism become identified with the Mosaic Law. The change-over from Wisdom to Word served in this respect a purpose which had ramifications wider than anything so far suggested. To some of these attention must now be directed.

---

[1] Typical examples are to be found in Isa. 20, Jer. 13[1-11], Ezek. 4.
[2] cp. Wheeler Robinson, *Inspiration and Revelation*, etc., pp. 170[f]

In our present line of thought it is assumed that the Johannine preference for Word over Wisdom is connected with the *proportions* of revelation.[1] Rabbinical Judaism affirmed that righteousness consisted in legal obedience to the precepts of the Law in their literal exactitude;[2] and the whole vast development of the oral law was concerned to define the range of such legal obedience with meticulous precision. In this way the Hebrew conception of righteousness was narrowed. Originally it included lovingkindness (or mercy) and faithfulness, represented in John 1[17] by 'grace and truth'.[3] Stripped of these qualities righteousness was inevitably reduced to formalism. Now in the prophetical demand for righteousness amongst men there is indicated a way of response to revelation; and this, in turn, seems to imply or involve a certain conformity with the divine character. That too was originally the Hebrew conception of wisdom.[4] For a son learns from his father a way of life exemplified in character. So the father-son relationship, in which the father (or teacher) represents God to the son (or disciple) implies a filial dependence upon God mediated through a human channel. This corresponds to the Johannine teaching that we become children of God through entrusting ourselves to the beloved Son who is the Word incarnate, and who in his sole-begottenness is the adequate exponent of the Father (John 1[12–18]). By identifying wisdom with pharisaic observance, however, the Rabbis had reduced divine revelation to the dimensions of their own casuistical cleverness. Thus it no longer displayed that quality of transcendent otherness which calls for man's whole allegiance, yet which, without weakening of awful majesty, becomes intimate with the humble (Isa. 57[15]).

[1] This is not to deny other considerations, such as the suitability of a masculine noun and the fashions of contemporary thought. For the latter see W. L. Knox, *St Paul and the Church of the Gentiles*, p. 114, note 4.

[2] This was a one-sided development of a traditional standpoint. The latter is accurately preserved by St Luke in his description of St John Baptist's parents, whom he evidently regards as an example of contemporary Jewish piety when seen at its best (Luke 1[6]).

[3] On this point cp. C. H. Dodd, *The Bible and the Greeks*, pp. 42 *ff*, and the relevant articles in G. Kittel's *Wörterbuch zum neuen Testament*, Vol. II, pp. 176 *ff*.

[4] cp. above, Ch. VII, § iii, pars. 7 and 8, concerning the teaching of Proverbs and its connexion with Ps. 82. Wisd. 6[1–21] reads like a commentary upon this psalm.

Nevertheless, in turning from Wisdom to the Word St John does not mean to depreciate the true wisdom, nor the proper functions of that *torah* with which wisdom had become identified. As we have already noted, he records as a word of Jesus the saying concerning Moses that 'he wrote of me' (5⁴⁶); and in the prologue he follows a model set up in the sapiential books, only taking care to transfer to the Logos descriptive phraseology previously applied to Wisdom.[1] This, however, would seem to imply that the true *torah*-wisdom is to be found in him who is the subject of the whole prologue, that is the Logos. From the beginning the qualities of wisdom were to be found in the preparatory ministries of the Word, in the work of creation and in the story of Israel. Now, at length, they are manifested in the Word incarnate, known in history as Jesus the Christ. The introduction of the Baptist, however, at verse 6 is a definite indication that the evangelist associates the Logos-theme with prophecy. Here, as in the other gospels, the prominence of 'John' signifies that the revival of prophecy in his person was itself a judgement upon contemporary Judaism and its rabbinical wisdom, involving a return from the self-sufficiency of human opinion to the authority of revelation.

In the authentic tradition Moses, the human inaugurator of both the theocracy and its cultus, was himself regarded as a prophet and as a prototype in this respect for the future course of revelation (Deut. 18¹⁵⁻¹⁸).[2] At this point, then, we may naturally ask, what is the typical relationship between revelation and prophecy? To this question there is the suggestion of an answer in the 'before and after' language of John 1¹⁵ taken in conjunction with John's own self-designation (1²³) in terms of a 'voice' through which the word sounds forth.[3] The word

[1] The model appears first in Prov. 8²²ᵬ which is broadly parallel to Gen. 1. Thence it is reproduced in Ecclus. 1, as a prologue to that work. The evangelist follows the model closely, except that he applies to the Logos (*a*) hypostatic pre-existence and (*b*) the functions of creative deity, where, in the model, *sophia* (*ḥokmah*) could be understood to be simply a created agent of the Creator-God; e.g. Ecclus. 1⁴,⁹, following Prov. 8²² (LXX). On Prov. 8²²ᵬ see further Addit. Note B.

[2] A reference to this passage is significantly introduced by the evangelist with the words: 'Art thou Elias? Art thou the prophet?' (1²¹) immediately before the new Elias points to the Servant-Lamb in whom the promise recorded in Deuteronomy was finally implemented.

[3] On these two texts cp. above, the final par. of Ch. VII with note

of the Lord comes forth out of the mouth of the Most High
and enters the mouth of the prophet with creative effect. The
word so uttered carries with it a divine guarantee that 'it shall
not return unto me void, but it shall accomplish that which I
please, and it shall prosper in the thing whereto I sent it'.
Thus launched from the prophet's mouth it passes beyond its
temporary vehicle, and continuing in its course (like the stone
from David's sling) it achieves with unfailing certainty its appointed end.[1] This certainty of fulfilment has its parallel in the
unchanging routine of nature—rain from heaven, the fruitful-
ness of earth, seed and harvest, bearing their corroborative
witness (Isa. 55^{10,11}).

ii

**The proportions of revelation: diverse types, each with its
own appointed function, combine and co-operate according to
measure in an organic unity. Wherever a functional unit preserves
its due proportion, there the Whole is represented in that particular respect. A single pattern of this functional unity is manifested in creation, scripture, and the body of Christ.**

In the last section it was suggested that the Johannine preference for the Logos-Christology had to do with the proportions
of revelation; and this, again, was connected with the restoration of the prophetic word in the person of the Baptist. Thus,
the association of 'John' with the Logos (1$^{6-9}$) is not to be taken
as meaning that prophecy is the only, or even *necessarily* the
pre-eminent, channel of revelation, or again that the Logos
should be thought of exclusively, or even primarily, in terms of
the *prophetic* word. For if the evangelist had intended this he
would surely not have modelled his prologue on the poem of
creation in language associated with Wisdom; nor would he
have adopted a key-word which his Greek readers would certainly associate with 'reason'. Actually, the conception of
Logos creating a *cosmos*, that is, an ordered world (1^{10}), could

[1] Every prophetic word was a partial embodiment of the hypostatic
Word. Its full significance, therefore, became manifest only when its
characteristic 'thinghood' came to fruition in the *person* of the incarnate
Word.

with no great difficulty be common ground to Jew and Greek,[1] and that because the Hebrew way of thinking had already laid suitable foundations. An order of creation in which all things co-operate harmoniously is a familiar idea in the Old Testament, an idea which was steadily emphasized, first by the prophets and then by the sages of Israel.[2]

St Paul's use of the organic idea in unfolding his conception of the church as Christ's body further illustrates our present thesis. Moreover, the idea of proportion (*analogia*) comes to verbal expression in one of his leading expositions of that doctrine. In Romans 12[6] he tells his readers that one who has the gift of prophecy should exercise that gift 'according to the proportion of the faith'. The connexion of thought is as follows: Gifts are bestowed for the edification of the whole church, not for the satisfaction of the individual's natural propensity to self-expression. The gift, therefore, should be exercised by each one according to the divinely apportioned 'measure of faith' (12[3]) which each has received. It seems to be implied here that, as each tribe and family of Israel received its appointed 'portion' (*meris*) in the Holy Land,[3] so each member of the new Israel receives a 'portion' of faith. A Christian does not receive individually an unlimited endowment of graces. For grace is given according to need; and the supreme need is that each one should fulfil his appointed function in the Body. Only so can he enter into the 'wholeness' wherein 'salvation' consists.[4] He receives, therefore, that 'measure of faith' which equips him for this function. Again, it follows that this 'measure' is not to be determined by the individual's intensity of feeling or of con-

[1] For the evangelist *Logos* is logical as well as creative; and that which *Logos* creates is a *cosmos* ordered to an end. He would surely regard the representative of prophecy as a witness to this truth; and the testimony would be such as only Judaism could give. See below, § iv. of this Chapter.

[2] Among a wealth of passages which could be cited from the former compare the striking sequence in Hos. 2[21,22], quoted by Wheeler Robinson, *op. cit.*, p. 13. Here 'Jezreel' receives an 'answer' from Jahveh through a chain of creaturely co-operation. The 'answer' of the elements to their Creator is interpreted in Zech. 8[12], as it is dramatized in Isa. 48[13] and in later writers (Ecclus. 43[10], Judith 9[6], Bar. 3[35]).

[3] Josh. 14[1-5] (LXX), where *kleros*, with *meris* and its verb, appears among the terms used. The verb is employed by St Paul in Rom. 12[3], and the two nouns together in Col. 1[12].

[4] cp. above, Ch. III, § ii, pars. 2 and 3

viction; for that might easily override the interests of mutual edification. Faith, in a member of Christ, bears a 'proportion' to the common life of the Body, being itself a constituent of 'the faith' which is common to all. He who preserves 'the proportion of the faith' will make his own particular contribution, as believer, to the treasure of corporate faith, in which all share, and by virtue of which the church is enabled to fulfil her bridal vocation in fidelity to her Lord.

But further, he who preserves 'the proportion of the faith' in this sense will, as an individual, be exemplifying the true life of the church in respect of its structure. He will, like the blind man in St John's Gospel, be showing 'the whole from the part'.[1] Thus he will bear a representative character, as one who *in that particular respect* stands for the whole. He will, to a limited yet real extent, be a microcosm of the new *cosmos* which Christ as Logos has brought into being.[2] He will, indeed, exhibit only one facet of the multiform beauty which adorns the city of God. Yet in so doing he will truly represent the law of functional unity which characterizes the one Body, the rule whereby the parts are completed in the Whole, the many justified in the One. Here we may recall what was said in Chapter VI concerning the rôle of Adam as a microcosm of creation's order. In our analysis of Genesis 2 it was suggested that this rôle was fulfilled in Christ, and that the recapitulation doctrine, both in the New Testament and in St Irenaeus, was to be understood in that light. Moreover, when we examined more fully the implications of the doctrine thus envisaged it became evident that recapitulation was to be understood in an inclusive sense. That is to say, the new Adam's function as microcosm extended to all his members. The scriptural way of setting forth this truth is to be found in those texts which refer to the reproduction of the divine image. As Adam begat a son in his own image, so the image restored in the new Adam is reproduced in his members who are the children of his bride, the new Eve.

The ascription, therefore, of a representative character to each member of the Christ, in the sense outlined above, can

[1] cp. above, Ch. VI, § iv, penultimate par, with the long note on the phrase quoted in the text

[2] For this use of 'microcosm' see above, Ch. VI, § i, last par. with notes, and (for what follows) § ii, par. 5 and the whole of § v in the same chapter.

be seen to agree perfectly with an interpretation of scripture already reached under the guidance of St Irenaeus. It is clear, then, that the doctrine of 'the extended image', as thus understood, is capable of still further development so soon as we begin to explore its bearing upon the life of the church. Such an inquiry would open up new vistas, and that in two directions. For, first, it would be concerned both with the process of new creation in Christendom and with the character of the structure so created. Since, however, both the process and the structure in question belong to the organism of revelation, such an inquiry would, in the second place, tend to throw light upon the character of revelation and upon the modes of its operation. This also would be a following in the tracks of St Irenaeus. For, as we have seen, his doctrine of the extended image is nothing else than the form in which he understands the facts of revelation as actually given.[1]

Let us now resume the argument at the point where we introduced from St Paul a picture of organic 'proportion' in the new creation. This was intended to serve as an illustration of the wider biblical conception of creation as an *order* in which the various elements co-operate harmoniously to fulfil the purpose of the Creator. The collaboration of these cosmic elements is reproduced, so to speak, in the higher harmonies of that mystical body in which creation comes to fulfilment. Thus proportion, harmony, and collaboration are complementary aspects of that divinely planned order which is recapitulated in Christ. In the organism of revelation, however, creation, scripture and the church form one interpenetrating whole. The like qualities of proportion and co-operation will, therefore, be looked for in scripture also, as in the other organs of revelation. This is, in fact, just what St Irenaeus was saying when he taught that the Hebrew prophets were members of Christ's body. For he saw in the unity and order of prophetic revelation, as fulfilled in Christ, precisely those characteristics which St Paul indicated in his language about 'the proportion of the faith'. That language was actually applied to *Christian* prophets. The teaching of St Irenaeus may, therefore, have been influenced by this very passage in Romans, or at least by the mention of prophets in the various descriptions of Christ's body. Be that as it may,

[1] see above, in Ch. VI, § iii, par. 1 and § v, par. 1

his diagnosis is profoundly apt. For what is said concerning prophecy in the New Testament corresponds accurately to the parallel activity under the old covenant.

No single prophet could foreshadow more than was implicit in his own function and vocation as an individual member of the one organism. Yet through faithful fulfilment of his appointed part each prophet became representative of the movement and structure which characterized revelation as a whole. Each became a constituent element in that image which was already being moulded by the hands of God until at length it received its crowning unity and perfection in the Christ. At this point it will be relevant to recall another feature of the Pauline analogy which corresponds to the complexity of creation's ordered harmony, and which may therefore be expected to throw light upon the proportions of revelation in scripture. 'The proportion of the faith', to which the many are adjusted in the unity of the whole, is a norm or standard, not only in respect of one gift (or *charisma*), but in respect of all such gifts. Further, this rule will apply, not only as between all persons similarly endowed, but also as between all the types of function which correspond to the various kinds of gifts. So also in nature we see co-operation, not only between the members of one particular species, but also between different levels of being. Such are the forms of collaboration which we may observe as between the soil and the elements of wind and weather on one side, and again the soil and a variety of living organisms, on the other side, from lowly plants and worms up to trees, cattle and men, the last of the series being uniquely endowed to promote the co-operative unity of the whole *cosmos*, and, again, to build upon that creaturely kingdom the higher commonwealth of God's sons and daughters.

The *proportions* of revelation in scripture, therefore, will correspond to the general pattern which we have found both in the old creation and in the new. The unity of parts and of forms will be a unity not of one type but of many. It will not, for example, be a unity solely of prophets agreeing in consentient witness to foreshadow the Christ along one line of revelation; it will be a unity, rather of prophets with priests, of poets with lawgivers, of devotees with chroniclers, of wise-men with story-tellers, and of all these again with rabbis, seers, and philosophers, and with plain men of action. Nor is that all. In the balance of the whole there is another type of co-operation, of which a good deal has been said in the present volume, upon which also the proportions of revealed truth greatly depend. I refer to the diversity of cultural levels, fashions, achievements and interests, as between one age or country and another. Revelation is given in process. Ordered unity is manifested not only in space but also in time; and the process is one of slow movement through the centuries. The fulness of truth requires a broad platform of time and space upon which it may be deployed in all its varied significance. Moreover, whereas the New Testament itself may seem to be an exception to this law, yet it is so only in the sense that its relatively restricted span of time and space lies at the centre of a much vaster circle of revelation, that wider encompassing range being necessary to the accurate explication of the central mystery.[1]

iii

The unity of the single plan of creation and redemption as set forth in the prologue of St John's Gospel. Here there is an identification of the body-bride of Christ with the cosmic bride of the Creator-Word through a symbolic re-interpretation of Gen. 1-3. Three strands are woven into one pattern: (a) Adam and Eve; (b) Christ and the church; (c) the Logos and the *cosmos*.

The preceding argument may be epitomized by saying that there is a law of divine economy, whereby the proportions of truth are manifested through corresponding proportions of response in the organism of revelation. These latter are to be conceived in terms of co-operation, several types of co-operation being actively present in that totality of response which is gathered up into the beloved Son, to be by him presented to the Father. The general law of co-operation is that which is exhibited in the order of creation. This, again, takes a more specific form on the human level; and its norm is set forth in the three main stages of redemptive history which correspond

[1] This consideration serves to emphasize the immense importance of studies in historical theology, and that too in the closest possible connexion with allied historical researches. See also the concluding paragraph of Ch. I, above.

respectively to Israel, the Christ, and the church. Not only does this proportion operate horizontally, so to speak, on the different strata of the order of creation up to the human level; it operates vertically also. Within the norm there are proportionate relations as between its three stages; and with these are aligned corresponding proportions in the *corpus* of the scriptures. Moreover, throughout the process of historical revelation co-operation is always proportionate, not only to truth as a whole, but also to that precise stage of revelation and response within which the particular measure of co-operation in question is being rendered.

This way of regarding the various factors involved can best be illustrated in the concrete by resuming our consideration of the Johannine prologue near to that point where the figure of the Baptist first enters upon the scene. We have called that figure 'representative', although 'intrusive' might appear at first sight to be a more appropriate term, inasmuch as the abrupt manner in which John is introduced into the argument seems to interrupt the smooth flow of a statement concerning the cosmic and universal functions of the Logos. Such an impression, however, will, it is believed, be dispelled by a closer scrutiny of the facts; and among the facts must be included the relation in which the prologue stands to the rest of the Gospel. The place which John occupies in the prologue corresponds to his rôle in the scenes which follow. This correspondence has, in part, been obscured by a modern tendency to assume that the prologue is an independent entity, not closely integrated with the plan of the book as a whole. There are, however, grounds for thinking that any such view will have to undergo considerable alteration before it can be squared with all the relevant factors in the case.[1]

---

[1] Recent investigation into the Aramaic background suggests that 'the Fourth Gospel is, in the sayings it attributes to the Baptist, a Greek translation of an Aramaic poem or prophecy' (Dr Black in *An Aramaic Approach to the Gospels and Acts*, Oxford, 1946, p. 111). Among the sayings so characterized some part, at least, of 1^{15-18} is included. Moreover the theological tone of 1^{18} offers a literary problem closely parallel to that of $3^{35,36}$, which is the corresponding conclusion to the other main group of 'Baptist' sayings (3^{27-36}). This evidence serves to forge a fresh link between the prologue and the rest of Chs. 1-3; and it looks as if this link will hold firm, whatever view be taken with regard to the problem of the 'theological endings' in question.

There is an allusiveness about St John's Gospel which suggests that the author is moving about in a territory familiar to his first readers, but largely unknown to ourselves. On the other hand this ancient territory is being extensively explored, with the result that definite landmarks are beginning to appear. Some of these, already indicated in the present work, may prove serviceable to our immediate inquiry. There are, for example, the widespread ramifications of the early Christian parallel between the form of the revelation in Christ and the narratives of creation in Genesis. There are also those all-important idioms of Hebrew thought which have a way of persisting into the pages of the New Testament. With these new-old clues let us make a fresh approach to that section of the prologue into which the Baptist makes his 'intrusion'. We will begin with a literal rendering of verses 3 and 4, following the better attested punctuation which finds a place in the margin of the Revised Version:[1]

3. All things came to be through him,
   And apart from him there came to be not even one thing.
4. That which has come to be was Life in him,
   And the Life was the light of men.

In this statement there are four distinct points to be considered: (1) The double use of the singular in lines 2 and 3 ('one thing. That which'); (2) The identification of created being with 'life' in line 3; (3) The position of the entity so identified, that is, 'in him'; (4) the meaning of 'Life', as intimated by my use of the capital letter. We begin with the first point, the singular number at the end of verse 3 and at the beginning of verse 4. 'Not even one thing' may well be directed against heresy of the type which undermined our Lord's unique

[1] The various attempts to emend John 1[4] on the basis of Aramaic idiom are set aside by Dr Black (*op. cit.*, pp. 56*f*), as being unsatisfactory. On the other hand he concludes with an interesting suggestion. He thinks that the original Aramaic of 1[4a] may have been: 'Because in him was life'. On the other hand, on the supposition that the prologue, as we know it, comes to us from a 'Greek writer or translator', he suggests that the two Greek verbs in our present text (as given, e.g. by Westcott and Hort) 'look very like alternative renderings of the Aramaic verb, combined, by the Greek writer, in an entirely new and individual interpretation'. I understand this to mean that the evangelist reshaped his material to elucidate a theological truth; the sentence as rewritten now became: ὃ γέγονεν ἐν αὐτῷ ζωὴ ἦν.

position as mediator between God and the world. If so, however, it also serves to introduce another idea, namely the unity
of all creation, as expressed in the opening phrase of verse 4.
This conception of the created order as a single entity is the
counterpart of the preceding statement. Monotheism implies *one*
order framed by *one* Creator. To this there can be no exceptions.[1]
Our second point brings us to an important idiom of thought
for which there is ample evidence in the Old Testament. The
evidence is conveniently summarized by Wheeler Robinson in
his posthumous lectures.[2] Whereas the modern mind makes a
sharp distinction between 'material' objects (such as stones) and
'living' objects (such as birds and beasts), the primitive Semite
knew no such distinction. 'The material objects of Nature were
conceived as having a psychical life of their own, making them
capable on occasion of more special manifestations of life.' The
text from Hosea 2[21,22] is given as an example.[3] Here is scriptural
basis for the conception of creation as 'an order in which the
various elements co-operate harmoniously to fulfil the purpose
of the Creator'.[4]

Our first two points must now be brought together. The
single created order is alive. It is, therefore, an organism which
can fulfil the functions assigned to it by its Creator. In that
respect the first creation is the counterpart of the second creation, the body of Christ. The analogy between the two, already
emphasized in preceding pages, is seen to have its foundation
in the whole mechanism of Hebrew psychology.[5] The *theological*
basis of this complex conception, however, lies in the dual

[1] This use of the singular (adjectival noun or relative pronoun) is a special
characteristic of the fourth gospel. The evangelist refers, in precisely the
same way, to the new creation, in his rendering of Christ's words, e.g.
6[37,39] and probably 10[29]; cp. also 11[52], and, for the divine unity to which
the 'one order' corresponds, 10[30] and 17 *passim*.

[2] *Inspiration and Revelation*, etc., pp. 12-16

[3] see above, p. 232, note 2

[4] as stated above on p. 234. In the text from Hosea the heavens 'answer'
the divine call by sending rain to the earth, which in turn 'answers' by
producing the harvest, and so on. Robinson notes the agreement of other
scholars on this point. Thus Robertson Smith: 'all things appear to them
to live'. See also Pedersen, *Israel I-II*, p. 479.

[5] Wheeler Robinson links up the psychic character of all material objects
with the Hebrew conception of human personality as 'extended' in the
members of the body, *ibid.* pp. 14, 15.

function of the Logos. He is not only Creator, but also the *site* of creation. This doctrine is common to primitive Christianity and to contemporary Judaism.[1] With it we pass to our third point: 'Life in him'. The divine site or 'place' of creation could also be expressed in the Wisdom terminology. For 'in wisdom thou hast made them all' (Psalm 104[24]).[2] So also St Paul speaking in terms of 'Wisdom Christology' says of our Lord: 'In him all things consist' or 'hold together' (Col. 1[17]). So also the members of the mystical body 'hold together' in Christ in the redeemed order. But the full meaning of 'Life in him' depends upon the meaning of 'Life' in John 1[4]. So we pass on to our fourth point: What meaning did the evangelist intend his readers to find in *Zoë*, the Greek word here employed for 'Life'?

For the answer to this question we must turn to the story of Adam and Eve in the Garden. After the narrative of the Fall and the divine judgements thereon comes this note:

> And the man called his wife's name Eve; because she was the mother of all living (Gen. 3[20]).

The Hebrew word corresponding to 'Eve' is *Havvah*, which means 'life'; and in its rendering of this text the Greek bible reads:

> And Adam called the name of his wife *Zoë*, for she is the mother of all the living.[3]

We may, then, conclude with some reason that in John 1[4] the evangelist is suggesting an identification of the created order with the figure of Eve. On the assumption that this was his intention, one obvious difficulty in the clause is at once removed. If the evangelist merely wished to characterize the creation as a single living organism, there was available a suitable term meaning 'living being'.[4] His use of the word which means 'life' would, therefore (on that supposition) be quite inexplicable. It remains to ask what would be signified by the

---

[1] cp. Philo, *De Somn.* I, 61-71, cited in part by C. H. Dodd, *The Bible and the Greeks*, pp. 20, 21. Cp. also above, p. 221, note 3, and refs.

[2] This text forms the climax of a creation-poem which follows the *order* of Genesis 1, giving to it a teleological interpretation.

[3] LXX afterwards reverts (Gen. 4[1,25]) to a Greek transliteration of *Havvah*, from which comes the Latin *Eva*

[4] ζῷον would have exactly suited his purpose

identification in question. An obvious clue is to be found in the parallel between the two creations; and here we can surely see our way to a straightforward solution.

The author saw in creation a single living organism, in part at least because he was familiar with the Pauline conception of Christ's body as the organism in which creation comes to fulfilment. But in that cycle of thought the relation of head to body or *vice versa* could also be stated in terms of the relations between husband and wife. This combination of images had already been effected in the Epistle to the Ephesians, in a passage which is based upon the story of Eve's creation (Gen. 2^{18-24}).[1] In the Christian re-interpretation of Genesis, therefore, body and bride are one. The church is the new Eve because she is the body of the new Adam. But, as we have already seen, the body of the new Adam is a 'world-body'. In terms of current thought primitive Christians would regard the mystical body of Christ as the *soma-cosmos* of the new creation.[2] Since, therefore, body and bride are one, the new Eve has identity with the order of creation as fulfilled in Jesus. In John 1^4 the evangelist is simply reading the story of Genesis in the light thrown back upon it by the revelation in Christ.

The story lent itself readily to this mode of exegesis. For Genesis 2 depicts the creation of the animal world as incidental to the provision of a 'helpmeet' for Adam. The creation of Eve is the successful conclusion of a process. She crowns creation's order in the second story just as 'Adam' crowns the series of creative works in the preceding poem.[3] This might well have special significance for the evangelist and for his readers. The first order of creation was completed in the new Adam, in whom the image of God was finally manifested.[4] On the other hand the second order of creation (represented by Gen. 2) begins with the new Adam, Jesus Christ, who collaborates with his heavenly Father in the process of the new creation.[5] The

---

[1] Eph. 5^{22-33}. Verse 31 quotes Gen. 2^{24}; and there is good authority for adding a further quotation, from Gen. 2^{23} (as in AV) to verse 30. On the literary connexion between this epistle and the fourth gospel see W. L. Knox, *Some Hellenistic Elements in Primitive Christianity*, pp. 62-64 (notes).

[2] see above, Ch. VI, § i

[3] The Hebrew text of Gen. 1^{26} has 'Adam' without the article.

[4] cp. Gen. $1^{26,27}$, the conclusion of which, on this view, anticipates the story of Gen. 2^{21} ℓℓ   [5] Gen. 2^{19} ℓℓ. Cp. above, the first note to par. 3 of Ch. VI. § v

goal of that process is the new family constituted in the church, where, in the children of the new Eve, 'the image' is reproduced from generation to generation. On this reading of the creation stories the figure of Adam merges into that of the Christ, a phenomenon which we have come across in St Irenaeus; and this peculiarity extends to the whole story, as already indicated in our commentary on the diagram of Gen. 2.[1] The phenomenon in question, however, is already present in the bridal section of Ephesians just now mentioned;[2] and in the prologue of St John it may serve to explain a further peculiarity which would otherwise be perplexing. This is connected with the meaning of the phrase: 'life in him', to which we must now return.

If for 'life in him' we read 'Eve in Adam' we have a formula which sums up the mode in which Eve was created. If, again, we read the formula in terms of the new creation, it summarizes the familiar truth that the church is 'created in Christ', 'bone of his bones and flesh of his flesh' (Eph. 2[10], Gen. 2[23]). But this phrase ('life in him') has already been explained to mean that the Logos is 'the place' of creation. That, then, is the peculiarity which might prove puzzling to us, if we had not learnt to think in terms of the ancient idioms. From the scriptural standpoint 'creation in the Word', the origin of Eve, and the new creation in Christ, are not three separate events in a causal series. They are rather three strands in one pattern, compresent together in the counsels of God.[3] The pattern 'repeats' itself in fresh phases. But none the less the whole pattern is one; and, moreover, *repetition is a fundamental form of the unity which the pattern exhibits.* Not only is the story of Eve's creation 'repeated' in the recreation of Israel in Christ, but also each of these mysteries has its ground in the more ancient mystery whereby all things are created in the Word of the Father. Thus once more, by a fresh route, we return to the elemental truth that there is only one plan of creation. Its foundations were laid 'in the beginning';

[1] Ch. VI., § v

[2] On this cp. above, the final note to par. 1 in Ch. VI, § ii

[3] To this 'compresence' corresponds the 'co-infancy' section in St Irenaeus, and further, his whole conception of the operation described in Gen. 2[7] (i.e. the moulding of Adam) as completed in the incarnation and 'extended' in the church.

and its structure is completed in the new Adam who is the incarnate Word.[1]

iv

Further aspects of this same theme expressed by the fourth evangelist in terms of light and in terms of nuptial imagery (the bride and the friend of the bridegroom). The function of the Baptist in the prologue; he typifies Israel's vocation to be fore-runner of the Word's age-long and universal mission.

The conclusion just reached can also be stated in a way which gathers up the themes of this chapter into one. The perfect reflection of the Father's glory is manifested in the Son. Scripture shows us a revelation of divine paternity in its perfect counterpart which is filial response. So too in the order of creation the scriptural teaching shows a world of finite response set within the filial relation of the Son to the Father. The Son, therefore, in his rôle as creative Word seeks to embody his own filial obedience in that world which he holds within his embrace. This drama of the Word and the world is set forth under various scriptural images, the multiplicity of images corresponding to the proportions of truth, whereas these, in turn, correspond to the multiplicity of functional responses to the Word within that living whole which is the medium of revelation. For example, the creative Word is life-giving Light; and this uncreated light is refracted variously in and through the manifold of creation's order. That order again, in its fulfilment, is set forth in the closing scene of the bible where the city-bride glows with the indwelling light of the Lamb's sacrifice. If that closing scene is allowed to enter as background into the opening scenes of the other great Johannine book we may get a clearer view of the whole which is implicit in the terse sentences of the pro-logue.

The eagle wings of the fourth evangelist bear us up to a vantage-point from which the End is seen to be implicit in the Beginning. The bride as luminary of the Lamb already begins

[1] For the interpretation of John 1[4] in this section by reference to Gen. 3[20] we can appeal to Philo, *De Agric.*, 95, where, in an allegorizing allusion to the serpent as 'the friend and counsellor of *Zöe*', the double meaning of the last word is rightly preserved by Colson and Whitaker (Loeb ed., Vol. III, pp. 156, 157). See further the final note of the present chapter.

to shine forth in the opening page of creation's story. So 'the Life was the light of men'.[1] The living Word had found entrance into the *cosmos* of his creation. Thus, despite the on-rushing darkness of sin (1[5]), created lights in the firmament already reflected the uncreated light and heralded its full uprising. At the point where John enters as the chosen herald we seem to have a conjunction of Malachi's prophecy with the poem of creation.[2] Before the heavenly chariot-wheels of the rising Sun of Righteousness, Elijah the prophet girds up his loins and runs.[3] As the divine bridegroom comes forth from his chamber to run his course, the friend of the bridegroom is present to prepare the way to the nuptial rites. For the Word of God is already the predestined Lamb on his way to the supreme sacrifice; and the bride of the Lamb must make herself ready. Thus the prologue already foreshadows the coming scenes by the river Jordan, where 'the friend' points to the bridegroom, and thereupon members of the true Remnant of Israel begin to form up into a bridal train.[4]

The uncreated light of the Word is the fire of the Lamb's sacrifice, predestined from the foundation of the world (1 Peter 1[19,20]). This is the genuine light of truth's fulness, out of which every man is enlightened by virtue of his creation 'in the image' and 'according to the likeness' of God.[5] To that intent the Word who is light[6] 'was always coming into the world'[7] (John 1[9]).

---

[1] The concluding clause of John 1[4] completes the author's re-interpretation of Gen. 3[20]. The Word illuminates what he creates; and his light is received and refracted to mankind by the created matrix of life, his cosmic bride.

[2] With the former in the order of the LXX; cp. above, pp. 222 with note 2 and 223 with note 2. On the other hand for western Christians, in whose bibles Malachi closes the old Hebrew canon, this conjunction appropriately shows the end in the beginning!

[3] Mal. 4[2-5] (LXX); cp. 1 Kings 18[44-46], 2 Kings 23[11], Ps. 19[4-6]

[4] And that in two senses of the word. For the saints form the pattern of the bride's wedding-dress (Rev. 19[8]).

[5] Gen. 1[26,27], where, however, LXX has 'according to' in both phrases. The sentence in the text is so worded as to suggest a correspondence between John 1[9] and 1[18f].

[6] The two aspects are summed up in Dr Carrington's term: 'word-light' (*op. cit.*, p. 83, note 2).

[7] Following the rendering of Dr Knox, *Some Hellenistic Elements*, etc., p. 56, note 1

This statement concerning the Word's age-long ministry to mankind *comes after* the corresponding statement concerning the Baptist's mission. Here, once more, the order of the prologue leaves an impression which must affect our interpretation. As the figure of the bride is introduced into the story of creation, so also the friend of the bridegroom is brought on to the stage with a priority which seems to make him forerunner to the universal mission of the Logos in history. This, again, adds piquancy to the disclaimer of priority by the Baptist, twice repeated in what follows ($1^{15,30}$).[1] For however far back John's mission is set it cannot go back to 'the beginning'. All that has been here said, however, only serves to raise the question: why is John given such prominence and such priority in the prologue?

To this question there seem to be two possible answers which correspond broadly to two aspects of the prologue. These have already been mentioned in what was said at the end of the last section, where we found in a single phrase three facets which were compared to three strands in one pattern. The pattern repeats itself in such wise that 'repetition is a fundamental form of the unity exhibited'. The two aspects of the prologue, then, are 'repetition' and 'unity'. Let us see what this implies. The evangelist repeats the story of creation in the story of its fulfilment, the beginning in the end. That involved showing some regard for the traditional forms of the creation story. In the main, Genesis 1 is followed as to order, but modifications are introduced to convey nuances of the second story. Now broadly speaking Genesis 1 has three main divisions: (1) the creation of heaven and earth; (2) the ruling lights set in the firmament; (3) the animal kingdoms and man. Of these the first and last work

---

[1] All the more so as the word which we render 'coming' in 1^9 is echoed (in verb and tense) three times over in the phrase: 'he that cometh after me' ($1^{15,27,30}$). Jesus as Messiah and Son of Man is 'the Coming One' (Matt. 11^3, Luke 7^{19}) whom the Baptist awaits. But in the Johannine writings our Lord's 'coming' is associated with the past as well as with the present and the future. For this cp. the language of Rev. $22^{12,13,16}$ with Rev. 1^4, where 'the Coming One' is a title of deity. Nevertheless, it seems probable that the peculiar use of the present participle in John 1^9 is, in part, due to a traditional connexion of 'the Coming One' with the Baptist's witness as evidenced in the form of the question put by John in his message from prison (referred to above in this note).

up to a climax. In (1) the climax is the emergence of earth as matrix of life; in (3) we have the creation of man in the image. Between these come the created lights which complete the external order and give guidance for the routine of human life.

These main divisions are repeated in the prologue. But first, fruitful earth is identified with fruitful Eve.[1] Secondly, whereas the Christian fulfilment identifies Eve with the new Jerusalem so that $Zo\ddot{e}$ is 'the light of men', there is still room left for the figure of him whom, later on, the voice of Jesus will designate as 'the lamp which burneth and shineth' (5[35]).[2] As such the Baptist appears as a satellite of the Sun of Righteousness or as a star of the dawn which in its waning heralds that Sun. Moreover the Sun's light illuminates mankind before the visible orb appears above the horizon. This helps to explain the order of John 1[3–10]. In effect, however, it sets the Baptist within the *preparatio evangelica* rather than in the gospel narrative itself. Here we pass from repetition as a literary *motif* to the unity of the whole within which repetition forms its pattern. From the Hebrew point of view a whole repeats itself in its parts. Adam is present in all his descendants; and again, although in a different sense, the one divine Word is serially embodied in a succession of prophets. Each of these embodiments is only a part of the whole revelation. Yet each prophet by fulfilling his function represents the whole. Thus the whole may be symbolically presented in one of its parts. This idea was reinforced, as we have seen, by St Paul's use of the organic conception, and in that form this biblical idiom of representation entered upon a wider inheritance. For its biological truth still holds good; and its sociological applications are manifold.

It is this representative conception of the individual rôle which runs through all the biblical typology, as employed by the writers of the New Testament. Its application to St John the Baptist, however, had peculiar sanction. For our Lord had

---

[1] For which cp. a definite parallel in Rom. 8[19]*ff*, and above, the first note to § iv, par. 2.

[2] The heavenly bodies were apparently regarded by the ancient Hebrews as lamps hung from the under side of the firmament. But since all things in that world were 'alive' (see above, Ch. VIII, § iii, par. 4, with notes), these celestial lamps could control the destinies of earth and its inhabitants; and this, as we have seen, was a dominant notion when St John's Gospel was written. Cp. above, the third note to Ch. VII, § iv, par. 1.

identified his forerunner with the Elijah of Malachi's prophecy;[1] and this again would be connected with the representative character of Elijah in the Transfiguration scene. The connexion is clearly seen by St Mark; and the fourth evangelist appears to be following in the same tradition.[2] Indeed the parallel with the Transfiguration is in this respect quite definite. In the synoptic story Moses and Elijah are set forth pictorially as contemporaneous with our Lord in the days of his flesh; and so too in the prologue the new Elijah is made to appear as a witness to the age-long activity of the Word.[3] This becomes intelligible when we set aside our western notions of causal

[1] Mark 9[13], explicitly interpreted in Matt. 17[13]. The evangelists also clearly make the further identification of 'Elijah' (Mal. 4[5]) with 'my messenger' (Mal. 3[1]). Thus Mark 1[2], in accordance with a further dominical testimony (Matt. 11[10], Luke 7[27]). Mark's own identification of 'my messenger' with 'the Voice' (Isa. 40[3]; cp. John 1[23]) is agreeable to the thesis of note 3 below.

[2] cp. above, the closing section of Chapter VII

[3] There is a further possibility: The close connexion of John with the ever-coming Logos (1[9]) is based upon the language of Mal. 3[1] with its verbal echo of Exod. 23[20] ϑ. It would be natural to identify 'the angel of the covenant' with the angelic leader of whom Moses was told that he would bring Israel to the land of promise. There are several points to be noted here. In Mal. 3[1] there are two messengers. The first prepares the way of the Lord, whereas the second (the angel of the covenant) appears to be identified with Jahveh. This agrees with Exod. 23[21]: 'My name is in him'. The language of Exodus, however, is now extended, in part, to both messengers, a point to which we shall return. If, following the traditional testimony of Jesus (Matt. 11[10] etc.), the fourth evangelist identifies John with 'my messenger' (Mal. 3[1a]), the Logos will then be 'the angel of the covenant'. This agrees with John 2[13] where 'the Lord' comes suddenly to the temple, and again with John 14[2] where Jesus assigns to himself the function of 'preparing a place' in accordance with Exodus 23[20]. The last-mentioned text precedes the inauguration of the covenant in Exodus 24[1-8]. So when Jesus 'repeated' the covenant-inauguration he also 'repeated' the promise of preparing a place. Finally our Lord's title of 'the Coming One', employed by the Baptist (see above, § iv, par. 3, last note), corresponds to the conclusion of Malachi's oracle: 'Behold he cometh' (3[1]).

Thus the order of John 1[6-9] corresponds to the order in Malachi 3[1]. Even the typically Johannine word: 'Sent' (1[6]; cp. 9[7], 10[36]) introduces John in the prologue, as the kindred verb introduces 'my messenger' in Malachi 3[1] and the covenant-angel in Exodus 23[20]; and this again brings in the *shaliach* nuance (cp. John 13[20] etc.). As 'the Lord' (Jahveh) is identified with 'the messenger of the covenant' (the Logos), so the 'man sent from God', 'my messenger', preparing the way of God in his Logos (Mark 1[2] etc.), is

sequence, and think instead in terms of Hebrew wholeness transcending the time series.[1]

V

The doctrine of creation forms the essential background for 'the extension of the Incarnation'. What is extended is the fulfilment of the created order. In the prologue, however, the Fall is not minimized. For the duality between creation and the Fall is represented by the disparity of types, Israel being typified both by the bride and by the friend of the bridegroom. Moreover, this duality is included within the larger plan of the whole.

The sequence represented by 'Israel, Christ, the Church' has now been defined in terms of a set of relations symbolized by the bridegroom, the bride and the friend of the bridegroom. Our analysis of St John's prologue was, indeed, strictly limited to the elucidation of this cycle of relationships so far as it seemed to be there adumbrated. That very partial analysis, however, has brought us to a point where the one organism of revelation, both in its unity and in its manifoldness, can be more clearly envisaged by reference to the Irenaean conception of the extended image. That conception, it will be remembered, implied a great deal more than is commonly understood in our modern way of speaking about 'the extension of the incarnation'.[2] Revelation and redemption are certainly carried to their fruition in the church. But it is only too easy so to restrict 'the extension' as to leave unexplored its foundations in the doctrine

mysteriously associated with the universal activity of his principal. There is one last touch, however. The description of the 'man sent from God' concludes: 'his name is John'. This is almost verbally identical with the traditional utterance of John's father when he named his son in obedience to revelation (Luke 1 [13,63]). But the name of John means 'Jahveh is gracious'. So here the fulfilment surpasses its foreshadowings. For the words of Exodus 23 [21] ('My name is in him') are literally true of 'my messenger' (John 1 [6]) as well as of Jesus his Lord (John 1 [17]) whose name means 'Jahveh is salvation'.

[1] G. F. Moore has pointed out how Jewish writers could group their historical figures together by association in the unity of an epoch rather than in strict chronology (*Judaism*, Vol. I, pp. 6-8 with note 3 on p. 8). This merely illustrates a tendency which, for special reasons, could be carried much further, in the movement towards the Whole.

[2] or (as some would prefer to say) 'of the atonement'

of creation. Whenever this happens a corresponding distortion is bound to occur in the use made of the Old Testament. For the biblical doctrine of creation (with consequent implications for the whole range of theology) shows its ground-plan most explicitly in the writings of the old covenant, even though the foundations are not laid bare apart from the fuller light which is given in Christ. Moreover, some such restriction and distortion will occur just as surely, whether it be in the first instance located in one or in another of the various organs of revelation. A weakened contact with one particular channel of revelation will certainly limit our capacity to apprehend truth through all such channels. That is an inevitable consequence of the interpenetration which pervades the Whole.[1]

Let us return to the group of relationships symbolized under the nuptial imagery. If the preceding analysis be accepted as a starting-point, the figures of the bride and of the 'friend' stand over against one another in a series of contrasts. Both represent Israel and both are orientated towards the heavenly bridegroom. For the rest their characteristics are altogether different, although, as we shall see, they are also complementary. The function of 'the friend' is to prepare for the nuptial union by pointing to the bridegroom. As a witness to the true light he leads all men to believe. The 'all' here (John 1[7]) corresponds to 'every man' enlightened by the universal activity of the Word (two verses later). The witness of 'the friend' thus represents the prophetic function of Israel, as reinforcing the wider revelation granted to all men by their creation in the image.[2] Therein lies the appropriateness of two other details in the fourfold gospel portrait of the Baptist, to both of which we have already

---

[1] What is here said about 'the extension' being grounded in the plan of creation is the counterpart of a corresponding assertion made in the opening section of this chapter, namely, that the plan of creative revelation in Christ will be misunderstood unless we see the living embodiment of the creative Word extended in the church.

[2] It is noticeable, however, that the evangelist prefers to employ here a terminology different from that of Gen. 1[26,27]. In 1[9] he falls back upon the implications of 'Let there be light' (Gen. 1[8]). Nevertheless, this corresponds to 2 Cor. 4[4–6], where the light of creation is connected with the image in Christ, and to Heb. 1[3], where the light is traced to its source in the Father. So, too, in the prologue the light is eventually identified with the glory of the Son (1[14]).

given some consideration. The first of these is the synoptic tendency to prefigure the life, death, and even resurrection of the Christ in his forerunner. This served to indicate a fore-shadowing of the Servant's form in the mission of Israel to the world. With that should be connected, secondly, a peculiarity of the Johannine prologue whereby Israel's mission, so under-stood, is placed on the background of creation. This is effected by the representation of John as a created light in the firma-ment of the creation story.

At first sight there is here a duplication of functions, since already 'the life was the light of men'. In the transition, how-ever, from first beginnings to redemptive history, the prologue passes on from one type to another, because the two symbolic figures of Eve and the Baptist represent two different aspects of Israel's relation to the Creator's plan. In the former of these the relation is represented as one of continuity and even identity. For the bride of the Lamb is simply the living matrix of created life as fulfilled in the true Israel of God. From another point of view, however, the world-order (*cosmos*) of creation is not rightly ordered towards the ever-present Creator-Word. Eve has fallen from her true function as 'help-meet'; and, although the light of creation has not been extinguished by 'the darkness', yet Israel's mission must now appear as a way of recovery and restoration. Accordingly that mission is here represented by a prophetic voice through which the divine Word calls men back to their true beginning in himself. The disparity between these two typical figures corresponds precisely to the duality of Creation and the Fall.

This duality at the heart of the prologue agrees with the function of the Baptist in the scenes which follow, for which it prepares. The forerunner here (even as the bride in the Apoca-lypse) is the counterpart of the Lamb. Indeed, the duality which breaks the smooth flow of creation's story with John's 'intrusion' corresponds to the conflict of light and darkness, of faith and unbelief, in the Gospel as a whole. When the prologue is read in this way it is also inevitable that the flame of the Lamb's sacrifice should be discerned in the uncreated light of the Word by whom the world was made. In the order of the Gospel, how-ever, the theology of the Word (1^{1-14}) and the revelation of the Lamb (1^{19-36}) are linked together through the statement con-

cerning the beloved Son and his human relationships (1^{11-18}).[1]
To this sequence corresponds the line of thought developed in
the present volume. The revelation of God (his 'Word') is given
in the Son's response to the Father; and that response has
become manifest in 'visible and tangible form',[2] that is to say,
the Form of the Servant.[3] The form is that of the divine image
'made flesh', the one image (*eikôn*) which is not an idol (*eidôlon*)
because it is God's own image in which he wills to be seen and
known, loved and adored.[4]

Our analysis of the nuptial symbolism in St John's Gospel
has brought to light certain characteristic features of primitive
Christian thought which we have also found in the writings of
St Paul and, again, of St Irenaeus. Both the symbolism and
the technique of presentation vary as between one writer and
another. Yet amid all the diversities an underlying unity can
be discerned. This unity of interpretation is itself Christological
in its significance. For Christ is the sphere within which the
interpretation takes place, since he is actually the *locus* of creative revelation in which and to which the response of his members is made. As he is the original mould within which the entire
manifestation of deity receives shape and form, so he is also
the Whole within which the divine plan comes to fulfilment.

[1] The links are clearly discernible: (i) The Word enters into the statement
concerning Sonship at the crucial point (1^{14}); and the Sonship is affirmed
in the record of the revelation (1^{34}); (ii) Into each of these three sections
the witness of John enters as a connecting thread. When that witness becomes vocal, its two utterances are linked, as by a refrain, through the
repetition (verses 15, 30) of the 'before and after' saying which refers back
to the Beginning.

[2] Irenaeus, *The Demonstration*, Ch. 6.

[3] Of this Pauline phrase 'the Lamb' is the Johannine equivalent, both
phrases corresponding in a general way to the picture in Isa. 53. Detailed
evidence was given in *The Common Life* and in *The Apostolic Ministry*.

[4] Contrast 'the image of the beast' (Rev. $13^{14,15}$, combining elements from
Dan. 2, 3 and 7). The victory of the Man over the beasts (Dan. 7) restores
creation's order and consecrates the whole world to be the abode of a re-
created family (Gen. 2^{18-24}, Rev. 19, 21). Within this new world of filial
response to divine paternity all images are re-hallowed to be incarnational
in their refraction of the One Image, to which all in their various degrees
may point. In that great re-hallowing the type-images of the old covenant
have likewise been re-born. This transformed situation has, perhaps,
scarcely received adequate recognition in a recent article on *Art and Religion*
by Prof. H. A. Hodges (CQR, No. 292; Vol. CXLVI).

In his condescension, moreover, he is not only the mould within which the treasures of creation come to be what they are; he is also the image which is being moulded out of those treasures into a completeness, which, nevertheless, he already possesses in its fulness by divine right of his essential being.

So when the disorder of sin found entrance into the framework of the divine plan, it entered into unfathomable depths of unity which it could modify indeed, but which it could not undermine, and still less destroy. Into that mysterious order of finitude whose beginning and end is Christological sin could penetrate, so as to arrest, and partially reverse, the law of wholeness within the whole. In this way there appeared a rift which affected the entire moulding of the image in head and members. One thing, however, sin could not do. It could not change the essential form of the sacrificial victim prepared from the foundation of the world. It could furnish only the occasion and some of the conditions under which the Lamb of God should come to claim his bride. Thus the history of this finite order has the character of a palimpsest, first the writing of creation, then the reverse writing of the Fall, and finally the original story of creation re-written, as it were, in the blood of Jesus, and upon his torn flesh. Moreover, the complete document may be regarded as the single act of God in Christ, into which has been interpolated man's rebellious counter-act. That complication, however, was provided for in the divine plan. For there the ruling factor is not causal necessity, but rather the dependence of the parts upon the whole; and in *this* Whole dependence is of such a kind as to secure the freedom of the parts to be (or not to be) their true selves, as they will.

The metaphor of the thrice-written document, however, must not be allowed to conceal what it cannot convey, namely, the grim intensity of the conflict by which the pre-ordained harmonies of creation are restored. Deity is manifested in that conflict and in its victorious issue, in both together. God is manifested in the humiliation by which all is subjected to vanity, as well as in the exaltation by which all is restored. Moreover this condition of revelation extends from the beginning to the end, from the primeval light shining in the darkness to the last trump of judgement. The conflict, therefore, sets its mark, not only upon the combatants, but also upon the conditions of the combat. At some of these we have glanced already. We must now attempt a more general survey of the whole field.[1]

[1] The interpretation of John 1[3,4] adopted in this chapter, being unusual, should properly be supported by a much fuller display of evidence than could be set out within the limits of the present volume. It can be said, however, that whereas the traditional explanations, ancient and modern, of this difficult passage have never been quite satisfying, the evidence (direct and indirect) in favour of a connexion with Gen. 3[20] has a cumulative character which could not lightly be dismissed. I shall hope to return to the subject more fully elsewhere. The indirect evidence would include everything which belongs to the new psychological approach to scripture, of which much has been said in the present work. We may recall the following particulars of early Christian thought: the earthy origin of man, the 'identity' of Christ's body with the order of creation, the analogy from virgin-soil to a Virgin-Mother, the repetition of creation stories in new and higher forms, the tendency to identify man with the 'all flesh' of creation; and lastly, in the contemporary environment, the widespread ancient notion that the world is a single living organism.

In the OT a passage like Isa. 26[17-19] points unmistakably to the whole 'new creation' cycle of primitive realism (to be explained more fully below, in Ch. IX, § iv), wherein man hopes to participate in the periodic re-birth of nature. In this cycle of thought every woman has potential identity with 'mother earth', the land which is married to her god. We may compare 'the virgin daughter of Zion' and similar personifications. So Hosea threatens Israel, the foolish bride of Jahveh, with the penalty of becoming a barren wilderness (Ch. 2); and to this corresponds St Paul's identification of Hagar with Mt. Sinai (Gal. 4[25]). So too the prophet suggests that the body of 'mother Israel' may become the pit of Sheol to her offspring (Hos. 13[13 θ]). A similar idiom in Ps. 139[13-15] equates the mother's womb with 'the lowest parts of the earth'. Once more, the apostle makes a corresponding 'identification' of Sarah's body with the tomb of Christ (Rom. 4[17-25]). In Rom. 8[19 θ] the 'Adam' sequence of 5[12 θ] is resumed. Here the background is Gen. 3; and the travailing of Eve has been transferred to a fallen creation. The sentences upon Adam and Eve have become blended with the curse upon the soil; and the offspring of the new Adam share the birth-pangs of their mother, a cosmic Eve in process of redemption. The corresponding figure in the Apocalypse (Rev. 12) shows the path of transition to St John's Prologue. The double function of Eve, as bride of Adam and mother of the Promised Seed (Gen. 3[15]; cp. 1 John 3[1-12], Rev. 12[17]), necessitates an alternation of images with the usual phenomena of 'oscillation'.

Such are the bare bones of the argument. It will be obvious that the new biblical sciences have brought fresh light of a sort which was partly accessible to Irenaeus, but which had faded out by the fourth century of our era. It does not follow, however, that 'the cosmic bride' is a radical alternative to the older interpretations. In the Apocalypse (22[17]) 'the Spirit and the bride' are closely linked together; and in this the End corresponds to the Beginning, when the Spirit hovered over watery chaos to bring out of it a

Additional Note B.

Three Problems connected with Wisdom

The purpose of this note is to discuss briefly three problems incidental to early Christian theology, all of which are connected with
the argument of the preceding chapters. 'Wisdom' provides the
connecting link.

(1) *Creation and Sonship.* The theology of Wisdom starts from
Proverbs 8[22ff], where there are complications arising from ambi-
guities of language. Disagreement continues about the keyword in
verse 30. Does it mean 'nursling child' or 'architect' ('clerk-of-the-
works' is Wheeler Robinson's phrase, *op. cit.*, p. 260, note 2)? The
punning tendencies of the Semite peoples must be allowed for here.
Conceivably in Colossians 1 St Paul has both meanings in mind.
But a more radical difference of opinion arises over verses 22-25,
the section to which we must here confine our attention. Was
Wisdom begotten or created? This question raises another: are the
two ideas mutually exclusive in OT? Of three verbs describing
Wisdom's origin in this passage only one *must* refer to generation or
birth. It occurs in verses 24, 25, where Wisdom says twice: 'I was
brought forth'. But in Psalm 90[2] the same word is used of Jahveh
'giving birth' to the world (cp. RV margin). On this ground C. H.
Toy (Proverbs, ICC, *ad loc.*, p. 174) concludes that the word is
simply a metaphor for 'creation'. On the other hand, Briggs finds
in such language 'a paternal conception of creation' (Psalms, ICC,
Vol. II, pp. 272 *f*, 496), tracing it back to the language of Genesis
2[4], and giving Proverbs 8[22] as a parallel. Moreover, in Job 38[8] the
birth of the sea 'from the womb' is described; and here the Driver-
Gray commentary (ICC *ad loc.*, p. 328) assumes a mythological
background such as may be traced elsewhere in OT. Cp. Skinner

cosmos. So in the New Beginning of the Prologue a new Eve cannot be wholly
dissociated from the promise of the Paraclete in the same Gospel. Perhaps
there is a hint of this in the proximity of that promise to a 'new birth'
parable (John 16[21-23]): cp. Isa. 66[5-14] and above, Ch. VI, § iv (2), for
background and foreground to the gospel theme. Thus there was a certain
justification for the patristic identification of *Zöe* with the Holy Spirit,
although this notion was definitely read *into* the thought of the evangelist
rather than read *out* of it. Finally, the text of John 1[4] (as read by WH and
RV margin) could be understood to mean: 'That which has been made
was life in him' (i.e., before it was made). This would support the theories
respectively of St Augustine (*In Joannis evangelium tract.*, 1.17) and of
Bishop Westcott (in a full note *ad loc.*). The evangelist may have intended
here (as elsewhere) a double meaning; in which case the reference to Gen.
3[20] was not necessarily meant to be extended by the reader to 'life' in the
Gospel as a whole.

(ICC) on Gen. 3^{20} (*Havvah*) and 4^1 (*kanah*). See *op. cit.*, pp. 85 *ff*, 101 *ff*. It seems, then, that Toy has by-passed an important phenomenon of ancient thought without giving it serious consideration. His treatment of Proverbs 8^{22-30} assumes that creation and generation are mutually exclusive concepts. I venture to think that this assumption cuts clean across the Hebrew way of thinking, and secondly, that it reflects a doctrine of creation remote from the thought alike of scripture and of primitive Christianity. If so, this would be a particularly clear example of the defective technique referred to above, in Chapter II, § iv, par. 4 ('the working theory of Liberalism').

When the Hebrew monotheists ironed out the polytheistic background of their beliefs, they did not suddenly change over to the sharp dichotomies of later European thought. For example, in Malachi 2^{10} the prophet says to Israel: 'Have we not all one father? Did not one God create us?' The parallelism implies that the two clauses of this saying not only refer to the same event, but actually *mean the same thing*. A similar use of language can be observed in Deuteronomy $32^{6,7,18}$; and note how here 'thy father' refers first to Jahveh, and then, in the next breath, to the human parent. But further, 'the paternal conception of creation', as Briggs clearly saw, includes the whole world in its scope. This, again, illustrates the depth of continuity as between 'nature' and man in scripture. It also provides further biblical reinforcement for the view, implicit in Irenaeus, that by virtue of man's inclusive character as the microcosm, the image which becomes visible in the Christ is spread out to include in its scope the 'all things' of the *cosmos*. I conclude, therefore, that in the biblical doctrine of creation the fatherhood of God is *presupposed*, which, again, means that, when God creates, he gives something of himself. This must be understood to imply, not a lowering of sonship in the scale, but rather an elevation of all creation to share in the glories of sonship. It is precisely this doctrine which is outlined in Romans 8^{19-30}.

(2) *The law in the heart.* The divine promise to put 'my *torah*' in the hearts of Israelites (Jer. 31^{33}) has a twofold parallel in St Paul. The Christian fulfilment of the promise is set forth in 2 Corinthians 3, 4. But in Romans 2^{12-16} it would seem that both promise and fulfilment are referred back to their ground in the plan of creation. This, however, raises a question posed by Dr E. de Witt Burton. In an excursus on νόμος attached to his great commentary on *Galatians* (ICC, p. 457) he concludes that 'the law' (twice with the definite article) in Romans $2^{14,15}$ refers, not to the Jewish Law as such, but to the divine law in a more general sense. In this long note, however, (seventeen pages of small print) the Hebrew word

(*torah*) occupies less than one page, while the Jewish identification of *torah* with Wisdom is ignored. Thus the close connexion between revelation and creation in the Jewish background of St Paul does not enter into Dr Burton's purview in his judgement upon this text. Moreover if, for Judaism, *torah* is, in G. F. Moore's words, 'the whole content of revelation', then the notion that the Christian rabbi had in mind two distinct and parallel concepts of divine 'law' becomes remote and improbable. Again, if *torah* is the 'instrument' of creation, its impress can be present in men's hearts by virtue of the divine image, which (on the authority of Genesis) St Paul clearly held to have been not wholly lost through the Fall (Gen. 5$^{1-3}$, 1 Cor. 11^7). Accordingly the νόμος φύσεως of contemporary thought would be for the apostle simply a gentile way of bearing witness to the truth that 'in wisdom' God 'made them all' (Ps. 104^{24}). The speech at Athens (Acts 17) shows the same standpoint. Finally 2 Corinthians 3, 4 connects the fulfilment of Jeremiah's promise with the restoration of 'the image' in Christ. There is only one plan of creation; and it includes a universal revelation which comes to fruition solely in the Son (cp. Rom. 8^{29}).

(3) *Scriptural imagery and the development of doctrine.* In primitive Christian thought the figure of Wisdom is utilized in three different ways: (i) In St Paul a simple identification of Wisdom with the Christ; (ii) in St John a transference of 'Wisdom's' attributes to the hypostatic Logos (Heb. 1$^{1-4}$ is an intermediate phase); (iii) in St Irenaeus, following Theophilus of Antioch, a simple identification of Wisdom with the Holy Spirit. The transition to (iii) might be effected partly under the influence of such texts as Isaiah 11^2, Wisdom 1^7, 7$^{22 ff}$; but also, partly through the language of St Paul in 1 Corinthians 2$^{6-16}$, 10^4, 12^{13}; cp. John 4^{14}, 7$^{37-39}$, Rev. 22^{1,17}. This peculiar development illustrates what one may fairly call the kaleidoscopic character of the transition in theology from Hebrew to Greek modes of thought (on this see above, Ch. V, § iv, par. 4, last note). In the new Christian *cosmos* of thought, as it develops, the various biblical images which provide the forms of revelation seem to jostle one another in their orientation towards the Whole. No image is adequate to that Whole, although every image has its place in the revelation (cp. above, Ch. VIII, § v, par. 4, last note). In the advancing movement of the Whole, moreover, as it is assimilated into the mind of the community, no single image can at all times occupy the foreground of conscious thought. For, apart from other considerations, no single image could correspond appropriately to every phase of developing apprehension in the corporate Christian consciousness.

Time alone, therefore, could show how the developed pattern of interpretation would look, when the kaleidoscopic movement had attained a relative stability in its new mould. What we seem to see, however, as we look back upon the development of doctrine, is a concentration of attention upon first one and then another biblical image in accordance with the shifting pressures of a continually changing historical situation. As each image fulfils its rôle, it retires and gives place to another. Thus, in three or four centuries of Christo-logical development Wisdom was succeeded by Logos, and this in turn gave place later to Sonship. In the flux of Hebrew thought, however, deity could be identified *in turn* with Wisdom, Word, Spirit (or again with 'the Angel of the Covenant'). This influence is apparent well beyond the end of the second century. We notice, in particular, the 'jostling' of the Logos tradition by incursions of 'Spirit-Christology' during this period. Moreover, when these lines of thought eventually gave place to a theology of Sonship, this was, in a sense, a return full-circle to the starting-point. For if—as we concluded under (1) above—Fatherhood is, in the Old Testament, a presupposition of creation, then it would reasonably follow from the fuller revelation in Christ that Sonship is a correlative pre-supposition of creation, to which in the last analysis a corresponding metaphysical status must be assigned. Such an explication of Christology could occur, however, only through a dogmatic develop-ment organically one with scripture *within the one organism of revelation.* In that respect, moreover, the very confusions generated by the intermingling of Semitic and Greek modes of thought are signs of continuity. The patristic development of the apostolic *paradosis* has in it, indeed, just that sort of continuity which scripture itself exhibits under the characteristically Hebrew category of 'extension'. Finally, since every image has its place in the revelation, *nothing is left behind* in the passage of thought. Some of these points will receive fuller explication in what follows. For this see especially Chapter IX, § vi; and for the disparity and interaction between Hebrew flux and Greek 'forms' see above, Chapter V, § v.

CHAPTER IX

THE MEASURE OF THE CHRIST

i

The living tradition of the new Israel is an indispensable key to the world of scripture. A return from disintegrated tradition to the form of the Whole is a return to the form of the Servant in which the conflict with sin's dispersiveness is continuously carried on.

At an early stage in this investigation it was suggested that the form and the content of revelation are mutually inseparable. This was connected with the thesis that revelation is always given in, as well as to, response, so that the Word of God comes to, and is embodied in, persons or communities of persons. Thus we were led step by step to a vital unity of revealed truth with the community of believers, and of the written word with those who received it as scripture. Finally, scripture and ecclesiastical tradition were seen to be two organs or channels within one vehicle of revelation. This vehicle was, at first, identified provisionally with 'Christendom' or 'the entire organism of historical Christianity'.[1] Without withdrawing this provisional conclusion we passed in review some of its complications,[2] and then turned to an alternative conception as presented in the writings of an early Christian theologian. Our study in the thought of St Irenaeus may at this point be compared with a recent paper by Père L. Bouyer on *Holy Scripture and Tradition as seen by the Fathers*.[3]

The writer in question points out that there is a fallacy in all polemical attempts 'to derive from the Fathers a one-sided answer to the question of the primacy of Scripture or Tradition'. In their thought there is no conflict between these two; for in their eyes scripture is 'not primarily an authority' but 'a whole

[1] Above, Ch. III, § i, penultimate paragraph
[2] Chs. III B, and IV, §§ i, ii
[3] Printed in *The Eastern Churches Quarterly*, Supplementary issue, Vol. VII, No. 1 (London and New York)

world'. Their minds are imbued with scripture 'to the point of reading everything in the world through it and finding the whole world in it'. This all-embracing conception depends, however, upon the unity found in the object of faith (as revealed in scripture); and the key to this unity is the ecclesiastical tradition. The recognition of such a unity is, moreover, the test of orthodoxy. When the grain of patristic exegesis is winnowed from the chaff it amounts to this: 'The Incarnation and all that it implies is a key to the whole history of man and to the whole Bible'. Scripture and 'cosmic history' alike belong to the unity which has its focus in Christ; and, on the other hand, the object of faith is inseparable from the church. Finally, the organic continuity is made clear when it is affirmed that 'the object of faith' is transmitted through the channel of tradition 'in conformity with the *vital*[1] manner in which the life of the Church itself is disseminated in time and space, without ever ceasing in the least to be one and the same as in the beginning'. Development is recognized, not however in the object itself, but 'wholly in the apprehension of the object'.[2]

The close similarity between this summary of patristic teaching during the first five centuries and the doctrine of the single organism of revelation with which we have been so largely occupied in the present volume will be sufficiently obvious. For our present purpose, however, it is the concluding quotation, given near the end of our last paragraph, which is particularly relevant to the argument of the present chapter. Like Dr Carrington, Père Bouyer sees the function of tradition as something organic to life. It is 'a living biological phenomenon'.[3] Moreover, the agreement of these two authorities in employing such language with regard to two quite different

---

[1] Italics are Père Bouyer's.

[2] This paper was read at a conference at Oxford, sponsored by Roman Catholics, and attended also by Orthodox and Anglicans. In the paper which followed, Père Bouyer's estimate of patristic teaching upon scripture and tradition was warmly endorsed by the well-known Orthodox theologian, Professor N. Arseniev (*op. cit.*, p. 16).

[3] see above, Ch. VII, § iii, par. 3. Tradition is something which lives and grows, not merely a deposit which is passed on. It is not a wall separating persons from their God, but an environment within which they receive the living word. Imperfections in the tradition may restrict, but do not eliminate this function.

stages of revealed religion reminds us of the fact that the
church in which the Christian fathers lived and taught was
still the Israel of God. Accordingly, 'the *vital* manner in which
the life of the church itself is disseminated in time and space'
is of one piece with that continuity of Jewish tradition which
enters into the texture of the New Testament. Just so far as we
take this fact seriously, however, we have to go a good way
further. For however one-sided rabbinical Judaism may seem
to be from the Christian standpoint, its continuity with the
older Hebrew traditions cannot be denied; and, further, something very similar must be said of a like continuity between
patristic teaching concerning tradition and the witness borne
by the New Testament to the teaching of our Lord and his
apostles.

To all this it will be replied that there is such a thing as a
false and corrupt tradition, and that the stern words of Christ
upon this subject (Mark 7, Matt. 15, etc.) have their bearing
also in church history. The fullest acknowledgement of that
unhappy truth, however, only serves to complicate the problem
of tradition without in the smallest degree eliminating it.
Herein lies the significance of Père Bouyer's observation that
in the teaching of the fathers scripture and tradition are still
complementary to one another, and not as yet the rival
authorities which they afterwards became. Concerning this
difference of attitude one observation may be made immediately. The change of outlook corresponds to an altered situation. So long as the visible unity of the church was in the main
preserved, divergences of tradition could be held to be complementary to one another, and therefore complementary also
to scripture. Only the more extreme divergences of heresy were
incompatible with this position; and they were cast out precisely in order to preserve the organic unity of tradition with
the scriptural revelation.

But further, it is important to observe that, when the idea
of a radical conflict between scripture and tradition at length
came into prominence, those who ranged themselves with
scripture against what they believed to be a corrupt tradition
did not thereby succeed in eliminating tradition from their own
version of the Christian religion. They merely substituted a
new process of tradition for that which they rejected. For the

misleading half-truth that 'religion is what a man does with his own solitariness'[1] here breaks down completely. Indeed, not only religious beliefs, but also all knowledge is mediated through tradition of some kind, and that too in a community which corresponds to, and is the trustee of, the particular tradition in question.[2] When once this fact is clearly seen, several further facts come to light. In the first place, since tradition cannot be eliminated, the question at issue is seen to be no longer one of competition between scripture and traditional authority as such, but rather the question as to what sort of tradition may prove to be the adequate complement of scripture within the one organism of revelation. It may also be remarked that this way of stating the problem of tradition should also prove to be the most hopeful method of approach to the problem of Christian disunion. Indeed, in the long run, it might conceivably be found that the two problems are two sides of one problem.

Let us now turn to another aspect of tradition already implied in the fact of disunity. The breaking up of Christendom into a number of competing traditions is primarily a product of sin's destructive effects; and the age-long processes which led to this result and perpetuated it are evidences of the power of evil at work in Christian history. The whole record of that history, therefore, is a manifestation of the 'subjection to vanity' which St Paul found to be a consequence of man's Fall.[3] The utopian or 'meliorist' attitude which has worked so strongly in recent generations has promoted a frame of mind capable of believing that our present subjection to vanity can be removed by a little patient exercise of goodwill. Such an outlook would logically imply that by a like exercise of goodwill our Lord could have prevented his own betrayal and crucifixion. What Jesus actually achieved was something much more difficult, namely an acceptance of humiliation involving an entry into the lowest depths of our human conflict with the powers of evil. Into this mission of the Servant the church was from the beginning initiated; and the character of our age-long conflict

---

[1] A. N. Whitehead, *Religion in the Making*, p. 16.

[2] This question was fully discussed in the first Book of the present volume. See especially in Ch. II, § i, pars. 6-end, and § ii, pars. 1-3, Ch. III, §§ i-v.

[3] Rom. 8[19] *ff*; cf. above, Ch. VII, § iv, last par. and notes

with sin determines much in the vital processes by which the unity of the Whole is sought and won.

The integrity of Christian tradition and its adequacy to the scriptural whole is something given from above, yet never to be taken for granted as though we possessed it by good fortune or by goodwill, something rather to be striven for, attained and maintained through ceaseless warfare with the dispersive power of sin. It would, however, be a complete mistake to suppose that the disintegration of Christian tradition and the consequent distortion of its witness to revelation are sufficiently explicable in terms of human selfishness and illwill. For that, again, would seem to imply that selfishness is a self-explanatory phenomenon, whereas it is in fact the perversion of an exquisitely ordered plan.[1] It is the disharmony which creatures have introduced into the original harmonies of the Creator's handiwork. This, however, implies that those original harmonies were through and through capable of distortion, and that this possibility was a characteristic feature of the plan as divinely ordained. All the gold was of such a kind that it could turn to ashes, just as all the ashes of our present exile are of such a kind that they could be converted once more into gold. These considerations are relevant to our understanding of the disparity which operates in a fallen world. We are naturally disposed to think that things are essentially that which they seem to be in the world as we know it, whereas in fact the blight of sin has left nothing precisely as God intended it to be; and this subjection to vanity includes our own subjection to spiritual blindness about the essential facts.

If then we seek to enter into the form of the Whole as divinely planned, we must engage in this task with one further consideration in mind. The whole which was divinely planned was from the beginning Christological in structure. The Christ is both its ground and its end, its site and its goal. This is as much as to say that, whether with or without the incursion of evil into the divine plan, the form of the Whole is and must be

---

[1] What is wrong is not the movement of the self towards a desired end, but the dislocation of that movement from its proportionate place in the divine plan. So too, *un*selfishness as a mere negation of self can be wholly misplaced. 'Self' finds its meaning in the order of creation renewed and fulfilled in Christ.

none other than the Form of the Servant. For that is the form
in which deity has been self-projected upon the screen of created
being. It is, in short, the only form in which we can securely
begin to understand what God is like. The importance of this
consideration may emerge more clearly as we proceed further.
For the form of the Whole is to be understood in terms of what
I have called 'the extended image', that is to say the image of
God inclusively[1] restored in Christ. Scripture is that world of
discourse in which Christ is seen to pervade the whole pattern
of things, so that his image is stamped upon the entire universe;
and the church is the place where this vision enters into the
continuous unfolding of human thought and worship and life,
as the restored image is reproduced in the holy community.

ii

The New Testament shows the compresence of diverse strands
of imagery, belonging to different epochs of redemptive history,
woven into a single pattern of revelation (Ch. VIII, § iii). This
is to be connected with the *soma-cosmos* theme—Christ the
microcosm in whom creation is repeated and fulfilled. The
working out of this conception in the recapitulation thesis of
Ephesians.

In the preceding chapter reference was made to a single
pattern wherein several strands are conceived to be compresent
together in the counsels of God.[2] Whether the particular application of this notion, as there worked out, be accepted or not
is of small importance, for it is seldom that the exegesis of any
particular scriptural text will fail to provoke diversities of
opinion. What matters greatly, however, is the general conception there adumbrated with regard to the *structure* of the
divine-human organism. The alleged example of this general
conception there put forward (in the exegesis of John 1[3-5])
was not fully elaborated. If now we take this example simply
as an illustration of the general conception, it will serve our
purpose to examine more fully the details of structure implied
in the given instance. Following this procedure, then, we can,
in the first place, set the three strands in a temporal sequence

[1] For the sense in which this word is used see above, Ch. VIII, § ii, par. 3.
[2] above, Ch. VIII, § iii, last paragraph

corresponding to their actual presentation in scripture. We
do so, however, in accordance with a principle which will be
found to be firmly grounded in the facts. This principle may be
stated as follows: The rich and diverse imagery of scripture
cannot be simultaneously present in equal measure to any one
mind; yet every image has its due place in the revelation.
Accordingly, whereas scriptural images are employed selectively
both by the inspired authors and by their successors in traditional exegesis, in accordance with the pressure of circumstances, yet in the passage of thought nothing in the form of
revelation becomes permanently irrelevant.[1]

Turning next to the details of our illustration we recognize,
of course, that the story of Eve's creation out of Adam's side
belongs to the distant world of ancient mythology. But here, at
once, the principle just now enunciated comes into operation.
St Paul found himself able to argue from this story as from a
record of revealed truth which could furnish guidance for the
life of the Corinthian church in the first century of our era.[2]
For obvious reasons we ourselves would not be justified in
adopting precisely the same procedure. On the other hand we
are bound to pay respect to the form of revelation; and the
form of revelation here is not the story in Genesis taken by
itself, but *the use made of it by the apostle.* As to how much is
covered by the italicized words will inevitably be a matter
leaving room for difference of opinion. But that a great theological issue springs from the use here made of Genesis is
already evident in the opening pronouncement (verse 3) where
an analogy is implicit between the headship of Adam over Eve
and the headship of Christ over the church, the headship of
the deity over Adam being also reproduced in two contrasted
forms: first, the headship of Christ over all men, and secondly
the submission of Christ to the Father.

In the light of this passage it is difficult to suppose that the
apostle's use of the 'second Adam' Christology in the same
epistle and in Romans did not already imply the nuptial
analogy which is set forth explicitly in Ephesians, particularly
when we take into account the way in which the figure of Eve

[1] For illustrative details see above, Additional Note B (3)
[2] 1 Cor. 11³⁻¹²; for a later elaboration in a similar vein of thought cp.
1 Tim. 2¹³⁻¹⁵

is employed in this group of epistles.[1] Whether the 'Eve' typology was *consciously* present to the apostle in the 'Adam' passages, however, is comparatively unimportant. What is clear beyond controversy is the fact that common idioms of thought bind together St Paul's use of these creation stories and his thought about the new creation in Christ. This, however, is a minimizing statement. The thought of the writer does not really become intelligible except on the presupposition that he sees in Christ a fulfilment of creation's order which involves a repetition of creation's events. It is this last point which receives specific elaboration in Ephesians 5^{22ff}. There the conception of the church as a new creation in Christ is referred back *into* the story of Genesis 2 as though it properly belonged there. Here two of our three strands are present together in the author's mind as though they formed a single mystery. This appears to involve the consequence that for the inspired writer the two strands are similarly juxtaposed (or superimposed one upon the other) in the plan of creation, and therefore also in the mind of God.

There was another line of thought which would ultimately lead to a similar type of juxtaposition. The formula 'in Christ' is bound up, on one side, with the Hebrew idiom which includes many persons in one (such as Adam or Abraham). This, however, could in rabbinical logic[2] be easily linked up with associations arising from the identification of Christ with Wisdom. Texts like: 'in wisdom hast thou made them all' (Ps. 104^{24}) would readily combine with Proverbs 8 and Genesis 1 to identify Christ as the site of creation, thus providing in him an identical 'place' for both creations. This, in turn, would be reinforced whenever the 'Adam' Christology coalesced either with Wisdom or (as in St John's prologue) with Logos, as invested with Wisdom's attributes. For then the conjunction of Christ and the church with Adam and Eve would be superimposed upon the connexion of Logos-Wisdom with the order

---

[1] In 2 Cor. 11^{1-3} an analogy is made between the temptation of Eve and the temptations of the Corinthian church, that church being here regarded as the spouse of Christ. Again in Rom. 8^{19ff} the background is Genesis 3. A similar use of OT stories appears in Gal. 4^{21}-5^1

[2] i.e. the logic of verbal association, for which see above, Ch. VI, § i, pars. 1*f*

of creation.[1] There is a possibility, also, that the three strands of which we have been speaking already meet in the Epistle to the Ephesians. Dr W. L. Knox has shown that the Wisdom-Logos background is present in this epistle (for example in 1[23] and 4[10])[2], and again that on this particular theme there is an affinity between Ephesians and the fourth gospel.[3] It can also be shown that the language of Ephesians 3 and 4, when connected with the current Jewish background, easily suggests a conjunction of Adam with Wisdom-Logos in the divine-human figure of the Christ. The details are here relegated to a footnote. The possibility of such a conjunction is, however, important for our present purpose, as will appear presently.[4]

---

[1] For this further conjunction in St John see my essay in *The Apostolic Ministry*, e.g. pp. 97-101 with the footnotes.

[2] *St Paul and the Church of the Gentiles*, pp. 186 *f*, 195.

[3] cp. above, Ch. VIII, § iii, par. 7, note on Eph. 5[22] *ff*.

[4] Wisdom fills all things (Wisd. 8[1]; cp. 1[7], 7[22-28]); and this rôle now belongs to the ascended Christ (Eph. 1[23], 4[10]). More fully, if we survey such passages as Job 28, Ecclus. 24 and Baruch 3[9]-4[4], we find the following: Wisdom, present in the universe, mysteriously eludes human understanding. Her 'place' is inaccessible; yet God who possesses her secret made her accessible to Israel, his beloved. In this connexion the quotation of Deut. 30[11-18] in Bar. 3[29] *ff* is important. The same quotation is applied by St Paul to Christ as 'the end of the law unto righteousness' in what is probably a baptismal context (Rom. 10[4-13]); and this passage has obvious affinity with Eph. 4[9,10]. The connexion of thought is as follows: as Wisdom was brought near to Israel in the Law, so we Christians have no need to climb the heavens; for we have union in the church with the ascended Christ who fills heaven and earth. If a late date for Baruch be accepted (for which see H. St John Thackeray, *The Septuagint and Jewish Worship*, pp. 86, 87), then the literary connexion with Ephesians can be only indirect. But there is a common stock of ideas, and perhaps of language. Cp. ἀμέτρητος (Bar. 3[25]) with the four dimensions in Eph. 3[18], and (by contrast) with the threefold use of μέτρον in Eph. 4[7,13,16]. In Baruch (following Ecclus.) Wisdom has two habitations. Of these one is the cosmic 'house of God' which is 'the place of his creation', the other being Israel (Bar. 3[24,37,38]). The cosmic temple appears in Ps. 29[9], and, again, in Isa. 66[1], a text which is significantly quoted by St Stephen against the Jewish temple; for the Shekinah is now with the ascended Jesus (Acts 7[48-56]). The new cosmic temple is the body of Christ which unites heaven and earth, whereas in Philo (*De Somn.* I, 215) the two temples, cosmic and human, are distinct, although parallel entities.

At this point we may legitimately introduce the graphic imagery of Wisd. 18[16], where the personified Word of God, having leapt from heaven 'into the midst of the doomed land . . . stood and *filled all things with death*;

Upon evidence assembled in the note it will here be assumed that the picture of the new organism (head and body) set forth in Ephesians 4 conforms to the *soma-cosmos* type of thought which has previously been explained in this volume. The special character of this imagery to which attention must now be drawn is its inclusion of temporal process within the new cosmic whole. The body of the ascended Christ includes within itself the entire range of redemptive history. In one sense the epistle here says nothing which had not already been said, in principle, in the earlier teaching of the Pauline *corpus*, and in accordance with the biblical idioms.[1] In Ephesians, however, the scattered

and, while it touched the heaven, it trode upon the earth'. In the fulfilment (Eph. 4^{9,10}) the Christ descended 'into the lower parts of the earth' (Hades) and 'ascended above all the heavens that he might fill all things', not only with his presence, but also with the sweet savour of his own sacrificial death (cp. Eph. 5^2). Earlier, the attribute of gigantic size was apparently assigned to the angel of divine vengeance (I Chron. 21^{15,16}; cp. Rev. 10$^{1-6}$). Somewhat later, again, the rabbis assigned the same characteristic to Adam. 'He was a mass that filled the whole world to all the points of the compass' (G. F. Moore, *op. cit.*, Vol. I; p. 452); and the initials of 'the four cardinal points' corresponded to the letters of his name, so that Adam 'somehow represented the whole world' (*ibid.*, Vol. III, p. 130, N. 180). In view of Adam's prominence in Chapter 5 we may surmise that current ideas about Wisdom-Logos and Adam are fused together in the thought of Eph. 3-5. The four points of the compass correspond to the language of Eph. 3^{18}, already noticed. But the new Adam has heaven for his throne and earth for his footstool (Isa. 66^1, Eph. 1$^{19-23}$); and accordingly the reference to 'the measure' of his $\dot{\eta}\lambda\iota\kappa\iota a$ in 4^{13} must be taken realistically. Moreover, $\dot{\eta}\lambda\iota\kappa\iota a$ can refer both to spatial size and to length of time. Hence the two renderings ('stature' and 'maturity'). The English word 'span' covers both meanings; and perhaps this corresponds to the thought of the author. For the biblical contexts cp. above, Ch. VII, § v, par. 5, final note.

[1] On this see above, Ch. V, last 4 pars. The crucial section in the epistle centres round Eph. 4^{13}, for which see the concluding remarks of the preceding note. A possible Jewish-gnostic background to Eph. 4^{13} is discussed by the late Eric Burrows, S.J., in an essay entitled 'Speculations on the doctrine of the two Adams', published in a volume entitled *The Gospel of the Infancy* (The Bellarmine Series VI, London, 1940). The 'speculations' in question correspond broadly to the Jewish background which we have sketched above in the preceding note. But there is one further detail of special interest. The gigantic figure in human form is, in *this* Jewish version, ascribed *alternatively* to God and to Adam. The author of Ephesians, however, had no need of the alternative. If our interpretation of his thesis is correct, the divine image and its Adamic counterpart (Gen. 1^{26,27}) are, in that thesis, shown to be united in the single figure of the Christ.

267

indications of earlier epistles are assembled into one picture and brought under a relatively new concept, that of recapitulation (1^{10}). Briefly the theme is twofold. Christ, as *consummator*, is the heir of all the ages, in whom all the treasures of this world-order are gathered up. They are gathered into the unity of that whole which corresponds to the perfect harmonies of the Creator's original design (3^{9-12}). Thus all things in the order of creation are brought to fruition in Christ; and this fruition involves oblation. For the living unity of Christ's body has also the significance of a temple (2^{20-22}), and of a sacrifice (5^2). That is one side of the thesis. The other side brings into the picture the individual members of the body, or their collective representation in the bride (5^{22ff}).[1] Corresponding to these two aspects of the theme there is a double use of the word which we render: 'measure'. To 'the measure of the span of the fulness of the Christ' (4^{13}) corresponds 'the measure of each several part' (4^{16}) in the cosmic temple; and this refers back to 'the measure of the gift of the Christ' (4^7). Here we are once more in a world of 'proportion' which was considered at length in the preceding chapter. In its Ephesian context it can open up fresh horizons for our contemplation.

iii

'The measure of the Christ' distinguished from the measure of his gift to us. Recapitulation involves a wider application of principles implicit in the structure of Christ's body. Repetition and transformation. Proportionate growth and dialectical conflict.

In all the biblical descriptions of Christ's body there is an immediate practical aim. The writer, in each case, is concerned to show the *ethos* of the Christian church in terms of right personal relationships, with a corresponding emphasis upon those qualities by which such relationships are sustained. There are, however, three further considerations which are essential to a correct estimate of this teaching. First of all, the conception of Christ's body is *theological*. It is concerned, not simply with ethical relations which fulfil the precept: 'Love thy

[1] Of the details on this side I have written elsewhere. They will be further elaborated in the next section.

neighbour', but also with the relationships proper to humanity redeemed by Christ and united with him in one organism. Secondly, the concept itself corresponds to the biblical doctrine of creation. It affirms a *creaturely* relation of the redeemed to God in Christ. Thirdly, it presupposes a conflict with sin victoriously sustained by Christ to the uttermost, yet also still continued in the members of his community. With these three implications the scriptural image of the *corpus Christi* covers implicitly every aspect of the church, her life and her mission.

It follows that, notwithstanding the immediate practical applications of such a passage as Ephesians 4^{1-16}, wider principles are involved which are truly integral to the scriptural revelation. In seeking to clarify these principles, however, it is essential that we start from the original applications. In this respect Ephesians 4 does not differ in substance from the earlier texts (such as 1 Corinthians 12 or Romans 12). All these statements with their contexts are aimed against the dispersiveness of sin, whether this takes the form of quarrelsomeness, or (as probably in Ephesians) of destructive types of thought. Moreover, reading between the lines of these descriptions, we can see that the disruptive tendency may intrude into the ranks of things good in themselves and subvert their good qualities. Thus the gold of human excellence is dimmed and corroded, or even threatened with dissolution. For example, knowledge can be used to the glory of God; yet the Corinthians allowed their intellectual powers to minister to individual vanity to the detriment of the community. Personal qualities, however, are bestowed for the benefit of all. The qualities, therefore, which count for most are those which can minister to the building up of the community, so that it becomes conformed to 'the measure' of the Christ.

From one point of view 'the measure of the Christ' is infinite with the infinity of deity. Yet the writer of Ephesians prays that his readers may know 'what is the breadth and length and height and depth'. More exactly, he asks that they 'may be enabled to comprehend' what their minds could never grasp unless aided by divine grace. This is completed with two further paradoxes. They are to know what passes knowledge, and to be filled 'unto all the fulness of God' (Eph. $3^{18,19}$). Here we are confronted with the 'mystery' language which we discussed in

an earlier chapter.[1] As we there saw, human analogies show all
knowledge to be infinite in respect of its goal, and yet positive
in its limited achievements. So it is with our knowledge of
God; and the same law prevails in the relations which obtain
between the Christ and the members of his body. In this
respect the language just now cited throws light upon the main
statement in Ephesians 4[13]. Great love is appreciated more
easily than a lesser love. From this point of view size can aptly
symbolize imponderables. As in Romans 5[1-11] and elsewhere,
the very greatness of God's love in Christ opens the mind to
its warmth and light, as the sun opens the bud; and by this
illumination we are enabled to penetrate ever more deeply
into the mystery of the Christ.

For the illuminating power awakens in us a response; and
'the exceeding greatness of the power' at work in us liberates
all the possibilities of growth which are already latent by
virtue of the divine image in which we were created. Thus, as
we penetrate more deeply into 'the mystery of the Christ', the
image which is mature in him imparts its likeness to us.[2] In
this way the image is ever being extended from head to members. In this way also 'the measure of the Christ' which 'fills
all things' is reproduced in his members; not, however, with
the infinity of degree in which it exists in him. Here we come
upon the difference between his measure and ours, a difference
which is fundamental to this exposition. The image of God in
Christ has in it all the divine glory as reflected in the order of
creation as a whole. Otherwise there could not be a recapitulation of all things in Christ. He, then, is the Whole in which
the glory of the Father is to be seen and known. We, on the
other hand, are only constituent members in that whole; and
that fact determines 'the measure of the gift of the Christ'
which is imparted to us.

The 'measure' thus imparted to each constituent member is
limited in the manner which has already been explained in our
discussion concerning 'the proportion of the faith' and its
bearing upon 'the measure of faith'.[3] It was there pointed out
that grace is given in accordance with the fundamental law

[1] above, Ch. II, § i
[2] This is explained in 2 Cor. 3, 4
[3] Rom. 12[3,6]. See above, Ch. VIII, § ii

of the Body, namely, that each member should fulfil his appointed function. For a cell or organ to fulfil its biological
function is, quite simply, to fulfil the law of its being. There
can be no higher destiny than that for each member of Christ's
body. It follows, however, that in this sphere of thought
equality must not be confused with uniformity. Every organ
in the mystical organism fulfils a different function from that
which every other organ fulfils.[1] Equality, therefore, involves
difference and requires it. But by the same biological analogy
equality of fulfilment involves limitation. We can grow into
the infinite measure of the Christ *only* if we observe the limitation imposed upon our own individual measure. The limitation,
therefore, is not fettering but liberating. For it enables us to
become our true selves in the whole to which we belong;
and that constitutes 'salvation' as understood in the New
Testament.

The preceding paragraphs have been concerned with the
structure of the Christ-organism in its bearing upon the individual members in their personal relationships, Godward and
manward. For this lies on the surface of scripture in the context
of its immediate practical pre-occupations. What was there
said, however, concerning the direct implications of membership
in Christ's body has also a wider bearing which corresponds
to the vast sweep of the recapitulation doctrine. For Christ is
the whole into which all things are gathered in fulfilment of the
divinely ordered plan of creation. The form of this whole is,
in a sense, always the same. Yet it presents to us different aspects
according as we think of it in terms of individual life or, again,
in terms of the deep historical perspectives of revealed religion.
It is to this larger aspect that we must now turn. In so doing
we shall expect to find the same fundamental structure, the
same dominant principles.

The moulding of Adam to the image involves the age-long
assimilation of earthly material to the divinely ordained form.
Various aspects of this process have already engaged our
attention in detail. It remains only to survey the whole field

---

[1] On the other hand, in the Christ-organism, as in its biological counterpart, there may be *classes* of functions which are shared by all organs
falling within a particular group, e.g. fulfilling a particular type of vocation
or serving in a particular ministerial order.

afresh, and if possible to carry the analysis further still. The process of assimilation is one of continuity through change. An unchanging pattern is reproduced in fresh material or in novel situations. This characteristic combination corresponds, it would seem, to an all-pervasive feature of the universe. At every level of finite being there are cycles of repetition which give stability to nature, but which may also be subsumed into new forms of combination without losing their original and unchanging pattern. *Repetition*, then, is a fundamental element in the order of creation.[1] But over against these unchanging uniformities man has a creative power of transforming his environment so as to modify profoundly the combinations of things. Upon the basic phenomena of repetition, for example, he builds new forms of repetition which are of his own devising, although they correspond to his psycho-physical make-up and to the needs of a being rooted in repetitive nature.

It is not surprising therefore that repetition is prominent in the recapitulation doctrine. It is already present in a number of different forms in scripture. Moreover the very notion of the extended image, which we have found to be rooted in scripture, is a notion which implies that the divinely ordained form of the whole is reproduced or repeated in the parts. This has already been examined in detail in our previous discussions of the image-doctrine, especially in connexion with the diagram based upon Genesis 2.[2] There, however, we were thinking primarily of individual embodiments of the image, whereas here we are concerned with the wider transformations of history. Recapitulation involves *transformation* as well as repetition; and the most difficult problems of theology are, perhaps, those which concern the interaction of these two principles respectively upon one another. This interaction of repetition and transformation is, however, 'spread out' through the successive epochs of redemptive history 'in conformity with the vital manner in which the life of' the *ecclesia*, old and new, 'is disseminated in time and space'.[3]

We shall proceed presently to some illustrations of this

[1] see also below, Ch. X, § iii, pars. 2 *ff*
[2] above, Ch. VI, § i
[3] For this language see above, Ch. IX, § i, par. 2; and for 'spread out' see next note

process; but, before doing so we must indicate briefly two further points of correspondence with the scriptural language about the body of Christ. The first of these is the principle of growth enunciated in the statement that we are to 'grow up in all things unto him who is the head' (Eph. 4^{15}). This principle applies, not only to individuals in their personal relations, Godward and manward, but also to the life of the church as a whole in its passage through history. The image is reproduced in redeemed humanity as a whole, not only through individual sanctification, but also through all those corporate developments of life and thought in which unity is manifested. These can come to fruition only through extended processes which may involve centuries of development. These processes are necessary for the 'building up . . . unto the unity of the faith . . . unto the measure of the span of the fulness of the Christ' (*ib.* 4^{12,13}). They are, therefore, indispensable parts of that age-long response within which revelation is first given, and then made accessible to mankind.

The second point is closely connected with the first; and it has already been enunciated in this section in its individual application. If the building of the Body is to be healthy, the life-giving powers of the whole must be distributed proportionately to all the parts. The dispersive tendencies of sin, however, obstruct the due fulfilment of this law, hindering the proportionate development of the parts into a measured harmony. Such a measured harmony would in its ideal fulfilment be nothing less than 'the measure of the span of the fulness of the Christ', whereas, on the other hand, the schisms of Christian history indicate how far short we are from that ideal goal. In so far, therefore, as growth has preserved the proportions of truth which belong to 'the unity of the faith', that result has come about through a dialectical conflict. In this the partial claims of particular interests have ultimately been resolved in the larger whole which could do justice to them all. The moulding of the image *takes time*. The material becomes dry or brittle through exposure to an unfriendly atmosphere; and so there appear breaks and fissures which delay the age-long task of the divine artist. On the other hand, in the degree in which the body has grown up 'in all things unto him who is the head', there has been a 'gathering up' of the resources of redemptive history into the whole with a concentration which makes possible a yet wider 'extension'.[1]

iv

Two illustrations: (1) The primitive theme of new creation through death and resurrection passed through the fire of prophetic criticism to fulfilment in Jesus. The final 'repetition' of the ritual pattern takes nature into history, and includes all redemptive history in a mystical order of identity with Christ.

The process outlined in the latter part of the preceding section must now be exemplified in detail. For this purpose we will consider two quite different strands in the development of revealed religion, each of which will be found to embody some aspects of the pattern just now stated in general terms. Our first example covers the whole course of revelation in scripture, whereas our second example will, it is hoped, throw light upon the interconnexion between that revelation and the subsequent development of Christian doctrine in the patristic period. In both instances alike we shall be contemplating forms of interaction between religion and culture; and this will lead on (in Chapter X) to some final considerations concerning the functions of the Christian religion in its relation to human society and history.

(1) In a previous chapter a contrast was drawn between the nature-religions of the ancient Semitic world, which form the geographical background to Hebrew religious *praxis*, and the historical religion of Israel which formed the more immediate prelude both to Christianity and to Judaism.[2] Each of these two religious domains (the 'natural' and the 'historical') has now been scientifically and impartially explored; and the resultant situation is peculiarly interesting. It has, for example, led one authority to speak of 'a curious dualism, or dichotomy, in the history of Hebrew religion'.[3] In the context of this verdict the writer has shown that the prophetic accounts of Canaanite religious practices are too hostile to enable us to

[1] For this phraseology see above, Ch. VI, § v, par. 3
[2] see above, Ch. VII, §§ i and ii
[3] Professor S. H. Hooke, in *The Origins of Early Semitic Ritual* (Schweich Lectures, 1935), p. 26

understand 'their significance for the people who practised them'. On the other hand, the same writer goes on to say that 'the prophetic recasting of the national traditions has almost entirely obliterated the traces of the pre-prophetic religion of the Hebrews themselves'. It is as though there were two religions struggling for the mastery. Yet in the final issue neither the one nor the other could be said to have completely won the day.

For what happened? Jeremiah's passionate hope of a new covenant ('*not* according to the covenant that I made with their fathers')[1] is succeeded by a new and yet restored version of the old nature-religion. Moreover, whereas the earlier 'writing' prophets denounced this kind of religion, the later prophets, from Ezekiel onwards, are its inaugurators and supporters! Yet these contrasts can easily be exaggerated. For the restored cultus of the post-exilic temple has, in its return, undergone a transformation. It now *presupposes* the ethical monotheism of the prophets instead of being, as formerly, in radical conflict with it. The nature-religion could not be suppressed. Under the fire of prophetic criticism, and after an interlude of total suspension,[2] its whole pattern is *repeated* in history in a form more compatible with a developed religious consciousness. The new form has assimilated the prophetic revelation, and has thereby struck a new balance between the religious forces which had previously been locked in conflict. The conflict had been dialectical in its general character, because both sides in the struggle were essential to the future of revealed religion. Conversely, if either side had succeeded in exterminating the other, the victorious form would, in its victory, have destroyed the proportions of truth which were vital to that future. Lastly, the conflict was necessary, because the old nature-religion was stained with much that was both false and immoral. The dialectical character of the conflict cannot conceal the fact that its *necessity* is to be traced to our fallen and sinful condition.

It would be a mistake, however, to suspend our analysis at this point, as though we had reached the end of the matter.

[1] i.e., not according to the pattern of an external cultus such as even the 'Book of the Covenant' (Exod. 20-23) contains, but, by contrast, an interior religion of the heart (Jer. 31$^{31-34}$)

[2] although perhaps not quite so 'total' as has been supposed

Christians, at least, cannot do so, inasmuch as they have in view a yet greater transformation of Israel's religion which took place in Christ. If, however, we are to carry the analysis forward into the New Testament, we must first, for our present purpose, carry it back again to the beginning. Christ is 'the first and the last, the beginning and the end'; and nowhere is that title more applicable than in this matter of religious development. Let us go back, then, to the typical religious ceremonies of those countries which are now commonly referred to as 'the Middle East', Egypt and Babylonia with that strip of coast-land lying between them, the latter including Syria and Palestine. All of this, except Egypt, may be called Semitic; and Egypt had strong cultural influences over Semitic territories throughout the epochs of biblical history. In ancient times the type of religion prevalent in these territories bordering upon the eastern Mediterranean was what is known as the 'fertility' cult. Man was dependent upon the forces of nature for his daily bread. Religion, therefore, was largely concentrated upon those acts by which, it was believed, the fertility of the soil and of those living organisms attached to it might be promoted and secured.

The most obvious fact about nature, from the farmer's point of view, is the regular round of the seasons upon which depend seed-time and harvest. Every year nature seems to die. The vital forces seem to be driven underground by the weather, until in the spring they rise to the surface again with renewed force and energy. So also the gods of the fertility cults, being identified with powers of nature, were supposed to die year by year, and then, each year, to rise again once more to a new life. Thus, in a religious regard, there was at the end of twelve months a New Year in the sense of a New Creation.[1] By the ritual acts in the temples of Babylon a new annual round of agricultural activity was literally created; and 'by this ceremony was secured the due functioning of all things, sun, moon, stars, and seasons, in their appointed order'.[2] Here we notice

---

[1] From the human standpoint the crucial periods were spring and autumn. The former was the season of actual renewal, whereas the latter was the beginning of a new agricultural round after the sun had finally destroyed all the old vegetation. Accordingly the religious rites of the new year were celebrated at either or both of these seasons.

[2] Hooke, *op. cit.*, p. 19

that the idea of 'new creation' is associated with the dying and rising of a god, just as in the New Testament a new creation is effected through the death and resurrection of Jesus Christ. Moreover, the fertility cults of primitive history had actually returned in a new form as 'mystery' cults about the time of the rise of Christianity. Can we wonder, if scholars supposed that St Paul had 'borrowed' from the mystery religions, when we reflect that the combination of 'new creation' with death and resurrection is one of the most marked features of the apostle's religious system?

This, indeed, is to anticipate. Yet, at every point the extraordinary recurrence of the old religious pattern meets the eye in the pages of the New Testament. In St John's Gospel, for example, the approaching death and resurrection of Jesus is actually described in terms of seed-sowing and harvest (John 12²⁴). Moreover, since this saying is ascribed by the evangelist to our Lord himself it may well be that this apostolic writer understood our Lord's 'sower' parables, as reported in the other gospels, to have a like significance. However that may be, we have now indicated the direction in which our previous analysis of biblical religious development can be extended. For, whereas nature-religion 'returned' in one sense in the post-exilic cultus of the Jewish temple, it may be said to have returned in a more complete sense in the Christian religion. In order to make this point clear we must go back to further details of the original fertility cults.

The basis of all these cults is the annual return of nature. This return is repeated each year. So also the 'new creation' ceremonies are repeated annually; and, since the ritual religion of the Hebrew people was of the fertility type, an annual repetition of the same ritual acts is fundamental to the Hebrew cultus in both its earlier and its later forms. But, secondly, there is another sense in which 'repetition' occurs. It is a characteristic of the fertility religion that the dying and rising of the nature-god is *repeated in another medium*, that is to say in ritual acts which somehow *represent* the original processes of nature and so induce their recurrence. Moreover, besides 'repetition' the cult-actions also imply another idea, namely 'identification'. The king, who in urban communities was originally the main actor in the ritual drama, was qualified for this vitally important function by virtue of his identification with the god. He was himself a divine being descended from gods or deified by virtue of his office.[1] The identification therefore was manifold. The god was identified both with the powers of nature and with the king; and the latter, as the representative of the cult-community, brought it into identity both with the god and with the order of nature. In this way what was done in the ritual affected equally man and his environment.[2]

This multiple identification subsequently developed distinctions (as we might expect) with the fuller elaboration of society. So in Mesopotamia 'the distinction between the god, the king and the priest, originally aspects and functions of one individual, became established'.[3] Similarly, the Hebrew monarchy originally exercised priestly functions, as we see from Solomon's prayer at the dedication of the temple. But on the return from exile priest and prince exercise a joint-suzerainty for a time (Zech. 6[13]), somewhat as envisaged by Ezekiel; and soon the memory of a royal priesthood has been practically forgotten (2 Chron. 26[16-20]).[4] But here, too, a return to the old pattern eventually emerges in the pages of the New Testament. The argument of the Epistle to the Hebrews depends upon an interpretation of Psalm 110 which finds in the primitive priest-king a type of Jesus; for he, as Messiah, is the divine priest-king who displaces the Aaronic priesthood. Here again there were relevant factors in contemporary history, such as the revulsion from a ruling Maccabean priesthood to the ancient promise of a 'son of David'[5] and 'the revival of the old conception of the divine king as the centre of the hopes of the community'.[6]

[1] The same authority refers to an example of 'the ritual of the deification of a king' (*op. cit.*, p. 13).

[2] The sacred marriage of the king was a feature of the ritual which, by virtue of identification, secured human fertility to the community.

[3] Hooke, *op. cit.*, p. 17

[4] The inconsistency of the Chronicler is obvious in view of 2 Chron. 1[6]. These incidents add force later to the thesis of the Epistle to the Hebrews.

[5] *Psalms of Solomon* 17

[6] Hooke (*op. cit.*, p. 56). The authenticity of the 'Son of Man' passages in *The Similitudes of Enoch* is now considered doubtful. On the other hand the LXX rendering of Ps. 109 (110)[3] and other texts can still be cited for the revival in question. On this point see G. A. F. Knight, *From Moses to Paul* (London, 1949), p. 152.

The history of Semitic ritual exhibits some curious transformations in which the original notions are modified or overlaid by new refinements. Originally the dying god is probably represented by a human victim who is actually slain. Then the slaying is apparently transmuted into the form of a symbolic action; or again an animal victim is substituted. But still the victim has identity with the god; and so the eating of the slain victim becomes a means by which the offerer secures identification with the deity. For to participate in the death of the god is to secure the benefits which are consequent upon that death. Such ideas must have largely determined the outward form of the post-exilic Jewish cultus. For the restoration was necessarily traditional in character. Nevertheless the restoration supervened upon a changed situation. Jahveh was no longer regarded as a dying and rising god of nature. He was Israel's almighty redeemer-king who in no way depended upon the cultus.[1] Yet he demanded recognition from his covenant-people, and that too in the traditional way. Consequently, as the original cycle of 'identification' ideas faded into the background and passed out of mind, the emphasis now fell upon grateful commemorations for the redemptive acts in Israel's history. Sacrifices thus came to be pre-eminently gifts due from a grateful, although erring, people to the transcendent God.[2]

Considering the prominence of 'identity' idioms in Hebrew thought,[3] this change of emphasis is remarkable. Yet the very persistence of identity notions would provide a natural basis for a return of the ancient pattern, although, of course, in themselves these notions could not produce such a return. That was effected, however, when the Son of God took upon himself the rôle of the divine-human priest-king. In so doing he repeated the original pattern of nature-religion in historical acts of redemption. In this fusion of nature with history the original pattern is finally brought to completion. For the death and the

[1] cp. Isa. 40[16] and Ps. 50

[2] cp. Hooke, *op. cit.*, pp. 64, 65; and on some aspects of the transformation see above, Ch. VII, § ii, pars. 6 and 7.

[3] cp. above, Ch. V, § v, the whole of Ch. VI, and in Ch. VII, § iii. In reference to the Ras Shamra parallel I. Engnell speaks of 'the typical oscillation in the totality formed by the king and the god, who are identical . . . but at the same time two different persons' (*Studies in Divine Kingship in the ancient near East*, Uppsala 1943, p. 131).

resurrection are physical events wrought out in the flesh of the God-man. Moreover *this* 'repetition' is wholly unique in kind, since it has a once-for-all character which can never occur again in human history. All previous repetitions of the original pattern are here recapitulated. For in the death and resurrection of Jesus the truth of them all is included. For that very reason the divine-human victim in whom the gospel events were wrought out may be regarded as the Whole in whom all the age-long events of sacrifice are summed up. This agrees with the apostolic theology in which Christ is not only Adam, but also Wisdom-Logos, the site of creation, who, as the eternal Son, takes up the whole world into his high-priestly action.

The comprehensive character of the final repetition has two other leading characteristics which give it depth and fulness of significance as a 'recapitulation of all things'. For first, in the passage of Hebrew religion from the 'natural' to the 'historical' form yet another concept of repetition made its appearance. The basic facts of Israel's national life were, in the prophetic outlook, those historical events through which the theocracy came into being. These were the acts of God by which he chose a peculiar people, redeemed it from servitude, and gave it the promised land for a possession. This he could do because all the powers of nature were ready to serve his purpose. Accordingly, any future acts of redemption were expected to repeat in substance the same cycle of historical events with their attendant nature-transformations.[1] So when the Redeemer at length came to Zion his life-story was understood in terms of the classic cycle of past redemptive history so conceived. It was, in fact, the final recapitulation of that history in a form which fulfilled Israel's mission.

Secondly the redemptive history which summed up all the past also included implicitly all the future. Accordingly, the final repetition which could not be repeated in the same historical order of physical events, precisely because it was all-inclusive, could for that very reason be repeated in another

---

[1] This notion is particularly prominent in Deutero-Isaiah. But the 'return' to the wilderness before 'restoration' appears e.g. in Hos. 2 and in Ezek. 20³³⁻⁴⁴. In the latter passage the whole story of Israel's discipline in the wilderness is repeated between the new 'exodus' and the final resumption of the theocracy in Jerusalem.

sense and on another plane of being. The passage of the Christ from death to resurrection inaugurated, not a New Year of physical events in the cycle of nature, but a New Age of mystical events in the domain of history. Yet here too nature and history are fused together into one whole. For the mystical events have two *foci* of reference in the sacramental dispensation of the church. On the one hand elements of nature, such as bread and wine, are taken into redemptive history to become the *media* in which the historical redemption is continually renewed; and on the other hand the participants in this new order of ritual action are the persons who together make up the redeemed community. In that sacramental order the old cycle of identification comes to fulfilment in a more august manner. For, where in the primitive cultus all was magical, in the new Christian cultus all is spiritual and rational. Repetition now means a total, yet voluntary, surrender of human life and all its powers to be conformed in character to that eternal sacrifice of God's Son which is the heart of the church, as it is the core and centre of history.[1]

V

(2) The repetition of revelation through a teaching succession is another mode by which its living historical unity is maintained. The equation of the teacher-disciple and the father-son relationships links up enlightenment with regeneration (Ch. VII, § iii). Mutual submission according to function is a sharing in Christ's obedience, by which the knot of Adam's sin is untied. The theology of Christian initiation forms one pattern with the various forms of the repetition-*motif* and with the redemptive creation-process.

(2) The victory of life over death may also be regarded as a triumph of light over darkness. Creation is the medium of revelation; and the process of renewal in the one underlies the

[1] For further details bearing on the preceding argument the reader is referred to Engnell's book cited above. His substantial agreement with Pederson (*Israel III-IV*), although not quite complete, is noteworthy. An issue, not yet resolved, remains concerning the dating of Hebrew psalmody (cp. N. H. Snaith, *op. cit.*). If the anthropologists are right, their thesis presumes a long-drawn-out literary development of the Psalter for which analogies suggest themselves (e.g. Deuteronomy).

mode of continuity in the other. Accordingly, as our first illustration dealt with the single pattern of new creation in revealed religion, so our second illustration shall exemplify the unity of revelation in its mode of progression, as 'a living biological phenomenon', through redemptive history. We recall, first, what was previously said concerning (a) the double character of the word of God as creative revelation and (b) the Jewish emphasis upon a 'didactic succession' of 'elders' who have been authorized to teach. The connexion between (a) and (b) is seen in the fact that the relation of teacher to disciple is that of father to son. That this cycle of ideas was taken over by the primitive Christian church has been shown by Dr Carrington.[1] To 'receive the word' and to be regenerated were alternative ways of describing the meaning of baptism; and St Paul who normally preferred the language of death and resurrection also told the Corinthians: 'I begat you in Christ Jesus through the gospel'. He then proceeded to enjoin upon them the filial duty of imitating their spiritual father; and for their further instruction in 'my ways in Christ' (the Christian *halakah*) he announced the dispatch of Timothy, 'my child beloved and faithful in the Lord' (i.e. qualified, as disciple, to represent the accredited teacher).[2]

The function here assigned to Timothy is significant: 'He shall put you in remembrance of my ways' etc., 'even as I teach everywhere in every church'. The task of the disciple is to recall to mind teaching already given, in other words to repeat a tradition. Here we have 'repetition' in another form. The pattern of the Word is repeated, that the learners may

[1] *The Primitive Christian Catechism.* See especially his Chs. VII and IX; and cp. above, Ch. VII, § iii, pars. 6-end.

[2] 1 Cor. 4¹⁴⁻¹⁷. With this cp. also the maternal metaphor in Gal. 4¹⁹. In 1 Pet. 1²³-2² the new-born Christians are reminded that they were 'begotten again'; and this second begetting (unlike the first) was from incorruptible seed through the word of God who lives and abides. A comparison of this language with that of St Paul, cited above, suggests that, whereas 'the seed is the word of God', the duly accredited teacher is *identified* with the divine Father in the act of paternity in accordance with the regular Hebrew idiom by which the deity is identified with his agents. Moreover, to complete the agreement of the apostolic writers we note that in 1 Pet. 1³ the new birth is effected 'through the resurrection of Jesus Christ from the dead'. See also Jas. 1¹⁸,²¹, where the maternal metaphor of Ps. 90² (cp. Gal. 4¹⁹) is repeated, and see above, Addit. Note B (1).

become 'enlightened'. This corresponds to the Jewish back-ground. The rabbinical teacher was known as a *tanna*, that is a 'repeater' of the tradition; and there was a *'tannaite'* succession of teachers which traced its genealogy back through successive pairs of rabbis to the men of the Great Synagogue. From these in turn the succession was traced through the prophets to Joshua and the elders, and so to Moses. St Paul also regards himself as a *tanna*; for he repeats to the Corinthians what was 'delivered' to him by the older apostles (1 Cor. 11^{23}, 15^3). The Pastoral Epistles, with their watchword: 'guard the deposit', continue the same line of thought, whilst other epistles preserve the 'father-son' theme by their emphasis upon a 'subordinationist ethic'. If we follow Archbishop Carrington and Dr Selwyn[1] in associating this with 'catechumen virtues', the subordinationist *nuance* is then seen to belong to a wider plan of order connecting the above-mentioned cycle of ideas with the 'repetition' of creation. To this wider plan we now turn.

Adam's act of insubordination is cancelled in us by 'the obedience of the Christ' (2 Cor. 10^5). When St Paul used this phrase he was exercising his apostolic authority to bring his spiritual children into the path of that obedience from which they had diverged by their 'disobedience' to his rule. Our Lord's obedience to the Father is mentioned in Romans 5^{19}; and it is there explained by reference to the 'act of redress'[2] by which Jesus recovered for man all that was lost through Adam's disobedience. Accordingly the phrase in 2 Corinthians 10^5 might be paraphrased as follows: 'obedience to the Christ as practised by those who have been made sharers in his messianic obedience to the Father'. The test of this obedience in the baptized is their sharing in the mutual submission of all members of Christ's body to one another (Eph. 5^{21}).[3] The exposition which follows (5^{22}-6^9) makes use of the 'natural' scheme of

[1] Dr E. G. Selwyn, Dean of Winchester, *The First Epistle of St Peter*, London, 1946. See his Index VI, for refs. to 'Catechumen Virtues' and kindred matters.

[2] Moffatt's rendering of the key-word in the preceding verse (Rom. 5^{18}).

[3] There should be no break in the paragraph, either before Eph. 5^{21} (Moffatt) or after (as in the texts of WH and RV). Verses 21, 22 form one sentence with one verb. The submission of wives to husbands, 'as to the Lord', is (*a*) an example of mutual submission in the church, and (*b*) an acted parable of the submission which the church makes to her divine spouse.

social subordination as understood in the civilized world of the writer's day. In that scheme the particular subordination expected of the individual corresponds to his or her place and function in the natural society. So also in the redeemed society mutual submission is in accordance with function and vocation. It involves, therefore, in the baptized a special kind or degree of submission to the fathers, teachers and rulers of the church, as had been the case in the theocracy of Israel from its first beginnings. We may compare here the language of Hebrews 13[17] as a typical example out of many which might be quoted in the apostolic writings. By pledging himself to this obedience at the time of his baptism the neophyte became a sharer in the 'reversed repetition' which unties the knot of Adam's transgression.[1]

The doctrine of mutual submission set forth in Ephesians corresponds to the general tone of those Pauline statements about 'the proportion of the faith' which we have already considered. The individual finds that wholeness wherein salvation consists by conforming himself to the laws of the organic whole to which he now belongs; and these laws are functional. A special contribution of Ephesians however is the fact that the entire 'subordinationist' section of the epistle is, as it were, anchored to the *mysterium* of Christ and the church as *included within* the story of Adam and Eve (5[22-33]).[2] A connexion with this wider thesis, which is latent in earlier epistles (especially 1 Corinthians and Romans),[3] here becomes explicit. There is a similar connexion of thought in the writings of St Irenaeus. We can point, for example, to the co-infancy passage, where the proportionate growth of the Christian church is deliberately inserted into the 'repetition' of Adam in Christ. In this light, too, we must explain the fact that in *adversus haereses* the doctrines of recapitulation and repetition are frequently interwoven with references to the *tannaite* succession of *Christian* 'elders' from whom the Christian readers of this work received 'the oral law' of the Christ.

---

[1] For this use of language see above, Ch. V, § iii, par. 4, note 1
[2] cp. above, Ch. VI, § ii, par. 1 with its final note
[3] e.g. 'the many' in Rom. 12[4,5] takes up the language of 1 Cor. 12[12-14] (which is completed in 15[45-49]) and echoes the language of Rom. 5[19]. For this see further *The Apostolic Ministry*, p. 75.

In the second century this 'oral law', handed down by the apostles, was, for that reason, known as the *paradosis*,[1] in contrast with the written *torah* of scripture (that is the Old Testament) which was called *graphê*. In that epoch the Old Testament alone was indisputably scripture, whereas the whole of the apostolic writings could be regarded as transcripts of the oral tradition. For the purpose of refuting heresy, therefore, appeal could not be made to the *exclusive* authority of the writings afterwards canonized as the New Testament. The apostolic *paradosis* was embodied, not only in the apostolic writings, but also in the accredited teachers of the Catholic Church who could show their 'didactic successions' from the apostles. Moreover, after the canonization of the New Testament we cannot point to any date when this appeal to the didactic successions ceased to be, in principle, relevant, although in practice it became complicated (in the course of history) by other factors in the tradition as well as by changing conceptions of authority. In St Matthew's Gospel the apostles are regarded as scribes who have been made disciples to the kingdom of heaven (13^{52}). As such they were to bring forth out of their treasure 'things new and old'. In due course, therefore, their words would eventually become 'a more serious matter'[2] than even the words of the old covenant. Accordingly, those who succeeded them in the 'successions', now called 'apostolic', were subject to the apostolic teaching; and the peculiarity of that teaching was the way in which the 'things new and old' were so interwoven that neither could be understood without the light thrown upon it from the other. As the New Testament writings were interlaced with ecclesiastical tradition before they became scripture, so both the new scripture and the new tradition were also interlaced with the ancient *torah* of Israel, written and unwritten.[3]

At this point we must indicate the connexion between the present argument and our survey in the previous section, where

[1] To which corresponds the Latin *traditio*. 'Tradition' could, therefore, mean that which is 'delivered' or 'handed over' from one teacher to another.

[2] For the context of this phrase see above, Ch. VII, § iii, par. 6 with its note.

[3] An example of the former point is the fact that towards the end of the second century Irenaeus could quote the Shepherd of Hermas (*mand.* 1.1) as 'scripture' (*adv. haer.* iv, 20.2).

we were considering the epochal unity of the new creation-pattern. As the Word is both light and life, so, in the holy community, the repetitions respectively of revelation and of creation belong to one concrete whole. Clearly the double theme of 'enlightenment' and of 'regeneration' has shaped the primitive Christian rites of initiation. Moreover, as Dr Carrington has pointed out, the Pauline teachings about dying and rising with Christ, about 'putting on' Christ, and about being clothed in the Christian armour, should probably be connected with the ancient king-ritual and with 'a light-darkness cosmology of the Iranian type'.[1] In other words all this phraseology should be associated with the baptismal rites by which the 'children of darkness' became 'children of light' in identity with the divine priest-king.[2] We have also to take account of the suggestion which connects this apostolic material with a primitive form of catechetical instruction lying behind several epistles of different authorship in the New Testament.[3] This thesis serves to strengthen the impression that the primitive theology of Christian initiation is of one pattern with the various forms of the repetition *motif*—with the apostolic form of *tannaite* succession as well as with the wider pattern of cosmic redemption in the new creation. It follows, moreover, that the several parts of this pattern throw light upon one another. If baptism is both enlightenment and regeneration, then the apostolic ministry should be regarded as a succession of fathers providing for their sons and daughters. These are, indeed, the channels by which the creation-pattern is perpetually renewed in the church, as well as the guardians of the traditional lore concerning the maintenance of the divine rhythm of action and interaction in the new creation.[4]

[1] *op. cit.*, p. 86, note 1

[2] Eph. 5[8]; cp. 2[1–10]. From this standpoint the whole of Eph. 4[17]-5[21] looks like a baptismal address. Moreover, after the subordination 'tables' the writer resumes this note in the 'armour' section (6[10] ff). In this way the whole epistle reads like a 'recapitulation' sermon to the newly-baptized.

[3] This is the main theme of Dr Carrington's book; it is further elaborated by Dr Selwyn.

[4] For the subject-matter of this paragraph the reader is referred also to my recent article on *The Holy Spirit in Christian initiation*, printed in *The Eastern Churches Quarterly*, Supplementary Issue, Vol. VII, No. 2, London and New York 1948.

vi

The mutual assimilation of religion and culture in its bearing upon the development of doctrine. The clash of cultures in the realm of dogma exemplified from 'Spirit Christology' and the doctrine of the Trinity. The relation of this conflict to the function of tradition.

The process outlined at the end of the third section in this chapter (the last four paragraphs) has now been illustrated in two ways. Moreover, the two illustrations have, in the conclusion of section v, been blended into a single picture. The second illustration, however, is still incomplete. For one whole aspect of 'the unity of revelation in its progression' through history has so far been left out of account. In the last section we emphasized only one of the factors involved, namely continuity through repetition. But in the preliminary sketch of the process involved it was pointed out that (a) repetition is subject to transforming influences, and (b) such transformation is bound to involve a dialectical conflict which is the necessary condition of proportionate growth. These factors, which were fully illustrated in the preceding survey of the 'new creation' ritual-pattern, were also operative throughout the development of doctrine in the early church. From the details of that development there is much to be learnt concerning the manner in which all things are recapitulated in Christ. It is possible also that some of the considerations here to be advanced may throw further light upon the writings of St Irenaeus. To this aspect of our subject, therefore, we must now turn.

One of the most perplexing features of theology in the first three or four centuries of Christian history is the variety of strange opinions which were received favourably, for a time, by high ecclesiastical authority, or which found shelter in the minds of men who actually laid the foundations of later orthodoxy. The perplexity, however, may perhaps arise from an insufficient understanding of the forces which were actually (even inevitably) at work, and perhaps also from an over-simplified notion of the task of orthodoxy, the latter defect being directly consequential upon the former. We ourselves read the New Testament in the light of successive dogmatic developments and definitions, aided by the experience of the centuries.

287

Christians of the earliest period, on the other hand, had no such sign-posts to guide them; and, moreover, they approached the sacred writings with the most varied presuppositions. It may seem a strange thing to say; but it is clear, at least to the present writer, that some of those Christians who largely shared the mental outlook of the Old Testament writers were by that very fact inhibited from moving forward along lines which could lead them to the later definitions of orthodoxy.

The last statement requires elucidating; and it will be well to begin by recalling the reader's attention to a fact which was explained in the first chapter of this volume. Throughout redemptive history revelation has received its outward expression in terms drawn from contemporary culture. Cultures, however, are in one degree or another transitory. For, unlike the major uniformities of nature, they are human adaptations of nature which are liable to lose their relevance and their suitability under the changing conditions of historical development. For this reason a living religion shows its vitality by assimilating itself to successive cultures through the advance of the centuries, whereas a religion which has less vitality may become fossilized in a particular form of culture, reinforcing it where it should have broken through to new forms of expression.[1] These, in turn, may be actually awaiting its co-operation, and for lack of it suffering permanent loss. The religion of Israel showed its vitality in precisely this respect; and the Christian church consequently entered, as the new Israel, upon a rich inheritance. Enough has been said upon this matter in Book I of the present volume. We have now to apply these considerations to the development of early Christian doctrine.

It might be said that the New Testament, as a collection of writings, draws its literary unity from the fact that it expresses Jewish thoughts and beliefs in the Greek language. In it two great cultures meet, the Semitic and the Hellenistic; moreover, for some centuries these two had already intermingled. In the apostolic writings, however, there is something more than a

---

[1] The assimilation is, of course, mutual. Revelation is ever stooping down to our earthly level in order to draw human formations and structures upward into its abiding orbit. These structures, however, have no *raison d'être* outside the main end of creation which is the glory of God. Accordingly the law of 'assimilation' fails when religion is merely domesticated for earthly ends.

mingling of cultures. There is a religious unity drawn from
centuries of historical revelation crowned and transformed by
the fact of the Christ. This transforming factor gave a new and
higher character to the existing unity of religious revelation.
But it did not in any sense supersede the general law of interaction between religion and culture indicated in the last paragraph. Consequently the Christian religion could find new
modes of expression which were not exemplified in the Old
Testament, and which could not be identified with any idiom
of thought characterizing the Semitic peoples. To some extent
this process had already begun in the Judaism which is reflected
in the New Testament. The fact of Christ, however, had a
revolutionary character, precisely because it transcended all
previous human thoughts, hopes, and imaginings. It changed
everything which it touched; and it could hold fast the historic
treasures of Israel's past, while reaching out to adapt and
assimilate for its own purposes those other treasures of the
western cultures.

This process can be observed in the development of Christian
theology. Some of the historic conflicts in this sphere are conflicts between modes of expression characteristic of divergent
cultures. But the interplay of forces is too subtle to admit of
simple demarcations. For our present purpose it will be sufficient to suggest one example of this clash of cultures, as it certainly appears to be, within the realm of dogma. I refer to the
prolonged rivalry (for such it is) between the 'Logos' theology
of which Justin is the typical exponent and the 'Spirit-Christology' which appears as early as the Shepherd of Hermas, and
which persists until at least the fourth century. In some writers
(as Tertullian) both modes of doctrinal expression are present;
and when this occurs no satisfactory harmonization seems to
be effected.[1] The Spirit-Christology is unfamiliar and puzzling,
and that, perhaps, for two reasons. In the first place, it did not

[1] For a detailed exposition see Loofs, *op. cit.*, Ch. II, from p. 103 onwards.
The analysis is not adequately discriminating. Loofs tends to ascribe to
Geistchristologie a systematic form within which most of the 'pneumatic'
theology of biblical and patristic writers is to be placed. Conversely theologians who are definitely of the 'Logos' school are assumed to be severely
'binitarian' or worse. This valuable piece of research is consistently fair-
minded; but it leaves many ragged edges and unresolved problems, most
of all the grim metaphysical problems of *der strenge Monotheismus*.

succeed in impressing its typical modes of expression upon the orthodox formulas accepted by the Ecumenical Councils; and secondly its idioms of thought and speech are of Semitic origin and could not be fitted into the Graeco-Roman ways of thinking. Of these two points the former is obvious to every student of historical theology. The latter, however, which runs back into the very beginnings of Hebrew religion, is the really decisive factor.

Any discussion of Spirit-Christology to-day should go back to the text in Isaiah 31[3]:

> The Egyptians are men (*adham*) and not God (*El*),
> And their horses flesh (*basar*) and not spirit (*ruach*).

On this saying Wheeler Robinson remarks: 'The poetic parallelism shows that man also is flesh. . . . It is equally implied by the parallelism that the essential substance of the divine is spirit'.[1] The author of this comment rightly regards the text in question as 'cardinal' for the biblical contrast between God and man. Elsewhere he writes:[2] 'God's essence is Spirit, though Spirit . . . is still conceived as that which could be poured out or divided, i.e. it is the sublimation of the material rather than the non-material'. With such a conception the Holy Spirit would naturally be regarded as an overflow of the divine energy, a substance or gift rather than a person. This way of regarding the Spirit of God is normal, both in the New Testament and in the Fathers. The personal language to which we are accustomed is less frequent in the apostolic writings and only slowly won its way to acceptance in the early church. It is, however, present from the first; and its presence constituted an unsolved problem for some four centuries.[3]

---

[1] *Inspiration and Revelation*, etc., pp. 50 *ff.* The whole section should be read, with its comments from other scholars giving expression to substantially the same conclusions. Cp. also p. 20. In Loofs' treatment much use is made of the flesh-spirit contrast in Rom. 1[3,4]. But the OT background is not discussed at all. His thesis was written in 1927-8. Yet in this matter of OT background he apparently had not moved since 1906 when in *Leitfaden zum Studium der Dogmengeschichte* (fourth edition) his preliminary survey of Judaism (pp. 36 *ff*) did not go behind the Persian period!

[2] *op. cit.* p. 20

[3] An example may be given from *adv. haer.* Irenaeus constantly refers to the Spirit as a 'gift'. Yet in iv, 20.12 he cites Joshua's spies (Josh. 2[1]) as types of the Trinity, *adding a third to the two spies of the biblical story*. The

There is, however, another aspect of biblical thought which must here be taken into account. For the Hebrews God is un-differentiated Spirit. But by the overflow of his spirit-energy he can enter into men or other finite agents; and in so doing he identifies himself with them. Accordingly, deity could, *on such presuppositions*, be ascribed to man *only* by such an incorporation of divine Spirit into a human person. The Jewish (or later Semitic) way of thinking[1] would, of itself, inhibit any suggestion that there was more than one person in the Godhead.[2] How then did a trinity of persons find entrance into the biblical revelation? There is, humanly speaking, at least one possible answer to this question. It seems certain that an opening for such a development of thought was made by the influence of Hellenistic culture upon Jewish mentality. Moreover, it is possible to trace two lines of influence which ultimately meet. The first of these is the Platonic conception of an eternal world which contains the archetypes of earthly things. This line of thought is clearly present in the Epistle to the Hebrews, where the Son of God is the archetype of Melchizedek (7^3). But further, this kind of influence had enabled Jewish sages to affirm the pre-existence of the *torah*. It would, therefore, be no difficult step to affirm the same also of the Messiah.

Secondly the conception of a second divine 'person' found entrance into the thought of Philo, the Jewish philosopher, (so it appears) precisely because his doctrine of God was more Greek than Jewish.[3] This opened the door for a parallel use of words in St John's prologue, where, however, the whole setting of thought is profoundly biblical. In Philo the divine is assimilated to Hellenism, whereas in St John a Hellenistic way of *speaking* is incorporated into the biblical revelation. What author here makes an analogy from human to divine personality. But the substitution of three for two by lapse of memory is a fact of deep psychological interest. For (a) the analogy implies an attribution of personality to the Spirit *in the same sense* as to the Father and the Son; and (b) the substitution of three for two presupposes such an attitude towards the three divine persons as something normal, if not habitual. All of this is missed by Loofs. For him, therefore, this passage is, in a sense which he did *not* intend, *eine ungeschickte Zutat* (op. cit., p. 414, note 1).

[1] For a more primitive and 'pluralist' type of Hebrew thought see below, the longer note appended to the penultimate paragraph of this chapter.

[2] On this see G. F. Moore, *op. cit.*, Vol. I, pp. 364 *ff*

[3] cp. Moore, *op. cit.*, Vol. I, pp. 416 *ff*

made this revolution possible was not a mingling of cultures, but the new revolutionary fact of the Christ taking up that intermingling into itself.[1] The two forms of Greek influence meet in the greatest of the Greek fathers, namely Origen; and he, in turn, makes possible a further step. The eternal Son can be identified with that eternal world of which Plato wrote. This would mean that the archetypes of all created things are to be found in God the Son, the image of the Father. But here we must do justice to the Spirit-Christology. The Origenistic form of Christian Platonism could easily be interpreted in a too pluralistic manner which might sink into a mode of belief indistinguishable from polytheism. This actually happened in the Arian heresy. The Semitic idiom of thought, however, though incapable of preserving the New Testament revelation out of its own resources, could and did keep up a dialectical pressure upon the rival theory. Its contribution was, in this respect, comparable to the sustained criticism of the prophets as against nature-religion. In both cases the negative thesis was essential to proportionate growth. The doctrine of a *coinherence* or mutual

---

[1] When, however, we ask, *What* did the new revolutionary fact 'take into itself'? a further possibility confronts us. There was an older Hebrew tendency to think in terms of 'corporate personality', not only in man (*Adham*), but also in God (*Elohim*). The 'return' of nature-religion in the mysteries, and of the divine-human king in Jewish thought or feeling (see above, Ch. IX, § iv, par. 8, with its last note), may not be the only phenomena of recurrence with which we have to reckon. A resurgence of the ancient Hebrew tendency to psychological pluralism would correspond to the return of 'identity' phenomena, e.g. in Paulinism, after they had faded out, at least from the official cultus in post-exilic Judaism. I owe this suggestion to A. R. Johnson who, in his important monograph on Hebrew religious psychology (*The One and the Many in the Israelite conception of God*), has shown how intimate was the correspondence in Hebrew notions between idioms of thought respectively about God and about man. This adds force to his suggestion that the Pauline conception of Christ's Body (many in one) would have for its counterpart a new tendency to affirm plural personality in God (*ib.* p. 41). In short, the new revolutionary fact of a divine-human *koinonia* in Christ would open up to Christian thought a corresponding concept of divine *koinonia* in the deity. It is, however, no easy matter to assess the relation of this tendency to other factors; for example, Spirit-Christology exhibited the characteristic Hebrew fluidity (Pedersen's 'movement') and oscillation, whereby 'identification' would always tend to fall short of genuine incarnation. This may serve to explain my remark about a Semitic outlook 'inhibiting' orthodox conclusions (above, in this section vi, end of par. 2).

indwelling of persons in the Godhead owes, perhaps, as much to the Spirit-Christology as to the alternative line of development.[1]

Orthodoxy, then, is something more than a matter of finding a correct formula. The *process* by which the formula was reached was all-important. This illustrates a fundamental principle in the thought of St Irenaeus. The *process* by which Adam is moulded to the divine image is as vital to truth as the final result of that process. Moreover, from this point of view we get new light upon the meaning of tradition, and, by consequence, upon the methods of a traditionalist like Irenaeus. This father included in his version of Christianity formulations of doctrine which we should be inclined to regard as mutually incompatible alternatives. But the true traditionalist clings, consciously or unconsciously, to an organic conception of truth. Every element in the tradition has *some* truth. It is better, therefore, to 'let both grow together', lest the attempt to make these elements into a harmonious system should destroy something integral to the organic whole which is still in process of growth. There are times when it is the part of wisdom to leave questions undecided until the developing force of truth puts the issue beyond doubt.[2]

[1] Similarly with regard to the Incarnation. Loofs drew attention to what is in fact a characteristically Semitic 'oscillation' between two ways of speaking about our Lord. This can be discerned in the Homilies of Aphraates, the East Syrian father (4th cent.). In close accord with Hebrew habits of thought this writer speaks now in terms of divine Spirit, now in terms of the human Saviour, and sometimes of *der ganze Christus* (*op. cit.*, p. 227, note 5). This shows the persistence both of psychological traits and of literary idiom in a particular culture. St Irenaeus used a Source (IQA) with a similar Christology and with markedly Semitic idioms. Moreover, his own tendency to display literary characteristics of the same type may be connected with the strongly Palestinian background of the Ephesian church, and with the unhellenic character of 'Asiatic realism'.

[2] The brief references to 'Spirit-Christology' in the text above say nothing concerning the wide-spread use of such words as *pneuma* and *spiritus* in the contemporary cultural background. This subject has been examined with some fulness in a recent monograph entitled: *L'Évolution de la Doctrine du Pneuma, du Stoicisme à S. Augustin*, by G. Verbeke (Paris and Louvain, 1945), a philosophical study which (in intention at least) abstains from entering the sphere proper to theology. This detailed and careful survey, however, inevitably throws light upon the history of Christian doctrine. In particular, the Stoic conceptions of *pneuma*, in their all-pervasive influence, provide, in some sense, a secular counterpart to the doctrine of 'Spirit' in its biblical

and Christian forms. Dr Verbeke's self-imposed limits did not allow him to explore this latter field of inquiry. Yet the Semitic antecedents of Stoicism and their possible relation to the Old Testament surely call for fuller investigation if the interactions of the Judaeo-Christian religion with Hellenistic culture are to be fairly estimated.

Such an investigation would carry us back behind Greek science and philosophy to those primitive idioms of thought in which 'matter' and 'spirit' are not yet differentiated into opposite categories. Such idioms are characteristic of the Old Testament and are by no means absent from the earliest Christian literature. This raises a difficult problem in the sphere of philosophical theology, a problem which scarcely seems to have entered into Dr Verbeke's horizon of thought. He claims to have shown that Christianity delivered the ancient world from pagan forms of materialism and secured for later ages the true significance of 'Spirit'. His survey also indicates the opposite error of 'idealism' as a permanent possibility of thought. The deeper problem, therefore, suggested by his stimulating book concerns the manner in which Christian spirituality can and does mediate between these two poles of thought by inclusion of their contrasted truths in the new concrete whole, that is to say, creation redeemed in Christ.

CHAPTER X

ASPECTS OF RECAPITULATION

i

An organic conception of redemptive history corresponds to the scriptural blending of metaphors in the doctrine of the body of Christ. Diverse cultures, in due measure and proportion, are assimilated and transformed in a single traditional whole, the *mysterium Christi*, which is conformed to the plan of creation and includes the scriptures and the church.

In the preceding chapter the Form of the Whole was defined in terms of Recapitulation; and with that 'definition' the argument of the present volume reached its conclusion. It remains to indicate some implications of that conclusion which might seem specially relevant to the mission of the church in her task of mediating Revelation to the modern world. Let us first recall briefly the line of thought which we have been pursuing. The doctrine of recapitulation has been stated in terms of an age-long historical process. The illustrations of this process which were given carried certain implications which may now be more fully elucidated. If the interpretation given to the facts was even approximately true, then our extended application of the *soma-cosmos* imagery has justified itself. For we have, in fact, arrived at what might be called a *functional* view of history. In this conception the unity of history is built up out of contributions from very varied sources, such as national or racial cultures, each of which, in turn, is built in to the living historical whole.

It will be noticed that the scriptural combination of biological and architectural metaphors has here been reproduced; and this has a significance of its own. Unlike natural processes architecture requires the conscious co-operation of many human minds and wills, if the single plan of the architect is to be translated into terms of the materials used. Such a collaboration is implied in the organic view of history which is the logical counterpart of the 'Body of Christ' doctrine. Here, however, the human collaborators of the divine artist are the various races and peoples of the world; and their collaboration extends throughout redemptive history. This conception is clearly present in the apocalyptic picture of the New Jerusalem with which the canon of the New Testament closes, although the time-factor is not there emphasized. In our interpretation that picture of the nations entering the city is combined with the Ephesian picture of the messianic organism growing to its full measure. The various cultural contributions enter the structure of redemptive history in successive epochs; and this factor carries with it certain complications of which we must now take note.[1]

In the development of our individual lives each of us passes through a number of stages. Each of these, in turn, has its peculiar human excellences, the freshness and vigour of youth, for example, or the wisdom and maturity of judgement which come only in later life. We cannot have all the values proper to human life contemporaneously; for each belongs to its own stage of development. Nevertheless, the fruits of each epoch in an individual life are, or may be, garnered into the next stage; so that in passing from one stage to another there can be gain which, on balance, outweighs the loss. The process is, therefore, cumulative; and this, in turn, illustrates the principle of 'dying to live'. We surrender a passing good in order to obtain another good, which is more appropriate to our condition. In so doing we have not merely exchanged one good for another. For that which belonged to the earlier stage has done its work in us. Its external manifestation passes away; but its interior contribution to the whole has been built in to the system. Each stage of our life fulfils a function in the whole; and this temporal or *epochal* manifestation of 'function' is as indispensable as the *simultaneous* manifestations of function which occur in the various organs of the body.[2]

Something of this sort is also true with regard to the continuity of redemptive history. The relevance of the analogy is

[1] It will be remembered that in Ch. I, § v (last paragraph) the picture of the New Jerusalem was introduced, as symbolizing the organic interpretation of redemptive history.

[2] The illustration employed in this paragraph owes much to a passage in the Gifford Lectures of A. E. Taylor (*The Faith of a Moralist*, Series I, pp. 94 ff). Note that the lecturer applied this principle also to the 'advance of civilisation', where 'the price of temporal good' is 'won by the loss of temporal good'.

implied in the biological imagery of the Epistle to the Ephesians.[1] Here, again, there are two aspects which must be taken into account, the one negative and the other positive. Each cultural contribution to revealed religion fulfils a strictly limited function relevant to a particular temporal situation. This corresponds to the strictly limited character of 'the measure of the gift of the Christ' accorded to each member of the mystical body, and (as we have seen) to the correspondingly limited 'measure' of each inspired writer in the canon of scripture.[2] Moreover, on each side of the analogy, limitation with a view to the proportions of the whole involves actual negation of positive good in order that some larger good may become possible. The tension involved in these forms of 'dying to live' was sympathetically indicated by our Lord in his reference to those who do not desire new wine because 'the old is good' (Luke 6[39]).

This necessity of the negative aspect in redemptive history rules out the merely sentimental appeal to a romantic past, as though something belonging to a by-gone situation ought to be resuscitated simply on the ground that it is 'primitive'. Such an antiquarian attitude would be as mistaken as would be the opposite tendency, namely, a cult of modernity claiming for itself a wisdom superior to that of past ages. In both attitudes there would be undue subservience to the time-spirit. In both the essential function of tradition would seem to be overlooked. The 'form of revelation' is neither an antique garment nor a modern fashion; for it is the flesh and blood of an organism which grows according to the complex laws of life. In that growth there is something more than *either* unchanging form *or* a chameleon-like succession of miscellaneous forms. There is, rather, a cumulative character by which the positive contribution of each cultural form is retained long after its external features have passed from the conscious memory of society.[3]

[1] This, in turn, rested upon the current use of the analogy from the individual to the social organism, e.g. in the Stoic philosophy.

[2] The reader is here referred back to the discussions of (*a*) 'proportion' in Ch. VIII, §§ ii and iii, par. 1, and (*b*) 'the measure of the Christ' in Ch. IX, § iii.

[3] The illustration of the body-garment cannot, however, convey the whole truth concerning 'the form of revelation'. (*a*) It is to be interpreted in strict relation to its context in the argument. Here organic growth is

This positive aspect of social tradition is not, of course, peculiar to redemptive history. It should, rather, be regarded as something belonging to the plan of creation. But, whereas our fallen condition gives an advantage to the dispersiveness of sin, recapitulation in Christ is the means whereby the true plan of creation is restored and brought to fruition. Accordingly *the creativity of revelation is manifested in its capacity for integration of many cultures in one traditional whole*. This 'traditional whole', again, is identically that same entity which, in previous chapters, has been designated by such phrases as 'the structure of orthodoxy' and 'the organism of revelation'. It is that *mysterium Christi* which includes within itself the scriptures and the church, and which, once more, conforms itself utterly to the plan of creation, since it is that plan restored and actualized in Christ. *Mysterium* is the right word to use in speaking of the traditional whole. For it has aspects which indicate its theologically unitive character in degrees of profundity baffling alike to thought and to imagination. To these an approach will be made in what follows.

ii

Parallels between a classic cosmology and aspects of recapitulation. The paradox of communication between incommunicables. Theological significance of Leibniz as prophet of things to come.

The cumulative character of 'the traditional whole', briefly indicated in the last section, has been adversely affected by the disruption of Christian unity. The divisions of Christendom certainly impede and restrict the manifestation of wholeness. They cannot, however, destroy its cumulative character, which is still represented in various forms and degrees in the separated parts of Christendom. It is still possible, therefore, to survey *from within* the structure to which, as Christians, we belong. That structure, it has to be remembered, is creation redeemed and restored in Christ; and this large conception is to be taken seriously. For in the present volume we are holding firmly to the thought that only in Christ can the plan of creation be clearly seen and understood. For that very reason physical and

emphasized. Earlier the emphasis fell upon the inseparability of form and content (Ch. II, end of § v, Ch. III, end of § i). (*b*) The limitations of this type of imagery must be corrected and supplemented by the alternative conception developed in Ch. IV, § vi. On this see below, § iv, pars. 2 *ff.*

social analogies have been introduced at various points in the preceding pages;[1] and to this way of approach we must once again have recourse in order to round off the argument.

It will be convenient to take as our starting-point the thought of the philosopher Leibniz concerning the structure of the universe. To this he gave mature expression in his *Monadology* towards the end of his life, in the early years of the eighteenth century. This thinker's conciliatory nature, which was ever ready to mediate between apparent opposites, led him to an interpretation of the world which contains several noticeable paradoxes. These may be attributed mainly to characteristic limitations of contemporary thought, limitations which did not suffer him to draw conclusions commensurate with his profoundly social outlook. For example, a ruling philosophical dogma of that age denied the possibility of any interaction between body and mind. Yet Leibniz saw creation as an ordered harmony, notwithstanding the fact that (in consequence of the above-mentioned theory) the units of which his world was composed had no direct cross-connexions with each other. His 'monads' may be regarded as 'spiritual atoms' shut up, each in its own private world, like houses which, as he put it, 'have no windows'. Nevertheless, within his cosmic scheme were included several remarkable features which give to it an almost prophetic character when regarded from the standpoint of our present situation.

It is with these special features of the Leibnizian scheme that we are now concerned; and there are four points which deserve special notice: (1) Every genuine unit[2] in creation 'reflects' the whole; (2) this is effected through the pre-ordained harmony of the whole; (3) The 'reflexion' occurs at all levels of creation; and (4) in all stages of each unitary development. In this four-fold scheme 'reflexion' has a peculiar meaning.[3] Every

[1] Especially in Book I, e.g. Ch. II, §§ i, ii (social), § vi (physical), and for both types see the whole of §§ vi-ix in Ch. III.

[2] I use this phrase as an equivalent of the less familiar term: 'monad'.

[3] 'Each simple substance has relations which express all the others, and consequently . . . . it is a perpetual living mirror of the universe' (from *Monadology*, 56, as rendered by Robert Latta in his English edition of Leibniz: *The Monadology and other philosophical writings*, Oxford, 1898/1925). For the significant emphasis on 'relations' see below, the penultimate par. of the present section with its final note ('Abstract formulae. . . .')

unit is a mirror of the whole in the sense that it is representative of the characteristic laws which prevail throughout the universe. Moreover everything which happens in each unit has 'effects', although indirectly, in the world as a whole, and *vice versâ*.[1] Thus, every unit is a microcosm; and this fact, with all that it signifies, may be said to carry with it an organic relation of each unit to the whole. Here there is a paradox. For this relation which I have ventured to call 'organic' cannot be effected *directly* from one unit to another. It is, however, effected through the pre-ordained harmony which covers all events in the universe.[2]

Before we complete our survey of the four points we may pause here to notice a correspondence which can be observed between the first two points, as explained above, and some details of recapitulation already examined in the present volume. As a Christian theist Leibniz attributed to God the Creator the pre-ordained harmony which he affirmed to be the supreme law of creation. We are, therefore, justified in understanding his cosmology to be, in intention, a contribution to religious thought. Circumstances compelled him to set the units of his world in sharp isolation from one another. But in compensation for this individualism he covered the collocation of units with the single divine panoply of pre-ordained harmony. Secondly, under the cover of that panoply he also diagnosed each unit to be in direct and typical relation to the whole. This interpretation of creation's order can be paralleled from characteristic features of the new creation in Christ.

The typical, or representative, relation of each unit to the whole corresponds to what has already appeared in previous chapters of the present work, where the doctrine of *proportion* in the body of Christ was unfolded. It will be remembered that, according to the exposition there given, each member of Christ's body becomes representative of the whole just so far

---

[1] For Leibniz, strictly speaking, 'effects' follow from 'material' causes. But they have their exact counterpart in a world of spiritual or mental relations. See last note.

[2] In affirming 'organic' relations on a cosmic scale I have tried to interpret the method by which Leibniz by-passed the obstacle of philosophic 'parallelism'. He was convinced of universal connexions; and he explained them in the only way which seemed open to him.

as he fulfils his function in the whole.[1] But, secondly, the members of Christ's body are uniquely bound together, *not* in the first instance by cross-connexions of human fellowship, but by the direct relation of each and all to Christ through the Holy Spirit. The pre-ordained harmony of the new creation is secured through the indwelling of the one Spirit in the one body (Eph. $4^{3,4}$). The panoply of Christ's righteousness covers all his members; and from another point of view this universal covering is the Shekinah cloud in which the Spirit is ever present (1 Peter 4^{14}). Just as the pre-ordained harmony makes possible the 'reflexion' of the Leibnizian world in each of its units, so the indwelling of Christ through the Spirit makes possible that functional fulfilment of vocation in all members of the mystical organism whereby each becomes significant of the whole *mysterium Christi*.

There is one further point in which, at this stage, a comparison suggests itself. Units which are like houses without windows must necessarily have an incommunicable character. Their insides are mutually inaccessible; and in this respect the monads of Leibniz are not unlike those persons who remain inscrutable to us, however well we may believe ourselves to be acquainted with them. We must, however, go further. There is a sense in which all human individuals are in the last resort inscrutable to their fellow-men. The soul is known perfectly only to God himself. Moreover, this fact of human inscrutability corresponds to the divine image in man, the image which is common to all, yet unique to each individual. Here, however, the Leibnizian paradox becomes positively illuminating. The houses without windows reflect the whole universe![2] So also in the plan of creation that communication of the divine image which is unique to the individual, and therefore ever mysterious, is the very means whereby human personality may reflect the glory of God manifested in the work of his hands, and so

---

[1] This thought underlay the whole of Ch. VIII. But see especially, in that chapter, § iv, last 2 paragraphs.

[2] 'There is no individual thing which is not to be regarded as expressing all others; and consequently the soul, in regard to the variety of its *modifications*, ought to be likened to the *universe*, which it represents according to its point of view, and even in a way to God, whose *infinity* it represents *finitely* . . .' (*Réponse aux Reflexions de Bayle*) (1702). I have reproduced Latta's rendering (italics included) *op. cit.*, p. 220, note 20.

exemplify what God is—inscrutable, yet, in his lowly love, self-communicating.

Our philosophic illustration has limits upon which we are putting a severe strain. Nevertheless, the concluding phrase of the preceding paragraph suggests one final consideration concerning the parallel thus far developed. The universe of Leibniz is a social order in which the character of the whole is somehow present in all the parts, and that notwithstanding the barriers of individual distinctness and separateness. This, again, corresponds broadly to the truth that, in the development of human personality, the more genuinely a human being 'represents' the spiritual world, the more distinctively does his individual character stand out in its separate uniqueness. If this truth be stated in more directly theological terms, it can mean that the self-communication of God to man creates a harmony of contrasts, or even of opposites. Individuals attain the maximum of contrasted characteristics in the very process which makes them members of one family, sharers in one life. Moreover, as members of one family are assimilated to one another in a common life, for example, in respect of habits and tone, so also in the family of Christ the developing divergences of sanctified character belong to a process which has for its other side a mutual interchange of virtues and graces. Thus there is in Christ's Body an interchange of qualities between his members; and this, in turn, corresponds to the more mysterious interchange of divine and human 'properties' in the Incarnate Lord.[1]

The limitations under which Leibniz framed his interpretation of the universe have now been largely broken through. The radical dualism which, in the seventeenth century, placed an unbridgeable gulf between body and mind, is now a thing of the past. Moreover, spiritual and psychological forms of atomism have, for us, become as obsolete as the old indivisible atoms of matter, which were propounded long ago by certain thinkers of ancient Greece. The world as we know it is so deeply interconnected that to-day we are seriously concerned to defend the individual units, which are now, as ever, inscrutable, and for that very reason an intractable nuisance to those who want

[1] The reference is, of course, to the doctrine of *communicatio idiomatum*, as between the two Natures in One Person.

302

a simple, easily constructed plan. This problem of the individual is, no doubt, at its maximum in *persons*, as bearers of the divine image. But there is also a sense in which inscrutability runs right down the cosmic scale to the lowest limit. At every level the concrete objects of knowledge are known only in their relations with the rest of the universe.[1] Apparently this fact is recognized so clearly to-day on the physical level that the pattern of relationships between entities is tending to absorb the attention formerly given to the objects themselves.[2]

It is possible that here we are confronted with a change of attitude which will become characteristic for the coming time. It may be that the interpretation of objects through their relations will, in large measure, take the place of attempts to know directly the things in themselves. If so, the change will have an immense significance for the theologian, as for thinkers in other fields. To this subject we shall return later in this chapter. Before doing so, however, we must complete our consideration of particular points in the Leibnizian way of regarding the universe. So far we have been contemplating that scheme in its surface characteristics only. In the third and fourth points, however, which still remain to be considered,[3] we descend the scale of being below the human level; and here the thought of this philosopher has a most surprisingly modern appearance. Moreover, it is here that we shall find peculiar affinity with some aspects of recapitulation already indicated in the present work.

iii

A theocentric interpretation of the universe which foreshadows recent developments of thought with regard to structure and process, thus mediating between the biblical revelation and the modern world.

[1] This is the proper justification for Kant's dictum that we 'cannot know the thing-in-itself'. The dictum, however, could so easily be understood in a sense which made of it a misleading half-truth.

[2] Abstract formulae of relationship replace the old attempts at imaginative description. Cp., in Ch. II, § vi, the last par. but two, and the final footnote of the chapter. The general trend of *The Logic of Modern Physics*, by P. W. Bridgman, and the other works cited at the end of Ch. II appears to support the statement in the text. See also, in the present chapter, the quotation from *Monadology* 56 in a note to § ii, par. 3.

[3] see above, § ii, par. 3

For Leibniz the 'representative' character of all genuine units is maintained at all levels of the cosmic scale and in all stages of individual development. By 'levels' I mean the grades of difference between classes of entities, from 'particles' of matter through the various biological kingdoms right up to man.[1] These exist simultaneously, whereas 'stages of individual development' are temporal cross-sections of existence in the life-process of each genuine unit. Thus the third and fourth points of those which are here singled out for examination, cover every phase in the existence of all genuine units in creation. But what are these units? Here the position of Leibniz is similar to that of 'pan-psychism', that is, the theory that all physical phenomena somehow represent, and in some sense share, those characteristics of life and mind which become manifest to us only at the higher levels of the universe. This was an interesting return to that primitive standpoint which we have found to be prominent in the Old Testament.[2] Leibniz, however, was not consciously 'going primitive'. He was re-acting against the serious one-sidedness of current thought.[3] For him the universe was functional throughout its whole range. At every level there could, in some measure, be a re-sponse to the creator. Every created thing can co-operate in the harmony of the whole. In short, the cumbersome jargon of the *Monadology* indicated a return from a secular to a re-ligious point of view.

It is scarcely necessary to point out the affinity of such an interpretation with what has been said about recapitulation in previous chapters. We have here a conception essentially re-

[1] As we shall see, the terminology of Leibniz did not directly suggest levels or grades of being. It did, however, foreshadow such a notion in-directly.

[2] see above, Ch. VIII, § iii, pars. 4 and 5 with notes

[3] Descartes had classified all sub-human objects as machines. Leibniz conceded that all 'bodies' are machines, to be explained in terms of efficient causes. But he held 'body' or 'matter' to be always a phenomenal mani-festation of mind. This might point towards the mentalism of Berkeley. But it might also foreshadow the inclusion of all sensible phenomena within an extended range of the 'organic', such as has recently been set forth by A. N. Whitehead. From this point of view the *Monadology* represents a remarkable protest against that undue separation of man from the rest of creation, which has characterized modern humanism. For this see above, Ch. III, § vii, last 2 pars., and Ch. IV, §§ i and ii.

ligious because it makes everything in 'nature' foreshadow the realm of 'grace'.[1] Thus the lowliest physical objects can symbolize the members of Christ's body, because functional response is a 'categorial'[2] feature of creation, and because in this respect, as in others, the plan of creation was in its very foundations Christological. Wherever the response of the creature to the Creator is made 'according to the working in the measure of each several part' (Eph. 4[16]), there the divine will is done; and such response can be as perfect in its own order at one level as at another. This principle of equality cuts across all degrees of importance or significance which are otherwise determined. It therefore undermines at a stroke all human pretensions to superiority which cannot be reconciled with the lowly form of the Servant. Above all, it cuts at the root of any notion of progress which implies that the latest in time must be the best in quality. A perfect response of creation to the Creator was manifested milleniums before the first appearance of man. The dust of the ground had to be rendered amenable to the divine artist before ever the moulding of Adam to the image could begin.

In these last few sentences a temporal aspect of nature's otherwise simultaneous panorama has been introduced. The rocks are older than the human race. It is, however, in stages of individual development rather than at levels of the universe that the time-factor becomes significant.[3] Thus we pass to the last of the four points. In all genuine units there are stages of development, although these vary enormously in their significance. At the physical base of our terrestrial existence movement consists predominantly in uniform repetition. Here development is at zero point; and yet the patterns of unchanging

---

[1] This corresponds verbally to the title of one of Leibniz's later works.

[2] I borrow this word from S. Alexander to indicate a cosmic characteristic which recurs in new forms at every level of the universe. My use, however, is necessarily more extended than his, because I have given to it a specific theological trend. Cp. his *Space, Time and Deity*, Vol. I, pp. 4, 184-186, 343, 345.

[3] It should be mentioned that for Leibniz the monads were graded according to the degree in which their substance was 'simple'. Moreover, whereas all monads had 'perceptions', more or less 'confused', the higher (more 'simple') had also 'apperception', which, in man, might rise to being both 'clear' and 'distinct'.

repetition are essential to all the significant changes that are to come after.[1] Repetition is built in to the foundations of development as its inseparable companion; thus it shares the representative character of all the stages which go beyond or rise above it. Continuity of development rests upon a basis of routine; and advance is registered by the subsumption of routines into new forms of unified activity.[2] This *cumulative* character of development, which has already been considered in the present chapter, is a distinctive trait of 'organic' continuity as understood to-day. It could not have been so understood in an era of spiritual and psychological atomism. Nevertheless a great step forward was taken when Leibniz affirmed that the 'reflexion' of the whole (with its pre-ordained harmony) occurred not only in every genuine unit but also at every stage of such a unit's continuity.

To affirm this was to affirm the significance of *process* as something integral to the manifestation of creation's order. The harmony of the whole includes temporal depth of perspective as well as spatially extended horizons. Moreover, since 'reflexion' occurs at every stage, the earlier stages are necessarily as significant as those that come later.[3] The working of a machine *can* be exhibited as a single simultaneous event, in which the functions of all the parts are fully manifest at one time. In an organism, however, functions develop at the stage appropriate to them, and continue so long as is necessary to the life-history of the whole. Moreover, in the slow process of growth the unfolding of functions may be largely hidden from observation within the concrete unity of the organism. Thus there may be a great deal more 'representation' of the whole in any one detailed phase than can ever become explicit to the human mind. All this is much more intelligible to us than it could have been in the aftermath of the Renaissance. Yet the Leibnizian doctrine of a representation of the whole *in* the continuity of the parts clearly pointed forward to a deeper and fuller conception of continuity and of all that it must involve.

[1] For fuller details see *The Incarnate Lord*, Index of Subjects: 'Repetitive energy'

[2] So that routine and repetition are 'categorial'. See above, in the present section, par. 2 with the note on this word

[3] For every stage 'reflects', as in a mirror, the harmony of the whole

Just how much is involved depends upon the connexion to be made out between the third and fourth points (here distinguished respectively by the terms: 'levels' and 'stages') which we have selected for consideration from the cosmology of Leibniz. Apart from his attempt to indicate a hierarchy of genuine units by reference to degrees of 'simplicity'[1] this philosopher recognized that a particular monad might have a dominant position in relation to others. The human soul had such dominance in relation to the vast group of significant units represented by the body with which that soul was somehow mysteriously associated.[2] Moreover, God himself was at the summit of the spiritual pyramid in which all such units were included. There is clearly adumbrated here an organic conception of the human individual not unlike that which in St Paul's day made possible an analogy between the corporeal body and the body corporate. We have only to think of the 'dominant monad' as 'head' in relation to 'members', or as 'spirit' indwelling 'body', and we are back once more in a Stoic-Pauline world of thought.

If, however, this affinity between two such epochs of thought is to be rightly appreciated we must pay attention to differences. Just now the image of the pyramid was introduced to indicate a graded scale of units with deity at the apex. The same image, however, could also be applied appropriately to the corresponding conception of each human individual. The units of the world-pyramid are themselves smaller pyramids. Here it is the soul which is at the apex; and, as before, the figure is built up out of 'simple substances' arranged at different levels, each rank being composed of units having the same general characteristics, or (as Leibniz would have said) the same degree of 'simplicity'. In this way the individual person is seen to have structural height as well as temporal development. His structure is composite, like that of the image which King Nebuchadnezzar saw (Dan. 2). Here, however, the likeness ends, the parts being (not kingdoms but) grades of being.

---

[1] see the note on this subject under par. 3 of the present section

[2] Every particle of which the body was composed might correspond to, and so manifest, a 'simple substance'; and this, in turn, would be one of the lesser monads in the 'pan-psychic' hierarchy over which the soul could be said to preside as the dominant monad of that group.

The hierarchical character of the structure is only faintly suggested by the author of the *Monadology*. Even now, the conception of a graded universe is relatively new. That is to say, the recognition that there are different *kinds* of laws operative, for example, in physics and in biology, and that these two levels are disparate, not only from one another, but also from other levels of mind and spirit still higher in the scale—such recognition could not become commonly possible until the differentiation of scientific disciplines had reached a point where it might have a noticeable effect upon philosophic thought.

Nevertheless the general conception of hierarchical structure in the universe, and of its reflexion in man, has now become sufficiently established;[1] and in this particular respect Leibniz was a principal mediator between the old world and the new. His description of the universe in terms of a social order which, in turn, is reflected in each individual corresponds broadly to the ancient threefold analogy whereby the human body is seen to be a microcosm, equally, of the universal community and of creation's order. There is, however, in some respects a more marked correspondence between his system and its modern counterpart. This is to be seen especially in his emphasis upon 'relations',[2] by which he secures the communal character of the universe. When this is combined with his other leading notions, such as the continuity of individual process and differentiations of rank or degree among monads, we have the outlines of a plan which has affinity, on the one hand with the unified scientific picture of to-day, and on the other hand with the early Christian theme of recapitulation. This two-fold affinity suggests an analogy which will require further consideration in what follows.

iv

Analogy between forms of interpenetration in the sphere of revealed religion and corresponding forms in the universe as known to-day. In both spheres there is interaction of distinct systems, without confusion, within a wider order.

[1] For a detailed survey see Chapter II of my book, *The Incarnate Lord*.
[2] see, in particular, the quotation from *Monadology* 56 in a note to par. 3 of § ii in the present chapter

We are now in a position to recall some of the aspects of Recapitulation which have been expounded in the present volume; and we shall recall them in order that they may undergo an interpretation which relates them to the modern world of thought. For this purpose the philosophy of Leibniz has served simply as a useful mediating factor. The truths of recapitulation cannot, of course, be *adapted* to modern ways of thought, as though our generation possessed a norm of truth by which primitive Christian thinking should be 'corrected'. Those truths, however, can and should be illustrated in a medium of knowledge which is part of our own way of life; and they may, perhaps, be greatly illuminated, if comparison should show a mutual relevance between the old and the new. A convenient starting-point will be found in the idea of *interpenetration* and in the various forms which it has assumed in the course of this discussion. With it we may also be able to associate the closely-related notion of *compresence* which came into prominence in the later chapters of the present volume.

Interpenetration confronted us first of all as characterizing the structure of orthodoxy in contrast to the disintegrating tendencies of heresy (Chapter IV, § vi). In this first form of the idea as presented in the teaching of St Irenaeus, we soon found evidence of the principle that interpenetration involves interdependence. (1) The triadic relationship—creation, people of God, scripture—is one in which priority could be awarded to each of the three terms according to the standpoint from which the threefold structure is approached. Yet, at whichever point we start, no one of the terms is securely based in isolation; and further, no combination of two is safe from distortion apart from the controlling influence of the third. The distortions which have actually occurred in history bear witness to this complex fact. Secondly, in other combinations interpenetration appeared as a relationship between two terms which are not on the same level. One of the two is either built upon the other or at least clearly transcends it in significance. Examples of this second form were the respective relationships between (2) Adam and Christ (Chapter V, §§ iv and v) and, again, between (3) the Old and the New Testaments. In Chapter VI, § ii, attention was drawn to the close interconnexion of (2) and (3) when the two creations are in question. We can also see that this relation between (2) and (3) is established under (1). For creation and scripture are interlocked in revelation.

In that section of Chapter VI it was also pointed out that, in what I have called the second form of interpenetration, examples of which are given under (2) and (3), the law of mutual dependence still holds good. Neither Testament is strictly intelligible without the other; nor can the Christ be rightly known except in the context of that which precedes his historical advent. The gospel is defined in terms of Israel and of the plan of creation.[1] Moreover, this mutual dependence in the second form also presupposes the first form. For Christ is the Whole manifested in that triadic relationship of creation, the people of God and scripture. This second type of interdependence, however, has always been liable to misunderstanding. Marcion repudiated it altogether; but many, since his day, have shrunk from it, minimized it, or misconstrued it in one or other of its applications.[2] It is, therefore, particularly fortunate that at this point a principle which is characteristic of revealed religion should receive striking corroboration from the structure of the universe as we know it to-day. The difficulty which we are considering arises from the fact that interpenetration here involves a dependence of the higher factor upon the lower. Can this occur without the higher factor losing its transcendent character? What light can be thrown upon this question by our present knowledge?

The two questions which have just been asked are, in fact, closely connected. This problem of relationship between 'higher' and 'lower' is by no means a specifically religious problem. In the modern centuries it has, in one way or another, been a key-problem of philosophy. In the seventeenth century it came to be commonly assumed that two entities of different orders (such as matter and mind) could not interact. Moreover, until recently this assumption generally tended to have one of two consequences. It was not unnatural to suppose that the

---

[1] It is noticeable that this general thesis covers all our Lord's parabolic teaching as well as other aspects of the New Testament.

[2] For example, the interpenetration of the two natures in Christ corresponds to the second type; and here it has not infrequently been assumed *within the orthodox tradition* that there could not be a thorough-going dependence of deity upon human conditions in the life of the Incarnate Lord, the distinction of natures being still preserved.

CH X, iv] ASPECTS OF RECAPITULATION

apparent conjunction of two contrasted entities should be understood rather in terms of one entity with two aspects. This, in turn, gave two alternatives. The real character of such an entity could be found in one of the two aspects, but not in both. Thus, in the apparent conjunction of mind and brain, the former might be the only reality to be reckoned with, brain being simply a manifestation of mind. On the alternative view matter is the only reality with which we are concerned. There would be no way of deciding this issue except by a fresh appeal to facts.

Neither of the suggested solutions would be compatible with the Christian revelation; and the very real dilemma of the religious man was well exemplified in the attitude of Leibniz. While he leaned towards a solution in terms of mind rather than matter, this did not really satisfy him. His difficulty could not have been removed except by his own removal, at least in thought, to a date some two hundred years later. Now, however, all is changed. The relation between higher and lower factors is still a mystery; but the mystery has become one aspect of a familiar pattern which is seen to run right through the universe. The conjunction of entities of *different* orders is a special instance of the hierarchical character which is normal to nature and to the life of man. Here we may recall what was said towards the close of Chapter III concerning the witness of natural science to the mysterious.[1] The development of sciences, many in number, has militated against the two notions, that all knowable reality is of one type and that all knowledge can be comprised within a single technique. Thus, any particular science has its own characteristic sphere; and this is delimited, both in extent and in general character, by the nature of the objects studied. There is, however, an overlapping of spheres, because each science depends upon the one next below it in the scale. The psychologist must take account of the biologist's findings, as the latter in turn must defer to the conclusions of the chemist. Here the principle of interaction comes into its

[1] In §§ vii-ix. There 'mystery' was affirmed of the infinitely complex and the unpredictable. Here I have in mind the apparent gaps between the grades in the hierarchy (e.g. between life and those physical substances to which life is not ascribed), gaps, nevertheless, which are bridged by some kind of inter-dependence (e.g. in a living organism).

own again in a new way.[1] The new way presupposes a scale or ladder, of which the various sciences are the steps. Each step takes us to a fresh level; and there is no point in pretending that the steps are all portions of one plane surface. Can we get clear, here, the sense in which the word 'level' is used? The chemist can analyse the characteristics of matter taken from a living body, in order to determine its processes in terms conformable to his science. The laws which he recognizes are thus ascertained to be operative within living organisms. His analysis, however, does not show him how these physical processes conform to the characteristic unity of the organism as a self-organizing whole. That is a problem which he has to hand over to the biologist. The latter, also, is concerned with physical manifestations, such as the functioning of the brain; yet here he, in turn, overlaps with the psychologist. He can recognize a connexion between matter and mind; but the laws of mind, as such, are not his business. In what sense, then, are the steps graded? Most obviously in the fact that mind presupposes living matter as the basis of its own activity, just as life, in turn, presupposes chemical and physical processes as a foundation upon which its own functioning is built.

But further, in the human organism all the steps are represented; and our justification for grading them as 'higher' and 'lower' is connected with that fact. Here, however, other presuppositions enter in. If it is believed that man is a spiritual being, existing for spiritual ends, then all the various laws exhibited in his complex nature will inevitably be regarded as ordered to those spiritual ends. In the terminology of Leibniz

---

[1] As the synthesis in a dialectical movement. The first phase was a crudely-conceived interaction which did not do justice to the gaps in the hierarchical structure (see last note). The negative movement of 'parallelism' followed with a denial of all interaction. This phase represented the truth that matter and mind, although connected in a regular manner, are in themselves distinct orders of being, each with its own system. Finally the new concept of interaction preserves the truth of parallelism by including one system within other systems without confusion of their respective laws. This type of interpenetration (without confusion) is clearly a 'categorial' feature which reappears in revealed religion. Its crowning example is that of the union of two natures in Christ. For here there is complete interpenetration 'without confusion', complete inter-dependence without loss of distinction.

the soul will be regarded as the 'dominant monad'. Other forms of unity in our being will then be seen to fulfil a subordinate function. The soul will be at the apex of the pyramid, and the various mental, biological and physical factors involved in our nature will be assigned to lower positions in accordance with the manner in which they appear to be mutually dependent, that is in a definite sequence or order. The divergence of scientific disciplines precludes us from treating the various factors as all of one type. They present the appearance, rather, of a series of interlocking systems, which have as good a claim to be regarded as forming a settled sequence as have the various entities comprising the periodic table in the modern analysis of matter. For the sequence and its order are firmly rooted in the co-operative system of the sciences. The picture of 'higher' and 'lower' grades, however, receives its fuller justification only from a religious interpretation of man's place in the universe.

When we ask what is the ultimate significance of this vast system of inter-dependence, a satisfactory answer can come only from the side of revelation. Yet, as in the pattern of the universe as a whole all forms of inter-dependence are mutually subservient, so also must it be between the pattern of revealed religion on the one hand and, on the other hand, the wider revelation which is implicit in the order of creation. That is to say, God's ways as presented to us in scripture and the glimpses of his wisdom which may be gleaned from a scientific account of the universe must be mutually illuminating. For the inter-penetration of the forms in which truth is presented to us implies the mutual dependence of those forms as channels of revelation.[1] The Form of the Whole, however, contains, not two interpenetrating forms subsidiary to itself, but three. With scripture and the order of creation the *ecclesia* and its tradition are interwoven. Here we have three interlocking systems; and this threefold order of the revelational whole is complicated by two types of sequence. (*a*) On the one hand there is the contrast and connexion between the two creations; and this, in turn, overlaps with the division of scripture and the

---

[1] The order of creation is the sphere in which interpenetration occurs as between the principles of revealed religion and the knowledge acquired through human investigations.

ecclesia into two covenants. (*b*) On the other hand, there is the regular sequence of cultural systems which are, in turn, taken into the order of redemptive history, there to be transformed.

In the preceding summary we see an order of revelation which has the character of a complex of systems. In that respect it is like the order of creation, which is itself, in turn, one of the systems within that same complexity of revelation.[1] In the analogy between 'nature' and 'grace', however, we must resist the temptation to be captured by too great an exactitude in making out parallels. The diversities of range and dimension are too far-reaching for anything like detailed correspondence. What is to be looked for is general guidance which will help us to see our way through crucial difficulties, and which will safeguard us from one-sided presuppositions and preoccupations. Four points may here be set down which indicate such general guidance as we need:

(1) In the revelational whole there is a compresence of systems without confusion of differences.

(2) The larger whole preserves characteristic laws of the included systems within a richer setting.

(3) Subsidiary parts do not make sense by themselves; knowledge involves relations.

(4) Each part represents the whole in its own way, but only through its relation to the whole and to the other parts.

V

In the general structure of the universe there is mutual dependence of 'higher' and 'lower' (Ch. VI, § ii). In this we can discern a parable of nature prefiguring the form of the Servant. The realms of nature and of grace are not only compresent. They also cohere together in one pattern which exhibits continuity through a series of transformations reaching into the very heart of the *mysterium Christi*.

If revelation 'has the character of a complex of systems', then it is likely to have innumerable facets which may easily elude observation. Recognizing this for a fact, we shall at least be on our guard against chasing will-o'-the-wisps, that is, grasping successively at false simplifications as they present themselves. The analogy which we are following may help us

[1] see last note

314

to avoid this mistake, and to be modest in our expectation of insights with regard to so difficult a theme. It will be simplest to proceed by way of examples. The human body contains minute physical structures (such as molecules) which follow their own laws. These laws are common to all such structures throughout the physical universe. Thus it is that a system, apparently in no way dependent upon 'life', enters into a 'living' system and becomes indispensable to it. The one system (the physical) penetrates the other system (the living) without change in its own character. Yet, for all that, it also acquires a new characterization; for, although still entirely physical, it is also 'living matter' and is, in some sense, controlled by new influences, subject to new laws. This may be taken as a typical example of 'interlocking systems'. The one system enters into the other without confusion of their respective laws. For, whereas the physical system retains its own character, the living system can maintain its own laws in being only through inclusion of the physical. Moreover, we must not overlook the fact that, whereas the physical system can maintain itself in being without entry into the living organism, it *can* also enter into that new set of relationships. In other words, its own laws, although peculiar to itself, are also *amenable to the laws of life*.

The concluding (italicized) phrase indicates the ground for holding that this interlocking of systems involves a definite sequence, in which significant movement is in one direction only—upwards (that is) and not downwards. Superficially the conclusion is paradoxical. For, whereas the physical system cannot exhibit all its possibilities without the higher grades, these, on the other hand, cannot exist at all in our world of experience without a physical foundation. This complete dependence of the human spirit upon what lies below it is for the Christian believer a massive illustration of the fact that the form of the Servant is stamped upon all creation, and again that dependence is a hall-mark of creaturely greatness. Conversely, the opposite view, namely, that dependence is humiliating, should logically suggest a materialistic conclusion, since the physical system alone *seems* to require no laws but its own. There is, however, another consideration which undercuts the plausibility of this argument. The physical system is interdependent within its own sphere. That is to say its units, down to the lowest level, have no significance except in terms of a vast network of relations amongst themselves. In short, they cannot even be known except by virtue of mutual dependence. To this point we shall return.[1]

The illustration employed in the first paragraph of this section could obviously be repeated for each of the levels represented in the human microcosm, and always with the same indication of sequence. For at each level the mutual dependence of systems has the same general character. Brain, for example, is the necessary basis of mind, whereas mind, on the other hand, manifests the possibilities of the cerebral 'grey matter'. The examples selected point to facts beyond dispute, which also happen to be familiar. The sequence, however, could be produced downwards into the microscopic world of quick-change inter-dependence between sub-atomic units, or, again, upwards into human society. Here, at the summit of the pyramid the continuity of the sequence is seen in the fact that ethical relations pre-suppose economic laws. On the other hand, the distinctively human relationships can have a character more permanent than any mode of inter-dependence in the lower systems. From this point of view tradition has rich spiritual significance as a typically human embodiment of the higher types of communal life, just as, conversely, its breakdown (for whatever cause) has a peculiarly devastating character. For when once 'the whole' has been broken, the parts cannot easily be re-united with their previous integral unity. Thus, as we ascend the cosmic scale we find reason for thinking that modes of relationship become more complex as they become more enduring. Moreover, as temporal process enters more deeply into their structure, so lesions in that structure have effects more permanent and far-reaching.

In the analysis just completed there was one point at which its theological relevance stood out starkly. I refer to the passage in which reference was made to 'the form of the Servant'. From this preliminary indication we can proceed to trace out the lines along which our parable from nature can receive its application in the realm of grace. The problem involved in the

[1] cp. again the final note to the penultimate par. of § ii above. For illustrative material in the biblical sphere see below, § vi.

dependence of 'higher' upon 'lower' factors is, in reality, *the* problem with which we have been occupied throughout the present volume. In its theological form it is manifold, and yet fundamentally one. Theologically speaking it *is* a problem to us primarily because we are fallen creatures. Because we have fallen out of the divine plan, we find it hard, even in our redeemed status, to appreciate the glory of God's condescending love, though it be spread out before us for our delectation. In itself, however, the lowliness of deity is not a problem to be solved, but a mystery to be adored as we reverently seek to apprehend it in the universality of its scope and range. This attitude is, for us, both legitimate and possible, because we actually stand within the mystery by virtue of our membership in Christ.

The mystery of which we are speaking confronts us in the fact that, as we are dependent upon our total environment, material and spiritual, so also our Lord has made himself to be dependent upon us. As we take into our bodies lowly things of earth, so also our Saviour takes us into his body. As earthy units enter into a living body, so we in our earthliness enter into the divine-human life of the New Man. Our 'earthliness', moreover, which thus enters into him makes him who is very God to be dependent upon everything which is characteristic of us, including our mental processes and our social life together with their characteristic products. In this way our achievements have, for good or ill, a necessary place in his existence as Man. Our corporate structures with their traditional concomitants enter into the orbit of his humanity, that they may be welded into its very tissues. This process has been going on through the centuries, since first the Son of God by his own voluntary act put himself at our disposal. Did that divine act of self-committal take place at the moment of the incarnation? Or shall we trace it further back to the call of Israel, or again further still to the *fiat* of creation when 'all things were created through him and unto him' so that 'in him all things consist'?

There would be no necessary inconsistency in returning an affirmative answer to each of these questions in turn. For the form of the Servant casts its shadow backwards from the incarnate life through the story of Israel into the obscure beginnings of history when the moulding of the divine image in our earthy substance was first taken in hand. In this way the analogy between nature and grace would resolve itself into one undivided pattern, in which all that belongs to the parable of nature is but the opening phase or the setting of the stage in a single drama of unfolding graciousness. We cannot, however, rest content with such a purely temporal sequence, inasmuch as in this larger plan there is, not only an interlocking, but also a simultaneity of systems. Interpenetration is thus seen to involve besides some degree of *compresence*. What I have called 'the setting of the stage' remains as the background of the ensuing drama.[1] The order of creation is the unchanging background to the play-acting of history, just as the systems which 'interlock' within the human frame are compresent in our bodies with all the changes and chances of this mortal life as it fulfils itself on earth.

Compresence and interpenetration may be regarded as two complementary aspects of *coinherence*, a word which has the highest significance for theology.[2] The order of nature is not only compresent with the order of grace. It is also taken into it in Christ. All things are summed up in him who is the true head of creation. This is the primary meaning of recapitulation. But it has manifold implications. For example, the relationship is mutual. Christ penetrated to the heart of creation that it, in turn, might be brought into his innermost being. This mutuality of coinherence, whereby the divine Son dwells in the creature that it may dwell in him, is a truth which has other applications. The Old Testament is present in the pages of the New Testament; and this fact means much more than that the one is quoted in the other. To begin with, the two covenants overlap; the first disciples belonged to both. Secondly, the apostolic minds, like that of their master, were wholly Jewish. They could not think of divine things, except in terms of the revelation to Israel. Consequently the new revelation was given in terms of the old; and the old showed itself to be amenable to the

---

[1] cp. above, Ch. V, § iii, par. 4 with its penultimate note

[2] The Greek word περιχώρησις which we so render was originally used to define the relations between the two natures in Christ. Later it became the normal term to express the mutual indwelling of the three Persons in the Godhead.

process. The two were welded together in Christ, with the result that each received something of the characteristics proper to the other. Coinherence involved an 'interchange of properties'.[1]

We began this phase of our argument by talking in terms of analogy. Now, however, we are thinking of a single pattern in which nature and grace coinhere. In such a pattern analogous features become repetitions, that is, characteristic formations of nature repeated in a new form in the order of grace. Two such repetitions confront us in the mutual coinherence of the two Testaments: (1) First of all, the New Testament writers show a constant tendency to bring together typical figures or stories of the Old Testament, so that they form a new whole in Christ. For example, Adam, the messianic king and the Servant of the Lord are frequently blended, either in pairs, or all together. Again, a single figure like the Lamb of God is a blending of the Servant (Isa. 53) with the paschal lamb and possibly with the cultus victims generally. (2) Secondly the Old Testament shows itself amenable to this process; for it already has a tendency to the same kind of thing. In deutero-Isaiah the Exodus is regarded as an act of new creation; and this idea is elaborated in the Wisdom of Solomon.[2] The new covenant, however, brings to fulfilment tendencies and possibilities which were already present in the old material. In these two points the structure of nature is *analogously* repeated. The former (the fusion of types) corresponds to the fact that in the cosmic scale the upward movement introduces more intensive forms of unity where the whole has a more permanent significance. The latter point (the

---

[1] This phrase has a special meaning with reference to the two natures in Christ. See the last note and a corresponding reference to *communicatio idiomatum* near the end of § ii above.

[2] This conjunction would be assisted by the re-association of the 'new-creation' cultus with events of Israel's past history. In this way the 'new creation' *motif* of natural religion was transformed into an expectation of historical redemption. Cp. above, Ch. VII, § ii, pars. 6, 7, and Ch. IX, § iv. There is, however, another aspect of this matter. Wheeler Robinson has pointed out that the 'transformations of nature' which are to accompany historical redemption 'are to be taken realistically'. They imply 'that, at any time, there may be a crescendo of the life of the world to reveal more of the divine energy, for man's good or ill'. This, in turn, is possible because all nature is 'alive, and able to respond to God's demands' (*Inspiration and Revelation*, etc., pp. 28-30).

amenability of the old order to the new) corresponds to the fact that matter is 'amenable to the laws of life'.[1]

vi

A partnership between religious faith and scientific knowledge (Ch. III, §§ viii and ix) has been exemplified in our argument (Ch. IX, § iv). The dialectical conflicts manifested alike in scripture and in its interpretation are incidental to wider laws of co-operation and of proportion which characterize the order of creation and its fulfilment in the Christ.

The transformations of religion which took place continuously under the old covenant reached their culminating point in Christ. Yet still we can trace continuity. St Paul's way of handling the Old Testament differed from that of his Jewish contemporaries only in the re-orientation of his material to an actual fulfilment of Israel's hope in Jesus. The method, therefore, was not different in principle from that of the old Hebrew writers who had re-interpreted the national traditions from the standpoint of their own situation. This raises a problem concerning the relationship between two quite distinct attitudes towards scripture, each of which appears to have a just claim to respectful consideration. The first of these is a 'traditional' attitude which accepts the verdicts and interpretations offered by the inspired writers, as theologically true and reliable within the total proportions of the biblical revelation.[2] The second is the critical attitude, which seeks to go behind the account rendered by scripture itself, and to reconstruct, so far as possible, the original course of events. Here we are faced with the

---

[1] The last sentence above corresponds to the first paragraph of the present section (concluding phrase), as the preceding sentence similarly corresponds to the third paragraph.

With the theme of cosmic continuity sketched in the above section may be compared a striking paper on 'The Psychology of levels of Will' by Margaret Masterman in *Proceedings of the Aristotelian Society* (New Series Vol. XLVIII, 1948).

[2] 'Proportion' is, once more, the key word. 'Truth' is not to be weighed by quantity, but judged by its relation to the whole. A subordinate truth may serve the proportions of truth in its fulness, as a subordinate musical instrument contributes to an orchestral effect.

issue raised towards the end of Chapter III,[1] where we were considering the conditions under which there could be a partnership between religious faith and scientific knowledge.

Perhaps we can now see our way towards a further clarification of the issue there articulated, an issue which was hanging over our heads like a cloud all through the Book on *revelation and culture* there brought to its conclusion. Once more, illustration will be the most direct method of procedure. In Chapter IX of this volume (§ iv) there was set forth an example of constructive results following from the application of empirical methods. The scientific scrutiny of Old Testament material was seen to have brought about, first a strange deadlock, and then an illuminating readjustment forming a pattern which did justice to all the relevant factors. The striking feature of this readjustment was its resolution of apparently irreconcilable differences between the inspired writers. The prophet Jeremiah and the authors of the priestly code, formerly considered to be quite contradictory in their respective attitudes to religion, were now seen to represent complementary 'moments' in the dialectic of religious development. The final reconciliation, however, has always been present in scripture; for there the author of the Epistle to the Hebrews actually quotes Jeremiah's charter of 'spiritual religion' to illustrate an argument for the abiding significance of the priestly cultus![2]

The above illustration may serve as an epitome of the argument implicit in the present chapter. Four stages in the religion of Israel were there delineated, in which a spiritual pendulum seemed to have swung to and fro through the centuries. At one point in the critical inquiry it looked as if the last of these stages, represented by the New Testament, would be divided into two parts, in which earlier contradictions would be found to have repeated themselves. In this 'repetition', indeed, there would have been no 'recapitulation'. For it would mean that Jesus had simply revived the prophetic protest against the cultus, only to be finally defeated by a Pauline surrender to 'the mysteries'! From St Paul himself, however, we may learn a more satisfying explanation of this whole epochal series—an explanation connected with his doctrine of proportion in the Body of Christ. What was previously said upon that

---

[1] §§ viii and ix   [2] Hebrews 8[8-13]

subject may now be brought into relation with *coinherence* in the overlapping realms of nature and of grace.

The pendulum-like movement of Israelite religious history may be partly explicable in terms of contrasted cultural situations.[1] Certainly every culture tends to be compact in itself, self-sufficient, and therefore capable of an unfriendly attitude towards its rivals. The religions which have died, or which remain static, are usually those which have been immured in a particular culture without ability to transcend it. If there was to be transcendence there would probably be conflict and tension; and this characteristic is certainly in evidence in the biblical religion. Such conflict and tension may be compared with 'the growing pains' of rapid individual development, as in adolescence, when old things are being left behind, and new vistas are opening up. Thus we may connect the movement of the pendulum in Israel's religion with what I have called the functional view of history.[2] On that view each epoch of revealed religion has its own peculiar vocation, its own special contribution to the truth of the whole. That special contribution has two characteristics of which we must now take account.

Every such movement, just so far as it fulfils its function in the dialectic of the whole, is in that respect representative of the whole. In Leibnizian terms it 'reflects' the pre-ordained harmony by virtue of its 'relations' with the whole, relations which also 'express' all the other parts of the whole. This language might seem strange and even extravagant, if it were not actually corroborated by what we know of the universe to-day. Every system in the interlocking hierarchy of systems represents the law of the whole in its fundamental character as a unity of disparate elements. Moreover, as each system within the whole has this general character, any one of them 'expresses' all the others *in that respect*. But secondly, any such

---

[1] The prophets sometimes appealed to the nomadic phase of Hebrew history as something to be idealized by contrast with its agricultural and urbanized phases. This attitude seems to be implicit in Jeremiah's prophetic testimony to the Rechabites (Jer. 35).

[2] cp. above, § i of the present chapter. What is said above concerning 'cultural religion' in general applies with equal force to the dangers attending national or racial forms of Christianity. The remedy would seem to lie in a humble recognition of the fact that such forms are not the whole, and that therefore they cannot be self-sufficient.

religious movement as that now under consideration fulfils its
special function by virtue of its *un*likeness to the contrasted
movements with which it is in conflict or tension. The leading
pre-exilic prophets could not fulfil their appointed function
except by hostility to the nature-religion of their day, and so
on. This disparity between the epochal units of religious history
corresponds to the inscrutability which we connected in a special
degree with the image of God in man,[1] but which, it was suggested, is also a characteristic of all entities in creation from the
highest to the lowest. The two characteristics just described,
namely, 'reflexion of the whole' and 'disparity of parts' must
now be considered together in their bearing upon the coinherence theme, into which questions relating to the interpretation
of scripture enter as one factor amongst others.

The conflict of priest and prophet in Israel, in so far as it was
a fact,[2] can be aligned in one particular respect with the
modern tension between traditional and critical interpretations of scripture. In both cases there is such disparity of
function that it has been difficult for either side to understand
the merits of the other. Yet it is precisely the second of these
two conflicts which makes it possible, not only to appreciate
the former, but actually to resolve it! It is largely through the
scientific researches of archaeologists, linguists, anthropologists
and the like that we are now able to see how the tensions of
Old Testament religion are reconciled in Christ. On the other
hand, the more traditional methods of biblical exegesis, in so
far as they have a certain continuity with the technique of the
inspired writers themselves, remind us that we cannot reconstruct biblical history without entering deeply into the mental
outlook of those writers, so that we can sympathetically re-think
their thoughts.[3] Here we must also remember, first, that tradi-

[1] By virtue of that image natural religion expressed a truth *hidden* from
the eyes of its radical critics, ancient and modern. The negative aspect of
prophecy is only one factor in religion.

[2] It was apparently limited to certain of the greater prophets. Cp. above,
Ch. VII, § i, last 2 pars, with notes. Moreover, behind it lay another
conflict, perhaps more significant—namely that between prophet and king.

[3] At the same time we are rescued from the puerility of *some* traditional
exegesis, only by the purifying effects of all forms of scientific knowledge
which can be made to throw light upon scripture. Cp. above, in Ch. III,
§ vii, par. 2, § viii, par. 1, and § ix, pars. 3*ff*

tion itself is continually undergoing modification for good or ill, and secondly that a knowledge of tradition in its most significant forms can be recovered only through critical and scientific researches.[1]

Thus at every point scientific criticism and traditional theology are mutually dependent. Each represents the truth of the whole, although in altogether different forms. Their very disparity is the condition of their mutual necessity and of their ultimate coinherence in the proportions of truth. This kind of co-operation, which is indispensable to a sound biblical theology, corresponds to the other forms of co-operation which characterize the realms of nature and of grace. Objects are known in their relations, and in no other way. But these relations are always of two kinds. Each system of knowledge can be seen to be, in this respect, analogous, on the one hand, to some one cultural grouping of human society or again to any one of the 'levels' which 'interlock' or overlap in the graded universe. Each of these units draws its character and its coherence from the uniform system of relations which it contains within itself. On the other hand the universe is a *cosmos*, and not a chaos, by virtue of the fact that disparate systems are amenable to one another's laws. Consequently each such system as we are envisaging has relations, not only of the internal, but also of the external kind. Each is capable of entering into co-operation with that which is, naturally speaking, alien to or at least different from its own type, as brain subserves mental activity or again as psychological processes may subserve the production of a great work of art.

It is in these external relations that what I have called nature's parable points to the higher mysteries of recapitulation. There is here a close analogy, but also a peculiar difficulty which brings us back to what was said earlier about inscrutability. In human society the general law of disparity between systems has been complicated by the facts of freewill and by the dispersive power of sin. Below the human level concrete objects may baffle us in the sense that they remain mysterious. Yet, notwithstanding this, we can know them in their relations, and

---

[1] The above paragraph retraces parts of the argument concerning 'the Liberal experiment' in our second chapter.

so manipulate them for our own purposes.[1] The inscrutability of persons, however, has a much more disconcerting character which affects all human relationships. Here the individual 'parts' can 'represent' the harmony of the whole solely through that creativity of grace which is the counterpart of creation's plan.[2] Recapitulation in Christ is the restoration of that plan with its correlative of grace. In the redeemed society the inscrutability of human personality ceases to be a vexatious surd which cannot be resolved or a perverse obstruction which must be suppressed. It becomes instead a mystery forming part of that greater mystery which is the *mysterium Christi*.

The image of God in its completeness has been manifested in Christ and is being reproduced in all his members. The image so extended includes the 'all things' of creation. All was originally created in the form of the Servant; and all is now being restored to that form in him who has ever shown it forth by his unchanging obedience to the Father. Yet there are also distinctions. The traces only of the Servant's form can be discerned in the order of creation as a whole; its detailed representation is unveiled in scripture; but its genuine lineaments appear most clearly in regenerate humanity, in personal character and in relationships between persons. Ultimately these involve all the other factors in creation, because of the mediatorial function which has been assigned to man. So the bride of Christ shares in her Saviour's work of reconciling all things to the Father; and the Servant's form is imprinted alike upon her structure and upon her mission to mankind.

[1] Knowledge through relations always involves 'interpretation'. Knowledge which was both *exact* and *direct* would have the character of a photograph, representing one momentary aspect of a much more mysterious whole. This has an obvious bearing upon interpretation of revelation in a traditional medium, where the overlapping of scripture and tradition through mutual interpenetration produces interchange of qualities. We know the revelation of scripture in a medium of tradition which has been partly created by the Word revealed; only partly, however, since another factor involved is the creativity imparted to man by the Creator-Word.

[2] cp. above, Ch. I, § iv

INDEX

The numbering of biblical chapters and verses follows RV. Under (i) (a) the letter G indicates the text of LXX; and a number in brackets is that of LXX. The letters 'n' or 'nn' indicate the footnotes of this volume.

(i) REFERENCES

328

[1] The arabic numerals refer to the sections as given in the Loeb edition.

332

(ii) PERSONS

(iii) SUBJECTS

ary meaning, 318; involves (*a*) repetition, and (*b*) transformation, 272; recapitulates previous repetitions, 280, and past redemptive history, 280; its connexion with *tannaite* succession, 283 *ff*; with the development of doctrine, 287 *ff*; with creativity of grace, 325; with the modern world, 308 *ff*. *See also* analogy, repetition, subordination.

'reflexion', 299 *ff* & *nn*, 306, 322 *f*; of whole and disparity of parts, 323

religion: (1) natural, 3 & *n*, 100 & *n*, 120, 194 *ff*, 274 *f*; defined, 195; and history, 198 *ff*, 202*n*; (2) revealed, 2 *f*, 6, 22, 24, 33, 41, 259 *f*, 275, 282, 310, 313*n*, 322; and culture, 6 *ff*, 10 *ff*, 20 *f*, 23 *ff*, 196, 201, 274, 288 *ff*; and science, 20, 50–52, 82 *ff*, 86 *ff*. *See also* dialectic, fertility cults, revelation.

repetition: physical, 305 *f*; as basis of development, 306; as routine, 198; of events, 141 *ff*, 151; of process, 143; of creation, 137, 245 *f*, 265; in nature, 155 *f n*, 193; of whole in parts, 272; as form of unity, 242, 246; continuity through, 287; cycles of, 272; magico-religious significance of, 155*n*, 277, 281; of revelation, 282 *f*, in tradition, 283; of creation in new creation, 137 *ff*, 283; of revelation and creation, 286; of Adam in Christ, 284; negative (reversed), 142*n*, 284; subject to transformation, 272, 287; and analogy, 319; *motif*, 137; forms of that *motif*, 286; in order of creation, human life, and scripture, 272; of naturereligion, 275, 277, 279–281, 292*n*; in ritual acts, 277; of historical events, 280; of history in mystical events, 280 *f*. *See also* recapitulation.

representation: of organic whole, 306; of whole by part, 233 & *nn*, 235, 246, 300 *ff*, 304, 314; of revelation by a prophet, 235, 246; of the Logos by the Baptist, 237, 246 *f* & *nn*; of Christ by OT types, 246; of Israel by symbolic figures, 249 *f*; of Christ's body by each member, 300 *f* & *n*; through creativity of grace, 325; as 'reflexion' of the

whole, 299 *f*, 306; of the whole as unity of disparates, 322. *See also* 'reflexion', whole.

revelation: its form and content, vii, 12, 16, 46 *f*, 60 *f*, 110, 114, 121, 129, 159, 225, 258, 297, & *n* to 297 *f*; special and universal, vii, 18 *f*, 33, 168 & *n*, 192 *f*, 194 *ff*, 248 *f*, 255 *f*, 313; creative and creaturely, 209 *ff*, 226 *f*, 325*n*; organic, 128, 132 *ff*, 149; its relation to:—

(1) religion, 4, 14 *ff*, 17–19, 22 *f*; (2) response, 18 *f*, 22 *f*, 32 *f*, 37 *f*, 60 *f*, 208, 211, 236 *f*, 258, 273; (3) culture, vii, 1–6, 287 *ff*; (4) a Christian order of society, 61 *ff*; (5) history, 192 *ff*, 198 *ff*, 208 *f*; (6) prophecy, 230 *f*, 275; (7) scripture, 15–17, 23 *ff*, 274; (8) development of doctrine, 274, 287 *ff*; (9) orthodoxy, 131; (10) sin, 103, 211, 215 *f*, 216*n*, 252

(*a*) core of, 60 *f*, 130; (*b*) complex structure of, 24–26; (*c*) unity of, 29, 50, 123 *f*, 131 *f*, 149, 224, 248; (*d*) manner of, 16 *f*, 60, 132, 191 *ff*, 197 *f*; (*e*) organs of, 22, 23 *f*, 25, 194, 211, 227, 234, 249, 258; (*f*) organism of, 90, 132, 194, 217, 225, 234, 236, 248, 257, 259, 261, 298; (*g*) three stages of, 40, 226 & *n*, 236 *f*, 248; (*h*) mystery of, 83, 89, 93, 129; order of revelation, 24, and order of creation, 313 & *n*, 314; creative revelation and (*a*) didactic succession, 282 *ff*, (*b*) integration of cultures, 298, 314

See also analogy, assimilation, creation, culture, mystery, prophets, religion, scripture, transformation.

sacrifice: ancient ideas of, 10, 11; the ancient institution of, 11 & *n*, 100 *f*

science, modern career of, 48 *f*; scientific thought, impartiality of, 48, 73 *f*; relation of, to biblical theology, 48–58. *See also* humanism.

scripture: and tradition, vii, 60, 204–209, 257, 258–263, 285, 325*n*; and other organs of revelation, 194; unity of, 8 *f*, 12 *f*, 23 *f*, 27 *f*, 40, 50 *f*, 75–77, 125–128, 160; inter-